California Pop

California Pop

The Evolution of Mid-Century, Sub-Cultural, Southern California

By Dorian MacDougall

Copyright © 2020 Dorian MacDougall

All rights reserved.

ISBN 978-17344834-0-6

californiapop.net

This book is dedicated to:
those who built the dream,
those who lived the dream,
and those who keep its memory alive.

Table of Contents

Introduction	xi
Chapter 1: California Dreaming in the Age of Conquest	1
Chapter 2: You Are Here	13
Chapter 3: The Padre's Progress	19
Chapter 4: Rancho Paradiso	31
Chapter 5: Johnny's War	39
Chapter 6: Going for the Gold	47
Chapter 7: All to See the Elephant	55
Chapter 8: At the Devil's Doorway	63
Chapter 9: Come and Get It... Please!	73
Chapter 10: The Surge of the Swells	81
Chapter 11: Nuevo Paradiso	91
Chapter 12: Some Assembly Required	105
Chapter 13: Hello-ha Hawaii	117
Chapter 14: A Tale of Two Cities	129
Chapter 15: Reveling Our Way to Ruin	141
Chapter 16: All Ahead Slow	153
Chapter 17: War All Over Again	169
Chapter 18: A World Away from Yesterday	179

Chapter 19: Futurama　　　　　　　　　　191

Chapter 20: Mid-Century Makeover　　　　213

Chapter 21: Dreamland USA　　　　　　　231

Chapter 22: The New Frontier　　　　　　253

Chapter 23: The American Riviera　　　　275

Chapter 24: California Popped!　　　　　289

California Pop Foot Notes　　　　　　　305
When my own personal experiences intersect with the narrative, it will be noted here.

California Pop Bibliography　　　　　　313

About the Author　　　　　　　　　　　327

"Print the words and post the pictures"
In order to keep the sales price low, images were not included. However, a continuously evolving photo display, organized by chapter, is available on the Cpop website (californiapop.net). Simply click on "The Book" dropdown menu and select Image Gallery.

californiapop.net

Introduction

As a child growing up in the salubrious suburbs of Southern California, it was only through the television set that I began to suspect there might be other worlds far removed from the one I knew. Big city dramas like *Call Northside 777, While the City Sleeps*, and *Knock on Any Door*, provided, what I considered to be, terrifying glimpses of claustrophobic, chaotic, concrete jungles of shadow, darkness, and dread. The visions were disturbing, but hey, it was fiction—right? Certainly, those grainy black and white images could hardly be considered conclusive evidence of the existence of an alternate universe.

Such youthfully ignorant reasoning allowed me to maintain a comfortable state of denial until the day I was dropped off at the Helix Theater for the Saturday matinee showing of *West Side Story*. Believe me, nothing makes an impact on a kid like wide-screen and Technicolor. In a matter of minutes, my vague fears were confirmed—we Southlanders were not alone! I left the theater that day nearly bursting with a renewed appreciation for my homeland, and a promise to myself never to stray beyond its borders.

Looking back, it's easy to see how a kid who had not done much traveling could develop such a mistaken impression. So many years after Southern California was first described as "an island on land," and "a country within a country," the characterizations were still valid. The Southland bore scant resemblance to anywhere else in the continental US. Through the 1950s and on into the mid-60s, Southern California was the most celebrated section of real estate in the nation.

Even now, when most people hear the words, Southern California, they envision a tropically tinged land of breathtaking beaches, sunny blue skies, and wistfully recall all the delightful and exotic folk arts and practices that were unique to the southwestern coastal region of the United States in the middle of the 20th century.

Though the period was so short it could practically be measured in dog years, it was during those years that the region achieved its most extravagant forms of aesthetic expression, and for that reason, the era remains fixed in the collective memory.

A truly remarkable achievement when you consider what a terribly long and arduous struggle it was to reach that pinnacle of pop progress. The first Europeans to land upon the shores of Southern California were not at all impressed. Spain's conquistadors came expecting to find a terrestrial paradise, and instead, found a dried-up desert that, 300 years later, was still judged to be *"so utterly desolate, deserted, and godforsaken that a wolf could not make his living on it."* Thoroughly dejected, they canceled their colonization plans and stomped off swearing never to return.

But despite the area's shortcomings, they eventually did return. Southern California's beguiling atmospherics and strategic location on the mid-eastern quadrant of the Pacific Rim made it inevitable that this most inaccessible and isolated region of North America would not only be colonized, but completely transformed into a tropicalized, and fervently romanticized American Riviera.

However, the process would not be an easy one. It would take all of three nations, a missionary movement, four wars, a gold rush, a transcontinental crossing, a gaggle of mythologizers, two railroads, legions of tourists, an army of hoteliers and chambers of commerce, and a thousand dissimilar individuals of far-flung imagination and fixed purpose over 400 years to turn that arid desert into mid-20th century America's most preeminent province.

Many unique elements would go into the making of this frothy, mid-century, pop-cultural soufflé, but the most essential of all was simply the accident of geography and atmospheric conditions that produced the picturesque shorelines, the wide-open spaces, and the mesmerizingly mild, sunny, semi-arid climate that naturally elevated the human spirit and kindled the kind of capricious creativity that culminated with the transformation of a seaside desert into the man-made, tropical oasis that once served as the universal symbol for the art of good living.

At the crest of its ascension, it was bankrolled by a cold-war defense and aerospace industry, by a Hollywood fantasy factory, by persistent waves of tourists, and by a host of merchandisers all struggling to keep pace with an insatiable consumer demand set free by high wages and the installment plan. Within this cloistered coastal realm, the pursuit of happiness became inextricably linked with the promise of a future thought to be soaring into a brilliant new world of progress and plenty. Intoxicated by an overpowering sense of optimism, and energized by ambient solar power, Southern Californians created a dazzling world all their own.

Here, home builders replicated the severe architectural styles of Europe, added a touch of tiki, and a pinch of googie, and so perfectly blended modernism into the landscape that it appeared to grow wild as the poppy. Here, teenagers transformed old, worn-out heaps into snarling, window-rattling, 400-horsepower chromed and candy-appled road rockets, and grown-ups toured about in luxurious factory jobs modeled after the latest space-age motifs. It was here that Hawaiian surf riders introduced the mainlanders to the island life, and it was also here that strange rhythms and exotic melodies would seep into the sub-conscious through the Stereo-Activated, Dyna-Grooved vibrations of a million rumpus room woofers and tweeters, as transistorized young primitives, awash in waves of twangy reverb and four-part harmony, celebrated the beach beautiful.

Shoring up this truly intoxicating cultural blend was the community brain trust assembled from the best and the brightest from everywhere else on earth, drawn to the Southland with the promise of good jobs, good schools, livable cities, and opportunities to enjoy the expanding leisure hours of the mid-20th century that could not be matched anywhere else. All these disparate forces converged at one time in one place and forever altered the lives of everyone who dwelled within their sphere. It was a golden era that has continued to define the image of Southern California long after its passing.

In this book, we will trace the period's development from the earliest flicker to the final fade. What you have before you is a valentine from a loving expatriate born of an affection that can only be achieved through prolonged absence. Yes, unfortunately, I was not able to keep my childhood vow of immobility; instead, as a part of my ceaseless effort to make those wondrous Southern California summers last a lifetime, I have created this modest remembrance—*California Pop*. I hope you enjoy it.

Chapter 1
California Dreaming in the Age of Conquest

Once upon a time...yeah that's right. Once upon a time. You didn't think we were just going to go jump on a surfboard and ride a wave of nostalgia through a world of mid-century, Southern California enchantment right from the get-go? Oh no. A civilization so colorful and so eclectic does not come into existence overnight. The bubbly, effervescent, lighter-than-air Southern California culture of the mid-1900s actually began fermenting centuries before it finally came into full bloom. If we are to really understand how Southern California came to be what it came to be, then we must go back a long, long time ago. And so, I repeat—once upon a time...

The Discoverer
It may seem hard to believe now, but it is nonetheless true that the event that set the great, cosmic wheels of progress in motion that led to the European discovery of the Americas, which in turn led to centuries of non-stop social and cultural mingling and maturating, which would eventually lead to the proliferation of civilizations so thoroughly enlightened that a film like *Beach Party* could actually become an international phenomenon began on the outer reaches of the near east in 1453 when the Ottoman Turks conquered Constantinople—really.

Prior to that date, the Holy Roman Empire generously allowed Europe's traders access to their lucrative overland trade routes to China and India. But with new management came a new business model, and the hard-nosed Turks decreed that the eastern trade routes were to become toll roads. To pass through their territories unmolested, foreign traders would now have to pay tribute to the Ottoman Empire.

The merchants of Europe were outraged. These meddlesome middlemen were cutting deeply into their profit margins. Something had to be done, but what? Wars were expensive and empires were fragile. Obviously, what Europe's business community needed was an alternate route; but the only other way to reach the Orient was by sea, and everybody at that time knew that the sea route was impossible—or was it? Enter one Christopher Columbus, Genoese business manager, trader, navigator, and most importantly—a man with a plan.

It wasn't a very good plan, but he had something down on paper and he was determined to run with it. Naturally, anyone planning to sail two thirds of the way around the world in those days was bound to run into a few logistical hurdles; however, the primary obstacle most often sighted in our old history books was not among them—the world was not flat; and nearly everybody of science, letters, and a reasonably sound mind knew it. The ancient Greeks had long ago observed that, on the ocean, objects did not progressively diminish into the distance; they sank below the horizon—hence, the world is round. It was a given, even in Columbus's day.

What really kept the European navigators from attempting a westerly voyage to the Orient was the accepted knowledge that it was just too far away. The ships of the day couldn't carry enough food and water to sustain a crew for the time it would take to complete a voyage of such distance. So, in order for Columbus to get the financial backing he would need to carry out his plan, he would either have to make the ships faster or the world smaller; counter-intuitively, it was in the latter solution that he saw an opening.

Columbus's brother had introduced him to a second-hand scheme to reach the Orient developed by Italian astrologer P. P. Toscanelli, which had already been rejected by Portugal's King fifteen years earlier. The king's ministers claimed Toscanelli got the measurements wrong, and they were right. Toscanelli had based his figures on those of Greek mathematician Ptolemy, who, 1500 years earlier, had underestimated the size of the earth by over a third. However, with the science of cartography still in development, there was room for debate, and so Columbus debated its merit before the new Portuguese king and got the same result—No!

From Portugal, he went on a fundraising tour to Genoa where he was rejected, and rejected again in Venice, but in Spain, he got a definite maybe. King Ferdinand was intrigued, but too busy fighting the Moors to seriously consider the proposal, so Columbus was asked to wait the two years it took Ferdinand to conquer his foes before he got his answer—No! Once again, royal ministers rightly concluded that Columbus's calculations were too far off the mark to entertain even the slightest hope of success. Discouraged but not defeated, Columbus was on his way to France when he was recalled before the Spanish court a second time. It seems, that the recent war had depleted the treasury to such a precariously low level that even a desperate long shot was beginning to look like a halfway rational investment strategy.

So, with lingering reservations, Ferdinand and Isabella agreed to finance the enterprise even though all the best scientific evidence at hand clearly indicated it was a surefire loser. Just exactly how hopeless the Spanish monarchs considered this venture is revealed by the outrageously generous terms Columbus was able to negotiate should he succeed:

- A royal appointment as High Admiral of the Ocean Sea
- A Governorship of all the new land he can claim
- A ten-percent share of all new revenue
- A one-eighth share of all new business enterprises

Judging from the size of the compensation package, one can conclude that the royals didn't believe they would ever see Columbus again and would never have to make good on their extravagant promises.

Nevertheless, a deal was finally concluded; and so, having made all the wrong moves in preparation for the voyage, Columbus set sail for China, or India, or anywhere thereabouts on August 3, 1492. Sixty-nine days later, exactly as predicted by all the naysayers back home, Columbus' found himself in big trouble. With nothing but ocean ahead, and the food and water almost gone, the crew was preparing to mutiny, when suddenly, from aloft, the lookout shouted, land ho! Columbus had made land right where he said he would. The disaster was averted by the most unforeseeable of circumstances—the accidental discovery of the Americas.

Columbus dropped anchor, lowered the boats, and rowed ashore thinking he had truly found a sea route to "the Indies," when, in actuality, he was over 10,000 miles short of his intended destination. It is believed Columbus landed on the island of San Salvador where he mistakenly declared the inhabitants to be Indians, made them subjects of the Spanish crown, and then forced them to hand over every golden trinket they possessed. The take was a modest one, for the islands he initially discovered were not rich in mineral deposits, but it was more than enough to build legends upon.

After taking a victory lap around some of the other islands in the region and leaving a small settlement on what is now the island of Haiti, Columbus returned to Spain a hero. Having seemingly discovered a viable sea route to the Orient, he was the talk of all Europe—he was a rock star! And while Columbus was basking in the glow of his celebrity, every other European nation was sending its merchantmen west to cash in on the Asian trade only to discover they could find no Asian traders on what was thought to be the west coast of Asia. Controversy ensued, and though he was loath to admit it, by the time Columbus set out on his fourth and last voyage, in 1502, the general consensus suggested that he had not discovered a sea route to Asia, but to a brand-new world, no doubt laden with treasure.

And so, throughout Europe, the race was on and any individual or group with the means, and the blessing of the Crown, which could be had for a standard 20 percent cut of the action, could organize an expedition to the new world. The original intentions of these expeditions were to colonize territories and bring the Catholic religion to the godless peoples of this new world. However, the most compelling motivation to venture out into the unknown was the lust for treasure and finding ex-soldiers, mercenaries, and daring young blades in search of adventure and the prospect of a quick fortune was a very easy task indeed. In the late 15th century, everybody wanted to be a conquistador.

Over the next few years, tales of their exploits would not only inspire others to follow in their footsteps, they would provide the inspiration behind some of the most imaginative literature of the age.

The Mythologizer
Garci Rodriguez de Montalvo, a writer of second-rate, chivalric, romance novels, was working on a tome called *Las Sergas de Esplandian* (The Exploits of Esplandian) at the time all the fuss was being made over the discovery of the new world. Surely, a man in his line of work must have been fascinated by these tales. And of course, it's not unusual for writers to take inspiration from the events of the day. But somewhere along the line, possibly swept up in a sudden burst of creativity, Montalvo stopped taking inspiration from the events of the past and started creating the inspiration for events yet to come.

The result was a spectacularly fanciful work of fiction so convincing that it inspired another generation of Spaniards to go treasure hunting in the new world years before any real treasure had been discovered. He also coined the word "California," attached it to a specific geographic location, and even enhanced it with an intoxicating bit of mythology so fantastic that it still ranks as the biggest mega-whopper ever associated with the region. With this novel, Montalvo became the very first purveyor of California mythology and thus established a grand tradition of regional mythologizin' that continues to this very day. Within the course of his narrative, Montalvo described a mythical island called California:

"Know, that on the right hand of the Indies there is an island called California very close to the side of the Terrestrial Paradise; and it is peopled by black women, without any man among them, for they live in the manner of Amazons. And there ruled over that island of California a queen of majestic proportions, more beautiful than all others...Their weapons were all of gold because in all the island there was no metal except gold."

For the young conquistador on the make at the turn of the 16th century, what's not to like about this scenario? We've got paradise, we've got beautiful Amazon women, and we've got lots of gold. In the age of conquest, this was the super trifecta, and when the book hit the stands, and news of the story of California spread throughout Spain, boatloads of treasure hunters began pouring out of Spanish ports faster than you could say, "hoist the main sail." As was the custom of the day, the Crown awarded each captain a royal commission granting the bearer a license to kill, steal, plunder, occupy, and enslave in exchange for a 20 percent cut of the spoils. With the aid of Mr. Montalvo, a growth industry emerged.

The Conquistadors

In 1504, partly influenced by the writings of Montalvo, Hernan Cortes landed upon the shores of Hispaniola (Dominican Republic) determined to make a name for himself in the new world. He took part in the conquest of both Hispaniola and Cuba and was richly rewarded for his efforts with lands and slaves. He was even appointed mayor of Santiago, but he had yet to make the big score he had come for.

Then in 1519, after years of distinguished service to the colonial Governor of Cuba, Cortes was rewarded with an appointment as Captain-General of a major expedition into the mainland of New Spain (Mexico) where rumors had been circulating regarding the existence of a large, up-scale, native civilization in possession of copious amounts of gold and silver located somewhere deep in the interior.

And though his commission officially stated that his mission was to acquire territory for colonization, he ignored it and shifted into quickstep conquest mode the minute he began receiving reports from rival tribesmen pinpointing the whereabouts of this huge, over-capitalized, native metropolis.

Here was the jackpot he was waiting for; this was what being a conquistador was all about. And with the aid of several of the neighboring tribes who were already in a dispute with the Aztecs over the punishing taxes they imposed, Cortes marched right up to the front gates of the fabulously wealthy Aztec empire with artillery, musketry, a detachment of bull mastiffs, a company of mounted lancers, and about 2000 Spanish and native light infantry.

Though the Aztecs had an overwhelming numerical advantage, the sight of the war dogs, which they mistook for demons, and the mounted cavalrymen, which they mistook for dragons, scared most of the fight out of them. Their legions retreated within the city walls and a small company of shamans were dispatched to make the invaders disappear. When that tactic failed, Cortez and his army were invited in as guests of the mighty emperor Montezuma, whom the Spaniards promptly captured along with his magnificent, golden city. Their land and riches were claimed for Spain, and their capital was leveled to make way for Mexico City.

Speaking strictly from the Spanish perspective, Cortes had done very well for himself; he had hit the mother lode. Once again, rewards were heaped upon the conqueror. He resumed his comfortable life as a Spanish gentleman, but that did not diminish his desire for new conquests, and neither he nor any of the dozens of other conquistadors working the territory had forgotten about that other great prize—the Island of California.

Go That 'a' Way

The news of Cortes' conquest of the Aztec empire, followed by Francisco Pizarro's equally rewarding discovery and conquest of the Inca civilization down south in Peru, re-energized every conquistador's hopes of finding some equally affluent native civilization yet to be discovered and conquered; and the Indian rumor mill had long suggested that there was just such a civilization in the northern regions.

Almost from the moment the Spanish set foot on the Mexican mainland, they began to hear tales of northern cities of gold located somewhere in what is now the American southwest. At nearly every village or watering hole, there could be found at least one Indian who knew the general location of a fabulous city of gold way, way, off in the distance that would set fire to the imaginations of the gullible Spaniards.

> "After the riches of the Aztecs and the Incas, the Spaniards were ready to believe in anything. "Richard F. Pourade

It was true that, in very rare instances, some of these legends bore fruit, as in the case of the Aztec conquest, but that was the rare exception to the rule. In most instances, these "gold rumors" were simply clever lures the Indians used to rid themselves of the annoying, gold-hungry Spaniards. And yet, no matter how many times the Indians would wryly recount the same, tired old "treasure tales," the Spaniards would have to take the bait.

Back home in Spain, fortunes had been spent on the hopes of finding even larger fortunes, and every conquistador in the region was determined to be the one to score the next big bonanza. This "rivalry of conquest" made it impossible for the upwardly mobile conquistador to ignore even the most insignificant wisp of native gossip, lest the oversight should lead the competition to the next Aztec empire, or the Seven Cities of Gold, or even the Island of California. The Spaniards were simply caught in a "you snooze you lose" situation, which led to some pretty wild escapades up in the northern regions.

Fool's Gold

In 1528, Álvar Núñez Cabeza de Vaca and his party of 600 were driven ashore, by heavy storms, upon the west coast of Florida. He had come to the new world as the treasurer of an expedition led by Pánfilo de Narváez to establish a colony on the northeastern coast of Mexico and then launch an expedition northward where Narváez believed the Aztecs had originally come from. The working theory being, that where there's Aztecs, or even where there used to be Aztecs, there must be copious quantities of precious metal.

But now, beached hundreds of miles off course, they just wanted to make it back to civilization; that is until some local tribesmen appeared and began regaling the Spaniards with irresistible tales of gold for the taking just a few leagues to the north. Narváez immediately changed his game plan and, along with Cabeza de Vaca and 300 others, headed off in the direction in which the smiling Indians were pointing.

Eight years and 6000 miles later, that same Cabeza de Vaca and just three of his original 300 compatriots wandered into the Spanish settlement of Culiacan, Mexico, nearly dead of starvation, exposure, and exhaustion. Finding nothing but angry Indians, and unable to locate their support ships, they wandered through the southwest into parts of New Mexico and Arizona. All along the way they were attacked by Indians and ravaged by diseases and starvation. The enterprise was a monumental disaster.

But once safely back in the bosom of civilization, and possibly enjoying a little celebrity status, de Vaca began spinning his own grand tales in which he claimed to have seen the Seven Cities of Gold. At any other time and place, he might have been dismissed as a dementia case. But following the Aztec acquisition, de Vaca's story was taken as indisputable evidence that, not only were the native legends true, but they converged upon a popular legend of their own.

The legend of the Seven Cities of Gold, known collectively as Cibola, was not a local saga, but a popular 12th-century Spanish import. According to the legend, to save themselves and some sacred relics from the Moors, seven priests fled to a faraway land where each founded a city of gold, which remained undiscovered until Cabeza de Vaca wandered out of the Sonora desert. This was the sort of news that spread like wildfire in the new world; and in just three years, the delusional account of de Vaca's misadventures prompted four major expeditions into the mysterious northern regions of the American continent.

The Lost Boys

Hernando De Soto, the governor of Cuba, who had won fame and fortune in the conquest of the Incas, was the first out of the gate in May of 1539, when he set out from Havana with a self-funded expedition numbering about 700. Starting near the area of present-day Tampa Bay, he worked his way north into Georgia where a local tribe graciously offered a basket full of low-grade pearls, but no gold. From Georgia, De Soto embarked on a three-year odyssey through what is now the Carolinas, Tennessee, Alabama, Mississippi, and Arkansas, and like the Narváez expedition eleven years earlier, was constantly besieged by warring Indians, diseases, and the threat of starvation.

Advancing into Arkansas, De Soto discovered the Mississippi River and then died of fever. The remainder of the expedition, now half their original number, abandoned the quest and made their way back to Spanish-held territory. No gold was found, no colonies were established, and no natives were converted.

Just two months after De Soto embarked on his ill-fated adventure, Hernan Cortes commissioned Francisco de Ulloa to sail up the west coast of present-day Mexico with instructions to find the mythical Northwest Passage, or the Seven Cities of Gold, or the Island of California, or, if possible, all the above.

With three ships, Ulloa departed Acapulco on July 8, 1539. Six weeks later, he unexpectedly ran out of ocean at the head of the Gulf of California, right where he had expected to find the Island of California. Although his charts clearly indicated there should be ocean to spare, Ulloa was forced to make a hard-left turn and head back down south along the east coast of Baja California. While stopped for supplies near the area of present-day La Paz, the crews began showing signs of discontent.

After months of skirting along desolate coastlines, they had yet to see anything at all resembling the terrestrial paradise promised in Montalvo's description of California, much less any gold-laden Amazon women. In fact, the crew was so discouraged that, among them, the word, California, was used as a derogatory term for the folly of those who would dream of easy fortune in the new world.

Yet Ulloa managed to persuade them to soldier on long enough to round the tip of Baja and sail out into the Pacific Ocean. But heavy seas, which claimed one of his ships, forced him back to Mexico where he was murdered by one of his disgruntled crewmembers. Once again, no gold was found, no colonies were established, and no natives were converted.

Francisco Vázquez de Coronado, conqueror and governor of the territory of Nueva Galicia and hero of the Aztec conquest, had no doubt heard of the failure of the previous two expeditions and was taking no chances. He wanted a second opinion, so he sent a small party led by Friar Marcos de Niza into the New Mexico area to reconnoiter before mounting an expensive, full-scale expedition.

When Friar de Niza returned, he not only backed up Cabeza de Vaca's claims, but he augmented them further by describing the golden city as being situated atop a hill overlooking the Pacific Ocean, even though his directions to the location placed it squarely in the vicinity of present-day Albuquerque New Mexico. However, two reported sightings were all the encouragement Coronado needed. He was so sure he had found the Seven Cities of Gold, that he and his partner, Antonio de Mendoza, Viceroy of New Spain, invested huge sums of their own money to finance the third Spanish expedition into the American southwest.

On February 23, 1540, the Coronado expedition headed north along the western coast of mainland Mexico and then veered off east towards Arizona and New Mexico. Along the way, Coronado noted that the lands they passed through were so barren and inhospitable that foraging for food along the trail would be impossible should their supplies run low. This really should have been a red flag, since everybody knew that, in legends, cities of gold were always located in what's commonly referred to as, "a veritable paradise."

Nevertheless, with no paradise yet visible on the horizon, Coronado pressed on into New Mexico. When they finally arrived on the spot where de Niza said they would find the great civilization of Cibola, they found only a tribe of pueblo dwelling, Zuni Indians of very modest means. Upon further cross-examination, friar de Niza finally admitted that, during his first visit, he had only seen what he thought was the Seven Cities of Gold from a considerable distance. He confessed that he had to maintain this distance to stay out of arrow range of the angry villagers, which he originally described as warm and friendly. He also claimed that the sun was in his eyes.

Hoping to salvage the expedition, Coronado pushed on in a northeasterly direction where he encountered other equally impoverished tribes. Occasionally these encounters led to skirmishes. Other times, the indifferent natives provided the Spaniards with fresh legends of golden cities just around the next mountain range, which they followed all the way into Kansas, where the search was ended. The Coronado expedition is given credit for having discovered the Colorado River and the Grand Canyon but finds like that didn't pay the bills. After two years, Coronado returned to Mexico with only 100 of the 1700 men who had originally signed on. No gold was found, no colonies were established, and no natives were converted.

Fantasy Island

Now you would think that after having experienced three major disasters in their quest to discover fabulously wealthy civilizations known only to have existed in romance novels and ancient, medieval legends, the Spaniards might want to consider scaling back their conquest operations. But these conquistadors were nothing if not determined, for, within two years of the Coronado debacle, another big-ticket expedition was underway.

On June 27th, 1542, Juan Rodriguez Cabrillo and his three ships departed from Navidad, Mexico. Once again, this very costly expedition was financed by the Viceroy of New Spain, Antonio (never say die) de Mendoza, who had personally lost a fortune on the Coronado expedition. Unlike Ulloa, Cabrillo bypassed the Gulf of California and sailed directly out into the Pacific Ocean heading north along the west coast of Baja California with the usual to-do list: find the Northwest Passage, and/or the Seven Cities of Gold, and/or the Island of California.

Fighting his way north through heavy winds and strong southerly currents, he made his way to Ensenada where he stopped to make repairs. It was during this brief period ashore that Cabrillo and his crew had a chance to get a close-up look at the landscape and the locals. All the way up the coast of Baja, they had observed "high, naked, and rugged mountains," and once ashore, they found the flatlands to be just as barren and severe.

Like those who had preceded him, Cabrillo entered a world far removed from the earthy paradise he had hoped to find, and his meetings with the simple and conspicuously insolvent native peoples did nothing to ease his fears that this expedition may prove to be just as ruinous as all those that had gone before. But he wasn't being paid to second-guess; so, with his ships repaired, Cabrillo battled the Pacific's southerly currents northward up to the San Diego area, making land at Point Loma. He stayed just long enough to name the place San Miguel and note that it had a nice, natural harbor. Again, the local Indians showed no outward signs of affluence.

> **Smoke Signals**
> Cabrillo noted, as they sailed past the Los Angeles area, that the smoke from the Indian campfires on shore did not dissipate into the atmosphere, as was usual, but tended to just linger in air. What he was witnessing, of course, was L.A.'s notorious inversion layer, which still traps the airborne smog and pollutants the residents have been suffering with since the introduction of the automobile.

From San Diego, they continued north and came ashore again somewhere near Oxnard where they met the Chumash Indians. The Spaniards found the Chumash to be an amiable group willing to share all that they had, which, unfortunately, did not include anything in the way of hard currency. From Oxnard, the Cabrillo expedition sailed up into the Santa Barbara area and engaged in some island hopping, possibly still hoping to find the Island of California. While landing on San Miguel Island, in the Santa Barbara Channel, Cabrillo's party was attacked by Indians. In the scuffle, Cabrillo splintered his shin on some rocks. Twelve days later, he died of gangrene.

He was buried on the Island and the expedition proceeded under the command of his pilot. History is uncertain as to how far north they may have sailed. Some accounts say they went no further than Monterey, while others claim they ventured as far as the California/Oregon border. What is not nearly so vague is the outcome of the adventure—it was another spectacular failure. This time, the disillusionment among the Spanish was complete. After poking around the northern regions for twenty years, they only managed to discover what wasn't.

They discovered that there was no Northwest Passage, and there was no Cibola. There was no Island of California, no Amazon women, and worst of all, there was no gold. The celestial paradise Montalvo had promised turned out to be a burnt-over desert inhabited by aboriginal tribes of the most unaccomplished sort.

Four hundred years later this same stretch of Southern California coastline would be considered some of the most desirable beachfront property on the planet, but in the opinion of those 16th-century explorers who had first reached her shores, California was a desolate, God-forsaken, wasteland. Their reports concluded that the soil was bad, the rivers were dry, trees were nonexistent, and that Alta-California was not even worth the effort it would take to colonize it.

The failure of the Cabrillo expedition brought an end to Spain's great era of exploration in the Americas. They cut their losses and moved on. By royal decree, all gold recovery and colonization efforts were to be confined to those southern territories already conquered. Spain abandoned California and would not return for nearly two hundred years, and then only because they had to.

Chapter 2
You Are Here

A Two-Faced Territory

Even if it was centuries ago, it's hard to imagine the Spanish couldn't see any virtue in a region that would one day be recognized as the universal symbol of everything the good life had to offer. Didn't these people have any imagination? At the very least, you would think they would have been able to appreciate California's natural beauty, if not its potential for further development.

I thought the Spaniards completely blew the call, and who would know better than a native son. My days in Southern California were played out amidst the golden sunshine and lush tropical greenery of a South Pacific Island. So, what on earth were these Spaniards thinking? It was a paradise—wasn't it?

It's quite possible you may have got the same impression even though you may have never visited the place. In films, television shows, magazines, and newspapers, Southern California was often portrayed as a sun-drenched, tropical wonderland. The spectacular images they created were so prevalent in the 1950s and 60s that they have now become Southern California clichés: the young lovers walking barefoot in the moonlight along one of those fabulous beaches or sunning themselves beside a shimmering aqua-blue swimming pool, or sipping exotic cocktails in equally exotic, tropicalized settings.

This was the Southern California I knew and loved, so you can imagine my surprise when, years later, I discovered that what I called home was not the real Southern California at all. It was a clever ruse and I had been totally taken in by it. As it turned out, the Spaniards were right, and what I thought was Southern California was actually the culmination of a long-running, multi-generational, community art project.

This transformation from desert wasteland to pseudo tropical paradise began the moment the Spanish padres arrived in San Diego and culminated nearly two hundred years later with the blossoming of one of the most unique, iconic, and instantly recognizable sub-cultures on the planet. And all during that time, legions of regional promoters worked tirelessly to create fantastic myths and fanciful misconceptions specifically designed to lure the farmer, the settler, the invalid, the tourist, the dreamer, and the sucker out west.

Many of these far-fetched promotional efforts were so persuasive that their mythical manifestations endure to this very day. So, before we go any further, let's stop for a moment and clear up a few of the more common misconceptions.

Misconception #1: It's So Big

Looking at it on a map, the state of California looks like a fairly substantial piece of real estate. It measures 163,695.57 square miles, which makes it just about the size of Italy and England combined. The geographical center of the state is located about 38 miles east of the town of Madera, which is about 37° longitude, so it would seem logical to assume that Southern California would be anything south of that line, which is still pretty sizey. But the Southern California that most of us are familiar with is much, much smaller.

The real Southern California is one of the smallest regions in the United States and takes up only a fraction of all that sprawling territory south of Madera. It measures about 275 miles north to south from Santa Barbara to the Mexican border. In width, it measures no more than a hundred miles at best, and in some places, it dwindles down to just a few miles. It totals only 11,730 square miles. And yet, it is upon this narrow, coastal sliver of land that 90 percent of the population south of that 37° longitude mark call home.

Misconception #2: It's Conveniently Located

In the early days, the region was completely cut off from the rest of the state, as well as the rest of the nation, by the turbulent Pacific Ocean on the west, and a series of mountain ranges beginning with the Tehachapi range just north of Santa Barbara, which runs east/west and forms Southern California's northern border, and a continuous string of eight other mountain ranges running north/south, which make up the region's eastern flank. On the eastern side of those mountains is desert—a real, industrial-strength, *Lawrence of Arabia* style desert. And guarding the southern approach is still more seemingly endless desert. Southern California truly was, as Helen Hunt Jackson suggested, "an island on land."

Today, with our planes, trains, and automobiles, problems of accessibility would never occur to us; yet even with the completion of the first transcontinental railroad in 1869, Southern California was still one of the most isolated, inhospitable, and inaccessible regions in North America.

Misconception #3: It's A Tropical Paradise
Yeah, this is easily the most common misconception regarding Southern California. For over 100 years, one of the most indelible images of the region has been the profusion of lush, tropical flora, which seems to blossom from every square foot of the landscape whether it be public, private, commercial, residential, or just plain undeveloped. The presence of all this tropical plant life leads many people to falsely assume Southern California is a tropical region, when it's actually sub-tropical—a designation that covers a very wide range of climate conditions from benign to brutal.

The difference is in precipitation levels. Tropical is humid and wet whereas sub-tropical is hot and dry. But this description didn't fit in with the marketing strategies of the railroads, real-estate boosters, chambers of commerce, and land investment companies trying to encourage western settlement, and so they did all they could to re-align the public's understanding of the term to suggest something more like the pacific island paradise it would one day come to resemble.

The truth was that, although their obsessive quest for gold may have temporarily blinded them to the region's possibilities, the Spanish conquistadors were not far wrong when they pronounced the place to be a barren wasteland. Despite what all the promoters would have you believe, Southern California was, and still is, a barren, semi-arid desert. The summers are hot/warm, the winters are warm/mild, and the rainy season is generally modest though it can be interrupted by brief periods of flash flooding when it's not being interrupted by much longer periods of drought.

Misconception #4: Anything Grows
The notion that Southern California is a gardener's paradise is almost true, but certainly not under natural circumstances. The annual rainfall for a semi-arid region tops out at about 15 inches. In San Diego, where I come from, you can't really expect much more than 10 inches in a good year, and that's not near enough water to support the tropical vegetation the region is known for.

What it will support is bunchgrass, sagebrush, chaparral, and some gnarly looking scrub oaks. These are the plants native to Southern California in the lower, coastal elevations. Honestly, I'm almost ashamed to admit it, but I was well into my 20s before I discovered that a Californian did not invent the palm tree.

All that tropical plant life so strongly associated with Southern California, the birds of paradise, the hibiscus, the bougainvillea, the numerous varieties of palms, and thousands of varieties of shrubs and flowers have all been imported. All the trees generally thought to be indigenous to the region; the eucalyptus, the acacia, and the pepper tree have all been imported. All the state's famous citrus crops as well as all the varieties of grape have been imported. And all the water necessary to support all the imported vegetation has likewise been imported.

Nearly everything associated with the Southern California lifestyle has been imported from somewhere else. So, you have to wonder, with all the negatives associated with this region, why wouldn't the Spaniards stomp off in disgust? And who in their right mind would ever want to pick up where they left off? How does an isolated desert, lacking in nearly everything necessary to support even a modest settlement, evolve into one of the most popular and culturally influential localities on the planet? What has made this place so attractive to so many people for so many years?

The answer, of course, is the climate. The climate made Southern California, and a great deal of geological happenstance and dumb luck went into the making of the climate. Scientists whose job it is to ponder such questions have often labeled the whole topographical configuration of Southern California as a freak of nature—a random series of happy accidents.

The first of these happy accidents was the presence of the Pacific Ocean on the western border. The ocean's constant evaporation, and the persistent sea breezes blowing that cool, moisturized air inland over the desert landscape, lessens the force of the sun. But it would have little positive effect were it not for those ten consecutive mountain ranges running along the northern and eastern borders.

This wall of granite holds in the cooling sea breezes on their western slopes while blocking out the harsh, hot winds of the desert on their eastern slopes. It's this fortunate arraignment of a desert surrounded by ocean and mountains that constitutes Southern California's most valuable natural asset, the climate.

But it wasn't long before the first, determined colonists who arrived on the shores of Southern California discovered that this very hospitable climate enveloped a very inhospitable region. Anyone who expected anything more than blue skies and balmy breezes was going to have to manage on their own, and that is exactly what they did. Again, and again, and again, whether motivated by wild flights of fancy or desperate necessity, Californians were constantly required to improvise and get creative.

This reminds me of a witticism I've heard many times over the years. I think it was originally attributed to a reporter from the *L.A. Times*, and it went like this:

"*If California didn't exist, Americans would have to invent it.*"

Yeah, it's clever, but the premise is flawed. I figure this reporter must have been a new arrival; otherwise, he would have known the truth—Americans, among others, did invent it.

Chapter 3
The Padres Progress

The Russians are Coming!

The Spanish may have lost interest in California, but their inability to turn a profit in the region didn't stop other nations from entertaining notions of acquiring territory along the west coast. With its control of Mexico and the Spanish East Indies (the Philippines), Spain had completed the final link in a very lucrative sea/land/sea trade route to the Orient; but their main cultural and economic competitors, England, France, Portugal, and Holland had no foothold in the Pacific region. For those nations, a port on the coast of California would level the playing field. The English were the first to make a move.

In June of 1579, after a series of very successful raids on Spanish treasure ships, English privateer, Sir Francis Drake, landed at Point Loma near San Diego, or perhaps it was Drake's Bay north of San Francisco, or maybe it was Whale Cove in Oregon, nobody really knows for sure. What is known is that while he stopped to repair and re-provision his ships, he brazenly claimed the territory of California for the English crown. However, his sovereign, Elizabeth of England, perhaps not wanting to add the insult of jumping Spain's territorial claims, to the injury her privateers were already doing to their merchant shipping, never pressed this tenuous claim on California.

Things had remained relatively quiet along the California coast for another 190 years when word got back to the Spanish government that Russian fur trappers had set up several base camps in the San Francisco Bay area. This encroachment by a nation in a much better position to stake a claim in the region finally prompted Spain into action—such as it was.

Though all of Spain's previous colonization efforts had failed, and "nobody wanted to go to that desolate, dried out, flee infested wilderness," Alta-California was still their desolate, dried out, flee infested wilderness, and they meant to hang on to it. But the Spanish were way over-extended in the new world and had neither the money nor the military resources necessary to oppose a foe with designs on its remote northern frontier. To hold on to California, Spain was going to have to get creative. And it was at that moment, with their backs to the wall, that they came up with a barely credible but doable plan B.

Since they couldn't afford to send a conquering army into the region, and since very few Spaniards would freely volunteer to colonize California, why not just skip those two preliminary steps, and colonize those who were already there?

Basically, the plan was to run the standard Spanish colonization process in reverse: instead of seizing control of the region with a show of military might paving the way for civilian colonization and the subsequent Catholic conversion of the natives, the crown would send a detachment of determined Franciscan Friars to throw up a defensive barrier of missions along the California coast and then proceed to Hispanicize anyone who happened to be loitering in the general vicinity—cut-rate conquest!

After all, there were already about 130,000 native peoples living in California and they didn't seem to mind the fleas at all. The Franciscans would simply convert the Indians to the Catholic faith, teach them the Spanish language as well as a few useful skills, and thus transform them into industrious, God-fearing, taxpaying Spaniards.

Among the principals, reaction to the plan, which was to be fully implemented within ten years, would remain mixed. The Franciscans welcomed the opportunity to absorb whole native civilizations into the European cultural cabal, while the native peoples never really warmed up to the idea.

Calling All Padres

But cultural conversion was a long-term strategy; in the short term, the objective was simply to take and hold territory, and the man chosen to accomplish that task was California's new governor, Gaspar de Portola. With just a handful of soldiers, he was to occupy Monterey while the spiritual leader of the enterprise, Father Junipero Serra, was to build a string of missions from San Diego to Monterey converting the Indians as he progressed. 3-1

Early historical accounts would portray Serra and his Franciscans as kind and gentle guardians of their native flocks, but this idyllic interpretation was just one more bit of over-romanticized California mythology. Serra was, in fact, a grim, no-nonsense sort who practiced a medieval form of Catholicism requiring much self-inflicted suffering. According to his friend and biographer, Father Palou:

"He had no joys; He turned away from all sources of pleasure... He was habitually serious. Not a joke or a jovial action is recorded of him."

However, before this hardened taskmaster could begin the business of building the missions and converting the natives, he had to make his way to California, which, 200 years after the first Spaniards set foot on her shores, was still one of the most isolated and inaccessible regions in the Americas.

The Trip to Paradise

To increase the odds that some of the 300 participants would make it to the finish line, the expedition was divided. Three supply ships left La Paz for San Diego in January of 1769, and two overland parties departed a short time after. Both groups suffered heavy losses. The strong currents and frequent storms of the Pacific overwhelmed the small ships. One was lost at sea, and by the time the other two reached San Diego, half their crews had died of scurvy.

The overland parties, which included Serra and de Portola, fared no better. The hardships they encountered crossing the vast deserts compelled many of the native support troops to quietly slip away in the night. By the time both the sea and land parties arrived at their destination, death and desertion had cut their number in half. And like so many other cash-strapped, European colonization operations, foresight was lacking in the planning stages, for they had neglected to include any experienced hunters or farmers among their number.

With the provisions exhausted, their only hope was to go hat-in-hand to the local inhabitants and see if they couldn't negotiate a temporary bail-out program. This approach had worked in the past, but unlike the other tribes the Spaniards had encountered during their conquests (the Aztec empire builders and the majestic warriors of the Great Plains), the California tribes were somewhat unaccomplished. They didn't farm, and they weren't very capable hunters.

They were what future visitors would refer to as "digger Indians." Their diet consisted mainly of acorns, roots, and wild berries—a bill of fare not well attuned to the European palate. Yet, however humble the locals may have been, they had their pride, and they were not all that impressed with these pushy

The Enervation Generation

It's true, having adapted to an environment that placed few demands upon their cunning and ingenuity, the indigenous tribes of California were somewhat slack. In observing these natives, colonists became convinced that Southern California's climate induced intoxicating effects. This apparent state of laxity was referred to as enervation and was described as a weakening of vitality and mental vigor. As we'll see, the fear of enervation is a recurring theme in Southern California history as similar symptoms developed in other, "more industrious," societies. The indigenous peoples of California were probably just the first to succumb to the soothing spell of the Southland—the first of many generations of laid-back, Southern Californians.

newcomers. They preferred to keep their distance and were of little help to the Franciscans. This societal friction, and the Spaniard's inability to forage off the land, nearly derailed the whole enterprise before it even got started, when, at the very last minute, a long-overdue supply ship arrived.

So finally, two hundred and twenty-seven years after Cabrillo first discovered it, California would be semi-settled by the Spanish. It would be Imperial Spain's last venture in the Americas.

We're Here!

Gaspar de Portola took a small party north to establish a presidio at Monterey Bay, while Serra stayed in San Diego to build the first of the twenty-one California missions.

The 167-year-old directions furnished de Portola by an earlier expedition had so overplayed the majesty of the modest little port that he didn't recognize it and pushed right on past it to discover San Francisco Bay. Six months later, de Portola returned to San Diego claiming he couldn't find the bay or any other worthwhile build site. Like the conquistadors of two centuries past, de Portola saw no virtue in California.

In his first report back to Mexico City, he declared that if the Russians really wanted this forbidding territory the Spanish Crown should make them a gift of it as a punishment for their transgressions. But the government refused to withdraw, and so, accompanied by Serra, de Portola dutifully made a second foray up north, locating the illusive Monterey Bay on May 24, 1770.

Who's First?

As promising as the Spaniard's colonization scheme may have looked on paper, its practical application required the cooperation of the native population, and that provision would never be resolved to the satisfaction of either party. As it turned out, the California natives were quite comfortable in their ineptitude and generally resented the Spaniard's efforts at re-culturalization.

Their dissent, however, did not deter the Franciscans, and the relationship between the two groups, which began in an atmosphere of skepticism and miss-trust, progressively deteriorated over the course of the Franciscan's 65-year tenure in California. Tensions between the two occasionally broke out into open rebellion. Several serious skirmishes were fought, and some lives were lost, but the Indians of California, despite their overwhelming numbers, were poor strategists and somewhat hesitant in battle. Consequently, they would never be able to break the Spaniard's hold on them.

Move It!

One of the first conflicts between the Franciscans and Indians was over zoning regulations. The Indians located their villages on the very best sites with the easiest access to water, game, and vegetation. The Franciscans, also keen to have access to these necessities, as well as access to the Indians, built their missions right in the middle of the Indian villages, driving the two factions further apart as they came closer together.

Not far from the missions, the Spaniards also built presidios or military garrisons. Always under-manned and poorly supplied, these presidios were not very imposing structures, but it was believed that the presence of anything even vaguely resembling a fort would be enough to keep the Indians in line and fool most foreign intruders, but neither assumption proved to be valid.

> **Convict Company**
>
> To man these feeble fortresses in a time when a tour of duty in California was a very unpopular undertaking, the Spaniards launched an aggressive recruitment campaign in the prisons and jails of Mexico. Potential recruits could choose to serve in the Spanish army in California or face immediate execution of sentence. For those facing a death sentence, the military option turned out to be very popular; but so many of those convicted of "non-hanging" offenses chose to serve out their sentences rather than serve in California that the Spanish penal system had to be revised to include a sentence to California.

Let's Get Missionized

Once settled in, the Franciscans, backed up by their outlaw army, took charge. There was much work to be done in establishing Spain's territorial claims, and the Indians were slated to do most of it.

In the very early days of the mission era, many of the local Indian tribes could be lured into the mission system with gifts of food and the usual assortment of brightly colored trinkets; but it was a devil's bargain for the native civilizations of California. Once they were absorbed into the mission system, the relatively carefree lifestyle they had known was gone forever.

Inside the missions, the "neophytes," as the Franciscans referred to them, were strictly regimented. The workday in and around the missions, presidios, and out in the fields lasted from sunup to sundown. Calling in sick was not an option. Those who would not work were either starved and/or beaten. On the mission grounds, the men, women, and children (families included) were kept apart and always under the watchful eyes of the padres and/or the military guards. Any bending of the strict, militaristic, mission rules resulted in harsh punishment.

Contrary to the romantic images conjured up in the old folklore, the living conditions of the mission Indians were abominable. To keep them from running off, they were deliberately underfed, and the sanitation was so ghastly that diseases spread freely. This unhealthy condition was compounded by the soldier's frequent abuse of the Indian women, which quickly spread syphilis throughout the native population.

In this constant state of near starvation, and with the unchecked spread of disease, the Indians began to die off in vast numbers; and as word spread of the deaths within the missions, those still running free took to the hills.

> *"The Indians live well free but as soon as we reduce them to a Christian and community life... they fatten, sicken, and die."*
>
> A Franciscan Friar

Surf's Up?

On the third and last of Captain James Cook's great voyages of discovery, in 1779, he stopped at a rather attractive island group in the mid-pacific, which he named the Sandwich Islands in honor of his friend, the Earl of Sandwich. Once ashore, he and his men were proclaimed deities and lavishly entertained by the locals. While they were all "getting acquainted," the officers and men witnessed a most peculiar native ritual. According to a Lieutenant King, the natives were observed paddling out to sea on large wooden planks. Once beyond the breakers, they would turn these planks toward shore. Then, while propelled by the incoming waves, they would stand upright and ride these planks back to shore. In the ship's journal, Lieutenant King described, in great detail, what he called "surf bathing." His log entry for the *HMS Discovery* was western civilization's first recorded account of surfing.

With fewer and fewer neophytes available to work on their expanding ranches and farms, the padres expanded their recruitment program.

The Usual Suspects

To replenish their flocks, the Franciscans sent soldiers into the hills to capture escaped neophytes. Any "new converts" found along the way were rounded up as well. Sometimes, the padres would allow a few mission Indians to escape so the soldiers could track them back to their villages and round up the whole community.

Those who did escape and were caught faced severe punishment. The laying on of 50 to 100 lashes was a common deterrent. Serra's harsh treatment of the Indians prompted the territorial governor to file a complaint against him with the Spanish government, but Serra had the meddlesome governor removed and the floggings continued.

Dawn of the Good Life

With all the ugly goings-son at the missions, it might seem odd to suggest that the very first glimmerings of the good life, as it would come to be practiced in Southern California, arose amidst the chaos of this unfortunate period; but the seeds of that Arcadian lifestyle were indeed first planted in this era. After a few years of California living, the padres began to get a feel for their new environment. They discovered that the rich soil and mild climate made for a very productive year-round growing season that favored nearly all the crops they imported.

Ranching came just as easy as farming. The Mexican cattle and sheep that were left to graze on the oceans of California grasslands, rapidly multiplied. By the late 1770s, many of the missions had become profitable commercial enterprises with wheat fields, granaries, orchards, vineyards, and ranches running thousands of head of cattle, sheep, and horses, all of which supplied the needs of the territory and allowed the Padres to begin developing a little trade with Mexico and a new group of visitors to the region—the foreign traders, whalers, and ottermen who had begun operating up and down the pacific coast.

This trade with "foreign smugglers" was strictly forbidden by the Spanish government, but the Franciscans, way beyond the reach of the King's ministers, willfully ignored their edicts and established smuggling as early California's preferred trading policy.

As time passed, the padres shifted focus away from their original obligation of stewarding their native flocks, to the stewarding of their many enterprises. By claiming the natives were hopelessly barbaric and unable to adapt to European civilization, the Franciscans justified their de-emphasis of the colonization program; instead, the Indians would be kept in perpetual servitude to work the farms and ranchos of the Franciscans, who, in effect, had become the first of the California land barons.

With the natives doing all the heavy lifting, and the land producing so freely, and the genteel environment easing the usually heavy burden of a frontier existence, the Franciscans found they could work a little downtime into their schedules. Inadvertently, this new California mission culture had produced something unheard of on any frontier—leisure. In the 18th century, leisure was a condition unknown to all but the aristocracy; but in far-off California, even the humble servants of God were learning to enjoy the privilege of Kings.

The Spanish friars of the Franciscan order were the first Europeans to succumb to the warm, languid, intoxicating rhythms of the Southern California experience. Could it be they were suffering from a slight case of enervation? It's possible; but there would be no need to worry over a cure, for the golden days of the Franciscans were not to last.

There Goes the Neighborhood
As the California missions became increasingly more productive, they began trading even more surplus produce with Mexico. And to facilitate this growing trade, the government improved the roads between California and Mexico, which not only made trade easier but colonization as well. And although Southern California was still viewed by most Spaniards as a wasteland, many of Mexico's more adventurous, or more desperate, inhabitants were willing to give it a shot.

The government was glad to offload what it considered to be the dregs of society while adding to the head count of a distant and troublesome territory. And the Franciscans, always in the market for new parishioners, also saw it as a plus. And so they made welcome these new colonists. But it wasn't long before problems would develop between the Franciscans, the new colonists, and the Spanish government.

Once the settlers arrived in California, boundary disputes arose over the mission lands. With the Catholic Church in possession of nearly all the best farmland, the new settlers began challenging their claims. The Franciscans appealed to Mexico City for help, but Spain's interest in the California missions had waned, and the government had neither the willingness nor the ability to vigorously defend the Churches' authority.

A Circling Come the Sharks
In the midst of all these domestic squabbles, several outside groups were also beginning to speculate on the rationale of honoring certain, frail territorial claims. The Franciscan's foreign trading partners were very much impressed with the natural beauty and what they perceived to be the immense commercial potential of the region, and often shared their thoughts with the folks back home:

> "The soil is good and the climate pleasant. It's a country rather calculated to expand rather than to restrain the energies of man, a country where the creator has scattered more than an ordinary share of his bounties." Jedediah Smith

Because these private letters from the frontier were the only source of news coming out of the far west, they were often published in the newspapers where they would stir up the imaginations of the folks back home and encourage even more adventurers to trek out west. What was revealed in the pages of these letters was the developing myth of a promised land at the western edge of the continent. Though some accounts were wildly exaggerated, they had an almost hypnotic effect on easterners dreaming of a better life; and it's from these letters home that the vague perception of California as an enchanted land began to take shape.

But it wasn't all an unrestrained love fest; throughout the early history of the golden state, it was reviled just as much as it was revered. Continuing into the next century, California would be hounded by such wildly mixed reviews that it would remain one of the most difficult regions to settle in the continental United States.

> **Ah Paradise**
> On his 1786 voyage of discovery, the French scientist Jean François de Galaup de la Perouse visited Monterey, and in his reports, noted that California's mild climate was similar to southern France. It was the first recorded acknowledgment of what would become California's most acclaimed asset.

"People generally look on it as the garden of the world, or the most desolate place of creation." John Bidwell, 1841

Along with the usual complaints of stingy natural resources, there was growing dissatisfaction with the ramshackle quality of civic development: the Americans, Europeans, and Russians felt that Spain had failed to develop the territory to its fullest potential. Visitors complained of bad roads, deplorable accommodations, and a general shortage of goods and services. Infrastructure was non-existent. There were no schools and no manufacturing or industry of any kind outside of the missions.

> **The Peculiar Institution**
> California remained a wilderness mainly because the Franciscans dependence on native labor alleviated the need to progress and modernize, which hindered Spain's ability to attract enough industrious settlers to California to establish a stable society.

Throughout the Spanish era, California would remain poorly managed and poorly defended. It was a situation that did not go unnoticed by the foreign military men who coveted the strategic ports of San Francisco, San Diego, and Monterey.

"California was totally incapable of making any resistance against a foreign invasion."
                    Captain George Vancouver, British Royal Navy

Similar conquest fantasies were even starting to turn up in American newspapers and monthly magazines:

> *"The conquest of this country would be absolutely nothing; it would fall without effort to the most inconsiderable force."*
>
> William Shaler

And as these tales of a feeble, underappreciated "land of Eden" continued to drift eastward, the steady stream of adventurers drifting westward began to grow, progressively weakening Spain's grip on California.

What War?

In 1821, Mexico won its independence from Spain, and although the war itself (which began in 1810) had almost no impact on California and the missions, the regime change would. Many Mexicans were horrified when they learned of the Franciscan's enslavement of the Indians and demanded the government close the missions. A position supported by California's native-born settlers, or "Californios," who were eager to seize control of the church's huge tracts of farmland.

Notice to Vacate

When the Franciscans arrived in California in 1769, they were charged with the task of creating civil communities within a decade. By 1834, the deadline had passed six times over and no civil communities had been created; instead, the padres had created a series of feudal fiefdoms in which they were the lords and masters of California's most productive acreage and thousands of Indian slaves. But the Franciscans did not hold title to their kingdoms. They served at the pleasure of a government that had run out of patience with their procrastination.

On August 9, 1834, Governor Jose Figueroa issued a proclamation authorizing the California missions to be secularized. All the mission lands and properties were to be turned over to the people of California—the churches' native converts.

Though none of the neophytes who remained within the mission system had been well-schooled in the ways of a responsible and productive citizenry, the Mexican government held firm to the original Spanish plan and forced the Franciscans to hand over half the mission lands to the Indians. The rest of the lands and properties were to be divided up into land grants, which were to be distributed among worthy civil servants, soldiers, and well-connected Californios.

Dawn of the Dons

Though many of the mission Indians did receive grants of land, very few were able to maintain their holdings. Some, unable to fully grasp the concept of land ownership, just walked away from their property. Some were cheated out of their land, and some sold it for next to nothing. But few of the lucky ones, those who survived the mission experience, were left with anything to show their years of servitude.

The mission system came to an end in the 1840s, but the era would not quietly dissolve into a dark, misty memory. Fifty years after the last mission was abandoned, a middle-aged tourist from Amherst, Massachusetts, would write a popular novel romanticizing the mission period beyond the recognition of all who had experienced it. Scholars would denounce it as a historical travesty, but a fast-growing state in need of a romantic legend would embrace it as gospel.

> **X-tribes**
> Of the tribes the Franciscans were able to missionize, all are now extinct, while those that managed to avoid the missions have endured.

Chapter 4
Rancho Paradiso

Give me Land, lots of Land

As the process of secularization continued, California's provincial governors did their best to dispose of the mission lands as fast as possible. Ex-soldiers, friends, family, and well-connected Californios were rewarded with huge grants of mission land. Just about any Mexican citizen (natural born or naturalized) willing to promise to settle in the region would be granted a piece of Alta-California upon request. Between 1834 and 1846 more than 600 of these "land grant ranchos" were created. This mass transfer of mission property into private hands marked the beginning of Southern California's colorful rancho period.

The unrestrained generosity on the part of the Mexican government was not totally magnanimous; there was a very practical consideration involved. The great real-estate giveaway was a last, desperate effort to populate the region, for even before Mexico gained control of the territory, it was well known that it was only a matter of time before one of the many foreign powers prowling the Pacific would challenge Mexico's hold on the region.

> *"All informed men knew that California was a derelict craft ready to be picked up by any captain who will take it into the port of a strong and stable government."* Alan Nevins

The situation made it imperative to distribute the land quickly in the hope that the presence of new settlers and settlements would legitimize Mexico's territorial claims. As for the new grantees, they would soon discover the truth in the adage, *"ya get what ya pay for."* Shortcomings aside, the missions did provide some semblance of civic structure. Without them, California was just another hopelessly under-endowed frontier with no infrastructure and almost no government support.

The grantees, most of which were farmers, were on their own and only the very well-connected were fortunate enough to acquire some of the mission's select, grade-A bottomland; the rest got desert. But the outlook was equally bleak for both the well-connected and the disconnected. After 60 years of civilizing, California was still too isolated and underpopulated to support any kind of sustained commercial activity. It appeared that all these nouveau-Californians were likely to extract from their free land was a life of severe hardship and poverty.

The Hide Barons

The missions succeeded because they were a very small number of self-sustaining communities that consumed much of what they produced. Trade was merely a sideline. But now, there would be hundreds of small-time ranchers and farmers all producing the same products for a nonexistent market. A bare subsistence existence seemed the only reasonable expectation when, unexpectedly, the Yankee's fur trade began to flounder.

After 40 years of intensive trapping along the California coast, the sea otter population was completely tapped out; and this was at a time when the growing industrialization of the eastern United States was creating an insatiable demand for all manner of leather goods. With the source of the most fashionable furs exhausted, styles rapidly broadened to include the far less trendy, but readily available, cowhides. And cows were the one resource California had in abundance.

With too few inhabitants to support a cattle industry, the thousands of mission cattle were let loose to roam free and had since multiplied into the hundreds of thousands. Overnight, those underappreciated, free-ranging cows had become the precious raw materials for California's first mega-industry.

California's hapless grantees suddenly found themselves positioned to become the territory's first true entrepreneurs. Every ranch in the territory requisitioned every available horse and rider to scour the countryside rounding up and branding every wayward cow they could find. Gone were the ottermen and in their place came the Yankee traders, turning what had once been a niche market into Southern California's main métier.

The Californios were desperate for nearly every imaginable necessity and convenience item when the Yankees arrived on the coast loaded down with all manner of trade goods, tools, household items, foodstuffs, and gold and silver currency. In exchange, they filled their ships with piles of dried and cured cowhides and hide bags filled with tallow.

The remote ranchos of Southern California had become one of the main suppliers of raw materials for the U.S. market as well as the thriving markets of the Orient. By the thousands, cattle were slaughtered and skinned right out on the range, and because there was still no market for beef, their carcasses were left to rot in the sun. With the hide trade such an instant, runaway success, almost every

Californio involved became very wealthy very fast. It was as if they had been granted a license to print money. In fact, with real currency still very scarce, these cowhides became such common items of barter that the Yankee traders began calling them *"California bank notes."*

The Nouveau Rancho Riche

With new wealth came a new and extravagant lifestyle. Most of the new hide barons would build immense adobe palaces and spend lavishly adorning themselves in the finest of imported jewelry and apparel. Everything was trimmed in silver and gold, from mantillas and fans to hatbands, boots, spurs, and even riding tack. To complement their newfound status, they even created a new social structure like that of the Deep South.

Those of pure Spanish ancestry occupied the top tier and were known as the "gente de razon," or "people of reason," which meant, "people of quality." The Mexicans held the middle ground, and the Indians reprised their roles as the involuntary support staff. Between the end of the mission era and the beginning of the rancho period, the poor California Indians barely got a weekend off before they were once again forced into hard labor.

To the dons, the patriarchs of the landed elite, it was understood that the Indians were a part of their estates. Many who had run off to the hills after the missions shut down were rounded up all over again and put to work on the ranchos. However, under this new rancho regime, they would actually draw a paycheck.

The Californios could never really get comfortable with out-and-out slavery, and so they devised a new and insidious system of perpetual servitude. Every Saturday afternoon, usually on the front steps of the local saloon, the Indian laborers would be paid just enough to get roaring drunk. By midnight, most would be behind bars on

---

Tallow is the hard fat that was used to make soap, candles, and lubricants.

No Stinking Taxes!

With this sudden burst of commercial activity, the inattentive Mexican government claimed a share of the spoils in taxes and set up a customhouse in Monterey to collect. But the independently minded Californios cleverly sidestepped the intrusion by electing, as their territorial customs agent, one of the most prolific Yankee smugglers on the west coast. Under this arraignment, the customhouse stood vacant, while the smuggling trade flourished.

A Ranch in the Burbs

One hundred years later, a descendent of these Californios would draw upon the layout of their adobe ranchos to create a masterpiece of mid-20th century architectural design and a hallmark of the Southern California lifestyle—the California Ranch House.

charges of vagrancy and public drunkenness. Monday morning, they would be sentenced to a week of "community service" on one of the local ranchos in a self-perpetuating cycle of servitude. As it was with the missions, Indian labor was the backbone of a rancho economy that allowed the gente de razon the leisure time necessary to indulge in other, more enjoyable pursuits.

Among the most fashionable amusements of the day were sports, partying, and gambling. The Californios loved gambling and would bet on anything, a horse race, a deck of cards, a pair of dice, or any other jointly observable chance occurrence.

The ease with which fortunes were made in the hide trade spawned a reckless, carefree spirit, which was never more in evidence than during rodeo time when the cattle herds were rounded up for branding. It was an arduous task that took several days, but it was always undertaken in combination with a huge fiesta. Here, the hospitality of the gente de razon proved boundless; the festivities would go on for weeks and were often remembered for a lifetime. Many a foreign guest would marvel at the Californio's "celebratory expertise," and spread tales of their reveries across oceans and continents.

> **The First Rodeos**
> Many of the roundup duties, especially those requiring great skill on horseback, were often performed by members of the nobility for the entertainment of their guests; this spectacle would eventually be turned into the organized, competitive event known as the rodeo.

The Sweet Do Nothing

It was these Spanish aristocrats of California's rancho period that conducted much of the pioneering research into the art of leisure—what would one day be described as, "the good life." They were the first Californians to whole-heartedly succumb to what one British observer referred to as *"el dolce far niente,"* or *"the sweet do nothing,"* a regional affliction brought on by prolonged exposure to easy affluence, good living, and great natural beauty; and you didn't have to be a cattle baron to take part. Richard Henry Dana noted, in his 1840 novel, *Two Years Before the Mast*, that even his Hawaiian shipmates were able to indulge themselves in the leisurely verve of an emerging Southern California lifestyle:

> *"The Sandwich-Islanders... were living on the beach, keeping up a grand carnival... drinking, playing cards, and carousing in every way... so long as they had money, they would not work."*

So here it was, as early as the 1830s, on the beach at Dana Point (named for the author), that Hawaiian sailors were already hard at work codifying the laid-back character of advanced, mid-20th century, California surf culture.

The Yankee Dons

The Californios were having such a very good time, and they were so open and friendly, that many a lowborn Yankee sailor would jump ship, take Mexican citizenship, adopt the Catholic faith, possibly marry a daughter of the gente de razon, and become a "Yankee don." Some of these common seamen became well-respected members of the California aristocracy, acquiring large ranchos of their own.

Astonished at their amazing good fortune, these deckhands turned dons would often write letters home praising this beautiful country of unlimited opportunities. It was in the many exuberant scripts of this sort that California's mythological status as the land of second chances was slowly nurtured.

And these AWOL sailors were not the only foreigners crashing the Californio's party. American fur trading companies regularly sent illegal hunting parties into California's mountains and backcountry often squatting on the land and setting up permanent camps and trading posts. In their quest for beaver pelts, they had practically scouted the entire state and had become very familiar with the terrain. So familiar that U.S. government officials with an eye toward westward expansion frequently solicited reports of their observations.

But the United States was only one of several nations contemplating a possible "forced annexation" of California. More and more foreigners were drifting into the territory by land and sea, and it seemed that every one of them had concocted a plot to relieve Mexico of its northern territories.

In 1835, a member of the Royal Geographical Society of London proposed that Britain send all its poor and dispossessed to California as sort of an advanced guard. In 1839, the attaché of the French Foreign Office urged his government to land a ground force at San Diego and then conquer their way north to San Francisco. With no navy of their own, the Prussians tried to rent one from the Danes to implement their own invasion plan, and the business-savvy Scots tried to arrange a buyout by assuming Mexico's debt to England in exchange for California. Amidst all these idle intrigues, America took the initiative and invaded California—twice.

The Pre-Invasions

In October of 1842, Commodore Thomas Catesby Jones, commander of the United States Navy's Pacific Squadron, was patrolling the

California coast when he received an "unconfirmed communication," suggesting that the British Navy might be launching an invasion of California. Jones, acting without orders, made straight for Monterey, landed troops, captured the town, and raised the American flag in the town square as bewildered villagers looked on. Holding his position in Monterey, he awaited official orders, or the brutal onslaught of the British fleet; neither was forthcoming.

Within days, Jones realized his mistake. He quietly struck the flag and set sail for Los Angeles where he presented his formal apology to Governor Micheltorena, who graciously accepted and used the occasion as a pretext to throw a fiesta in the Commodore's honor. Unwittingly played for comedy, Commodore Jones's misguided imperial escapade posed only a slight menace to Mexico's dominion. It was that other, nearly undetectable, little incursion that occurred the year before that presented a much more ominous threat.

In 1841, the Bidwell family, along with 69 others, left the banks of the Mississippi River and trekked over 2000 miles across the great plains, and the great deserts, over the great Sierra Nevada Mountain range, and right into the San Joaquin Valley—the very heart of California. This was not the usual bunch of burly, leather-clad mountain men secretly slipping in and out of the territory on foot; it was groups of families in wagons. It wasn't easy; they nearly lost their lives doing it, but they proved it could be done. And because it could be done, others would surely follow.

Bad Company

Fearing just that very outcome, the Mexican government issued orders to the people of California to drive the Yankees out; but instead, they welcomed them in. By the time the Mexican government had really begun to feel uneasy about the presence of so many Americans in California, they had already become prominent members of the rancho society.

The Californios, bemused by the industriousness of these foreigners, found them to be much more dependable allies than their own government. And besides, to most Californios, it had already become clear that the persistent, westward momentum of the American was beyond restraint.

> *"We find ourselves suddenly threatened by hordes of immigrants whose progress we cannot arrest. They are cultivating farms, establishing vineyards, erecting mills, sawing up lumber, building workshops, and doing a thousand other things which seem natural to them." Pio Pico*

As for the foreign contingent, they were not always as charitable as their hosts. Most Yankee outlanders considered the Californios too laid-back and preoccupied with their socializing and merry making to reap the rewards made available to the go-getter in this bountiful land of opportunity. The American's protestant belief that hard work and frugality were qualities that could lift one's soul into heaven ran counter to the Catholic's more relaxed approach to labor and economics.

Like the Franciscans, the Californios were working a system that didn't really demand the same sort of dogged determination and industriousness one generally expected to see in the inhabitants of a frontier region. The operation of the ranchos was left to the Indian laborers and other assorted hirelings. Agriculture, other than subsistence gardening, was not practiced, and the development of industry was not pursued.

Commerce was restricted to a hide trade that was flourishing so effortlessly that even some of their Yankee compadres were slipping into the same comfortable lifestyle patterns. Maybe it was here, in the 1840s, with the fusion of these two contrasting cultures that blended the recreational and entrepreneurial arts, that some of the distinctive facets of the character of the Southern Californian began to evolve.

War Parties

But the cozy relationship between the Californios and their American neighbors would not be shared with the Mexican government. The management of such a distant and impoverished territory required a degree of expertise rarely found in California's bureaucrats. Among Mexico's competent and talented administrative officials, a posting to California was to be shunned. Any administrator of above-average ability was usually able to redirect such undesirable assignments to less experienced, and often less ethical officials.

After years of having to endure the Mexican government's ineffectual stewardship of the territory, the rancheros developed an independent streak that would often flare up into open hostility. Mini revolutions would erupt on a near-weekly basis. Evidence of some governmental corruption or the issuance of some burdensome edict would incite one or more of the dons to raise a militia and attack the governor's troops. Surprisingly, these uprisings generally produced more comedy than tragedy.

Since the government's soldiers were still recruited from its jails and prisons, military discipline was generally weak. Therefore, they were disinclined to put themselves in harm's way by mounting serious opposition to a bunch of unruly aristocrats. As for the Californios, they had way too much going for them to want to risk their lives over the shortcomings of a distant government they routinely ignored anyway. So, instead of horrific bloodlettings, these conflicts became symbolic carnivals.

The soldiers would fire indifferently aimed volleys in the direction of the Californios who would respond in kind and then break off for refreshments. A few volleys, a few drinks, and all in good fun. Often, bystanders would gather outside the line of fire to watch the show. Rarely was anyone injured, yet even without the threat of serious harm, the dons usually made their point; and in this manner, they sent more than a few third-rate California governors back to Mexico at the quick step.

This smoldering dissatisfaction with the Mexican government prompted some prominent Californios to consider declaring California's independence from Mexico, while others entered into secret negotiations with U.S. government officials for the annexation of California into the United States. But in the end, all the behind-the-scenes skullduggery would go for naught, for by the summer of 1845, unbeknownst to the conspirators on either side, events had already been set in motion which would take the matter out of their hands.

Chapter 5
Johnny's War

Let's just suppose that we've all gone out to the theater on a Saturday night to see one of the hottest shows in town. Inside the theater, two people are holding twenty of the best seats in the house for friends who have yet to arrive. As the house lights dim, and the seats remain vacant, what do you suppose will happen?

By the 1840s, Mexico's predicament had become just this acute. For years they had been holding territory they were not able to colonize; they couldn't fill the seats and a crowd was gathering. Foreign warships regularly put in at California ports in open defiance of Mexico's demands that they back off. Everybody seemed to be encroaching on California's territory and that was perceived as a serious threat, not only to Mexico but to the United States.

> **Misfirin'**
> The presidios were so woefully neglected that they often had to beg gunpowder from visiting warships just to fire the obligatory salute.

Cover Ye Backside

The conquest of California has often been described as the fulfillment of a nationalistic principle known as Manifest Destiny. This was not an official government policy, but merely an opinion shared by many U.S. citizens that it was America's destiny to expand her boundaries to the west coast and spread the American principles of freedom and democracy from sea to sea.

On this issue, the country was split along party lines with the Democrat-Republicans in favor of westward expansion, while the Whig party was very much opposed. Even the journalist who created the concept (John L. O'Sullivan, who opposed the war with Mexico) did not conceive of it as a call to arms, but as a gradual process in which neighboring territories, as they filled up with American settlers, would establish democratic governments and apply for admission to the Union.

There were, however, some factions within the country that wanted to skip the slow gestation period and just go for the jugular. But the desire to acquire more territory was never as strong as the desire to survive as a sovereign nation. For as much as some Americans might have coveted California's commercial potential, the more pressing issue was one of national security: could the United States possibly continue to exist with England in control of California and the southwest?

The conflict between Great Britain and the United States over the Oregon Territory threatened to draw the two nations into what would be their third war in just 70 years. That standoff ended in a compromise, but if Britain took possession of California, there would be no compromise; the United States, in effect, would be surrounded. To prevent that possibility, the United States made two attempts to buy California from Mexico; both offers were rejected.

With regards to what happened next, most of the who, what, when, and where, have been well documented. It's the question of why that will forever remain a mystery, for everyone involved took their secrets to the grave. So, depending on which theory you believe, the conquest of California was either a government-sponsored, covert, insurgence operation or the work of a single rouge operative gone way off the reservation. Judging from the clues history has left us, the truth probably lies somewhere in between.

Which Way to The Front?

In the spring of 1845, Captain John C. Fremont of the U.S. Army Topographer's Corps held open auditions for the 62 positions available on his third expedition out west. Even in the planning stages, there were clues that this operation was extraordinary. Unlike Fremont's earlier expeditions, which were made up of mapmakers, geologists, and botanists, this crew was made up of seasoned frontiersmen and ex-soldiers assembled based on their exemplary marksmanship.

The outfitting of the expedition was curious as well. Along with the usual, government-issued supplies and provisions, those who made the cut were also issued a long-range, high-powered, Hawken rifle, a brace of pistols, and a very large knife.

The Fremont party left St. Louis, Missouri in June of 1845. Official army records stated that their objective was to map the source of the Arkansas River. But the large troop size (three times that of his first expedition) indicated that there might be other, more militant objectives to be achieved. And, sure enough, early in their journey, even though the river was clearly leading them on a northwesterly course, Fremont ordered his men to break off and march due west.

The Guileful Gringos

By early 1846, Fremont and his party arrived in the Sacramento Valley. As protocol dictated, he went to Monterey and presented himself to Mexican commander-general Jose Castro as the leader of an American "scientific expedition," and requested permission to camp for the winter in the San Joaquin Valley. Although not thoroughly convinced these bawdy-looking galoots were real scientists, Castro granted the request. But instead of heading directly for the valley, Fremont hung around Monterey and paid a visit to the American Consul and suspected spy, Thomas Larkin, who was in secret negotiations with a "high-level Mexican official" for the peaceful annexation of California.

Though later events seem to indicate that Larkin did not reveal his activities to Fremont, some believe that, should this deal sour, Fremont was expected to nudge the Californios toward revolt. Years later, Fremont would claim that his orders were to keep the British from gaining a foothold in California. It's possible that he was "unofficially" assigned to perform either or both tasks as events unfolded.

Whatever his orders, from Monterey Fremont moved into Santa Cruz, and then relocated to Salinas. All the moving around was making General Castro very nervous. Fremont seemed to be stalling, waiting for something to happen. Finally, Castro ordered him out of California. But instead of leaving, Fremont and his fellow "scientists" moved to Gavilan Peak, just outside Monterey, where they defiantly raised the Stars and Stripes and began constructing fortifications.

> **Myth Makin'**
>
> In his journals, Fremont compared Monterey with the picturesque villages of Italy. He even spent a few days at the beachfront home of an American trader basking in what he perceived to be California's Mediterranean-like character. It was a most auspicious association that would prove invaluable to area promoters thirty years hence.

A few days later, Castro took the field facing Gavilan Peak and began menacingly maneuvering around Fremont's position. In a panic, Larkin sent off a dispatch telling Fremont to "get the blazes out!" Vulnerable, and probably with no authorization to commence hostilities against a foreign nation, the company waited for nightfall and slipped out the back door.

But once out of the range of Castro's guns, Fremont resumed his holding pattern, going here, and going there, and never really going anywhere. The group continued zigzagging all the way up to the Oregon border when they were approached by a Marine Lieutenant, disguised as a traveling merchant, carrying secret dispatches. All that is known is that Fremont received communications from the president, the secretary of state, the secretary of the navy, a senator, and his wife.

After the dispatches were read and destroyed, Fremont abruptly changed course.

Advise and Invent
After the meeting with the lieutenant, the Fremont party turned around and headed back to Sutter's Fort. Their standoff at Gavilan Peak had stirred up much Mexican military activity with troops scrambling here and there and often casting suspicious eyes upon the resident aliens, especially the Yankees.

When Fremont returned to Sutter's Fort, he immediately drew a crowd of anxious Americans. He explained to the fearful gathering that he had returned to assist them in a sort of advisory capacity. When they inquired as to exactly what advice he might have for them, Fremont coolly suggested that they might want to consider capturing the garrison at Sonoma.

As the stunned crowd pondered that bombshell, a group of thirty-three "rough specimens of humanity" organized themselves into a guerilla unit. Fremont then directed this band of backwoods adventurers toward the town of Sonoma, just north of San Francisco. The plan was to capture the commandant of Northern California, General Mariano Guadalupe Vallejo. This was clearly an act of war, and if it's true that Fremont was acting without orders, then this certainly has to be the single most brazen act of daring (or insanity) in the history of the American West.

The Bear Flagger's Revolt
On June 14, 1846, Fremont's irregulars arrived in Sonoma where they found the presidio deserted. From the presidio, they made their way to General Vallejo's hacienda where he greeted them in his full military regalia and gallantly invited the ragged band into his parlor for brandy and cigars. After the pleasantries had been concluded, the Americans arrested the retired general, spiked some old, inoperable canons, and seized the general's wine cellar. Vallejo was sent under guard to Sutter's Fort where he held court in Sutter's parlor for about a month before being released.

Though they had no way of knowing it, "Fremont's follies" had captured and imprisoned America's most valuable ally in California—the very same high-level Mexican official with whom Consul Larkin had been secretly negotiating. But the men holding Sonoma had no time to contemplate the subtle nuances of vague political alliances; they had a wine cellar to liberate and an enemy town to occupy.

It took them all night, but they succeeded in laying waste to Vallejo's wine cellar, thus ensuring it would be of no aid and comfort to the enemy. The next morning, when some of the more thoughtful combatants had sobered up enough to consider the thorny position they were in, one of them suggested that maybe the raising of a flag of some sort might give their reckless campaign that certain degree of legitimacy it seemed to lack. But what flag should they raise? Not knowing exactly who they were fighting for, they decided to improvise a banner of their own.

And so, they rummaged around the town and came up with a scrap of white muslin and the hem of a red petticoat. A red stripe was sewn along the bottom, and the best artist among them took a piece of charcoal and drew a star as a symbol of their support for Texas' fight for independence, and a grizzly bear as a symbol of their own courage and daring. Below the bear, they wrote the words "California Republic."

The villagers, who mistook the grizzly bear for a pig, found the primitive banner a bit puzzling, but the irregulars were so moved by it that they christened their campaign "the Bear Flag Revolt," declared California a republic, and elected a president, all of which remained in effect for about a week. When Fremont arrived, he inducted the Bear Flaggers into his "California Battalion," and then marched south to seize the rest of California.

A Prelude to War, Part II

A few weeks later, upon hearing of the Sonoma incident, and acting under the assumption that the U.S. government must surely have sanctioned the Bear Flagger's actions, Commodore John Drake Sloat sailed to Yerba Buena, (later renamed San Francisco) and captured the village without incident. While awaiting further orders, Sloat met with villagers to explain their new, American benefits package: political freedom, efficient administration, and a predicted rise in real estate values. Most seemed pleased with the new policies.

Shortly after Sloat took Yerba Buena, three U.S. warships landed American marines at Monterey. Along with the soldiers came the official news that the war between Mexico and the United States had begun two months earlier. Once it became known that war had actually been declared, events unfolded very quickly.

Fremont and his volunteer militia captured Santa Barbara with no loss of life, and a company of marines took Los Angeles, also without bloodshed. All the way down the coast they were met with indifference, curiosity, and sometimes, even hospitality. For young officers looking for a chance to distinguish themselves in combat, the whole thing was a great big bust.

"We simply marched all over California, from Sonoma to San Diego, and raised the American flag without protest. We tried to find an enemy but could not." John Bidwell

The easy conquest of California was all but complete, and it would have remained so were it not for the contemptuous attitudes of the American soldiers toward the Californios. For the thinly stretched American forces, wounding the pride of the Californios would prove to be the costliest tactical error of the entire campaign.

The war was so uneventful the soldiers complained they were being driven mad with boredom. But that malaise abruptly ended when a company of Californio Lancers organized from among the local vaqueros suddenly counter-attacked and drove the astonished marines out of Los Angeles. The lancers then managed to rout another force of marines when they attempted to recapture L.A. It was a classic case of "defeat snatched from the jaws of victory."

General Stephen W. Kearny, with a company of 139, had to be sent all the way from Santa Fe to rescue the foundering American forces. But at San Pasqual near San Diego, he marched into a trap set by another 150 Californio lancers. This time, some real blood was spilled, but Kearny's forces managed to dig in and hold off the lancers until more troops arrived.

Outnumbered three to one, the lancers disappeared into the countryside, and the Americans, now numbering about 600, marched on San Diego and Los Angeles. Two more small skirmishes were fought along the San Gabriel River as the Americans advanced towards Los Angeles, but by that time, the Californio's munitions and supplies were exhausted, and they sent up the white flag.

Can We Surrender Now?

You would think surrendering would be one of the easiest tactical maneuvers to execute, but the Californios ran into complications when both the Navy's Commodore and the Army's General claimed to be the ranking officer in the field. While the two debated the question of who shall accept the surrender, Fremont, the junior officer, had a treaty drawn up on January 13, 1847, ending the hostilities and declaring the Californios to be citizens of the United States. And the moment the guns were silent, the guitars began to play. After the signing of the treaty, Commander Pico threw a big

> **Fought and Bought**
> As is customary in war treaties, the vanquished (Mexico) ceded the disputed territory to the victor (the United States). As is not quite so customary, the victor (the United States) then paid the vanquished (Mexico) 15 million dollars for it.

fiesta for the new landlords. When the party was over, the Californios and the American civilians went home and resumed their lives as if nothing had happened. A year later, the war with Mexico would officially end with the signing of the Treaty of Guadalupe Hidalgo in Mexico City on February 12, 1848.

Now What?

With the war ended, the United States took possession of California as well as a good deal of the southwest, which put them in exactly the same precarious position as their predecessors. How could the US populate such a distant and inhospitable territory? America had been weakened by two years of war and Britannia still prowled the Pacific coast. If the United States were not to fall into the same predicament that had plagued Mexico, somebody would have to find some way to move a huge number of Americans all the way to California and do it fast. The odds against it were overwhelming. Half the U.S. population had opposed the war and opposed the prospect of becoming entangled in the affairs of another distant, derelict, territory.

"It spreads forth into undulating and treeless plains, and desolate and sandy wastes, wearisome to the eye for their extent and monotony." Washington Irving

It was a monumental problem that had already undone the two previous landlords. But unbeknownst to any of the policymakers in Washington, just nine days before the signing of the Treaty of Guadalupe Hidalgo, a carpenter from Coloma, California had already stumbled upon the solution.

Chapter 6
Going for the Gold!

John Augustus Sutter arrived in California in the summer of 1839. A few years earlier, he left his native Germany, a wife, four children, and a pile of debts associated with a series of business failures. In California, he had hoped to reinvent himself—this time as a successful entrepreneur. For even as early as the 1830s, the myth that, in California, one could start life anew had spread all the way to Europe; and for a while, it appeared that Sutter just might break his losing streak.

King for a Day
Within two years of his arrival in California, Sutter had become a Mexican citizen and been granted title to nearly 50,000 acres of prime California real estate at the juncture of the Sacramento and American Rivers. There, he began to build the empire he called, New Helvetia.

By 1844, Sutter's Fort and Trading Post had become the unofficial base camp for nearly every trapper and trader that passed through the Sacramento Valley as well as journey's end for the wagon trains coming out west on the overland trail. As his business grew, he opened a blacksmith shop, a distillery, a freight and passenger service, and then expanded into large-scale wheat farming and cattle ranching.

No one could deny that Sutter had fulfilled his California Dream, but there was still more to do. To grind the wheat, he would need to build a flour mill. And to produce the lumber to build the flour mill, he would need to build a sawmill. And to that end, he hired carpenter and all-around handyman, James W. Marshall.

The sawmill was nearing completion on the morning of January the 24th, 1848, as Marshall was inspecting the waterwheel when he accidentally stumbled into the feed-stream and noticed something gleaming next to his boot. He bent down, picked it up, and carefully examined it. It was only a pebble, but the color was interesting. To Marshall, it looked a lot like gold.

"My eye was caught by something shimmering in the bottom of a ditch... The piece was about half the size and shape of a pea. Then I saw another." James Marshall

Sutter's Global Secret

Marshall called his crew over to get their opinion. Some laughed and chided him for his foolishness. But there were a few who also thought it looked a little gold-like. Not wanting to cause a commotion over an unsubstantiated find, Marshall asked them to keep it their little secret, and they all said they would, and he believed them. A few days later, Marshall dragged Sutter into a storeroom, locked the door, pulled down the shade, and dropped about two ounces of gold on the table. After having performed a few crude experiments gleaned from an Encyclopedia Americana, they concluded that gold had been discovered at Sutter's Fort.

The next day, Sutter and a few of his crewmen met Marshall at the sawmill. They all fanned out and began poking around along the banks of the stream bed, and within a short time, each had come up with a handful of gold nuggets. Sutter considered the discovery as nothing more than a nuisance that would distract his workers from their duties and so he asked the group to hush it up for just a few weeks, so he could get the flourmill finished. Once again, they all agreed.

Of course, with the hills and streambeds littered with gold, it was a promise they were not able to keep. During their off-hours, Sutter's laborers would head out to the mill site, and within days of having given their vow of silence, they were proudly showing off their finds all over the valley.

They began making purchases at Sam Brannan's Supply Store with gold nuggets, and just days later, Sam Brannon himself was seen marching up and down the streets of San Francisco waving a bottle full of gold dust and shouting at the top of his lungs, "gold, gold, gold at the American River!"

The Real Bonanza

It might seem foolish to publicly announce the location of so rich a find when you could be out in the hills gathering it all up for yourself. But Brannan, along with many other cunning, frontier entrepreneurs realized that the real money would not be made mining the hills, but rather in supplying the miners who mined the hills.

Brannan's logic proved to be sound, for he earned a fortune with his mercantile store by mercilessly price-gouging the armies of hopeful treasure hunters who poured into the gold fields.

Within two weeks of Marshall's find, nearly the entire population of San Francisco was out digging around the mill along with Sutter's employees, which had all deserted him. Trading and whaling ships carried news of the California gold strike to cities along the Pacific Rim long before the story got any attention in the east. In fact, when the story first appeared in the eastern newspapers, it was widely thought to be a government-sponsored hoax to lure settlers to the newly acquired California territory. But while easterners scoffed at prospect of gold in California, the first waves of gold seekers, from Hawaii, Peru, Chile, New Zealand, Mexico, and China were already making their way to the digs.

It would be seven months after gold was discovered before California's military governor toured the area and finally dispatched a courier to President Polk with his official report along with a canister containing 230 ounces of California gold.

Polk received the report along with the gold on December 7, 1848, and then, at a meeting of Congress, made the content of the report public:

"The accounts of the abundance of gold in that territory are of such an extraordinary character as would scarcely command belief were they not corroborated by the authentic reports of officers in the public service." President James K. Polk

This presidential statement, and a public showing of the gold samples, finally caught the attention of the American people, and the country suddenly went wild with gold fever. When Horace Greeley wrote in the *New York Daily Tribune*, "We are on the brink of the age of gold," that was it. The gold rush had officially begun, and thousands scrambled to be the first to light out for America's newest and richest frontier.

Going My Way?

But all those ready to leave everything behind and head out to California in hopes of finding their fortune were suddenly faced with the same disquieting dilemma—how does one get there? For those Americans east of the Mississippi River, the journey to California was more formidable and perilous than that faced by those who would approach it from nearly any other point on earth.

Until the completion of the transcontinental railroad in 1869, it was much easier, and far less hazardous, to get to California from China, or India, or Australia than it was from Independence, Missouri or Boston, Massachusetts. But it was exactly this ordeal that tested the courage and determination of the American gold-seekers that made the gold rush "the" pivotal event in the development of early California.

Pick Yer Poison

If you wished to go to California in the spring of 1849, you had only two choices: if you had a little money, you could take passage on a ship out of New England. It was long, boring, and somewhat hazardous; or, if you were on a tighter budget, you could go overland by wagon, which was long, brutal, and really hazardous. Either way, here's what lay in store for you.

Blow Winds Blow, We're off to Californio

With all the rush to get to California, every vessel, no matter its condition, was hastily rigged up, including many ships that were way past their prime. And once fitted out, they were loaded to capacity, for there was no shortage of eager, paying customers. The most popular route was around Cape Horn. It was 15,000 miles and took from five to eight months.

If you were to book passage on one of these decaying vessels, seasickness would probably keep you down for the first few weeks at sea. Ship owners often cut corners by stocking overripe provisions. Sickness brought on by tainted meat and fowl water was common, and the shipboard diet, lacking in fruits and vegetables, increased the risk of scurvy, and possibly a burial at sea. If you were fortunate enough not to have fallen prey to this common hazard, you may envy those who had when faced with the white-knuckle thrills of going around Cape Horn or taking the equally harrowing shortcut through the Straits of Magellan.

If you were like most of the gold seekers, you were a God-fearing soul who had given your solemn oath to the congregation that you would steadfastly adhere to your faith when faced with the wicked temptations you were sure to find in California. But after several months at sea alternating between crushing boredom and excruciating terror, a deck of cards to check the boredom, and a bottle of whiskey to steady the nerves, might have already become indispensable necessities. In fact, most California sojourners had become experienced sinners long before they ever set foot on the San Francisco docks.

As soon as the ships did arrive in San Francisco Bay, most of the sailors, officers, and often captains, would desert them, leaving their cargos to rot at anchor while they set out for the gold fields. By the summer of 1849, there were over 300 abandoned ships cluttering up the bay; the following year, there were over 650. Whole army platoons deserted their garrisons, and so many American sailors deserted that the Pacific Fleet had to suspend operations.

Going Coach

If you could not afford passage on a Yankee schooner, then you were forced to take to the trail in a prairie schooner on the much more difficult and dangerous overland route.

It's just not possible to overstate how perilous this journey actually was back in 1849. In recounting this event, authors and moviemakers always played up the action, with the westerners circling the wagons to defend against the inevitable attack by wild savages. But this overwrought fiction only served to trivialize the truly hazardous nature of the undertaking.

"You needed oxen, a wagon, provisions, and way more luck than one has a right to expect." An unidentified 49er

Forget the Indians; the main hazards of the journey were time and distance.

It was 2,200 miles of vast stretches of prairie, blistering alkaline deserts, and immense mountain ranges to get from Independence Missouri to Sutter's Fort. You could complete the trip in about five months if all went well, and it really had to go well, for you had to cross over the Sierras before the first snows fell to have any hope of a happy ending. But even within those two parameters of time and distance there dwelled a thousand "sub-hazards" just as deadly.

The average speed of the wagons was about two miles per hour, the average distance traveled on a good day was 12 to 15 miles, and anything could happen anywhere at any moment. This made it nearly impossible to keep a steady pace on a journey in which timing was everything and luck played too crucial a role in the outcome.

The Spanish Trail to Los Angeles, which bypassed the Sierra Nevada range, was the easier route, but it was longer, and everyone was in a big hurry to get to the diggings; so most took the more difficult, but more direct, Truckee Trail right over the top of the Sierras.

"Once you started, the only problem you faced was to finish. It was simply a desperate undertaking." An Unidentified 49er

Do You Feel Lucky?

The first deceptively simple and potentially terminal decisions you had to make were departure time and group size. It was thought that a group should be limited to 60 wagons; any more might overtax the available grass and water. A departure date between late April and early May was best. Start too early in the spring and there may not be enough new grass along the trail to sustain the draft animals. Start too late, and the animals of earlier trains might have eaten all the good grazing grass.

So right out of the gate, you may be faced with a life-altering decision: if there's no grass, do you push on and hope for better grazing ahead, and risk starving your draft animals out from under you, or do you leave the trail in search of grass and risk losing precious time and the possibility of a late crossing in the Sierras. You see what I mean? And you're just barely getting started.

But once you did start, you couldn't stop, not even on Sunday, for you never knew when some unforeseeable incident might delay you up ahead, and delays were deadly. Now, if your departure was timely and the grass and water plentiful, the first few weeks could seem deceptively easy, but as the weeks wore on, the hardships began to mount. Although there were some rare accounts of Indian attacks on small parties, by far the most common dangers were accidents and disease.

The food supply had to be packed very well, for if it spoiled...well, it just better not. The provisions, which had to last for months in a harsh environment, could not include perishable fruits or vegetables. This omission left the overlanders susceptible to scurvy, but the most common killer on the trail was cholera.

Without the antiseptics so common today, any little cut or wound could develop into gangrene. If it did, a trailside burial was usually only days away. A sudden summer storm or flash flood could wipe away a trail in minutes and swell rivers making them impassable for weeks. It was inopportune delays like these that could seriously reduce the chances of survival.

Are We There Yet?

If you were on schedule, you reached Fort Laramie by late June. This meant you were less than a third of the way there and already the nights were beginning to get cooler. Just ahead lay the Rocky Mountains, which were a challenge, but nothing near that presented by the Sierras. At Fort Hall, Idaho, you reached a fork in the road; you could turn right for Oregon or left for California; but in 1849, everybody was turning left.

Continuing along the California trail put you on a collision course with the Great Salt Lake. It was at about this point that you would begin to see evidence of the troll the journey had taken on previous groups of sojourners. All manner of personal belongings were dumped along the trail. Further along, you would begin to see more animal carcasses and broken-down wagons; and then there were the graves. Toward the end of 1849, it was said there was at least one grave every 80 yards. By the next spring, you could find your way to California by following the grave markers.

Next on the itinerary was the Great Basin, or what we now call Nevada. A hundred years before it became a gambling Mecca and a nuclear test site, Nevada offered nothing but thousands of square miles of the harshest desert imaginable. What water that could be found, provided it wasn't drop-dead poisonous, was so tainted with alkali that it had to be boiled and mixed with strong coffee and/or molasses just to make it palatable enough for the animals to drink.

So, let's just say that the water wasn't poisonous, and the wagons didn't fall apart, and the food didn't spoil, and you didn't get scurvy, or cholera, or smallpox, or malaria, or typhoid fever, or dysentery, and you didn't get snake bit, or drowned crossing a river, or trampled by an ox, or run over by a wagon, or accidentally shot, or possibly even purposely shot. If you were really that lucky, then you had earned the right, after about four months on the trail, to try to climb up and over the Sierra Nevada Mountain range. Now at this point, if you wanted to indulge in a little self-pity, you go right ahead. Who could blame you after what you've been through? You just go ahead and have a good cry, because the worst is yet to come.

Hordes of overlanders stood right where you're standing now, and must have looked up at that mammoth wall of granite, and thought to themselves, how could life be so terribly unfair? You may be thinking the same thing, but I wouldn't waste too much time pondering the cosmic injustice of it all; if you made it to the eastern slopes of the Sierras by early October, and you didn't get caught in an early blizzard, and you suffered no other delays or setbacks, then you just might have enough time to make it over the top.

If you were late getting to that point, the odds narrowed but you had to chance it. You couldn't survive the winter where you stood, and you couldn't turn back out across the desert. If you are fortunate enough to make it to the summit, do not stop to enjoy the view, keep moving; you won't be reasonably safe until you reach Sutter's Fort, and every minute counts—really. Oh… didn't I mention it? This trail you're on, the one that's going to take you over the summit and into the valley; this is the same trail the Donner Party took in 1846. You never heard of them? Well… just keep moving.

O.k., I'm going to give you a little push here, you've earned it. You made it over the summit, down the valley, and into a hero's welcome at Sutter's Fort. You're there; you're safe—almost. In one last cruel gesture of fate, some of the overlanders who made it all the way to Sutter's Fort lived only long enough to be buried there having succumbed to the ravages of the journey and having never set eyes upon the California gold fields.

Who Goes There?

Now the reason I've gone to such extravagant lengths to relate to you just how challenging this mass migration really was is because this event directly shaped the character of the Californian of the 19th century and continued to influence the character of the native Californian for many years after.

"The gold rush established, for better or worse, the founding patterns, the DNA code of American California." Kevin Starr

The hardships and the dangers presented by this desperate quest limited its appeal to a very narrow segment of the population. Most of them were young men between the ages of 18 and 35 representing nearly every profession imaginable: soldiers and sailors, farmers and ranchers, bankers and merchants, doctors and dentists, lawyers, clerks, blacksmiths and the list went on and on. What set these people apart from most of the folks back home was their willingness to accept risk and embrace adventure.

Those who took part in the great westward migrations of the gold rush were not the genteel, the affluent, nor those in reasonably comfortable circumstances. Instead, they were the bold and daring adventurers, the dreamers in search of a better life, the desperate in search of a purpose, and the failed in search of a second chance. They were what President Woodrow Wilson would, years later, refer to as "the colts of our society," and they had all amassed themselves in one very specific location.

They were not interested in establishing any roots or in building a civilization out of a frontier. Very few planned to stay any longer than five years. The universal plan was to get in, "make your pile," and go home a hero. The newspapers called them Argonauts after the legend of Jason's Argonauts and the search for the Golden Fleece. They came from every corner of the earth, which made Central California the most cosmopolitan region in the world at that time.

By the end of 1848, there were over 10,000 of these Argonauts flailing away in the California gold fields. By the end of the following year there would be 100,000, and the problem of how to populate the most isolated region in North America, the problem that had stymied Spain and Mexico for nearly 400 years, had finally been solved in just one.

Chapter 7
All to See the Elephant

Ready or Not, Here We Come
So, where were we? Oh yeah... out combing the hills, valleys, streams, and riverbanks of Central California with about 100,000 of the wildest, most desperate adventurers from seven continents all searching for a fortune in gold. Civilization's nearest outpost is over 2000 miles away. Welcome to California!

Yeah, there were still some logistical problems that needed to be worked out; it certainly wasn't a terrestrial paradise. But where else on earth could a poor man wander out into the hills one day and emerge the next day as rich as a king. Every civilization creates its own escape myths of an earthly Valhalla where the bunch grass is always greener. By word of mouth, California had developed just such a reputation, though the details remained somewhat vague. For many Americans of the 19th and early 20th century, the west became a symbol of unlimited opportunity; it was the universal plan B for those who felt the dream of a better life in the industrializing east was beyond their grasp.

And though the truth was often at odds with the myth, it was the persistence of the myth that brought many a hopeful American to the edge of the west in the decades leading up to the gold rush. But in 1848, the California dream was no longer just a myth. It was as real and as solid as the precious metal it was now based on, and the image of California as a land of dreams fulfilled would, forever after, be indelibly etched upon the collective consciousness of the nation.

Camp California
California happened in the blink of an eye. It happened so fast that there was no time for the government to establish an effective civil authority; therefore, it was impossible to buy land, file a mining claim, or call a constable when the occasion warranted. It was an out-and-out free-for-all. Anyone who could get there could participate unencumbered by federal regulations, civil laws, or moral codes. It was the wildest place on the planet.

"Mingling together were Missouri farmers, Yankee sailors, Georgia crackers, English shopkeepers, French peasants, Australian

sheepherders, Mexican peons, heathen Chinese, and a liberal sprinkling of assassins manufactured in hell all drawn to California by the magnet of gold." Ray Allen Billington

Who Stays There?

The brave souls willing to venture out to California were a diverse group. Yet, they generally shared certain personality traits that identified them as a distinct subset of humanity. Supporting those qualities already attributed to this assemblage was an overwhelming degree of self-confidence, optimism, and can-do spirit. Unbridled courage, and a better than average capacity to absorb physical abuse were also common character traits that helped to ensure the survival of this exclusive species.

> *"The cowards never started, and the weaklings died by the way."*
> *An unknown 49er*

Once out in the diggings, it was apparent that life there demanded much more than a love of adventure. To exist in this harsh environment, the Argonauts had to become self-reliant, resourceful, and able to improvise. And a century after the last 49er had pulled up stakes, the same elevated levels of adventurousness, risk-tolerance, self-assurance, independence, wanderlust, and ingenuity were still perceptible in much of the native population.

Sooner's Better

For the lucky ones who arrived in the first year (1848), a fortune could be found lying on the ground. Some claimed to have dug up their pile with a teaspoon. But by the time the majority of the Argonauts arrived in 1849, most of that surface gold was gone. However, it was still remarkably easy for even a moderately industrious miner to scrape together a very respectable ounce of gold a day using the traditional pick, shovel, and pan.

This earning power made the Argonauts the wealthiest wage earners in the nation. It was an ironic distinction, for they were also experiencing the lowest standard of living in any American territory. Despite the free flow of easy money, there was no commercial infrastructure in place to provide them with even the barest necessities.

The gold camps were often just a ramshackle assortment of filthy tents and impromptu shacks. Rodents and insects spread disease, as did the often-contaminated water. Other common gold camp hazards included snakebites, bear attacks, and landslides. The most prevalent man-made hazards were clubbings, stabbings, and shootings. And although the miners "improvised" their own laws and courts to try to curb the tendency toward anti-social behavior, these makeshift attempts at frontier justice only added to the mayhem. For the most part, the gold fields were governed by "revolver rule." Conditions were so disagreeable that some considered the destination to be just as horrific as the journey to get there.

"A residence here at present is a pilgrimage in a strange land, a banishment from good society, a living death, and a punishment of the worst kind, and the time spent here ought to be considered as a blank in existence, and accordingly struck from the record of one's days."
Franklin Langworthy

But the deprivation would not last very long. Among the new arrivals for 1850 were as many merchants as miners. These were the entrepreneurials, the civilization builders, the men, and on rare occasion, the women that would really kick the gold rush into high gear.

Cities of Gold
Businesses seemed to materialize overnight: supply houses, mess halls, outfitters, and hotels catered to the needs, while gambling dens, grog shops, and bordellos catered to the desires. Far from home and completely cut loose from society's restraints, the Argonauts enthusiastically indulged themselves in whatever frontier diversions were provided, spending their gold with reckless abandon—and why not? You could always go out and dig up some more.

In this manner, many a magnificent fortune was made, not in prospecting, but in merchandising. Industries grew to fill the needs of the miners as well as their suppliers. Lumber mills, iron foundries, grain mills, freight companies, stagecoach lines, fishing fleets, farming, and countless other industries suddenly came into existence all financed with California gold.

The isolation of the region forced these new industries to design and develop their own product lines, while it protected them from outside competition. The locals had the hottest market in the nation all to themselves, and it allowed them to grow at a phenomenal rate. The California dream was expanding into the commercial sector.

Boomtowns began popping up anywhere there was room. An abandoned schooner broke loose from its moorings and drifted upriver until it finally ran aground. The beached vessel was discovered by a couple of shopkeepers who converted it into a storefront, and before a year had passed, that single old hull had grown into the city of Sacramento. Within a few more years, San Francisco grew from a sleepy port village into an international center of world commerce. The word coming out of California was that no enterprise would fail in this "golden state." The whole territory had itself become the mother of all get-rich-quick schemes, and California fever was spreading all over the world.

Where's the Beef?

This runaway, economic engine had very far-reaching effects, and it wasn't long before the spillover reached down into the Southland. God only knows what the Argonauts had been eating out there in the gold camps, but now that they had money, they wanted a better grade of grub; they wanted beef, and it just so happened that the dons of Southern California were sitting on vast cattle herds.

While all the commotion was going on up in central California, down south life remained unchanged. At the sleepy ranchos, the hide business remained steady. The dons were getting an average of two to three Yankee dollars per head. Then, within a single year, the demand for beef exploded, and that very same scrawny three-dollar cow was worth as much as $500.00 in Central California; all you had to do was move it there.

Overnight, the hide business gave way to the newly conceived Southern California beef industry. Once again, anyone who could sit a horse became a cowboy. Whole herds, one after another were rounded up and driven north. For the southern ranchos, the cattle drives of the early 1850s were an economic boon even greater in magnitude than the hide and tallow trade. No one south of the Tehachapi Mountains had ever dreamed a bunch of dumb-looking cows could be worth so much.

An old proverb suggests that "a candle burns brightest just before it burns itself out," and for the rancheros of Southern California, the candle burned brightest from 1849 to 1851. Huge sums of money flowed into the hands of the rancheros and just as easily flowed out again.

Unfortunately, like the Argonauts, the masters of the Southern California ranchos could not claim caution and frugality among their virtues. Their unrestrained passion for gambling and high living, combined with a general disregard for market forces and U.S. property law, would soon lead most of them into financial ruin; but while the good times lasted, oh what a party it was.

The Do-It-Yourself State

In 1850, the United States Congress began squabbling over whether the new territory of California was to be slave or free. But while congress debated, a handful of impetuous Californians banded together to form their own legislature, elect their own delegates, and draw up their own state constitution, which outlawed slavery. And then, as if to prove the indisputable validity of the old adage, *"money talks,"* the home-made California constitution was boldly submitted to a stunned Congress, which meekly acquiesced and admitted California to the union on the ninth of September 1850, skipping over the entire mid-west and completely bypassing the territorial phase altogether. It would take Arizona 64 more years to achieve statehood.

> **Grogged Governance**
>
> The California Legislature was known as the "the legislature of 1000 drinks," for its frequent adjournments to the local saloon.

Panned Out!

Those first few years of 1848 and 49 were known as the "flush years," when the 49ers took an estimated $300 million out of the California gold fields. But by the time California became a state, the placer gold was gone and so were the days when a man could work a claim with simple hand tools. By the early 1850s, it was becoming almost impossible to scratch out a reasonable take without the use of heavier and more costly equipment.

The work was backbreaking, and while the level of effort required to work a claim was escalating, the rewards were progressively diminishing. By the mid-1850s, it was all but over for the iconic 49ers. From that time on, the gold country would be the almost exclusive preserve of the new corporate mining companies with their heavy equipment and even heavier financial backing.

Quitin' Time

As the easy pickings petered out, the original 49ers began to drift away. Some became merchants, some became farmers, some hired on with the big mining corporations, and some just wandered. For many who made their way to California during the gold rush, it was the greatest adventure of their lives. They had seen the elephant, and that would be their only reward.

Fortunes were made in California, but few were made by men working the claims. It was the merchants and captains of industry who were the real winners. But the biggest winner of all was the state of California itself for, after 400 years, it was finally getting a little recognition. The gold rush made California world-famous, and by 1854 its population had increased by 2500%. But the boom was

> **Seein' the Elephant**
>
> The phrase, "going to see the elephant," or "I saw the elephant," was a common 19th century expression meaning that the subject either would or had witnessed some spectacular sight or event, usually at great personal sacrifice.

primarily confined to Central California; down south, things had begun to take a turn for the worse.

Adios Rancheros

Of course, cutbacks in the mining industry soon resulted in reduced orders for the Southern California beef industry, and most of the dons were ill-prepared for a downturn in the market. Many, who had run up high expenditures during the boom, were forced to borrow to maintain their extravagant lifestyles.

This fiscal vulnerability could not have occurred at a worse time for the lords of the ranchos, for in March of 1851, the United States Congress passed the "Land Act of 1851," which required holders of Spanish and Mexican land grants to prove their validity to a state land commission. This usually proved to be a very difficult task, for the Spanish and Mexicans did not actually survey their holdings. Instead, they just marked off their boundaries with rocks, trees, and bushes.

> *"A large oak was taken as a boundary, in which was placed the head of a beef and some of the limbs chopped."*
> *Original Mexican title to Rancho San Jose*

American law required that the original documents be authenticated, and accurate surveys made. It was a long and costly process. On top of all that, the Californios were hit with property taxes, which were unheard of under Spanish and Mexican rule. And then the squatters came. Just as some of the Californios had squatted on the land of the missions, refugees from the gold fields were squatting on the lands of the gente de razon, who often had neither the resources nor the will to drive them off.

About three-quarters of all the land grant cases brought before the commission were found to be valid, but as the years passed, and the expenses mounted up, the old ranchos would be sold and subdivided again and again into smaller and smaller parcels until each one was just big enough for a three-bedroom two-bath ranch house with a fenced yard and an outdoor patio.

Trail's End

It is equally unfortunate that, for the two original cast members in this sweeping drama, the play would end in tragedy. John Sutter grossly underestimated the negative impact the discovery of gold would have on his once emerging empire. Within a few months of the finding, his land was overrun by hordes of well-armed squatters. His cattle were run off and killed, his wheat fields trampled, and his storerooms and warehouses looted. In the 1870s, he left California for Washington D.C. where he filed numerous petitions begging congress to compensate him for his losses; but he never received the reparations he sought, and he died alone and destitute in a D.C. hotel room in June of 1880.

The man who picked up the first gold nugget along the south fork of the American River fared no better. James Marshall tried his hand at winemaking and even invested in a gold mine, but neither endeavor succeeded. Having fallen on hard times, he was given a pension by the state, based mostly on sentiment, which was later revoked when his alcoholism became an embarrassment to the legislature. He died forgotten and penniless in 1885 and was buried within sight of the very spot where he had earned his place in history thirty-seven years earlier.

The gold rush jump-started California as a state, and San Francisco as the jewel in its crown. A leader in commerce and culture, it had become known as "the Paris of the west," while San Diego and Los Angeles languished as backcountry cow towns. During the closing stages of the gold rush, all roads led to Frisco, and the devil could take the rest!

Chapter 8
At the Devil's Doorway

The Wild, Wild, West Coast
In mid-19th century California, all roads led to Frisco, and amongst the general population, it was universally acknowledged that the devil could have what's left—and he didn't need to be asked twice. While San Francisco was becoming the cosmopolitan, go-to place on America's new west coast, the cow towns south of the Tehachapis were filling up with losers, loners, miscreants, and malcontents of every possible description; and by most accounts, the longtime residents were no shinning beacons of society either.

In September of 1781, twelve local families got together to christen the pueblo of Nuesta Senora la Reina de Los Angeles or City of the Angels. But if the founders intended this homage to the heavens to ward off evil, it failed miserably. By 1850, Los Angeles had become so rough and unruly a town that its few civic-minded residents couldn't hire a lawman nor keep a churchman.

Never mind what you've heard about the wild and woolly cow towns of Abilene, Kansas, or Tombstone, Arizona. In the 1850s, Los Angeles, California was the undisputed capital of misdeeds, mayhem, and cold-blooded murder. Nearly all residents walked the streets armed to the teeth. Between the years 1849 to 1854, they collectively spent over six million dollars on weaponry and were more than willing to use it.

From 1850 to 1857, Los Angeles had the highest murder rate in the nation with a least one killing a day, not including Mexicans, Indians, and Chinese, which were generally not listed in the daily body count. For Southern Californians of the 1850s, a premature parting under unnatural circumstances awaited one in every ten residents.

> *"California is just 3000 miles closer to Hell."*
> *Henry David Thoreau*

So how, in just a few short years, did Southern California go from a sleepy, pastoral province to a southwestern version of Sodom and Gomorrah? Well, for decades, Mexican authorities had forcefully herded their criminal class up into the northern territories. And San

Francisco, transitioning from a lawless boomtown into that "Paris of the West" thing, was cracking down on the wild, frontier hooliganism that was so common during the gold rush days. To rid itself of this felonious element, the city organized some very effective vigilante committees.

These regulators managed to shoot, hang, lynch, beat, and deport so many of the criminally inclined that most of their brethren voluntarily relocated to Santa Barbara, Los Angeles, and San Diego. Outlaws, gamblers, drifters, whores, tinhorns, and much of the disaffected rabble of the gold rush all converged on Southern California where civilization had yet to advance. Saloons, gambling halls, and bordellos dominated the business districts of these towns and gave them that boisterous, border town ambiance that's so attractive to the social renegades among us.

Ranchos Mirages

Another impediment stunting Southern California's development was the confusion over the Spanish and Mexican land grants. The old ranchos were being broken up, and land was available for sale, but many of the titles were still in question, and very few solid, upstanding immigrants of the kind Southern California desperately needed were willing to buy and work land that may later be determined not to belong to them.

Also, the difficulty and expense of getting water to the fields and moving produce to distant markets left little incentive for the average, family farmer. Thus, the Jeffersonian ideal of neat little sections worked by industrious, yeoman farmers was very slow to catch on in old California.

However, these obstacles were not enough to put off the less scrupulous settlers migrating into the area. Squatters and rustlers and those of a low character found there were opportunities in this uncertainty, and many of these outcasts settled in the backcountry areas. A visiting newspaper columnist described the Southern California settler of the 1850s in this way:

"He is the Anglo Saxon relapsed into semi-barbarism. He expectorates vehemently, takes too whisky, has little respect for the rights of others, distrusts men in store clothes, venerates the memory of Andrew Jackson, and dislikes trees." Bayard Taylor

With the whole region collapsing into chaos, those respectable, God-fearing people of the territory offered an annual salary of $10,000 to anyone who would execute the office of Los Angeles County Sheriff. However, there were no takers for it was no secret that the previous two office holders were themselves executed in the course of performing their routine duties.

The Reverend James Woods, a Presbyterian minister who arrived in 1854, believed the town was simply in need of some of that old-time religion. But despite his heroic efforts to bring the Gospel to the murderous masses of Los Angeles, he was forced to abandon his ministry and run for his life after only six months.

Release the Hounds

Finally, the good people of Los Angeles realized that if they were going to effectively combat the unchecked lawlessness that was overwhelming the territory, they would have to do as San Francisco had done and organize vigilante committees of their own. And so, at a local L.A. saloon, a mounted vigilante group was assembled and sworn in on August 1, 1853. They called themselves the Los Angeles Rangers, and they too became deadly regulators tracking down and dispatching 22 repeat offenders in their first year together.

Word of the Ranger's lethal prowess quickly spread throughout the Southland, which again convinced many of the local perps to seek out some less perilous environment in which to conduct their affairs. The vigilante system proved so effective that most of the other Southern California towns organized their own hometown vigilante teams, and by the late 1850s, the wanton bloodletting had subsided enough for a marginally stable social system to emerge.

> **Justice Delayed**
>
> According to legend, the Rangers never brought em' back alive because Los Angeles had no jail facilities. However, in order to avoid the appearance of impropriety, the deceased were always given a fair trial at a later date.

This was good news for the community builders of the Southland, but it was only a partial fix to a small part of the Southern California conundrum. Establishing some law and order would certainly make the region a much more attractive option for those seeking to improve their lot in life, but it would not resolve the persistent problems of limited career opportunities and transportation options.

By the late 1850s, Northern California had it all: a mining industry, a timber industry, and a shipping industry with an international port-of-call. They had everything they needed to attract a large, productive population and build a prosperous, commercial economy; while, on the plus side, all Southern California had was a placid climate and some attractive coastal areas.

"Los Angeles, San Diego, and Santa Barbara were considered fossiltowns, down at the heels." Cary McWilliams

If the Southland was going to develop into anything other than the desolate, sparsely populated, backcountry province it was, somebody was going to have to find a way to lure throngs of solid settlers into what was generally considered to be the badlands of California.

To accomplish that task, impressions would have to be altered. What was needed was a halfway believable re-branding model that would focus attention on the area's attributes and away from its many shortcomings. And as it turned out, some very clever fellow had already imagined a very workable new concept that, when put before the public, would slowly begin to sweeten their assessment of the Southland.

Johnny Came Marching Home

Following the war with Mexico, ex-Bear Flagger John C. Fremont made good on his promise to relocate to California where, in 1848, he wrote a book called *Geographical Memoir upon Upper California*. That is, he recounted events to his wife, Jesse, and she, being the more scholarly of the two, wrote the book for him. In fact, Mrs. Fremont wrote all the books attributed to Mr. Fremont, including several lengthy government reports on his early expeditions out west. And because there were no copyright laws at the time, all these reports were reprinted by numerous publishers and circulated throughout the United States and were quite popular and influential reads in their day.

One of the recurring themes that would drift in and out of nearly all of Fremont's narratives was the favorable comparison he made between California and the Mediterranean regions of Europe, especially Italy. And indeed, the seasoned traveler could not fail to recognize the similarities between the two regions. In fact, since the passing of the gold rush, California had even developed some of the same light industries commonly found in the Mediterranean. Vineyards began proliferating throughout southern and central California, as did the wool trade.

Basque and Mexican sheepmen and their herds were becoming common sights in California, which, along with the picturesque vineyards, contributed strongly to the general Mediterranean aura visitors were just beginning to appreciate. And it was that Mediterranean aura that,

Magic in the Air

In 1857, Lorin Blodget, of the Smithsonian Institute, not only backed up Fremont's Mediterranean claims in his scholarly work *Climatology of the United States*, but went on to suggest, for the very first time, that this warmer, dryer climate might be beneficial to those suffering from respiratory ailments. As a scientific theory, the notion was entirely speculative; nevertheless, it provided the root source of a new and very seductive myth that would pay big dividends a few years hence.

when properly promoted, would turn public attention toward the area's extraordinary aesthetics and slowly reshape the state's image.

So, by the late 1850s, the Southern California climate was finally beginning to garner some favorable notice, but it would still be many years before these marketing schemes could be effectively implemented. In the mid-19th century, California was still way too remote for most dreamers to act on their fantasies.

It was one thing to get people to risk their life for a fortune in gold, and quite another to run the same risk for the pleasure of watching grapes grow. However, this does not mean that there was no in-migration at all. There were some people so desperate they would accept any risk, even a trip to Southern California, for a chance at a life better than the one they knew.

The Persecuted Pilgrims

The religious beliefs and practices of the Mormons often put them at odds with mainstream American society and forced them to seek shelter from both persecution and prosecution in some of the most out-of-the-way sections of the western frontier, and Southern California was as far out-of-the-way as one could go. So, in 1855, a group of Mormons ventured out to California and established the community of San Bernardino. It was just 55 miles east of Los Angeles, but the contrast between the two towns could not have been more distinct.

Although many Americans took exception to some of their lifestyle choices, it could not be argued that the Mormons knew how to build and maintain a rock-solid community. In their towns, there was no shooting, no robbing, no gambling, and no drinking. Churches and schools were often the first buildings raised. They worked their land without imposing upon the Indians, and they even advanced the art of desert farming by introducing irrigation. Most travelers found them to be reserved but civil, and thus, when they had a choice, preferred to stay in San Bernardino rather than take their chances in L.A.

Two years later, a group of German settlers, who had come to San Francisco in 1848 to escape a revolution back home, migrated south after hearing rumors of the great land bargains to be had. They bought a 1200-acre plot about 45 miles southwest of San Bernardino and raised the community of Anaheim. Like the Mormons, the construction of schools and churches came at the top of a to-do list which even included an opera house. And though there wasn't a single farmer among them, they taught themselves the art of grape growing and wine making and made Anaheim one of the most prosperous communities in the Southland.

These refugees were the real frontier tamers of the Southland. Most came with nothing into a region that might just as well have been on another planet, for there was nothing in the way of the familiar to reassure them. Home, wherever that was, was no place like this. There was no Farmer's Almanac to guide the new arrival. No one knew the weather patterns. The soil had never been analyzed. All undertakings were conducted on a trial-and-error basis, and many traditional customs, beliefs, and time-tested modus operandi had to be either abandoned or revised to suit the new environment.

These sojourners were just the kind of committed, hardworking, civilization builders Southern California needed, but the region could hardly rely on a slow trickle of desperate religious and political refugees to colonize it. For civilization to grow on this isolated "island on land," there just had to be a better way to get there. There had to be a cheaper, safer, faster way for the not-so-desperate to experience California.

Railroaded
The notion of building a rail line linking the east coast with the west had been knocking around the halls of Congress since the late 1830s, but at that time, interest in such an ambitious project was very limited. Many in Congress still believed that the whole southwestern shebang would never be worth the trouble it took to get there:

"What do we want with this vast and worthless area, this region of savages and wild beasts, of deserts of shifting sands and of whirlwinds, of dust, and of cactus and of prairie dogs? To what use could we ever hope to put these great deserts? I will never vote for one-cent from the public treasury, to place the west one inch closer to Boston, than it is now." Daniel Webster

But after the territory became a state, the tune had changed considerably; it was no longer a matter of if, but when a transcontinental railroad would be built. Pressure to get the project underway was brought to bear from several different quarters. San Franciscans wanted it to give them access to the markets of the east. Easterners wanted it to break their shipping magnet's monopoly on transport to and from the Asian markets, and Congress wanted it to join the west with the rest of the nation.

Most of the country agreed that the project should be given the green light, however, instead of moving forward, it hopelessly stalled out in the planning stages. By the time the country was finally ready to have a go at such an ambitious undertaking, the secessionist fever had split congress in two, and the bickering between northern and southern factions blocked any chance of progress.

Right from the start, the decision on where to lay the tracks was a deal-breaker. The northern states favored a central route that would provide them with a political, economic, and strategic advantage over the southern states. The southern states favored a southern route that would provide them with that same leg up on the northern states. What resulted was an ironclad stalemate that delayed progress for years. It took the 1860 presidential election of Abraham Lincoln to break the deadlock that would eventually allow work to begin on a Transcontinental Railroad.

The Civil War

To the south, Lincoln's election was proof that their voices would not be heard within the new administration. It was the final straw in a bitter rivalry that had been raging for decades between the northern free states and the southern slave states. Now it would get ugly. Just days after Lincoln's election, South Carolina seceded from the Union. By February of 1861, six more states seceded. And the following April, with the flare-up at Fort Sumter, four more states joined the Confederacy, and the war was on.

With the southern states out of the debate, the question of which route the Transcontinental Railroad would follow was settled, yet the project was repeatedly delayed. With the Civil War raging in the east, many government-sponsored projects and proposals had to be postponed, like the building of railroads and the very popular proposal to divide the state of California into two separate states, north and south. Even in far-off California, the secessionist fever appeared to be spreading, and that was exactly what the north was afraid of.

Although the movement to divide California into two states was strictly a local dispute based on interstate rivalries, to put pressure on Washington to begin the construction of the railroad, the California Legislature let rumors leak that the state was considering seceding as well.

The Californians were not particularly concerned with the war, but their secessionist rumblings worried Washington so much they fast-tracked the transcontinental line, not necessarily to facilitate commerce, but to facilitate the rapid movement of Union troops into the state if California should try to make good on its threats to join the rebels. So finally, after ten years of congressional bickering, Lincoln signed the Pacific Railroad Act into law on July 1, 1862.

The Rail Rogues

The Central Pacific Railroad Company was created by four San Francisco shopkeepers: Leland Stanford, Collis Huntington, Charles Crocker, and Mark Hopkins. Together they were known as the Big

Four. Though they were some of the most formidable merchant hucksters of the gold rush era, as railroad entrepreneurs, they were considered so clueless, and the enterprise so impossible, that banks refused them loans, forcing them to use their own funds to begin the task of linking a nation—at least their half of it. The plan was for their Central Pacific to begin laying track in Sacramento and continue east, while the Union Pacific Railroad would start laying track in Omaha, Nebraska, and head west. Somewhere along the line, they were to meet.

The project was financed with government bonds and huge grants of government land which would be awarded to each of the companies as they progressed. The deal was simple: the more track a company laid, the more land and government bonds they got.

To lay those tracks, the Union Pacific hired tough, hard-living, hard-drinking army veterans and Irish immigrants. The Central Pacific had planned to hire equally lusty ex-miners, but the silver mines around Virginia City, Nevada were still working the Comstock Lode. With the mines in full production, and the Central Pacific about to start work, the competition for labor was high and the mines paid better than the railroad.

With less than a fifth of the manpower it needed, the Central Pacific was stymied. In this desperate pickle, a construction boss boldly suggested that they try the only sizable group of men available—the Chinese.

The proposal was not well received. After all, how could the diminutive and frail-looking Chinamen ever stand up to the grueling conditions on the line? But when the construction boss reminded management that these were the same people who built the Great Wall of China, orders were given to hire fifty Chinamen as a test group. The railroaders were astonished

---

First in Surf

Samuel Clements, correspondent for the *Sacramento Union*, arrived in Honolulu in the spring of 1866 to observe and record the color and culture of the Hawaiian Islands. Though he'd yet to write his first novel, he was already using his famous nom de plume, Mark Twain, in his dispatches to the home office. Missing among the many adventures he described, was the story of his pioneering exploit on a surfboard. It wasn't until 1872, that the details of this historic encounter came to light in his first book, *Roughing It*.

"... I tried surf-bathing once... but made a failure of it. I got the board placed right... but missed the connection myself. The board struck the shore in three-quarters of a second, without any cargo, and I struck the bottom about the same time, with a couple of barrels of water in me..."

It was the first description of surfing to appear in popular western literature, written by the first westerner to ever have a go at the Hawaiian sport of kings.

to find the Chinese to be ideal employees. They showed up for work on time and sober. They were tough, agile, and resourceful. They put in a full day's work and were not inclined to shoot each other.

A few days later, the word went out to hire as many Chinamen as could be found. The Central Pacific filled its employment quotas and never looked back. The race was on to lay tracks, hoodwink the United States government, and bleed the American taxpayer of every penny possible.

The Gravy Trains

When Leyland Stanford turner over that first, ceremonial shovel-full of earth to mark the start of their great railroad project, on January 8, 1863, neither he, nor his partners were certain a transcontinental line was even possible, but that didn't matter. What they were certain of was that big money would be made building it, not finishing it, and certainly not running it. As the principals of a paper railroad, they had secured the largest government contract ever awarded.

Through backroom deals, Stanford was elected governor, which paved the way for millions more in state support. They formed their own construction company and overcharged the government for every inch of track laid. They submitted false surveys, making mountains where there were only molehills. But twenty miles east of Sacramento, they struck some real mountains and progress slowed to a snail's pace as they began blasting their way through the Sierra Nevada range.

The Union Pacific began work a month before their California colleagues, yet with nothing before them but wide-open spaces, they were stalled as well. With a rewards system that paid by the mile, and a federal government too distracted by war to oversee their progress, the Union Pacific management decided to forgo the more efficient straight-line method of linking two distant points in favor of the much more profitable corkscrew pattern. For two and a half years they laid tracks in circles never straying more than forty miles from their original point of origin. It wasn't until July of 1865, three months after the end of the war, that the government would begin to monitor their progress and force the Union Pacific to lay tracks in a westerly direction.

> **Upscaled Pay**
> The railroads collected $16,000 per mile over flat terrain, $32,000 over mid-level grades, and $48,000 over mountain grades.

For over six years the two companies battled mountains, deserts, floods, snowdrifts, and disgruntled Indians, when finally, the two crews came within sight of each other, and just kept on going. Since the government hadn't designated an official link-up sight, they kept laying track in opposite directions, each trying to take the treasury for all they could until the omission was discovered and orders were hastily issued to meet at Promontory Point, Utah on May 10, 1869. And there, at the peal of the last hammer blow, delivered by Governor Stanford, a telegraph operator sent out a one-word message to both coasts —"done!"

With the completion of the Transcontinental Railroad, travelers could get from the east coast to the west coast for $85.00 and do it in one week. Now, the only question was, would anybody want to?

Chapter 9
Come and Get It...Please!

Trains to Nowhere

In 1869, the railroad opened California up to western migration and finally gave the state a practical means of exporting its products and produce. But contrary to the expectations of thousands of hopeful Californians, railroad executives, and railroad investors, the completion of the transcontinental railroad did not set off a mass pilgrimage to the Promised Land. No matter how easy it was to do so, settlers and farmers were still reluctant to migrate to a land where corporations were buying up much of the prime acreage and the lack of natural resources severely hindered the development of job-creating industries.

As a result of the anemic demand, land prices went into decline. And if that weren't shocking enough, the railroad, having finally breached the isolation of the golden state, opened its market to competition from eastern merchants and manufacturers. In the short term, the railroad plunged California into a depression, which spread throughout the rest of the nation.

This depression, known as the Panic of 1873, was partially the result of the wild speculation in railroad construction, which included the transcontinental line. In addition to all the generous government grants the two railroads had been collecting, both the Union and Central Pacific operated as joint-stock companies and raised even more cash by selling their own stocks and bonds and by reselling their government bonds to private investors. As long as the easy money kept flowing in, the tracks kept getting laid, even to places nobody wanted to go. When the tracks were completed, and the returns on these investments didn't materialize, the bubble burst, and many banks and financial institutions, which had invested heavily in railroad bonds, began to fail, which triggered a nationwide depression.

With the completion of the transcontinental line, the government money machine shut down, and the railroads suddenly found themselves going deep into debt with lines that weren't paying off. For the principals of the Union Pacific, the unprofitable lines combined with major scandals involving government overcharges and bribery brought their tenure to an end and sent the company into bankruptcy.

Ironically, it was the rookie railroad men of the Central Pacific who remained solvent during the tough times and eventually made railroading immensely profitable. But first, they had to overcome another epic challenge possibly even more daunting than the actual construction of the railroad.

In for a Pound

The plan was to sell out once the task was completed and their fortunes were made. But somehow, they missed the moment; before a buyout could be arranged, the panic hit.

> *"We built that road for the profits we could make in building it, and when we got it done, we didn't know what the devil to do with it."*
> *Charles Crocker*

Several unsuccessful attempts were made to sell. Now, there was no other option but to hold on and make it pay or lose everything. In this desperate fix, the Big Four were forced to get creative in the formulation of a very risky, two-part survival strategy. The first part of the plan to save their failing railroad was to buy more failing railroads. To get a monopoly on all California rail service, they bought more tracks to nowhere. It seemed a crazy idea, but they wouldn't be buying tracks to nowhere if nowhere could be transformed into somewhere. And that was the objective of part two: They had opened the door to California; now they had to sell it—that was the crazy part!

The railroad had to sell the very same desert acreage that Spain and Mexico had trouble giving away. They had to convince a bunch of hard-nosed, Yankee skeptics, few of which had ever traveled more than 30 miles from their birthplace, to relocate thousands of miles from their home and start anew in a sketchy, untested region that had once been described by explorer Kit Carson as, *"so utterly desolate, deserted, and godforsaken that a wolf could not make his living on it."*

It's quite possible that the history of the west might have evolved much differently had the gentlemen of the Central Pacific not been scrappy frontier merchants before they were railroad men. As consummate hucksters, they were masters of the hard sell and the deceptive pitch. And in the selling of California, they would use these techniques incessantly. To push this beguiling but flawed product, they concocted a plan to transform the public's perception of California and then lure them in with promises, promises, and more promises. And to achieve that goal, they instigated one of the most gargantuan, enduring, and relentless marketing campaigns ever mounted in the history of corporate enterprise.

Boostermania

To spin a completely new "web-of-perception," the Central Pacific (which bought and became known as the Southern Pacific) hired an army of journalists and travel writers to overwhelm all the rest of the country with an inexhaustible deluge of guidebooks, pamphlets, magazines, and magazine and newspaper articles highlighting the endless business opportunities and magnificent natural wonders waiting to be realized and experienced in California.

One of the railroad's first, and most celebrated, troubadours in this major public relations assault was Charles Nordhoff, the former editor of the *New York Evening Post*. Nordhoff drew up the blueprint for all the California "rebranding exercises" for the next 70 years with the 1872 publication of his guidebook, *California for Health, Wealth, and Residence*.

In this tome and thousands of others, the railroad's scribes attempted to dispel the lingering perception that California was "a dangerous and barbarous land," by systematically de-emphasizing the many awkward rumors that, for years, had been drifting eastward, while creating new and extravagant mythologies much more sympathetic to the marketing strategies of the Southern Pacific Railroad. And they didn't confine their efforts merely to literary publications; if the public wouldn't come to California on their own, the railroad's reps would bring them there.

Go Get Em!

The publishing of books and newspaper articles left way too much to chance. So, the management at the Southern Pacific concluded that they could eliminate at least some of the uncertainty in the sales process by hiring even more promo men to travel the nation in special "excursion trains" rounding up as much of the population as possible and personally escorting them back to sunny California.

The most celebrated of these "tourist wranglers" was Nathaniel C. Carter, who was known as "the great excursionist." Every winter, beginning in 1872 and continuing for twenty-five years thereafter, Carter would barnstorm the cities, towns, and villages of the mid-west, the south, and

---

The Magic Box

Forever the gambler, railroad baron Leyland Stanford bet a friend $25,000 that a horse on the run lifts all four hooves off the ground and then hired photographer Eadweard Muybridge to prove it. That was in 1872. It took Muybridge five years to perfect a system of 24 cameras laid out in a row and triggered by a tripwire as the horse passed. Leyland won the bet and Muybridge developed the principal behind Hollywood's paintbrush—the motion picture camera.

the northeast on behalf of the state and the Southern Pacific Railroad. Like a tent-show evangelist, Carter would mesmerize the crowds with his sermons on the splendiferousness of Southern California, and then pack up the Pullman with the recently persuaded and head due west; only a few days' ride to the promised land where polite, well-groomed, estate guides were waiting to conduct visitors to what could be their own little bit of heaven, with prices starting at only one dollar per acre.

California Dreamin'

What Nordhoff and Carter and the rest of the railroad's boosters were selling to the people of the United States was the California Dream: a bright, shiny, newly re-imagined version of the old American Dream.

The American Dream was all about freedom and rights: freedom from the oppression of monarchies, aristocracies, and religious institutions and the right to life, liberty, and the pursuit of happiness among many others. But even with the barriers to individual self-fulfillment lifted, life was still pretty rough for most 18th century Americans, and by the latter part of the 19th-century, conditions had not improved much.

The average Yankee farm family toiled year-round from sunup to sundown just to get by. The tradesmen, laborers, mechanics, and factory workers of the big eastern cities could expect to put in the same long hours in far less favorable conditions. The Southern Pacific sought to improve upon the American Dream by offering one where the drudgeries and perils of 19th-century existence would be significantly reduced if not eliminated while accentuating life's precious little pleasures.

And through the efforts of their lecturers and writers for hire, the railroad restructured the image of California from a parched desert into a sub-tropical, Mediterranean-styled paradise that beckoned to the struggling minions in the east to venture out west and experience for themselves this California Dream built upon the promise of a better life through natural upgrades in geology and atmospherics. By marketing the climate in this most aggressive manner, the railroad spread the myth and mystique of the California Dream to all corners of the earth.

The program was certainly intended to have widespread appeal, and efforts were made to connect with every conceivable demographic in the quest to lure warm bodies out west, but in the initial stages of the campaign, the railroad's hired guns directed special attention toward three key groups—tourists, invalids, and farmers, with special emphasis placed on the latter.

Searchin' for Sodbusters

By the 1870s, California's leading economic generator was no longer mining, or cattle, but agriculture. And, though rumors of large landholders limiting small-scale agricultural opportunities persisted, the truth was that most of the state's square footage was still available, especially in the southern regions. The growth potential was enormous, and with no real industrial possibilities yet visible on the horizon, the need was great.

The Southern Pacific especially wanted to bring farmers into the region because they could quickly jump-start a stalled economy. They bought the railroad's land, planted crops, built houses, raised families, sold and shipped produce, and bought merchandise. They were the civilization builders, and to lure them out west, the Southern Pacific fashioned a special, "agricultural edition" of the California Dream just for the eastern planter.

Plowing Eden

According to the boosters of the Southern Pacific, farmers coming out west could expect to enjoy the pleasures of west coast style husbandry working on land where the soil was said to be so rich and bountiful that nature practically did all the work herself. Some of their claims bordered on the supernatural:

> *"So prolific was the soil, that the pioneer bed posts, table legs, and benches would put forth verdure and take root, re-attach themselves to the soil, and again become real estate."* Horace Bell

And rich, productive soil was just one of a multitude of blessings enjoyed by the California farmer. Where eastern fields had to be cleared for cultivation, California land, being mostly desert, came naturally "plow ready." California farmers didn't have to hold to strict planting and harvesting schedules nor build expensive outbuildings to protect produce and livestock from the ravages of a contrary climate. While easterners waited out the harsh winters, Southlanders were out in the fields enjoying the year-round growing season.

In California, the theory went, the environment was not an adversary but an ally, which helped the farmer to increase productivity while reducing his workload and operating expenses, leaving him with more income and more free time to pursue other, more agreeable interests. All this could be had for just 20% down and easy terms of five years to cover the balance.

The terms were agreeable, and the land was cheap—really cheap. California real estate, including beachfront property, could be purchased from $1.00 to about $20.00 an acre. If the prospective grower could be persuaded to consider the even more isolated community of San Diego, some real bargains could be had. Alonzo Horton built the entire city on land he purchased for just 27 cents an acre.

As these guidebooks proliferated throughout the central and eastern portions of the nation you might think that the east coast would raise up three inches and the west coast sink a similar amount with the added weight of all those farm families that ought to be rushing into California, but once again, results fell short of expectations.

The Devil's Own Details

As intriguing as all this ballyhoo might have sounded, there were still some major drawbacks associated with the railroad's relocation plan that had yet to be addressed: the first and foremost being that there was still no water. The dream world so imaginatively described in the pages of these guidebooks was still just a seaside desert with above-average ventilation.

Farmers, no matter how idyllically situated, must have a reliable source of water, and in California, that required the construction of elaborate and costly irrigation systems. It was a fact that was generally minimized in the promotional literature if not wholly omitted. The California farmer may not need to build outbuildings, but he will need to build windmills and storage tanks, and dig reservoirs and canals and wells, and lay miles of irrigation pipe. It was a very labor-intensive and costly undertaking.

The second hang-up in the railroad's pitch was the unusual product line they were promoting. Most farmers grew staple cereal crops like corn and wheat, which had to be raised on a large scale to be profitable. But, according to the railroad boosters, the future of California agriculture was not in those old-school staples but the recently introduced tropicals. Tropicals that the boosters claimed could be raised profitably on as little as ten acres. So rather than continue as they had back home working dozens of acres of staple crops, farmers were being encouraged to come west and bet their family's future working perilously small plots raising fruits and nuts.

Among the laundry list of exotic specialties, the boosters were recommending to potential newcomers were nectarines, lemons, oranges, bananas, citrons, quinces, almonds, walnuts, dates, and figs. In the 1870s, few people outside the temperate zones of Florida and California had even seen an orange or a banana much less bit into one; and fewer still were willing to try to raise these bizarre species in a remote desert on pint-sized plots with no water. And if that weren't too much already, nearly all these sub-tropicals required several years of maturing before they produced a marketable crop. Who among the potential prospects had the resources to wait that long for their first California payday?

Another in this growing list of awkward realities was the odd fact that very few of these eastern growers responded positively to the notion of extensive leisure time, which was one of the key components of the new California lifestyle.

Although they were not all practicing Puritans, Puritan values, especially the Puritan work ethic, still exerted a powerful influence over a great many 19th-century Americans. All this talk of higher productivity and ease

> **Labor Relations**
> America's early pioneers were fearful of leisure because, during the 18th, 19th, and even into the 20th century, most lived from day to day, hand to mouth. If you didn't work, you didn't eat. Therefore, both parents usually worked at something, and the very moment they were able, the kids worked too, and all without a social safety net. It would take many years of economic and social re-structuring before the pursuit of leisure would be recognized as a safe, and reasonably respectable, "part-time" undertaking.

of operation could only lead to extended periods of idleness, and many believed that it was during those empty hours that the devil did his best work.

This popular assumption threatened to undermine the whole concept of the California Dream on which everything was riding, and so efforts were made to re-structure the booster doctrine to balance the virtue of honest labor with the luxury of leisure, and to assure the public that California wasn't a land of laggards, but simply a place where the hard-working didn't have to work nearly so hard, but the public wasn't really buying into it—at least not yet.

The Steerage Class Coaches

In the campaign's first few years, results were disappointing. Most solid citizens were not easily uprooted, so the railroad began a program to target the already uprooted. In the mid-1870s, the railroad began running special, low fare, immigrant trains—just a few boxcars hooked on the back end of a westbound freight train loaded with poorer settlers and European immigrants.

It was an unpopular policy that got the railroad into trouble with some of California's leading citizen groups. With the region still struggling to shake off its reputation as a wild, lawless frontier, many Californians felt the emigrant trains were only adding to the problem.

"This afternoon the western-bound emigrant train disgorged the shabbiest lot of mortals it has been our misfortune to see for some time. The bell rang, all got aboard and went off. Reno was relieved, but we could not help feeling for California." The Reno Gazette, 1876

These new emigrants were not always welcome, were rarely well-funded, and worst of all, they were not coming in anywhere near the numbers needed to keep the Southern Pacific out of the red. So, despite the protests, the railroad refused to shut down the emigrant trains; but they did make some discernible efforts to target the God-fearing and industrious, while halfheartedly dissuading the slacker element:

"Men who have the sound sense to realize the situation will be made welcome...those who imagine that any other combination of elements (thrift and industry) will give them a home or an estate in this valley had better keep away." Benjamin Truman

However, most easterners remained unconvinced. Train or no train, in the minds of many, California's negatives still far out weighted its positives. To pave the way for civilization, California would have to rely upon a new breed of trailblazer to tame the last great American frontier; but not before brunch, or after the four o'clock tea.

Chapter 10
The Surge of the Swells

Spain may have first laid claim to the territory of Alta California in the middle of the 16th century, but it wasn't until the mid-1870s that it was really and truly discovered. It was not discovered by conquistadors, or padres, or rancheros, or even the 49ers; it was discovered by tourists—rich, "goggle-eyed, umbrella-toting" tourists.

Although the wealthy had been frequenting fashionable, eastern spas and resorts since the beginning of the 19th century, tourism did not begin to fully develop until the great railroad boom of the 1860s and 70s.

With tracks leading to many new and extraordinary western destinations, the race was on, among those who could afford the time and expense, to experience as much of this new country as possible; and it was exotic, far-off California that became the number one, "must-see" destination. In fact, among the American upper classes, a trip out to California was considered a patrician obligation.

"No man-of-the-world considered himself well-traveled until he went across America in the steam trains." Keith Wheeler

Recognizing this opportune trend, the railroads were quick to promote it with their own, not so subtle, directives:

"It is now the fashion to make a rapid run through California." Charles Nordhoff

Most of the serious settlers may have kept their distance, but the tourists began pouring into San Francisco and the surrounding burgs almost before there was a tourist industry ready to accommodate them. San Francisco had some very acceptable hotels, but little thought had been directed toward the establishment of any genuine points of interest suitable for the amusement and edification of vacationing out-of-towners. And here the streets were becoming clogged with persnickety, upscale tourists demanding to be shown a good time.

Overnight, this sudden, and somewhat unexpected, development thrust into being one of California's most durable industries—the tourist trade. Finally, here was an enterprise with unlimited growth potential that wasn't dependent on scarce natural resources.

Railroad boosters and local entrepreneurs began directing visitors toward anything that might be considered majestic, or picturesque, or just plain peculiar. Topping the list of the newly imagined California tourist attractions were the great natural wonders: Yosemite Valley, Lake Tahoe, and Mount Shasta.

Within the city limits of San Francisco, the top draw was Chinatown. Out in the hinterland, tourists flocked to see old, rundown mining towns and traipsed over hillsides still scarred by mining operations that had been shut down for years. Some enterprising locals even took to the streambeds with pick and pan recreating scenes of the 49ers for the delight and considerations of the roving bands of intrepid tourists.

For the truly courageous among the tourist hordes, there was the trip down into the southern region—the badlands of old California. One could take a steamboat to Los Angeles or hire a wagon and guide for an excursion along the old coast route as far as endurance permitted.

The railroad boosters portrayed the southern portion of the state as an unspoiled and underpopulated tropical paradise until it was discovered that some tourists associated the tropical metaphor with sweltering jungles teaming with poisonous reptiles, large, man-eating cats, and malaria-carrying mosquitoes.

In response, the travel writers toned down the tropical associations in favor of the much more refined Mediterranean comparisons. In hindsight, they probably needn't have bothered, for those vacationers truly determined to see America's last real frontier were not about to be sidelined by the uncomfortable conveyances, the crude, backcountry accommodations, or the possibility of chance encounters with bad-tempered wildlife.

For those who made the trek, nothing they had heard or had read could have prepared them for what they would experience south of the Tehachapi Mountains. Even before the first boats docked at Los Angeles, travelers were already succumbing to the spell of the Southland:

"Immediately after passing Point Conception we realize that we have come into a southern climb; and we almost seem to see a distinct line of demarcation separating the northern gloom from the southern glamour." An unknown tourist

By the time they had come ashore, the spell was nearly complete:

"Nowhere else on earth have I seen the light of the sun rest down on this beautiful world so tender as it streams down through this white-lilac autumn haze of California." Stephen Powers

By the time they progressed to this phase, most of them were goners. The landscape was so beguiling that some could not make up their minds where they thought they were; comparisons ran in all directions:

"Its mountains are Swiss, its valley Scottish, and its bay that of Naples." A Santa Barbara tourist

Some saw it as more Greek-like, while others saw a touch of the French, the Iberian, the North African, and the Near Eastern. California seemed to possess at least a piece of every panorama on the planet; it was a unique, environmental abnormality that would be gleefully exploited by pioneer filmmakers 40 years hence.

The tourists visited L.A. and the surrounding towns and villages; they picnicked at the beach; they stopped in at the missions, and the vineyards, and almost inevitably, they found their way to the land office. A short stay was usually all it took to put many in a mood to buy.

The climate and natural beauty of the landscape proved so intoxicating that land agents found there was practically no need to do any selling. When a newspaper reporter questioned one of the railroad's land agents over what the reporter considered to be inflated prices, the agent famously quipped:

"We sold them the climate and threw in the land."

Those truly smitten bought land, built huge winter homes, and began a long and very popular tradition among eastern elites of "wintering" on the west coast. When the Southern Pacific completed a new line linking San Francisco with Los Angeles in 1876, the tourist trickle became a torrent.

Now, it was no longer fashionable just to visit California; to be truly "in vogue," one had to buy a winter home. Many selected build sites in and around the San Francisco area, but for those enchanted by the Mediterranean myth, Santa Barbara, Pasadena, and Redlands became the favored locations of a new patrician class settling into Southern California.

Room Service

The annual migration of wintering elites was so pervasive that their presence began to give the region a resort-like appearance when, in fact, there was not a single guest facility south of Monterey that could honestly be described as, "habitable." Those expecting to check into their usual five-star accommodations were in for a rude surprise. So bad were the frontier hostels of Southern California that even the railroad boosters would not dare to represent them as anything other than dreadful:

> ### Victoriana
> The Victorian architectural style was a European import that became popular with Yankee blue bloods in the latter half of the 19th century. Built up rather than out, the heavily built, multi-story structures were adorned with elaborate trimmings, do dads, and bold, contrasting colors. These "painted ladies," as they were often called, proliferated east of the Rockies where the style better suited the various cultures and climates. But out on the warm, dry, west coast, these qualities were useless. Nevertheless, easterners stubbornly clung to the familiar, and so nearly all buildings associated with the tourist industry, as well as their stately homes, were done up in this mode. From Santa Barbara to San Diego, grand Euro-styled residences were erected, often within sight of the crumbling adobe walls of an old Spanish rancho. But in time, the natural compulsion to want to turn the Southland into New England west diminished as other, more appropriate, alternatives became available.

"...You will not find any of these places tasteful pleasure grounds or large, finely laid out places. Nature has done much and man has not, so far, helped her." Charles Nordhoff

One guest of the Bella Union Hotel in Los Angeles was so bemused by the establishment's shortcomings that he felt compelled to leave a record of his experience, possibly as a warning to future travelers:

"In rainy weather the primitive floor was... rendered quite muddy by the percolations from the roof above. The rooms were not over 6x9 in size. If a very aristocratic guest came along, a great sacrifice was made in his favor, and he was permitted to sleep on the little billiard table." Horace Bell

But, of course, with so many well-heeled guests popping in and out of the territory, the oversight was soon rectified. Santa Barbara's Arlington Hotel, completed in 1876, was the first of many opulent, 19th-century pleasure palaces erected during Southern California's thirty-year-long resort industry building boom. When it opened, it had to be one of the most absurd structures in the west. Here was an elegant, east coast hostelry standing alone in the middle of the California outback.

Yet, despite the remote setting, the accommodations and the service were equal to anything that could be found in San Francisco or even New York. Entertainments were provided nightly and organized activities were scheduled throughout the day, including "surf bathing parties."

The Backcountry Bourgeoisie

Within a few short years, the steady flow of blue bloods into Southern California transformed select pockets of the frontier into miniature, American Rivieras. This crowd came well cultured, well educated, and well financed. They also came with a sense of civic responsibility that would push the process of transforming a remote frontier into the kingdom of the sun.

This transformation was quite remarkable when you consider that in the same year that the ultra-posh Arlington Hotel was completed, Custer met his end at the Little Big Horn. Bourgeois refinement may have graced some small pockets of the landscape, but Montana was still the Wild West and so were Los Angeles and San Diego.

Despite the growing presence of so many refined, well-bred easterners, local newspapers in these Southern California towns were still sprinkled with stories of cattle rustlers, stage holdups, hangings, shootouts, and occasional skirmishes with the Indians. But none of these frontier dustups ever made it into the pages of the railroad's marketing materials. Instead, tourists were being fed travel advice that most locals would probably have considered downright reckless:

> *"You will hear... that it is a wild country in which everyone goes armed, and where you may with very little trouble lose your life or your purse. But it is not true. Contrary to the advice of friends, I brought no arms with me; I found everybody civil, and my precious person and property perfectly secure." Charles Nordhoff*

Ironically, the one threat the self-serving railroad hacks did take seriously was the one that didn't really exist. Most new arrivals became aware of this dreaded peril through cautionary tales of the poor souls who had fallen victim to the curse of enervation!

Forever Wild
To give you an idea of just how misleading the boosters could be, 40 years later (circa 1915), the *L.A. Times* reported that a Hollywood film crew, on location in Malibu Canyon, was robbed at gunpoint by two mounted highwaymen.

Psychosis de la Sol

A story had spread of a group of European emerges who started a colony in Southern California. But even before the first week was out, a strange spell had overtaken them.

People stopped showing up for their assigned work details, and instead, began writing poetry, dancing in the woods, singing songs to the far horizon, and basking in the golden sun. The fields went fallow, the livestock wandered off, and the neighbors helped themselves to the rest. One by one, they wandered off never to be seen again.

Did enervation, the dreaded scourge of Southern California, strike down these poor devils? Don't laugh; this was no joke to the tourists and settlers of this era. The guidebooks were full of warnings to avoid prolonged exposure to the mesmerizing California sunshine lest one succumb to its hypnotic spell and abandon a once productive life to wander up and down the beach looking for seashells.

"Sooner or later, there is a slacking, a toning-down...this is as sure as the sun shines for it is the sun that will bring it about." H. H. Jackson

Up San Francisco way, there developed a whole new school of tragic literature, which focused on the denizens of the local artistic community and their struggles to remain creative. Beautiful Carmel-by-the-Sea was an especially dangerous place to linger:

"Despondency lurked behind the laughter of the Carmelites. Many found their hoped-for period of creativity turning into an ordeal of apathy. They gave themselves over to daydreams, while their minds ran down like clocks, as if they had lost the keys to wind them up with and they turned into beachcombers, listlessly reading books they had read 10 times before and searching the rocks for abalones."

Van Wyck Brooks

O.K., so it might be wise to steer clear of Carmel; but that's up in Northern California and we don't care what goes on up there anyway?

"The droning of the shoreline knocked ambition out of me." Max Miller

Evidently, there was danger along the coastline as well. Maybe we better move inland.

"The perpetual sunshine baffles, confuses, irritates, and eventually maddens the inhabitants." Denis Ireland

Even inland, it seemed one was not safe. Was there nothing to be done? Was there no one who could resist this terrible menace?

"This feeling would vanish once energetic Yankees took firm possession of the land. The climate was not really enervating. One just got that impression from the low educational and moral status of the native population." Charles Loring Brace

Well, as silly as all this sounds now, the fear was very real back in the 1870s and it persisted for many years thereafter. Something did happen to these people, but it was not the result of a medical disorder. Enervation was just another of those amusing California myths. Mr. Brace was correct in his assertion that "the climate was not really enervating," but he could have cast his net a little wider in his estimation of those able to prove it.

Of course, you didn't need a New England pedigree to be able to withstand the sensual assault of the sun; you simply had to have the fortitude and strength of character to be able to keep your nose to the grindstone in the face of a steady run of absolutely glorious days in which you might be engaged in any number of more pleasurable pursuits.

What the Southern California climate did do was present an atmosphere in which the impulse to "go native" could be overwhelming, and some people just gave themselves up to whatever impulse arose. Southern California simply provided the perfect arena for those of truly great purpose to achieve miraculous goals, or for those of limited industry to indulge themselves.

By the end of the 19th century, most people had come to realize that enervation had more to do with character than climate. Simply put, the condition known as enervation does not exist—except when used as a placebo.

To Catch a Cure

The fact that enervation did not exist did not mean it did not have any practical applications. Enervation, taken in excess, often proved to have some very positive medicinal effects. There were some people for whom a dose of what they thought was enervation, could mean the difference between life and death.

This was good news for a nation in which nearly one-third of the population was in poor health. This collective infirmity was not the result of some terrible plague, but simply the result of the crude nature of life in 19th century America, where a poor diet, poor working conditions, poor sanitation, and even poorer proficiency in the practice of medicine undermined the general well-being of the nation.

Since the beginning of the century, wealthy Americans had been visiting backcountry hostels in hopes of restoring failing health. Most were acting on the advice of doctors who believed that the most common maladies (cholera, smallpox, malaria, and tuberculosis) were simply the result of "bad air," of which, according to some observers, California was naturally exempt:

"The friction of the winds, generating electricity and adding power to the health-giving ozone, bromide, chlorine, and the saline of the sea killed the noxious germs in the air." George Wharton James

Yeah... well, with that said, we now fast-forward to the 1870s, where medical science had yet to discover that it was not the air itself, but the bacteria and viruses that got into the air that were the causes of the most common killers of the day—the kind of microorganisms that propagated as easily in the damp cellars of stately mansions as in the tenement houses of the crowded and often filthy eastern cities of the 19th century.

Doctors who sent their malaria and tuberculosis sufferers (the only ones who lingered long enough to attempt a cure) out into the countryside to "ruralize" in the fresh air and sunshine, did see slight improvements in the condition of some patients. Naturally, it was assumed these improvements were the result of exposure to clean country air, when they were actually attributable to the patient's time spent away from a compromised environment.

This medical misinterpretation was picked up by the press and then pounced on by the Southern Pacific's marketing division. If nine out of ten eastern doctors say that fresh air and sunshine is the new miracle cure, then there can be no place more healthful than Southern California—all aboard!

When the Transcontinental Railroad opened the door to Sunny California it had seemed to America's infirm that salvation was at hand; and why not, they had the indisputable assurance of the Southern Pacific Railroad:

"I have seen on my journey dozens of people deeply gone in consumption when they came here who had been restored to health by residence in some of the southern counties." Charles Nordhoff

The first waves began arriving in the late 1870s, as did many of the quacks and crackpots that preyed upon them. So many tuberculosis sufferers came to Southern California hoping to find a magical cure that Los Angeles became known as the "one lunged town." To accommodate the influx of the sick and suffering, sanitariums began spreading all over the Southland, with those in Palm Springs, Sierra Madre, and San Gabriel becoming some of the world's most renowned invalid destinations.

The burden of caring for so many sick people might have strained the resources of the fragile frontier communities they settled in were it not for the fact that a great many of them went right from the train station to the cemetery. Despite all the boisterous ballyhoo, sunny days and balmy breezes could not forestall the inevitable. When asked if the environment of Southern California could really be of any benefit to the afflicted, a local newspaperman replied:

"No, sir, but I think it is a pleasant place in which to be sick, and, when my appointed time comes, an easy spot in which to die."

The movement probably would have petered out within a year or two if this journalist had been 100% correct in his estimation of the region's healing powers. But the fact was that, under certain conditions, a small number of invalids actually did experience some improvement in their constitution, if not their actual condition. If they were young enough and strong enough, and if the disease had not progressed too far, then maybe some relief could be found. A lift of the spirits triggered by the cheery atmosphere often convinced sufferers they were experiencing a recovery.

And so, believing in miracles, the desperate, ailing hordes migrated west in such great numbers that they became something of an embarrassment to the railroad. Had it not been for the irrepressibly buoyant nature of the Southern California environment, the presence of so many invalids might have overwhelmed the upbeat ambiance their boosters had spent years trying to create. But fortunately, by the 1880s, the years of pushing the hard sell were beginning to pay off. Ticket sales were on the rise as were land sales. And, in their quest to settle the west coast, the railroads still had one more card left to play.

> **Forever Cured**
> What hopeful eastern readers never knew was that quite a few of the "miraculously healed" who had gone on to write great volumes in praise of California's restorative powers had already succumbed to their afflictions by the time the books appeared on store shelves.

Chapter 11
Nuevo Paradiso

The Golden Orb

By the early 1880s, the Southern Pacific's unflagging publicity campaigns were finally beginning to produce some positive results. Yet, after more than eight years of non-stop ballyhooing, efforts to attract not only competent agriculturalists but also the kind of farsighted investors and entrepreneurs that were always essential in the transformation of a frontier into a commercial empire, had failed. Despite all the promising developments that had taken place, few could see any serious commercial potential in Southern California.

The tourist trade was still in its infancy and primarily a winter phenomenon. The sanitariums were doing well, but they could do damage to the region's prospects if they got to be too prominent. And neither the tourists nor the invalids came to stay, and therefore, they had little stake in the Southland's development. To go forward economically, Southern California needed an industry that could demonstrate the kind of serious, long-term growth potential that would encourage further development.

It was a momentous problem that would eventually be mitigated, not by the seasoned marketing professionals at the Southern Pacific, but by a middle-aged housewife and part-time spiritualist who had just arrived from Knoxville, Tennessee.

Eliza Tibbets and her husband, Luther, came to California with a colony of twenty-five families in 1871 and founded the city of Riverside California. It was Luther's job to select the colony's cash crop and he was convinced that citrus would do well in the warm, dry, frost-free climate of Riverside. The Franciscans had successfully imported a Spanish variety of orange for their mission gardens, and so he decided to bank on this proven commodity.

But Eliza thought she could do even better. She had heard favorable accounts of a new variety of Brazilian orange tree that Department of Agriculture researchers were experimenting with in Washington D.C. So, she sent away for two trees and planted them in her front yard and waited, and waited, and waited. Finally, in 1879, they had begun to bear fruit—a whole lot of fruit.

Unlike the small and seedy Spanish variety, this new "Riverside Orange," which was also known as the Washington Naval Orange, which came from Brazil, by way of Portugal, which had imported it from India, grew large and near seedless. It peeled easily, its flavor was exceptional, and it thrived in the hot, dry outback areas of Riverside and San Bernardino counties.

To show off her produce, Eliza hosted tea parties where she passed out samples of her big, plump, juicy, oranges and took orders for tree clippings at five dollars a pop. From there word spread throughout the state and the nation that this new "super fruit" had found an ideal home in Southern California.

> **Community Colonizers**
>
> One of the most common arrangements, for those on a budget looking to put down roots and earn a living in this underdeveloped frontier, was to throw in with a group of like-minded immigrants and establish a colony. Participants pooled their resources and sent a few elders ahead to buy land and sub-divide it into home lots. Then the advance units would send for the main body of the colony to begin the business of building a community. This was the blueprint for many Southern California townships such as San Bernardino, Anaheim, Riverside, and Pasadena.

Eliza's oranges not only provided a cash crop for the Riverside Colony, but within a decade, California citrus had developed into a regional industry serving markets all over the nation. By the time the citrus industry had reached its apex in the 1930s, the offspring from Eliza Tibbet's original two trees were spread out over 100,000 acres.

Eliza's oranges provided Southern California with a product that had the potential to transform a desert into an agricultural colossus. All that was needed to make it happen was some interested parties with very deep pockets, and they were arriving by the trainloads every winter.

The wealthy eastern tourists fell in love with Eliza's new California oranges. They loved how the vibrant orange color contrasted with the deep green of the leaves; they loved how their sweet fragrance scented the breeze; they loved their stately bearing, and the way elegant rows of mature trees could bestow upon a country estate the magnificence of a Mediterranean villa, and they tasted pretty good too. Best of all, a man of means, with no real interest in agribusiness, could become a distinguished gentleman grower and never have to get his hands dirty.

Just like the railroad boosters had been saying all along, what made the orange unique was that it was, relatively speaking, a non-committal crop. It wasn't necessary to cultivate thousands of acres of orange trees to be successful. The orange could be grown, at a profit, on a relatively small plot of land. With that, a little water, and a lot of patience, any eastern novice could become a productive California citrus grower. But it couldn't be done without a little seed money for they were slow-growing and required expensive irrigation. Thus, citrus growing had to be approached as a long-term investment rather than the usual California get rich quick scheme.

This prerequisite of time and capital excluded all but the wealthy from the citrus business, but most of the tourists coming to California in the early 1880s had plenty of both. Eastern retirees found the citrus business to be a charming little outdoor hobby, and soon, a whole new breed of Californian emerged—the gentleman citrus farmer.

More Fruit, More Flora

The success of the Riverside Orange prompted many of the local farmers to begin experimenting with other exotic species of fruits, and it was discovered that nearly all of them could find a welcoming habitat somewhere within the confines of Southern California. Apples, peaches, pears, cherries, lemons, and apricots all thrived, as did the date in, of all places, the Salton Basin. Groves of these other crops soon spread throughout Southern California adding greatly to the region's agricultural output, but it was Eliza's orange that always remained king. 11-1

Tropicalizin'

Though these cash crops certainly garnered the most attention, there were many other botanical projects underway as well. One of the most common complaints among the continuously expanding influx of wealthy winter tourists was the pitiable aesthetic quality of the inland landscape.

Wealthy part-timers and concerned, year-round residents generally agreed that something had to be done to enhance the desolate-looking terrain. Trees were especially rare, and so civic-minded organizations and influential individuals began importing, en-masse, those species that could survive in Southern California's natural, un-irrigated environment: the eucalyptus and acacia from Australia, the palm from northern Mexico, and the pepper from Peru were some of the most popular imports.

> **First in Flight**
>
> On August 28, 1883, on a hill overlooking Otay Mesa, near San Diego, James Montgomery took hold of a towrope and ran for all he was worth, successfully launching his brother, John, fifteen feet into the air aboard their own home-made glider. After covering a distance of six hundred feet, both man and machine returned safely to earth. It was the first "controlled" flight of a heavier-than-air "flying machine" in the United States.

Kate Sessions, a horticulturist who opened the first nursery in San Diego, began importing seeds from all over the world and experimenting with various forms of decorative, tropical foliage. Most of these foreign imports proved so successful that they were soon being spread all over the Southland initiating Southern California's gradual "surface" transformation from a barren desert to a tropical oasis.

The success of all this exotic foliage encouraged the railroads to ramp up their usage of the Mediterranean and tropical comparisons in their promotional efforts and, from the 80s on, none of the railroad's special excursion trains headed east without a few potted palms and several lugs of California oranges to pass around to the astonishment of the natives.

The message was not quite as refined as it would become a decade later, but just the experience of holding that exotic, golden orb in the hand said,to many a wannabe settler, that there had to be something very special going on out there in California to be able to produce such a truly wondrous harvest.

Mythologizer II

In 1879, Helen Hunt Jackson, a Massachusetts widower and writer of travel yarns, domestic advice columns, and second-rate romances, attended a lecture given by a Ponca chief on the unjust Indian policies of the United States Government. Mrs. Jackson was so moved that she joined his crusade, and after two years of passionate academic research, completed her first book on the subject that would occupy the remainder of her days.

The book, *A Century of Dishonor*, published in 1881, was a huge, tedious volume highlighting past violations of Indian rights. She sent a copy to each member of congress, none of whom acknowledged the gesture. There, her career as an Indian activist might have ended had providence not delivered her out west. *Century Magazine* sent her to Southern California to write a series of articles on the unique, outdoor industries of the far west; but as she toured the area gathering facts and figures, she became more interested, some might say obsessed, with the plight of California's diminishing Indian population.

The time spent out west rekindled her enthusiasm for the plight of the American Indian, which she forcefully pressed upon her return to the east. In countless newspaper reports, op-ed pieces, and personal visits to congressional offices, Jackson railed against the government's ruthless relocation policies and corrupt Indian agents. She made such a nuisance of herself in the halls of Congress that the U.S. Commissioner of Indian Affairs made her an agent of the Interior Department and sent her back out to California, in 1883, to better appreciate the situation.

On this trip, she visited Indian villages, mission ruins, and a few of the remaining old ranchos where she was entertained by aging dons and donnas with their personal reminiscences of the old days in Spanish California. Jackson was completely enchanted, and through their recollections, she imagined a bucolic California veiled in Spanish charm, grace, and beauty as she assumed it surely must have been in the years before the coming of the Yankees.

When she returned to Washington, she wrote her *Report on the Condition and Needs of the Mission Indians* and submitted it to congress. But again, her efforts were ineffective. Undaunted, she determined to have one more go at it; but this time, since her previous "scholarly" efforts had failed, she decided to try a different approach. Instead of writing a treatise, she would write a novel. She would disguise her sermonizing and social protest within the plot of a fictional romance. She would bypass congress and take her appeal directly to the people:

"I will write a novel which will set forth some Indian experiences in a way to move people's hearts. People will read a novel where they will not read serious books." Helen Hunt Jackson

She went to New York, where she settled into the Berkeley Hotel and began to write. Jackson's *Ramona* was published in November of 1884. In it, she told the story of Ramona, a half-breed orphan raised as Spanish, and Alessandro, her Indian lover. The two elope; they lose a daughter when a white doctor refuses treatment; their tribe is driven off their land by the white government; Alessandro is murdered by a white man, and Ramona re-marries her guardian's Spanish son and moves to Mexico where it is assumed there are no white people.

As this brief synopsis suggests, Jackson heaped all the blame for the mistreatment and exploitation of the California Indians solely upon the gringos. And though it was certainly true that they were responsible for countless random acts of cruelty, an unbiased chronicler would have distributed the blame equally among the Anglos, the rancheros, and especially the Franciscans, which Jackson portrayed as kind and gentle guardians of their adoring, aboriginal dependents.

"Grateful Indians, happy as peasants in an Italian opera, knelt dutifully before the Franciscans to receive the baptism of a superior culture." Kevin Starr

The book was publicly denounced as an unconscionable misrepresentation of history among those few scholars who were familiar with the true saga of early California, but the howls of protest were too late, *Ramona* was a sensational hit. Under the spell of her own overwhelming enthusiasm, Jackson created a tale awash in pastoral enchantment and romance. She had unwittingly hit a nerve with rapidly urbanizing easterners desperate for a nostalgic glimpse back into a dreamy, agrarian world of old-fashioned, rural splendor.

As a work of romantic fiction, *Ramona* became one of the most popular books of the era, but as a means to awaken a nation to their government's mistreatment of the Indians, it was a dismal failure. Nobody picked up on the social protest angle; instead, readers were captivated by a semi-epic romance with a fairy-tale ending.

The sudden popularity of the book helped to promote tourism to Southern California and therefore, the railroad boosters aggressively helped to promote it, for the publication of *Ramona* had given them a third attraction with which to lure tourists out west. Southern California had no marketable past. Egypt had its pyramids, Europe its castles and cathedrals, and even the original colonies had their revolutionary shrines, but until *Ramona*, all Southern California had was a few crumbling adobe huts; Jackson gave it a viable past.

The Master Booster

There is no doubt that *Ramona* would have been a popular book, but it's quite possible that it would not have had such a lasting influence on Southern California had its publication not occurred just prior to two pivotal events: the completion of a second transcontinental railroad, and the arrival of Charles Fletcher Lummis.

By the time he was twenty-five, the fortunes of Charles Fletcher Lummis were already in decline. He had failed at Harvard; he had failed as a newspaperman; he was failing in his marriage, and having contracted malaria, even his health was failing. Desperately in need of a fresh start, he decided to pursue a familiar self-improvement strategy and migrate to Southern California.

To finance his move, and hopefully secure a job, he contacted Harrison Gray Otis, the publisher of the *Los Angeles Times*, with an offer to write a series of articles describing the interesting people and places he was sure to encounter on his journey out west.

> **Royal Wave Riders**
>
> In the summer of 1885, two Hawaiian Princes, on leave from a San Mateo military school, shaped their own redwood planks, headed down to Santa Cruz, and made history as the very first surfers to ride a west coast wave. Bystanders showed little interest.

With travel literature becoming commonplace, it's possible Otis might have declined the offer had it not been for the unusual mode of transportation Lummis proposed. It was just the kind of gimmick no newspaperman could refuse. Lummis claimed that he would make the 3500-mile journey from Cincinnati, Ohio to Los Angeles, California on foot, and he did; after 142 days on the road, Lummis met Otis at the San Gabriel Mission where the latter offered the former the job of city editor of the *L.A. Times*.

In Southern California, Lummis recovered his health. Then he spent the next four years working, smoking, drinking, and carousing his way into a paralytic stroke and had to be shipped out to New Mexico for several more years of convalescence. But during those first four years in Los Angeles, he established himself as the Southland's premier "boostmeister." Over the course of his western trek, Lummis developed a deep affection for the southwest, which could barely be contained by the time he got to Los Angeles.

> *"God made Southern California, and he made it on purpose."*
> Charles Fletcher Lummis

Like Helen Hunt Jackson, Lummis became enamored with Southern California's faded and near-forgotten Spanish heritage and began to imagine that, with his help, a new Anglo civilization could arise in the west where eastern wealth, culture, and refinement would learn to blend harmoniously with the slower pace of life lived under the California sun. In time, the Yankee would learn to embrace the leisure hours and appreciate the Latin's love of art, beauty, and gracious living. It would be a Renaissance California style.

> *"California and the Southwest would be the theater in which for the first time an English-speaking race has the opportunity to repeat the glories of classic days -- the art, the music, the literature and the life of ancient Greece and Palestine and Italy."* Charles Fletcher Lummis

In the same spirit of hyper-romanticism that gripped Helen Hunt Jackson as she wrote *Ramona*, Lummis sought to reconnect with the region's early Spanish heritage. Like so many other new arrivals made giddy with the overpowering sense that absolutely anything might be possible in California, Lummis re-invented himself as "Don Carlos." In a Spanish costume complete with sombrero and sash, he became the model for the Neo-Californio.

In countless articles for the *Times* and other publications, he invited Californians to slow down, forget the pressures of industrialized society, and experience the virtues of leisure and the elegant, simple life as it was lived by the early Californios. He celebrated the architecture, music, and art that had been overlooked for decades, and created organizations dedicated to their restoration and preservation;

and just in time for what would become the biggest tourist rush the Southland had ever experienced.

Tusslin' Trains

Since the completion of the Transcontinental Railroad, the Southern Pacific extended its branch lines to all corners of the state and enjoyed a monopoly on all rail service within it, which, to the frequent consternation of the locals, often resulted in arbitrary freight rates, high fares, and shoddy service.

However, the railroad's expansion did finally give Southern California's farmers access to nearly all markets within the state including the population hubs of Sacramento and San Francisco. This made Southern California farming a little more practical and added some value to the Southland's depressed real estate, for it was a well-known fact that a railroad was good for business; therefore, two railroads, fighting for territorial domination, had to be a godsend!

> **Corporate California**
>
> Listed among the great robber barons of the 19th century was the Big Four, who controlled the state's rail lines, and consequently, the state's commerce. Cities lobbying for rail service would be forced to make huge concessions or see the tracks pass through "spite towns" just a few miles away. Their discriminatory shipping rates favored friends and ruined foes; they bribed judges and politicians and anybody else worth bribing and reigned practically unopposed for nearly 40 years.

For twelve years, the Southern Pacific profited greatly from their monopoly and did all it could to discourage competitors from trying to enter the California market. But they could not stop the steady, westward advance of the Acheson, Topeka, and Santa Fe Railroad, which reached Deming, New Mexico in early 1881, where it connected to the Southern Pacific's eastbound line from Los Angeles.

To complete their western progression, the Santa Fe was forced to lease track rights from the Southern Pacific. With the arrival of a second transcontinental railroad, competition between the two rival providers should have led to improved service and lower rates; However, the cost of maintaining their new lines and the tribute the Santa Fe paid for track use put them in no position to challenge the mighty Southern Pacific—at least not right away.

But over the next four years, the Santa Fe quietly bought several small, local railroads along the route from New Mexico to Southern California and, linking them together with new construction, pieced together their own line into Los Angeles, which opened in late 1885. To the Southern Pacific, it was an act of war, and for the next two years, the two great railroads would alternately manipulate their freight and passenger rates to modestly, and temporarily, undercut one other. It was more like polite skirmishing than total war, but anyone who knew anything about the railroad business knew that it was only a matter of time before the gloves came off.

The Rail Rumble
Retired Indiana railroad executive, Elisha Babcock, had come west for the cure. While recuperating in San Diego, he picked up a great bargain on a failed resort project on Coronado Island in the San Diego harbor. To help finance the completion of his new resort, he subdivided some of the project's land into home lots, and on November 13, 1886, he held a public auction.

Among the 6000 attending the auction was a Mr. Chase, who bought the first lot. And at the end of the day, when all the other lots had been sold, Mr. Chase resold the lot he bought just hours before for more than twice what he paid for it. Evidently, there was somebody in San Diego who knew something about railroad competition and its effect on real estate values. For in the calm of that fall evening, almost before anyone was fully aware of it, the first of the great California land booms had begun.

Then, less than four months later, on the morning of March 5, 1887, without any fanfare, the price of a one-way ticket from Kansas City, Missouri, to Los Angeles, California, on the Santa Fe line dropped from a staggering $125.00 to just $12.00. A short time later, the Southern Pacific matched it. Within minutes the Santa Fe's price dropped to $8.00. The Southern Pacific made it $6.00. They continued slashing and counter slashing until, by noon, the price for a one-way ticket to Southern California, on either line, was $1.00. The Great Southern California land boom had begun, and now, everybody knew it.

The Pullman Pilgrims
In 1887, one hundred and twenty-five dollars was an insurmountable obstacle to most Americans, but practically any cookie jar east of the Mississippi was probably good for at least a dollar. And now, that and five days would put you in the Promised Land. Who would not be willing to take a shot at a better life, or just a wild, impromptu spree, for a buck?

All westbound trains were filled beyond capacity. The result of the railroad's price war was a flood of migration into the region that would nearly rival the great gold rush. People with money earned elsewhere flooded into the Southland. Surely, it was thought, big eastern capital would now pour into California and fire up new industry and commerce. Affluent, moderately prosperous, and low-wage settlers and invalids all were quick to seize the opportunity to get in on the ground floor. So many people, who had heard so much about this land of milk and honey, now had a chance to go there and buy their own piece of paradise.

But this price war had been anticipated by promoters, speculators, sharpsters, and out-and-out swindlers from all over the country. They arrived early and bought thousands of acres, both useful and useless. They staked out imaginary towns and were waiting at the stations in Los Angeles and San Diego to greet the hordes of greeners as they stepped off the train. Carriages and wagons were in continuous motion transporting prospective land buyers from bars, hotel lobbies, and railroad depots out to haphazardly laid out town sites where home lots were sold on the promise that future development was a rock-solid certainty.

"We may say that San Diego has a population of 150,000 people, only they are not all here yet." A San Diego land speculator

Promoters set up observation towers near town sites where buyers selected their lots through a telescope, while others set up huge tents and beckoned buyers with brass bands, free lunches, and the convenience of selecting their lots right off the auctioneer's map. People from the lowliest stable boy to the grandest of railroad tycoons gambled in the over-heated real estate market, and more were arriving by the trainloads every day. Land values escalated by 300% and the constantly increasing demand drove prices higher by the hour; in the great frenzy to get hold of a piece of California, all caution was abandoned:

"...Take with you all the cash you can raise and buy at auction and keep buying until your money and credit are both exhausted. It will not be possible for you to make a mistake..." Thomas L. Fitch

During these boom years, the carnival atmosphere and rapid influx of easy money attracted every type of criminal and vice merchant. Gambling and prostitution were out in the open, and incidents of murder and robbery rose dramatically. Even ex-marshal Wyatt Earp, himself ducking a murder charge in Arizona, liked the odds in San Diego so much that he took up residence and opened three successful gambling halls. Though some of the locals welcomed the sudden blast of capital and commerce, most felt the boom had set the Southland back 30 years:

"The desecration of Sunday was complete, with all drinking and gambling houses open... Theft, murder, incendiarism, carousals, fights, highway robbery and licentiousness gave to the passing show ...many

of the characteristics of the frontier camp."
　　　　　　　　Walter Gifford Smith, The San Diego Sun

The Del
Though the legitimate hostelries were outnumbered by the bordellos and gambling halls, Southern California's tourist industry was also experiencing a ripple effect, which produced two of the greatest super-resorts of the era—the Raymond, and the Del.

The ultra-elegant Raymond Hotel opened in Pasadena, in 1886, as a winter retreat for eastern blue bloods ducking the harsh, New England winters. With the Santa Fe stopping at the front door, the Raymond was instrumental in introducing thousands of wealthy easterners to the soothing Southern California milieu.

The Raymond, like all the other big, fashionable, Southland resorts, was just a colonial outpost of east coast style and culture on the western frontier; but on Valentine's Day 1888, all that changed. On that day, the Hotel Del Coronado opened for business. The all-electric Hotel Del was the largest in the world with 399 rooms, and the first mega-inn on the west coast to fully embrace its Southland setting.

It was Southern California's first real beach resort and no effort was spared to emphasize that fact. The whitewashed all-wooden structure was located right on the beach with every room facing the ocean.

The grounds, which featured a Japanese tea garden, were landscaped with the new, imported tropicals. Outdoor amenities included tennis courts and an Olympic-sized, salt-water swimming pool. At the hotel yacht club, guests could even sign up for deep-sea fishing excursions. In the years to come, nearly every new inn within sight of the Pacific Ocean would incorporate a bit of the Del's shoreline ambiance into its presentation.

> **Tenting on the Strand**
> To handle the Del's summer overflow, the management laid out a tent city in a grid pattern along the Silver Strand, a sandy peninsula with the bay on one side and ocean on the other. The eight by ten-foot canvas tents came fully furnished with daily maid service and a trolley line connecting the camp with downtown Coronado. The tent city drew vacationers from far and wide as well as local guests from L.A. and San Diego and became such a popular summer attraction that it was duplicated by nearly every other upscale, seaside resort on the Southern California coast.

The After Boosters
Not content to rely solely on the promotional efforts of the railroads to keep those settlers coming, the L.A. city fathers formed the Los Angeles Chamber of Commerce in 1888 and began distributing its own promo material and sponsoring its own "California on Wheels" train to

carry the "life is lived better in California" message directly to the cities of the Midwest, south, and east, as well as the state and world's fairs and exhibitions. Resort hotels also began sponsoring tourism campaigns, hiring their own writers and artists, and organizing westbound excursion parties that began targeting an entirely new and fast-growing demographic yet to make much of an impact on the Southern California scene—the middle class.

The Bulge in the Middle

In addition to the demand for armies of laborers, the industrial revolution created an insatiable need for a better-educated, and therefore, better-paid workforce to fill the ranks of the managers, clerks, schoolteachers, accountants, engineers, and other professionals, all of which made up a new and fast-growing middle class. With their increasing prosperity and leisure time, they developed an urge to travel, to get out and experience something a little bit out of the ordinary.

The grand tour of Europe was out of the question, but a trip to Southern California was becoming a popular alternative. Railroad competition kept rates low, as did the competition between the scores of new, mid-level, tourist hotels opening all over the Southland. But just as Southern California's stock as a tourist destination was rising, its land asset value took a sharp nosedive.

Busted

Not all land speculators were driven by pure greed. Some were doing their very best to help build solid, prosperous communities; and some of the towns they staked out, like Monrovia, and Glendale, and La Mesa (where I grew up), did eventually succeed. But the sincere boosters were always outnumbered by those out for the quick buck—the so-called "escrow Indians." And by the spring of 1888, the imbalance was all too apparent.

The unscrupulous peddled to the unwary home lots located on cliff sides, in riverbeds, and even out in the San Diego Bay. Speculators sold worthless lots for top dollar with the promise of "soon-to-come" runaway civic development, but it was the speculators who ran away.

> *"...at least a quarter of a million dollars were thrown away upon alkali wastes." Theodor Van Dyke*

With all the boisterous boomtown commotion that had gripped Los Angeles and San Diego, there was a realization among banks and investors that, after three years, very few truly substantial townships had been created, and the easy money evaporated like morning dew on the desert. By the late spring of 1888, it was over.

"From whence the boom came I do not know, and I have never been able to learn... it reversed motion and went down like a chunk of sawed-off wood." Thomas J. Hayes

Within six months, most of the speculators, gamblers, whores, and hucksters were gone. San Diego's population dropped to half what it was during the peak of the boom, but even that was an increase from what it had been before. Los Angeles also lost thousands of disillusioned pilgrims, but like San Diego experienced a substantial increase from pre-boom population levels. In fact, in those tumultuous three years, Los Angeles had transitioned from a cow town to a city.

Those with the means to do so could chalk it all up to experience and return from whence they had come, while those who bet everything on a bust were forced to seek work wherever it could be found. The boom of the 80s did not bring civilization out to the west coast, but it did add to the head count. And though still a semi-sparsely populated frontier, the Southland had now grown large enough to begin developing a civilization all its own.

Chapter 12
Some Assembly Required

Ramona-nation

The real estate bust of the late 1880s left the Southland flattened—again! At the dawn of the 1890s, forty years after the gold rush, Southern California's commercial yield was limited primarily to tourism.

The basic laws of economics suggest that betting the future on a single, seasonal, service industry greatly heightens risk exposure; but while most other commercial enterprises were struggling, if not foundering, tourism was on the rise. And most of the credit for the upsurge in tourist activity was due to one lady—Helen Hunt Jackson. Six years after the publication of *Ramona*, the myth she created had become one of the Southland's top tourist attractions.

> *"Eastern visitors commonly read Ramona as a part of their preparation for a winter's trip to Southern California."*
>
> *Margaret Allen*

Much of the book's growing appeal derived from its stark contrast to the new, industrialized world many easterners were finding increasingly alien, unattractive, and disorienting. Within the pages of *Ramona*, readers could escape from the smokestacks and skyscrapers of the big city into a tranquil world of lazy days gone by. Modernization, urbanization, and industrialization had set a high premium on the antiquated, primitive, and picaresque. For those wishing to flee the foul metropolis, the Southern Pacific could have them in the middle of that scenic pastoral in just eight days.

And so, in a general state of hyper-nostalgic delirium, tourists began arriving in the Southland fully expecting to retrace the steps and visit the haunts of a character commonly known to have been purely fictional. Perhaps in any other part of the country, these seekers might have gone home disappointed, but not in the can-do milieu of Southern California. Recognizing the economic implications of this bewildering fascination, the locals were in a panic to re-discover their forgotten Hispanic culture.

By the 1890s, most of the ranchos had been subdivided into small farms, towns, and residential subdivisions. Few of the old adobe haciendas were still standing, and nearly all the 21 missions were in ruin. In the late 80s, faint efforts had been made to restore some of the crumbling structures, but with the *Ramona* craze gaining momentum, those projects were revisited with a fervent sense of urgency.

Local newspapers, eager to encourage this lucrative deception, began running stories about the people and places featured in the book, further blurring the distinction between fact and fiction. Nearly every county in the Southland claimed to be the home of Ramona and began directing tourists towards any adobe relics that might bolster those claims.

There was so much confusion over which sites were authentic that a team of archeologists were sent out into the backcountry to determine the true origins of this work of fiction.

There were two leading contenders for the title of home of Ramona: Rancho Camulos in Ventura County, and Rancho Guajome in San Diego County. Both locations had been briefly visited by Mrs. Jackson, but even though it was built nearly 20 years after the story was said to take place, Rancho Camulos got the nod.

As a consolation prize, San Diego designated an abandoned adobe hacienda as "Ramona's Marriage Place," shrewdly converting a civic eyesore into a cash cow that is still reaping dividends. The school Ramona "attended" was discovered in Los Angeles, and at any of those three locations, tourists could load up on refreshments and souvenirs and even have their pictures taken with one of the many local Indian women claiming to be "the real Ramona."

> **Mission Revival**
>
> With the overwhelming popularity of these spurious shrines, as well as the original missions, local builders jumped on the Ramona bandwagon and began incorporating the Spanish architectural style into their new construction. To satisfy the tourists desire for the exotic, as well as the locals desire to celebrate the region's new historic significance, the "mission revival" style spread throughout Southern California. Countless commercial, industrial, and residential structures were built featuring clay tile roofs, exposed wood beams, rough finished plaster, arched doorways and windows, and numerous other traditional design elements.

Orange Blossoms

Second, on the short list of Southern California's most promising commercial enterprises of the 1890s was the citrus business. In the years since Eliza Tibbets first introduced her Riverside orange, it had become the Southland's foremost fruit. However, the perishable nature of California's exotic produce restricted its export range to a few hundred miles, severely limiting the industry's growth potential. But with the advent of the refrigerated rail car, in the 1890s, California fruit suddenly began appearing on market shelves as far away as Augusta, Maine, where much of it was left to rot.

Unfortunately, most consumers considered the California specialty crops to be too exotic, and consequently, the supply ran way ahead of demand. To sell their produce, the California fruit growers would first have to create demand by selling the public on what was considered its primary virtue—healthfulness.

But reaching out to this many people would require another mammoth marketing campaign far beyond the financial and logistical ability of a scattered assemblage of independent growers. So, in 1893, they organized themselves as a non-profit cooperative called the Southern California Fruit Growers Exchange.

Commercial enterprises along with the numerous independent "status growers" pooled their resources to transform a regional industry into one of national prominence, with nearly all associated activities (irrigation, pruning, picking, packing, shipping, and marketing) coordinated through the exchange.

To boost demand, the exchange orchestrated the usual 19th-century media barrage of pamphlets, brochures, and newspaper and magazine articles highlighting the health benefits of a diet augmented by generous helpings of California fruit. Doctor's testimonials and highly imaginative fruit recipes were also prominently featured in the flood of promotional materials.

However, this advertising blitz played only a secondary role in the campaign; surprisingly, the real game-changer in the effort to introduce California fruit into the national diet turned out to be the lowly label on the box.

Billboard on a Box

To protect the delicate produce, oranges were packaged for shipment in sturdy wooden boxes. For quality control purposes, a label was glued to the box to identify its contents and packinghouse. The first labels featured an extensive assortment of arbitrary images (Indian Chiefs, locomotives, dogs, ships, etc.) that bore scant relation to their place of origin.

But it didn't take long for the growers to realize that they were overlooking a valuable marketing opportunity. Soon, all the California packinghouses had redesigned their labels into beautiful advertisements that featured both the delicious fruit inside the box and the enchanted land from whence it came.

To the rest of the nation, the California orange crate labels were like postcards from paradise. In radiant colors, every imaginable utopian theme was portrayed, but by far the most common scenario featured Southern California as a fantasyland of eternal sunshine where, in fertile valleys that stretched beyond the horizon, a cornucopia of exotic delights sprung forth from the fertile soil.

Fanciful images of the Southland's many natural wonders and its healthy, happy inhabitants were on display in the produce isles of nearly every market in the nation. There, they spoke to the huddled masses of sunshine, fresh air, and the freedom of the wide-open spaces of the west.

In the seventy years the railroads, hotels, and chambers of commerce actively campaigned to bring new settlers to Southern California, none of the marketing tools they employed were quite as effective in conveying their utopian message as the labels on the orange crates. A few years later, in another masterful re-branding action, the Southern California Fruit Exchange would change its cumbersome moniker to the one that nearly every 20th-century homemaker instantly recognized—Sunkist.

Bungalonia

From the 1870s through the 1890s, Southern California society was generally made up of two polar opposites: wild-eyed adventurers, and wealthy, winter tourists. In the middle was a smattering of shopkeepers, merchants, and tradesmen valiantly trying to hold this fragmented frontier civilization together. But by the late 90s, the Southland was beginning to attract more small businessmen and entrepreneurs looking for new opportunities out west.

This new, middle-class demographic created a demand for a new type of middle-class residential dwelling; something that would bridge the gap between the crude frontier shack and the stately Victorian. Introduced to Southern California by a small assemblage of well-traveled British émigrés, the housing model that best fit the demands of the environment and the needs of this growing market sector turned out to be the Bengalese bungalow.

Developed by the British in India as a cheap and comfortable type of temporary housing on the hot, dry, Bengalese frontier, the bungalow proved to be especially well suited to the warm climate and unhurried culture of Southern California. The boxy, single-story, wood-framed structure featured an

> **Ins & Outs**
> This blurring of the distinction between indoors and outdoors became an essential part of the Califormula that, from this point on, would be replicated in every successive style of residential architecture.

open floor plan and generous window space, which provided excellent ventilation and opened up the inside of the house to the outside. The overhanging rooflines and large porches, inspired by the old adobes, reversed the process and brought the inside outside.

The bungalow's low cost and simple design not only made it a very popular choice for middle and lower-income residents but an ideal second home for wealthier, part-time Californians. The informal character of the bungalow balanced so well with the casual, transient lifestyle of the vacationing tourist that it became the model for the west coast beach house.

By the turn of the century, the "California Bungalow" was so popular that it could be purchased in kit form from mail-order catalogs and shipped directly to the building site. At a time when Southern California land was cheap, the bungalow made suburbia not only possible but also practical; and for nearly fifty years it remained one of the Southland's most popular residential styles.

Tropicalizin'

To enhance the appearance of barren subdivisions during the land boom of the 1880s, real estate speculators decorated their properties with a dizzying assortment of ornamental foliage. With nature imposing few limits, Californians exercised few restraints, and during this period, the Southern California landscape began to solidify the distinctive image of luxuriant, botanical chaos it has since become known for.

Trees and shrubs imported from all corners of the globe were planted side by side in haphazard arrangements that could only exist within the balmy boundaries of the Southland. However, despite the limitless possibilities, it was the tropicals, especially the palm trees, that took precedence over all others.

Real estate developers found that palm trees liberally sprinkled over the desert landscape, suggested a biblical connection that appealed to the pious Midwesterners migrating into Southern California. Consequently, huge numbers of palms were imported and became a dominant presence in residential, commercial, and civic landscaping schemes.

Southern California real estate developers, business and tourist organizations, community planners, civic groups, and high-minded individuals sought to outdo each other in their efforts to carpet the region in tropical splendor. By the turn of the 20th century, the Southland's physical transformation from empty desert to tropical paradise had been firmly established, and henceforth, the tropical mode would be recognized as the unofficial regional landscape motif.

Land of Sunshine

In 1886, in a last-ditch effort to rid himself of the consumption that was killing him, Charles Dwight Willard moved to Southern California. Perhaps owing to his grim prospects, his initial impression of the Southland was decidedly unfavorable, and he missed few opportunities to express his pessimistic viewpoint:

> "It had no past. Its future reveals nothing but an ignominious scramble for dollars, its politics are odious and its population mongrel." Charles Dwight Willard

But as time passed, and the elements began to work their restorative magic, Willard's position softened. In fact, he began feeling so superior that he abandoned all thoughts of the hereafter and took a wife. An impulsive step that proved an exceptional stroke of good luck, for Willard chose for his bride a strong-willed Scotswoman who would force him down the path to recovery:

> "She insisted her new husband eat regularly, get off cocaine, and stay away from long conversations with morbid literary intellectuals." Kevin Starr

Evidently, the new Mrs. Willard had truly hit upon the miracle treatment; for not long after the honeymoon, Willard proclaimed himself to be fully recovered, and to prove the depth of his rejuvenation, he took the job of executive secretary of the Los Angeles Chamber of Commerce, in 1892, and founded *Land of Sunshine* magazine, the first of many Southern California lifestyle magazines. Targeting readers east of the Rockies, the monthly showcased the new, semi-luxuriant, Southern California lifestyle and provided guidance to newcomers adjusting to life in this charmed environment.

Readers found practical advice on everything from home construction and landscaping to west coast style decorating tips and cooking recipes. A host of passionate supporters, local novelists, and prominent guest writers provided the boosterish content, including poems, short stories, travel guides, and historical narratives, some of which might possibly have been true.

Back from the Brink

In 1895, Charles Lummis, having once again recovered his health, returned from New Mexico to become editor of *Land of Sunshine,* the magazine for which he contributed hundreds of articles promoting his dream of an Anglo/Hispano, co-cultural, leisure-based lifestyle until the magazine ceased publication in 1909.

Black Gold

Loitering around LA's downtown area on a hot, dusty afternoon in 1892, ex-prospector turned day laborer, Edward Doheny, noticed a delivery cart with wheel hubs greased with a black, tar-like goo. He asked the driver where he had acquired the intriguing substance and was directed towards a seep hole north of town.

As the existence of this anonymous cart owner clearly indicates, Doheny was not the first to discover oil in Southern California. Since the ice age, crude oil had been seeping to the surface in numerous locations all over L.A. County; the most famous breach being the La Brea Tar Pits. The local Indians used it to waterproof their canoes, and the Franciscans had used it to patch the roofs of the missions. Everybody knew it was there, but nobody really knew what to do with it.

Back east, crude oil was distilled into kerosene and used as fuel for lamps; but unlike the pliant eastern crude, California oil, with its higher asphalt content, did not respond as well to the primitive refining techniques of the day, which made it unsuitable for that purpose.

Nevertheless, Doheny was convinced he could find a market for this volatile commodity, so he leased a likely parcel and started digging. In true 49er fashion, the novice wildcatter tore into the earth with pick and shovel digging up the pitch to be processed into a crude fuel oil. When this manual extraction method proved too burdensome, Doheny improvised a drilling rig using eucalyptus tree trunks as boring bits and began extracting as much as 40 barrels a day. He then marketed his fuel oil as a cheaper substitute for coal, and by the century's end, nearly all Southern California's businesses and industries, including the railroads, were using it.

With his fuel oil, Doheny created the beginnings of a gargantuan industry, yet, in historical terms, this trade barely rates a footnote compared to the record of developments that were soon to be realized. The Duryea brothers of Springfield, Massachusetts, had been building and testing gasoline-powered motorcars since 1893, and by 1900, there were already 23 manufacturers of gasoline-powered automobiles in the United States. Four years later there would be 118, and the skyrocketing demand for that gooey, black sludge oozing through the cracks in the earth's crust would propel Southern California into a new era of prosperity.

The Purple Mother

Katherine Augusta Westcott Tingley (aka the Purple Mother), and several of her followers, arrived in San Diego in the winter of 1897. In a conversation with the old bear flagger himself, John Fremont, she let on that she was in the market for a "golden land" where she might build a "white city" to serve as the new world headquarters for the Theosophical Society of America, of which madam Tingley was the supreme leader. Her vivid description of the ideal location reminded Fremont of Point Loma, near San Diego, and upon his recommendation, she established, what the locals would blithely refer to as, Lomaland.

Tingley and her disciples were the advance guard of a subculture that would soon become very familiar to Southern California—the cultists. In 1894, Tingley, a New York social worker, joined the Theosophical Society of America. Theosophy was a pseudo-religious philosophy assembled from various notions lifted from other eastern religious, mystic, and philosophical beliefs by a Russian circus performer who immigrated to the United States in 1873.

In a nutshell, the sect's teachings integrated an awareness of the brotherhood of mankind with an eternal quest to unlock the ancient mysteries of the universe, humanity, and the world of divinity, as well as the cultivation of one's own psychic and spiritual powers to achieve human perfection.

And since the cult's creators considered this lofty goal too big a challenge for a single lifetime, the faithful were assured that a process of reincarnation would guarantee that their work in progress would continue uninterrupted until perfection had been attained, at which time, the newly enlightened would take their place among the divine ones. It was sort of a learn-at-your-own-pace program. And as bizarre a setup as it was, it was mild milk compared to what was yet to come.

Tingley called her white city Xanadu. There, her young, live-in students ran around in Greek togas, practiced yoga, studied painting and art, and

---

Look ma, no horse!

On May 30, 1897, the stillness of the Los Angeles morn was shattered by the unfamiliar clamor of a four-cylinder engine sputtering to life. The jarring racket was coming from the 5th avenue workshop of machinist S.D. Sturgis, who, along with his engineer partner, J. Philip Erie, had designed and built a "Gasoline Carriage." In an earlier test, the huge, noisy, oil spewing contraption caught fire, and so a very early hour was chosen for the trial run in order to minimize the risk of injury to the public and/or their livestock. As it surged out onto the roadway, the cumbersome vehicle made history as the very first automobile to traverse the streets of L.A. Though slow and ponderous, it covered several city blocks and returned to the barn under its own power and was thus considered a success. Now had Erie and Sturgis been able to turn their gas-wagon into a commercial success, Detroit might never have been. But the two inventors were never able to perfect their design beyond the experimental stage.

Xanadu is now the home of Point Loma Nazarene University.

performed in plays and pageants in the compound's beautiful Greek theater. San Diegans were of a mixed mind concerning the theosophicals. The city fathers feared Tingley's operation would attract the wrong kind of attention, but most of the locals considered them a batty but harmless bunch.

The public's general indifference to the cultists was an example of the escalating degree of tolerance most Southlanders were willing to extend to the unconventional. But even Southern Californians had their limits, as some of those new mid-western modernists would ultimately discover.

Great Blazes

Although Southern California has long been recognized as the nation's most fertile garden for the propagation of modernist architecture, that revolutionary style actually began its evolutionary process some 2000 miles away in a burnt-out section of downtown Chicago. On the night of October 8th, 1871, a flash fire destroyed a third of the city. To refill the void, the city called upon the nation's most innovative architects and engineers just at a time when advances in technology were making it possible for men of vision to re-imagine the metropolis of the 19th century, and by extension, the home of the 20th.

Going Up!

These advancements in design were made possible by advancements in the manufacture of steel, which made the steel I-beam strong enough, and cheap enough, to be used as a component in hi-rise construction. No longer were massive masonry walls required to support a building's weight; with the new load-bearing steel frames, wall mass could be replaced with plate-glass and lightweight, prefabricated concrete sections.

Stripped of all ornamentation, it was a radical departure from the Victorian norm and was met with fierce resistance. But the dramatic reduction in the cost of labor and materials it offered made it impossible to resist. And so, as ghastly as most 19th-century Americans thought it to be, modern industrial design would come to dominate the nation's commercial landscape.

Architect Louis Sullivan elegantly expressed the rationale for this revolutionary design theory with just three words: "form follows

> **Patsy on the Hoof**
>
> In case you're wondering, the answer is no; the cow didn't do it. Mrs. O'Leary's poor old milk cow, rumored to have started the blaze by knocking over a kerosene lantern, was framed by a newspaper reporter who made up the sensational story to scoop his competitors. It was later determined that the fire was the result of high winds, drought conditions, and inopportune circumstance.

function," meaning a building's design should be dictated solely by its purpose. Only on occasion would Sullivan apply that directive to his own work, but it would soon become sacred scripture for modernists from all over the world who made the pilgrimage to the heartland of America to marvel at the innovative structures on display along Chicago's main commercial thoroughfares and industrial avenues.

The Californians, and those destined to become Californians, would go west, and reinterpret modernism as a celebration of leisurely, suburban sophistication, while the Europeans would reinterpret it as a symbol of militant, social revolution.

The Prairie Schooler

One of the first of the American modernists to adapt this urban industrial mode to a suburban setting was Frank Lloyd Wright. Blending the modern with the rustic, Wright laid out his houses long and low to harmonize with the horizontal contour of the landscape. Roof angles were lowered, and windows were mounted in low rows of twos and threes, prefiguring the picture window and sliding glass door.

Anticipating the passing of sociable, carriage culture and the emergence of the noisy, noxious automobile, he eliminated the front porch and moved the outdoor social center to the backyard. Inside, the ceilings were low, and the floor plan was laid wide open with minimal room separation. Sliding panels, screens, and strategic furniture placement were used to suggest separate living areas.

His distinctive style became known as Prairie School, but it quickly spread well beyond the prairie. Wright would introduce nearly every distinctive feature of what would later be incorporated into the jubilant, modernist architecture of mid-century Southern California.

Throughout the 20th century, west coast modernism would be interpreted by four types of architects: those who worked with Wright; those who were trained by Wright; those who were trained by those who worked with Wright; and those who were trained by those who were trained by Wright.

California Modern

Acting upon his doctor's advice to relocate to a warmer climate, Irving Gill arrived in San Diego in 1893, after serving two years as a draftsman in the Chicago office of Adler & Sullivan, where he worked side-by-side with Frank Lloyd Wright.

Early examples of Gill's work on the west coast demonstrate his ability to faithfully duplicate all the popular, revivalist styles of the era, but Gill had absorbed too much modern theory to be completely satisfied cranking out copies of the old-world models. So, he began to gently urge some of his more malleable clients to accept some of his more progressive design concepts; and much to his surprise, some of them did.

Modernism may have had its champions in the commercial realm, but in the residential sphere, it was roundly shunned. In the older, more settled parts of the country tastes ranged from the traditional—period! But in California, which had no fixed architectural traditions of its own, things were a little different.

Many of Gill's wealthy clients were disinterested, part-time residents far away from the arbiters of east-coast fashion and respectability. Luxuriating out on the west coast, they were free to consider the unconventional without fear of reproach. And so, Irving Gill was occasionally given a degree of artistic freedom impossible to imagine in any other part of the country.

In San Diego, Gill blended elements of bungalow and mission style, to create a west coast hybrid of Wright's midwestern motif. By the turn of the century, most of Gill's Southern California structures were favoring the horizontal over the vertical and emphasizing geometric simplicity over revivalist clutter.

However, the cool severity of the straight line and flat plane were nearly always softened by the use of regional design elements. Even the landscaping was used to blunt the sharp edges of the new, modern look. And with his lively blending of old and new styles with organic shapes and materials, Gill created what would become fundamental elements of the architectural "Califormula" of the Southland.

> **The Califormula**
> I will use the term, "Califormula" to describe all the idiosyncratic elements that went into the making of this unique civilization just emerging on the southwestern coast of America.

Sunset

Acknowledged as a true architectural trailblazer, many of Gill's modernist structures were featured in the pages of the Southland's most iconic and enduring lifestyle magazine—*Sunset*. In what would become its final effort to promote tourism and settlement in the west, the Southern Pacific Railroad launched *Sunset* magazine in the spring of 1898, amid growing signs that the west was rapidly changing.

By the late 1890s, the majority of settlers heading for California were no longer poor, backcountry farmers, fortune hunters, or rich tourists, but middle-class families with resources and a preference for the suburbs. The creation of this polished, upscale magazine was, in part, the Southern Pacific's own confirmation of a pronouncement made six years earlier that the American frontier had finally been closed.

With the expectation of promoting a new surge of westward travel and investment, *Sunset* was aimed at America's emerging bourgeoisie. Taking advantage of recent improvements in rail service, *Sunset* showcased the newly refined pleasures of scenic rail travel along with the Southland's best hotels, combining the adventure and romance of the rails with genteel, Southern California style, resort living.

Though the magazine was a great success, its association with the Southern Pacific would be brief. By 1914, over six million people had already found a home in the west, and more were coming every day. Forty years after the Southern Pacific Railroad first began publicly advocating the settlement of the west, and just sixteen years after it had launched *Sunset* magazine, the principals at the railroad determined that their objective had been accomplished.

Promotional campaigns were terminated, and *Sunset* magazine was sold to a group of its employees. In the 19th century, the big question regarding the future of Southern California was "will they come?" Now, at the turn of the 20th century, that question had been answered and replaced by the follow-up question, "what are they going to do?"

Chapter 13
Hello-ha Hawaii

With a single schooner, Captain William Matson began the Matson Navigation Company in 1882, running merchandise, provisions, and a few intrepid passengers on a regular route to Hilo, Hawaii, and returning to San Francisco loaded to the gunwales with the island's sole export—sugar.

Business was good, and by the turn of the 20th century, the Matson Line had grown into a small fleet of larger, modern steamships; and when a British whiskey distiller opened the luxurious Moana Hotel on a desolate stretch of Waikiki Beach in 1901, Matson expanded his operation to include regular passenger service to Honolulu, opening the islands to the mainland tourist trade.

Right away, among California's well to do, the Hawaiian cruise had become near compulsory for the fervently fashionable who began, in earnest, the process of importing Hawaiian beach culture to the California coast.

Growing Pains
But back on the mainland, the Southern Pacific Railroad, another frontier enterprise of the last century, was struggling to adjust to this new century and not doing nearly as well. The Big Four had always run their railroad as they had their gold camp emporiums, ruthlessly charging all that the traffic would bear. It was a policy that won them no friends. But they were gone now, and with their passing came an opportunity for reconciliation; but the new overlords, the Union Pacific, made no efforts to mend the frayed relationship.

Adding further to the railroad's tarnished reputation was the publication of *The Octopus*, by Frank Norris in 1901, which falsely vilified (at least in this instance) the Southern Pacific and succeeded in spreading anti-railroad sentiment nationwide. And things weren't going much better out there in the field.

By the turn of the century, all the railroad's good land was sold; what was left was desert in varying degrees of intensity. Not only could they not sell it, but they were also losing revenue on land already sold as more and more farmers were abandoning their plots, and their mortgages, in frustration over their inability to cope with the region's water shortages and its maddeningly contrary mini climates. To reverse this alarming trend, the Southern Pacific teamed up with the agricultural schools at Berkeley and Davis to develop a desert farming program to go out on the road in a converted freight car as the University on Wheels.

> **Hollywoodland**
> The quaint little village of Hollywood California was incorporated in 1903 by a Kansas prohibitionist. City ordinances banned alcoholic beverages and limited the number of sheep that could be driven down the main thoroughfare to 2000.

For years, this mobile farm school traversed the state teaching Southern California's farmers how to sink wells, build irrigation systems, and how and where to cultivate all the strange, foreign fruits that were just beginning to gain widespread acceptance.

Though the railroad would not close the books on its real-estate program until 1940, the University on Wheels would be its last promo push in California. The leadoff years of the 20th century would also mark the decline of the locomotive as the nation's primary people mover as more and more ex-passengers were abandoning the railways for the roadways.

Henry Founds Ford

On the cusp of the 20th century, it seemed that nearly every machinist, bicycle mechanic, carriage builder, pipefitter, and part-time tinker was working on his own "concept car." One of the most promising of this lot was a Michigan farm boy named Henry Ford, who, on the strength of his first homemade automobile (a brakeless four horsepower pushcart with an impressive top speed of 20mph) was able to attract enough wealthy investors to establish the very first automobile manufacturer in Detroit, The Detroit Automobile Company.

But philosophical differences between the builder and the backers would force the dissolution of the enterprise before it really got started.

Not surprisingly, Ford's backers wanted to build cars for those who could afford to buy them—the very rich. But Ford, who had entered the business from a populist's perspective, dreamed of building an automobile that nearly everybody could afford.

So, once again, to raise awareness of himself and his dream, Ford went racing. Yes, racing! At a time when a driver stood a much better than even chance of experiencing a debilitating breakdown on even the briefest of motor excursions, the automobile race was already becoming a familiar attraction at county fairs and holiday picnics. It also served as a showcase where builders could prove the worthiness of their designs.

So, in 1901, with no money to hire an experienced driver, Ford built an underpowered entry, solicited tactical tips from a bicycle racer, ran against the country's most celebrated factory driver, won the race, promised his wife he would never do it again, and then collected the $1000.00 grand prize as well as the financial support he needed to establish the Ford Motor Company. The nation, and especially Southern California, would never be the same again.

Venezia di Americana

Though it had been well proven, by the turn of the 20th century, that enervation, the debilitating neurosis thought to be the result of prolonged exposure to Southern California's radiant atmospherics, did not exist, that did not necessarily mean that the environment was totally benign.

There was another school of thought that suggested the bewitching elements, rather than mesmerize, actually energized some individuals to such levels of climatologically induced euphoria they sometimes let their wildest dreams get the better of them. And if any one individual lent credence to this hypothesis, it was Abbot Kinney.

On the last leg of a trek around the world, tobacco magnate and asthma sufferer, Abbot Kinney, was delayed in San Francisco where he experienced some shortness of breath. Aware of the rumors surrounding the therapeutic qualities of the atmosphere found in the southern portion of the state, Kinney made a quick side trip to a Sierra Madre sanitarium.

He was so overjoyed to awake the next morning completely relieved of his respiratory ailments that he bought a 500-acre citrus ranch about 30 miles east of L.A. When his wife complained of the heat out there in the backcountry, he bought a summer home in Santa Monica and joined a consortium speculating in beachfront development. His very first venture, the Ocean Park Beach Resort, was a success, but the partnership was not, and so the principals agreed to split their holdings on the flip of a coin.

Kinney won the toss, but passed on the resort, and instead, claimed the marshy tidelands next to it, which he developed into a combination resort, entertainment center, commercial district, and residential subdivision. But this wasn't just any old seaside development. Kinney, a devout Mediterraneanizer, attempted to re-create one of Italy's most illustrious cities—Venice.

Ford Racing

This was truly an epic David and Goliath style contest. Ford, the novice driver with the homemade car was up against Alexander Winton, maker of the best-selling automobile of the day and considered to be the world's best driver. Winton's car had three times the horsepower, but Henry had the edge having devised a rudimentary but reliable form of fuel injection and a crude spark plug made by a local dentist. Come race day, reliability and nerve triumphed overpower and experience.

Having already built villas and resorts, perhaps a half-sunk, European city seemed like the logical next step, though not all Angelinos agreed. The local newspapers called it "Kinney's Folly." Kinney called it Venice of America and he would spare no expense in its creation. Seven canals were built in a grid pattern stretching two miles in all, with a 70-foot-wide grand canal with a salt-water swimming lagoon.

Homes were built on the small islands joined by footbridges and surrounded by waterways. Gondolas were imported from Italy, along with their singing gondoliers, and a light-gauge railroad served the entire facility. The surrounding commercial structures were erected in the Italianate style, and a huge pier was constructed with rides, dance and concert halls, hotels, a bathhouse, and a wide variety of lowbrow, carnival attractions.

On July the 4th, 1905, 40,000 attended the opening day festivities of Venice of America, Southern California's first themed development. Kinney's goal was to create a uniquely European-styled environment dedicated to the cultural enrichment and edification of a populace he felt could really use some polish; but the classic dramas, lectures, and concerts he presented played to near-empty houses, while the roller coasters, Ferris wheels, and shooting galleries were overrun with paying customers. Instead of a temple of high culture, Venice Beach became Coney Island West.

And so it remained; and in spite of an occasional fire, and intermittent problems with water circulation, this improbable exhibition continued to thrive for twenty more years until it was swallowed up by the city of Los Angeles and most of the canals, which had become a hindrance to the free flow of automobile traffic, were filled and paved over in 1929.

As the years passed, many of his original buildings were raised or remodeled, slowly phasing out the most ambitious effort to graft European élan onto the Southern California scene, but it would certainly not be the last. 13-1 Several Southland communities, including Santa Barbara and San Clemente, would adopt a similar theme into their zoning restrictions. As for his expansive amusement facility, a half-century later and just a few miles south, it would also be emulated on a much grander scale by a berry farmer and a Hollywood cartoonist.

The Sunken Sea of Salt

Had California colony builder, George Chaffey, not just returned from Australia where he developed several viable colonies in some of the most desolate areas of the outback, he might have dismissed the principals of the California Development Company (CDC) as just another bunch of over-enervated zealots when they approached him with a scheme to irrigate 100,000 acres at the bottom of a prehistoric sink hole in the Sonora Desert. But, having worked similar wonders in the past, Chaffey was willing to listen, and as he did, he too began to see some merit in this madness.

What this small group of land speculators had discovered was that centuries of natural runoff from the Colorado River had spread a layer of very fertile silt atop an area of the Salton Sink, which lay 234 feet below sea level. All that was required to turn this miserable, desert basin into the most productive agricultural region in the state was a reliable water source.

And so, in 1900, the CDC hired Chaffey to bring water to the desert by cutting an ever so insignificant little notch into the west bank of the Colorado River and rerouting the runoff through a series of ancient riverbeds and hundreds of miles of man-made canals while the CDC subdivided the valley into hundreds of farm lots.

Twenty-five years earlier, few farmers were willing to work Southern California's "good land." Now, despite the desolate location, all 100,000 acres of scorching desert were under cultivation and five new farm towns were under construction.

The region was growing so fast the company couldn't keep up with the constant demands for more water. So, to appease the populace before they took to the streets with pitchforks, the company, acting without the benefit of Mr. Chaffey's expertise, widened that insignificant little notch in the riverbank. More water flowed, and all was well until the following spring when the annual floods jumped the bank and emptied the Colorado River into the Salton Sink transforming it into the 34-mile-long, 10-mile-wide Salton Sea.

Silent Light

Even though short, narrative films, like Edwin S. Porter's *The Great Train Robbery*, were already beginning to appear in storefront nickelodeons by 1903, the public's fascination with the sheer novelty of moving pictures would hold steady for years. Early cinematic impresarios could turn a profit by setting a camera in front of anything that moved—a trotting horse, a sputtering motorcar, a passing train—anything. The humdrum of the here and now was absolutely mesmerizing when projected against a blank wall. Nobody knew this better than Thomas Edison, the inventor of the motion picture camera and one of the world's first movie moguls. In 1906, Edison sent a camera crew to Honolulu to film trotting horses, sputtering motorcars, passing trains, and a bunch of surfers riding the swells at Waikiki. His two-minute, Hawaiian home movie played in nickelodeons from L.A. to Boston. For most mainlanders, the flickering images of dark figures gliding on silver surf provided a rare glimpse into an exotic world they would never come to know; but for Southlanders, it was a vision of things soon to come.

The entire valley was submerged, and the California Development Company, unable to respond to the catastrophe, was taken over by the Southern Pacific Railroad, which required 16 months, over three million dollars, and an earth-moving operation larger than the Panama Canal job to finally stop the flow on February 10, 1907. Gone was the farming community and in its place, was a man-made, oceanic water park in the middle of a desert, which, for the next 65 years, would remain one of Southern California's most popular tourist attractions and vacation destinations. 13-2

Neptune's Nephew

Henry E. Huntington knew he would not turn a profit with the Pacific Electric Railroad when he created the L. A. based light rail service in 1901. A consummate railroader, Henry E. (nephew to the Southern Pacific's Collis P.) expected to lose money transporting people and freight; but he expected to make a fortune selling real estate.

From his main terminal in downtown L.A., Huntington laid tracks out to the huge, barren tracts of land he had purchased in the outlying areas of San Gabriel, San Fernando, San Bernardino, and several beachfront tracts stretching from Long Beach to the Venice Beach breakwater.

Subdivided into town lots, with downtown L.A. just a 30-minute train ride away, the land was potentially worth many times its original purchase price. To sell his lots, Huntington ran special, weekend excursion trains out to his many developments. He lured prospective buyers to

---

The Wave Writer

With the royalties he collected from his enormously popular novels, author Jack London bought himself a 55-foot ketch and set out on a voyage around the world. Just days later, he was strolling along Waikiki Beach when something caught his eye:

"Suddenly... rising like a sea god from out of the churning white... appears the head of a man. Swiftly he rises... flying fast as the surge on which he stands. He is a Mercury... His heels are winged, and in them is the swiftness of the sea."

As you can surmise from this effusive excerpt from his October 1907 article in the *Woman's Home Companion,* London was astounded by the sight of a man riding high atop the rollers at Waikiki. He discovered the wave rider was not Mercury, but George Freeth, who gave London a few lessons, which was all it took, according to the author, to become an accomplished surfer:

"Inside of half an hour I was able to start myself and ride in. I did it time after time."

In his travelogue, *The Cruise of the Snark,* London would revisit this episode and offer a most eloquent description of the power and majesty of the sea, and the immense thrill one gets from riding it, which marked only the second time in 35 years that surfing was presented in popular print.

his inland subdivisions with the same old, stale refreshments, bland entertainments, and tasteless gimmicks real-estate speculators had been employing for nearly half a century. But it occurred to him that, to draw crowds out to his beachfront locations, he might do something out of the ordinary.

Huntington vacationed in Honolulu the year before and was treated to a surfing exhibition performed by Waikiki's George Freeth, who had also appeared in Edison's surf film. This, he thought, would be an ideal diversion. So, he decided to hire a surf rider to thrill the throngs milling around his beachfront sales office. But he found his publicity stunt was so original that he would have to send all the way to Hawaii to get one.

In the summer of 1907, Huntington wired an offer to Freeth to come to California to perform daily surfing exhibitions and manage the huge, saltwater plunge he was building on Redondo Beach. Having been instrumental in rekindling interest in surfing after a century of neglect imposed by various groups of repressive, western missionaries, Freeth welcomed the chance to expose the sport to a new, mainland audience.

And so, at two and four o'clock every weekend afternoon, for the rest of the summer and into the fall, a man with a megaphone would walk out on the beach and beckon the crowd to behold, "the Hawaiian Wonder, the man who could walk on water." Freeth would then charge out into the surf with his weighty redwood plank tucked under his arm. Crowds of men and women wrapped in heavy woolen garments, from their high button shoes to their stiff, starched collars, lined the beach to watch as he paddled out; they held their breath as he lined up; and they cheered as he took off, stood up, and hurtled back towards the beach, looking, for all the world, as if he truly could walk on water.

For the next few years, Freeth taught swimming and surfing, but nearly all his pupils were children. During his days on the beach, few Southlanders would accept surfing as anything more than a curious, carnival stunt.

The Count of California

Chicago filmmaker William Selig was in a bind. Winter had come early to Chi-Town in the fall of 1907, and he still had a few scenes left to shoot for his epic, twelve-minute version of *The Count of Monte Cristo*. So rather than wait out the winter, Selig sent a skeleton crew to Los Angeles to complete the last few scenes with local talent.

> ### Runaway Productions
> Edison controlled the patents on his cameras and projectors with an iron fist. Filmmakers who refused to pay his licensing fees were often visited by lawyers with lawsuits and hired thugs who busted equipment as well as heads. Southern California, with its excellent shooting conditions and its proximity to the Mexican border, should things really get sticky with the patent police, became a haven for film makers from all over the country.

The shoot went so well, and the conditions were so agreeable, that he told them to rent a barn and start shooting their next opus, *In the Sultan's Power*. But when Edison's process servers showed up at Selig's Chicago office to shut him down, he sent word to his men out west to buy the barn and keep shooting. And with that, Southern California had entered the movie business.

T Time

By the time the Ford Motor Company was incorporated, on June 16, 1903, there were literally hundreds of American automakers scattered throughout the nation, building handsome, handcrafted, and very expensive motorcars for the well to do. Ford, knowing he would never be able to make "a motor car for the great multitude" unless he could streamline this costly and time-consuming process, went searching for a solution and found it on a visit to a Chicago meat packing plant where he watched cow carcasses pass by a series of butchers on a moving "disassembly line." Ford would just run the process in reverse.

Starting with a simple, no-nonsense design using standardized, interchangeable parts, he assembled his cars in 84 steps along a moving production line manned by an army of assemblymen. This mass production process, developed and refined over a ten-year period, was first incorporated into the manufacture of the most successful and revolutionary automobile in history, the Ford Model T.

Introduced in 1908, the Model T was everything the competition was not. It had a 20-horsepower engine that could be pushed to a top speed of 45mph. With its lightweight, 1200-pound body mounted on 30-inch artillery wheels, it could nimbly navigate the worst of roads in the worst of conditions. Hardly more than a tractor with bench seats, the "T" was extremely durable, reliable, easy to operate, simple to repair, would run on practically any combustible liquid, and at $850.00, was one-third the price of the average automobile of the day. Ten thousand were sold in the first year.

Americans so eagerly embraced the Model T that it would take nearly 15 years to catch up with the demand for what would affectingly become known as "The Tin Lizzie." As Ford continued to perfect the manufacturing process, prices continued to drop to where, in 1924, a brand-new Ford Model T could be had for just $260.00, putting automobile ownership within reach of almost everyone.

> **Easy Terms**
> Alarmed by the willingness on the part of a significant percentage of the population to empty their savings and mortgage the farm in order to buy a new Ford, several banks established their first automobile financing programs in 1910.

The Model T changed the world as it was known up to that time. Prior to the advent of the T, most average Americans lived out their lives within a few miles of their birthplace. In building the "universal car," Ford freed the common man from the isolation of the big city borough and the small-town hamlet; he had literally put the world on wheels and made it possible for those with the will to wander to do so wherever the spirit, and the roads, might lead them. And for a great many, the spirit, and the roads, were leading west.

Just Add Water

Fred Eaton was a visionary; he saw it coming back in the 1880s when he was the superintendent of the privately-owned Los Angeles City Water Company—the growing disparity between the city's limited water supply, and its steadily rising population.

Los Angeles had grown to 100,000 by 1900, and just five years later, it was twice that and growing still greater by the day. For most Angelinos, the steady flow of new residents was a source of immense pride and hope for the future. But to Fred Eaton, it was a catastrophe in the making that might be the very making of the man who would prevent it.

Water-wise, L.A. was living on borrowed time. The annual rainfall was never enough to support its population. The city's water supply came from an artesian basin that had been accumulating for millennia, and nobody knew how much was left in the tank. What Eaton and his friend, William Mulholland, the superintendent of the now publicly owned Los Angeles Department of Water and Power, did know was that, in the 18 years since Eaton held that job, the aquifer had lost half its flow pressure. It was clear to both men that if the city continued its current rate of growth, it would run out of water within ten years, and this great western empire in the making would be left to crumble into dust.

But there was an out. Eaton had devised a very creative, cunning, and utterly unscrupulous plan that would not only save the city from terminal drought but make him a wealthy man in the bargain. The concept was simple: The easiest way to get more water into Los Angeles was to steal it. And Eaton had already lined up a target.

The nearest reliable source of water was 250 miles away, in the Owens Valley, an idyllic little farm/ranch community northeast of Los Angeles with a Sierra-fed river flowing into a lake 4000 feet above Los Angeles. If a canal could be made to cover the distance, gravity would propel the water all the way to L.A. Eaton would secretly buy up a controlling interest in land and water rights and then sell the Owens Valley's water to Los Angeles. All the city had to do was provide a flow pipe.

The execution of the plan would be a little more complicated. The Owens Valley, and its water, was already spoken for. The United States Bureau of Reclamation, the federal agency charged with developing the nation's water resources, had claimed the area for development. But it turned out that the bureau's own top engineer was an old employee of Eaton's who was secretly hired to conduct his ex-boss, posing as a representative of the Reclamation Service, around the valley on a land-buying spree gobbling up all the strategic land and water rights he could get his hands on.

Back in L.A., Mulholland was secretly lobbying the city's water commissioners for approval of Eaton's plan to build a 233-mile-long aqueduct from Owens Valley to L.A. The plan was approved, and the Reclamation Service agreed to relinquish their claim on the valley provided the project would be publicly owned and operated; it was agreed, and Eaton was forced to sell his Owens Valley interests to the city.

To keep all this legal, but morally questionable, chicanery a secret until the deed was done, a news blackout was arraigned with the principals of two of the three L.A. newspapers (the *Los Angeles Times* and *Los Angeles Express*). When the Reclamation Service bowed out, and a grant of right-of-way over federal lands was secured, the secrecy ban was lifted and the headline of the July 29, 1905, edition of the *L.A. Times* heralded the heist with great jubilation:

"TITANIC PROJECT TO GIVE THE CITY A RIVER"

The howls of protest coming from the Owens Valley could be heard all the way to L.A. city hall, and an even bigger scandal blew up when that other paper, the *Los Angeles Examiner*, accused a syndicate of very well-connected business leaders, including the editors of the *Times* and *Express*, of acting on insider information, leaked from the water department, to buy up 16,000 acres of near-worthless land in the San Fernando Valley north of L.A., where the aqueduct was to feed into the L.A. aquifer, making the parched valley a potential Garden of Eden.

The paper also accused Mulholland of trying to sway voters by orchestrating late-night dumpings of L.A. water into the ocean to create a drought scare. Both accusations turned out to be false. The land syndicate had indeed acted on insider information but from an earlier, aborted land scheme. As for the drought scare, L.A. was already

> **It's Chinatown**
> If all this is beginning to sound vaguely familiar to you, it might be because the incident was used as the source material for the classic, 1974 film, *Chinatown*.

in a three-year drought and reservoir levels were dropping of their own accord.

Though most Angelinos truly sympathized with the plight of the Owens Valley folk, they overwhelmingly approved the Owens Valley bond issue on September 7, 1905. Work began in 1907, and was completed six years later, on November 5th, 1913. But the fix was only temporary.

Twenty years later, consistent population growth would require another infusion of water siphoned off the Colorado River through an even more elaborate system of dams and canals, and twenty years after that, still more water would flow through canals that stretched all the way to the Southland's last accessible water source in the heart of northern California. 13-3

Californulatin'

In spite of the strain on the resources, within the first decade of the 20th century, the seeds of Eden were taking root. Though still way outside the norm, the paint had dried on the first few examples of the modernist, structural style that would come to define the Southland as indelibly as the marble and limestone edifices that characterized the great civilizations of antiquity.

Making much less of an initial impact was the sport of surfing, which, with only one practitioner, got off to a very slow start. But California waves had been publicly "board ridden," and the example was set that others would eventually follow.

Further inland, pioneer filmmakers, in their efforts to dodge patent enforcers, had founded the first production outposts on the west coast. There, they would grow and prosper, exporting myth, fantasy, and dreams throughout the world.

But of all these, now familiar, "Califormulants," it was the automobile that was the first to gain immediate and unmitigated acceptance. Just two years after the introduction of the Model T, there were more cars registered in L.A. County than in most European countries.

A subject of reverence and adoration in Southern California, the automobile not only represented personal freedom and independence, it was also prized as a platform for technological experimentation and artistic expression—the early cultural trappings of a newly emerging coastal civilization. The frontier was indeed fading out of existence, and ever so slowly, rising up in its place, was Xanadu on the Pacific.

Chapter 14
Tales of Two Cities

Smokestacks vs. Geraniums

After decades of unsuccessfully battling Los Angeles over commercial domination of the Southland, San Diegans began battling with themselves. Having lost the bid to become the southern terminus of the second transcontinental railroad to L.A. in the 1880s, San Diego languished as a branch line town, and for some residents, that was just dandy.

Los Angeles had embraced industrialization and some areas were already experiencing the sort of commercial blight typical of big eastern cities, and there was fear bucolic San Diego could suffer a similar fate. Yet, another, equally determined, contingent wanted better-paying factory jobs and were willing to sacrifice aesthetics to get them. In the newspapers, the controversy would be referred to as the "smokestacks vs. geraniums" debate.

As the smallest and most isolated big city in an isolated region, circumstances in San Diego naturally favored the geranium party. Unable to attract heavy industry, the town developed as a retirement community and tourist destination, and in 1908, prominent, geranium-minded San Diegans hired a city planner to reinforce that pastoral inclination by re-designing the city in the image of the great Mediterranean port towns of Naples and Seville.

In response, the smokestackers doggedly developed a tobacco plant, a broom factory, a salt works, and a small fishing and canning industry; but neither faction would ever be able to declare victory. For those favoring geraniums, the re-design was way too ambitious and costly to win taxpayer support. But the geraniumizing impulse would persist through thousands of other public and private initiatives.

For the smokestack crowd, it would be many years before they would be able to secure the railway connections necessary to attract bigger business. San Diego would eventually become a significant player on the Pacific Rim, but it would take the full force of both the United States Navy and Marines to do it.

Fair Weather Flyers

In their quest to industrialize, San Diegans got some unexpected help from their Angelino cousins in 1910, when the Merchants and Manufacturers Association of Los Angeles sponsored the first-ever International Air Meet in January of 1910.

Just six years after the Wright Brothers proved flight was possible, daredevil pilots in their rickety "flying machines" were proving it was not only possible, but probable that aero business would one day become an enterprise of unimaginable proportions, and L.A. planned to get in on the ground floor by, once again, drawing attention to the region's exemplary climate. Invitations were sent to aviators worldwide to come to Southern California, in the dead of winter, and experience the sunny blue skies and gentle wind currents of the most idyllic flying environment on the planet.

Fifty aviators and nearly 200,000 spectators attended the event where new records were set for speed, distance, and altitude. And first among the winners, was the Southland itself. The meet was a great success, and as a result, within 15 years, most of the biggest names in aircraft manufacture would be located in Southern California, adding one more developing industry to a region desperate to build a solid and well-diversified economic foundation.

Location Nation

While planes were circling just a few miles away, ex-writer, ex-actor, and now film director D.W. Griffith was out at Mission San Gabriel shooting a couple of quickie shorts, *In Old California,* and *Ramona*. Griffith, who worked for the Biograph Company of New York, had set up winter working quarters in Hollywood, and he wasn't alone.

Mack Sennett, another Biograph director, had a studio turning out a steady stream of slapstick comedies, and producer Jesse Lasky, along with director Cecil B. DeMille, had taken refuge from Edison's patent agents in a Hollywood barn where they began shooting the first feature-length (74 minutes) movie, *The Squaw Man*.

With no real film stages yet in operation, these early filmmakers did much of their shooting out on the streets of L.A., and through their films, they revealed to moviegoers around the country, a land of perpetual sunshine, warm breezes, and swaying palms. Before the advent of "the flickers," the Southland's 40 years of promo campaigns to attract new tourists and residents were primarily reaching only those in the middle class and up—the most settled segments of society.

But the movies were reaching everybody, and in the nation's nickelodeons, California was being discovered all over again. Though they were not yet the most revered members of Southland society, it was the movie makers (along with the development of the affordable

Ford) and not the railroads, or the hotels, or the Chambers of Commerce that would play the most significant role in the launch of the third of California's four population booms—the great auto-migration of the 1920s.

Pioneering Politics

Since its inception, regardless of what party was in power, the Southern Pacific Railroad governed the state of California. Nearly all public servants served at the pleasure of the railroad, which paid for the pleasure of dictating state policy favorable to its own interests. With a disinterested and distracted pioneer population struggling to tame a willful frontier, governmental corruption spread freely.

But by the turn of the 20th century, the complexion of the Southern California populace was expanding beyond the usually detached vacationers, speculators, cultivators, and pensioners. A civic-oriented, professional class was emerging in Los Angeles, and they were declaring war on the Southern Pacific and all the other "boodlers" operating within the halls of state government.

In May of 1907, a handful of progressive reformers got together in an L.A. café and founded the Lincoln-Roosevelt League to push back against the state's corrupt government, corporations, and labor unions. Though small in number, they had one thing going for them—the fiercely independent, free-wheeling, and capricious character of average Californians, who were transitory in nature, preoccupied with their own business, and as such, not terribly interested in local affairs.

In such a mercurial society, it was impossible for the railroad to run a political machine and organize voting blocs like those found in the older, more established communities of the east. This made it possible, in 1911, for league members to get elected to office and then completely re-structure the political process by giving to the people the three keys to the kingdom—the initiative, the referendum, and the recall. With the petition process, the initiative, referendum, and recall, voters could directly make or revoke laws, express opinions on bills up for consideration, and remove officials from office.

Through these three measures, the Southern Pacific's stranglehold on California politics was broken and fair regulations were put in place. The old patronage policy of civil service was replaced with a merit-based system and numerous laws were passed for the protection of children, women, and workers. With this system of direct democracy in the hands of such an autonomous society, California would remain, until recent years, one of the most wildly unpredictable political environments in the nation.

The Loos Cannon

In 1893, Austrian architect Adolf Loos toured the United States to make a study of its architecture. He visited soaring skyscrapers, sprawling estates, and grand government edifices, but what really blew him away were the factories and grain silos of the mid-west—yes, grain silos!

What Loos saw in these bare-bones, utilitarian structures was an industrial model that could serve not only as cheap, livable shelter for the masses being squeezed into the decaying slums of Europe's industrialized cities, but a modern symbol of a new socialist order of workers and their struggle for recognition against a European aristocracy still clinging to the old-world traditions of inherited privilege.

Back in Vienna, he wrote scathing pieces for architectural journals in which he denounced Victorian extravagance and praised the "untattooed" simplicity of the new industrial form. But as his own work began to resemble that industrial form, angry mobs demanded his building permits be revoked until he properly embellished his unadorned facades.

Exasperated over the shortsightedness of what he called "ornamentalists," Loos wrote another of his contemptuous essays crying out that, "Ornament is a crime!" The audacious pronouncement would never be written into law, but it would become the second great tenant of modern architecture after Sullivan's "form follows function." Guided by these two assertions, 20th-century, modern architecture would be thrust upon the world—like it or not.

No Mo Mod!

With his lively blending of old and new styles with organic shapes and materials, Irving Gill had created what would become fundamental components in the architectural "Califormula" of the Southland. But then, quite possibly influenced by the writings of Adolph Loos, he abruptly began to push off into uncharted territory.

Straying from his well-received formula, he began designing projects in the very severe European style, and by doing so, he inadvertently upended several emerging myths concerning Southern Californians and their legendary tolerance for all things new and novel.

In 1910, Gill was hired to do a low-rent, courtyard apartment in Sierra Madre. The complex consisted of twelve freestanding concrete cubes with flat, eaveless roofs, white walls, and concrete floors. But the target demographic, blue-collar renters, shied away en masse, and a more affluent group of tenants moved in. The rents were raised, which pleased the client, and therefore, the project was considered a success. He had another go at hard modern in 1912, when he was hired to design worker housing for a Tustin factory town. This time, his stark, angular designs so offended the aesthetic sensibilities of working-class homebuyers the project was shut down before it could be completed. Then, in 1914, he went upmarket and created a spacious house composed of simple, concrete squares and rectangles. The client, a Mr. Dodge, was quite pleased with the results—San Diego's city fathers were not.

Hoping against hope that San Diego could win the lion's share of business coming through the Panama Canal when it was to be completed in 1914, the city planned to throw a big party in Balboa Park requiring the design and construction of a city within the city to announce to the world that San Diego was ready to be the nation's port-o-call on the west coast.

Irving Gill was the clear frontrunner on a short list of architects under consideration to oversee the project; but when news of his L.A. experiments in modernism reached the architecture committee, he was passed over in favor of a neo-gothic revivalist from Boston, who dressed his buildings in a highly ornamental, Spanish Colonial motif.

Unfortunately, Mr. Gill had gotten out ahead of the moment. The Dodge house marked the end of his ascendancy as one of the Southland's premier architects. Through his pioneering projects in modernism, Gill had exposed an unassailable truism regarding modern architectural style, which is that it never really appealed to the average Joes and Josephines it was designed for. Modern architecture found favor among better-educated élites and liberal-thinking intellectuals.

> **Port of Last Call**
>
> Once again, San Diego's hopes would be dashed when Los Angeles annexed the coastal communities of San Pedro and Wilmington and built their own deep-water harbor. When the Panama Canal opened, the traffic sailed right on by San Diego to L.A. and San Francisco.

From the 1920s on, modern architects would continue migrating to Southern California, and none of them would go hungry, but they catered to a high-end, niche market. The popular 1950s myth that we all lived in Jetsonian earth modules was a creation of the media. Only after decades of tweaking to achieve a perfect blend of resort-style comfortability and theme park whimsicality would average, middle-class Southlanders warm up to the modernist mode.

Hapa Haole Oe

Hawaiian merchant seamen had been "putting in" at west coast ports since the early days of the great ranchos; and in the grog shops along the wharves, they often entertained themselves, and other patrons, with their unique brand of folk music, which remained an obscure curiosity until 1915, when several Hawaiian folk groups were invited to perform at the two Panama-Pacific expositions in San Francisco and San Diego.

The dual engagements ignited what was probably the first inexplicable, populist fad of the modern age. Suddenly, Hawaiian music, or what was thought to be Hawaiian music, was all the rage, especially along the California coast.

Actually, by the time the exposition closed, Hawaiian music had already undergone a transition incorporating elements of jazz, ragtime, and popular styles sung in English; it was what the native boys called Hapa Haole or "half-white," meaning mixed style. But for nearly 10 years, it was this hybrid style of "Anglicized" Hawaiian folk music that remained one of the most popular entertainment genres on the mainland.

Island tunes, mostly written by Manhattan islanders, sold more sheet music and records than any other style. Hawaiian dance bands toured incessantly spreading their escapist magic to millions. Thousands bought guitars and ukuleles from department store catalogs and subjected themselves to a series of mail-order music lessons in hopes they could learn to strum and warble just like the guys on the Victrola discs.

It seems that no sooner had a sizable contingent of pilgrims amassed on the west coast, the promised land of the Americas, then they began to fantasize of a new earthly paradise floating somewhere out there in the deep blue Pacific.

And so, for years, in ballrooms and in parlors all over the Southland, Hawaiian-styled music brought a sense of the exotic romance of the South Seas to those who would never experience it for themselves. It was one of the first layers in the application of a Polynesian patina that would eventually spread over all of Southern California.

Polynesianism

Of all the imaginative escape fantasies that found form in Southern California, this Polynesian spree, of which the Hawaiian music fad was a part, was the most picaresque, prolonged, and pervasive. The fascination started in the 18th century with the widespread publication of the ship's logs and officer's journals of a thousand voyages of discovery, which described in lurid detail the primitive, pagan tribes strewn among hundreds of pacific islands.

Based on these reports, and in many instances, their own colonial experiences, 19th-century authors like Herman Melville and Robert Louis Stevenson created an entirely new literary classification of romanticized South Seas travel and adventure novels. Originally intended as a source of edification and entertainment, these exotic tales were received as a welcome means of escape, both literally and figuratively, for millions of city dwellers trapped within the workings of the modern, industrialized world.

Through their quixotic narratives, they beckoned modern man to leave the stress and strain of civilization behind and join the primitives in paradise where the skies are always blue, the seas green, the living leisurely, and the native women beautiful and indiscriminately affectionate.

Yeah, it was mostly a guy thing; a universally venerated dropout scenario, which omitted awkward details like the numerous diseases, the monsoons, the bugs, the barbarism, and the fact that not all islanders lived up to their idealized image.

But none of that would matter on the mainland, where this most favored fantasy would be re-created, minus the imperfections, as an exotic backdrop for Southern California's tourist and leisure industry, and even find widespread acceptance within the suburban wards of the 20th century.

Wheels 'R' Us!

It's not possible to over-emphasize the dramatic effect the automobile had on Americans in every part of the country. Ford's introduction of the Model T was truly one of those rare, "earth-moving events."

> *"The automobile changed our dress, manners, social customs, vacation habits, the shape of our cities, consumer purchasing patterns, common taste, and positions in intercourse."* John Keats

But nowhere else on this fair earth was the automobile more rapidly and fervently absorbed into the very core of the culture than in Southern California. The reasons the Southland became the Mecca for motorists, begin, as always, with the climate.

Within this placid environment, motoring was never out of season: cars started as easily and ran as smoothly in January as they did in July. The predominantly horizontal layout of the landscape made for easy passage, and the roads (most of which were still dirt) once built, pretty much stayed built, and passable, and tended to propagate rapidly due to an exponentially growing public demand for more of them.

Originally conceived, not as a utilitarian necessity, but as an amusing toy for the rich, the early automobile was used almost exclusively for pleasure outings. And as automobile ownership became more and more common among the less well-situated strata of society, that original perception did not diminish. With the beautiful beaches, mountains, and deserts all within reach of any reasonably determined motorist, pleasure touring became a favorite means of entertainment for commoners as well.

But automobility wasn't just about amusement; come Monday morning, most people did have to get to work, and one of the most compelling reasons why the automobile was so readily accepted by Southlanders as such an indispensable necessity was the elongated layout of the suburban landscape they had to negotiate to do so.

Guided by the west's wide-open spaces, the expansive real estate schemes of the railway companies, and a general desire on the part of the populace to live in a countrified, single-family home far from the city center, Southern Californians built out, not up, and often lived several miles, not blocks, from their place of employment. Mortgage aside, the price one had to pay to live in these far-flung suburbs was complete dependence, for all transportation needs, upon one of two light rail companies.

The Los Angeles Railway, with their Yellow Cars, and the Pacific Electric, with their Big Red Cars, laid tracks in all directions running from downtown L.A. to the outlying suburbs. It was these "traction companies" that made the Southern California suburbs possible, but not necessarily practical.

Nobody liked the traction companies. Their cars were grossly overcrowded during peak hours, slow, unsafe, prone to breakdowns, and unable to maintain schedules. When the automobile became a viable option, Southern Californians abandoned the rail lines en masse for the freedom and independence of their very own motorcar. Within just six years of the introduction of the Model T, most Southlanders had made the transition from transit slog to T jockey. 14-1

> **End of the Line**
> An ancient, yet enduring, urban legend suggests that several large auto, tire, and oil companies banded together in a conspiracy to buy these rail companies and destroy them in order to eliminate the competition. The fact was that these rail lines were never profitable; they were a means with which to sell real estate. By the mid-thirties, with most of the viable real estate sold and developed, the rail lines had become an even greater liability. After the war, a conglomerate of transportation related companies did begin to buy up these failed traction companies in order to replace them with more modern, flexible, economical, and most of all, profitable, bus lines.

> *"The day is here when the smallest tradesmen, builder, or skilled mechanic can own an automobile economically."*
> *The Los Angeles Examiner, 1914*

The Bronze Duke

On his way to the 1912 summer Olympics at Stockholm, Sweden, Hawaiian swimmer, Duke Kahanamoku, stopped off in Southern California to confirm reports he had heard of some very respectable surf spots along the California coast. It was he, along with George Freeth, who brought the long-lost art of stand-up surfing back into style.

Tall, handsome, and gregarious, Southlanders couldn't get enough of "the Bronze Duke." The surfing exhibitions he gave at Santa Monica, Redondo, Huntington, Corona Del-Mar, and Laguna Beach were well-attended events that brought the sport to the attention of more and more mainlanders but did little to coax them out into the water, partly because most couldn't swim.

Swimming was not the popular leisure activity it would later become, and instruction was generally limited to those wealthy enough, and interested enough to afford private lessons or those that might have picked it up in a physical enrichment class in college. The YMCA had only begun to offer swimming instruction to the general public in 1909. In fact, up to that time, most professional sailors, both military and merchant, never bothered to develop the skill.

The second obstacle in attracting devotees to the sport was the unwieldy surfboards of the era. Made of heavy hardwoods, the first surfboards ranged in size from 16 to 24 feet long, weighed as much as 200 pounds, and were about as buoyant and maneuverable as a church door. They were flat on top and bottom, squared along the edges, with a rounded nose and a square tail. These were the type of surfboards Kahanamoku and Freeth brought to California.

And although the two masters could make the surfing experience appear effortless, the public was not fooled. It was obvious surfing required much more physical strength and sea skill than most mainlanders could muster. Freeth even cut his giant board in half to make it seem less intimidating to the novice, but even that effort proved unconvincing. It did, however, mark the very first step in a fifty-year-long trial & error process that would eventually see the heavy, cumbersome, plank board evolve into a stick so light and nimble, that even a teenage girl could manage it quite nicely in the hard, fast waves at Malibu.

Ford Performance

With the proliferation of the Model T, most backyard tinkers abandoned their dream of building their own automobile and began to focus their energies on how they might make Ford's better, which usually meant faster. Built economically and designed with an emphasis on durability and reliability rather than maximum performance, the Model T left a lot of room for improvement, and by 1910, a small cottage industry emerged to produce performance parts for the T.

As horse tracks around the country began hosting the much more exotic, exciting, and dangerous, auto racing events, the Model T became a very popular racing platform due to its low price and the interchangeability of its parts. Of course, neither attribute was going to win any races and so several of the most talented auto tinks throughout the Midwest began turning out an astounding array of high-performance components for the Model T. And it soon became apparent that most of their mail orders were coming from regular street drivers, and great many of those regular street drivers were located in Southern California where the auto-virus had reached epidemic proportions.

> *"So prevalent is the use of the motor vehicle that it might be said that Southern Californians have added wheels to their anatomy."*
> Gordon Whitnall

Even before America's involvement in World War I, hopping up, or hot rodding the Model T had become such a popular hobby among Southern Californians that many of the performance parts manufacturers kept sales reps in Los Angeles.

For those who wanted to improve the performance of their automobiles, there were two routes they could pursue—reduce weight, and/or increase horsepower; and since weight reduction was the cheaper of the two options, it was usually the first taken in the creation of a hot rod. All non-essential parts—fenders, hoods, running boards, bumpers, windshields, seats, headlights, ornaments, and sometimes even the front brakes, if it had any, were removed.

> For clarity, we'll use the term, "hot rod," to describe a home-built performance car even though its usage didn't become commonplace until the mid-1940s.

> *"Many a Ford owner had stripped the fenders and body from his car, strapped a pillow onto the gasoline tank, and entered the races at the Hometown fair..."* Ford Owner Magazine, September 1914

To boost horsepower, you could replace stock parts with the new high-performance varieties. In this way, a determined tink could raise the T's horsepower by 50% and increase its top speed to around 80mph. However, these performance enhancements could rarely be fully appreciated for there were so few places where such power could be let loose. Most dirt roads were hardly more than single-lane wagon trails, and the few paved roads in existence were in crowded urban areas. Even the oval track races were more a test of driver skill and machine endurance than flat out, all she's got, top speed, which was what most of these backyard builders were really interested in; but that would have to wait until after the war.

Over Here

Very few Californians would have been able to find Sarajevo on a map prior to June 28, 1914, when a Serbian radical shot an Austria archduke and touched off World War I. Even then, there wasn't a great deal of interest. Most thought a war 5000 miles away would have no effect on Southern California, but it immediately became apparent that they were wrong; the war's effect would be immense.

The first shockwaves were felt in the agricultural communities. Orders for beef, vegetables, and citrus almost overwhelmed the state's production capacity. With Europe's film industry gone dark, Hollywood's fledgling little movie colony had suddenly become, and would remain, the entertainment capital of the world.

Wealthy eastern tourists, cut off from their usual European haunts, turned up in Southern California in such huge numbers that most of the Southland's sanitariums permanently transitioned into tourist hotels. And in San Diego, the Navy and Marines moved in for good. Over 150,000 Californians marched off to war in 1918, and not all returned, but those that did would find a once rusticated Southern California fully engaged in the 20th century.

Chapter 15
Reveling Our Way to Ruin

Throughout the decade of the 20s, America continually transitioned away from a rural agrarian to an urban industrial society. Even in far-off California, the frontier was succumbing to the onslaught of the 20th century. Postwar prosperity and technological progress fueled a social and cultural transformation that swept the nation.

By 1920, the automobile had gone from a regional to a nationwide obsession that spun off scores of subsidiary industries. And as more and more cities and towns hooked up to the national power grid, a whole galaxy of new electric appliances began to enter the marketplace. Five years earlier, few had heard of a refrigerator or a washing machine; now everybody had to have one. The radio, the most popular of all the new household gadgets, brought a new mode of entertainment directly into the home as well as a new mode of mass marketing, which sparked a nationwide surge of job-producing, wage raising, consumerism.

With the certainty that they had just fought, and won, the war to end all wars, public optimism ran exceptionally high. The economy was flush with cash and banks, unencumbered by federal regulations, were eager to lend it out for the purchase of houses, cars, appliances, and a brand-new consumer product—common stock.

First introduced to the concept of capital investment through the Liberty Bond program during World War I, Americans dove into the stock market with total abandon, and why not; stock values had been steadily rising since the war's end, everybody seemed to be getting rich, and the banks would loan out 90% of the purchase price and accept the stocks bought on margin as collateral on the loan! Though President Hoover publicly worried that this "orgy of mad speculation" could lead to problems down the road, few Americans were willing to listen; after all, stock speculatin' was just a way of investing in the future of a nation on the rise; it was an act of patriotism—where's the harm in that?

California Here We Come—Again!
By 1920, there were twelve million automobiles on American roadways and Detroit was producing over two million more every year.

As the coming of the railroads had done forty years earlier, the automobilization of the nation provided the means for another mass resettlement to the west.

"The age of the automobile was the age in which the average American vacationer first found the west within his reach."
Earl Pomeroy

Roads now stretched from coast to coast and, as traffic began to build along the roadways, businesses sprouted up like weeds to provide goods and services to travelers on their way out west. So keen was the competition for the tourist dollar that roadside establishments began to rely on outlandish architectural features and ornamentation to attract customers.

Diners were erected in the shape of huge ducks, teapots, dogs, milk bottles, and even elephants. Motor lodges were done up like Indian villages, frontier outposts, and fairytale kingdoms. There were snake charmers, dancing bears, acrobats, and reptile farms—anything that might draw a crowd in off the road.

During the decade of the 20s, about one and a half million new California residents arrived by car making the great auto-migration the largest in the state's history thus far. Those coming from the northeastern regions took the Lincoln Highway, the nation's first transcontinental thoroughfare, which stretched from New York to San Francisco.

Farmyard Fantasy

Hoping to make a little something extra off his berry farm, Walter Knott set up a little fruit stand on highway 39 in the rural community of Buena Park. The stand did well and a small diner was added. But it wasn't until 1940, when Knott finally gave in to the popular, sideshow impulse and amassed a collection of old frontier buildings around his stand, that Knott's Berry Farm would begin to transition from just another roadside curiosity into the state's first world renown theme park.

As was the case with the great railway migration of the 1880s, most of Southern California's new "auto-emerges" came from the south and mid-west. 15-1 The roads of the southwest, like the Old Spanish Trail, weren't quite as well finished as those further north, but the Model T performed well in the rough, was cheaper than taking the train, and for many, that one trip out west would be the greatest adventure of their lives.

What they found when they arrived in L.A. was a city in the process of restructuring itself to accommodate the automobile, and a populace so devoted to its exploitation that the right to own and drive one was practically thought to be guaranteed by the United States Constitution.

"Our forefathers in their immortal independent creed set forth the pursuit of happiness as an 'inalienable right' of mankind. And how can one pursue happiness by any swifter of surer means then by the use of the automobile." Los Angeles Times, 1926

In Fields of Black Gooey Gold

With the meteoric rise of the automobile, gasoline, the once worthless byproduct of the oil refining process, had become the industry's primary yield along with asphalt, another petroleum waste product useful in the making of roads.

The market for gasoline was metastasizing daily, but Southern California's reserves, worked by a hodgepodge of wildcat operators, were only good for a modest million barrels a year. It wasn't until some big outfits with geological know-how started poking around the hills that the Southland's full potential was realized.

Standard Oil Company scored first when they drilled into a major gusher at Long Beach in 1920, followed by Union Oil's strike at Santa Fe Springs in 1921, and Shell Oil's hallelujah moment at Signal Hill. The combined output of just these three fields was over 400,000 barrels a day and suddenly, a third-tier industry had become a leader. For the next 30 years, Los Angeles County would be blanketed with fields of oil derricks in the west coast's second great oil boom.

The Empire of Entertainment

By the early 20s, Hollywood movies had gone from bizarre curiosities shown in vaudeville houses and amusement arcades to the number one entertainment medium of the masses, shown in movie palaces all around the world.

One reelers grew to be two, three, four, and full-length five-reel epics shot on location, not only on the city streets, but in the mountains, deserts, prairies, oceans, and skies surrounding L.A. and vicinity. Most city dwellers went to the movies at least once or twice a week, and through that regular exposure, Hollywood emerged in the 1920s, as the nation's trendsetter in fashion, style, manner, and thought.

Through thousands of films turned out by hundreds of newly relocated film companies, Hollywood itself became a leading L.A. tourist attraction drawing thousands of vacationers every year to the place where American's dreams were made.

Land of Shiners

For nearly 100 years, various ladies' organizations, church groups, and a dedicated Anti-Saloon League had been pressuring the government to ban the manufacture and sale of alcoholic beverages. Many Americans considered alcoholism to be a scourge upon the welfare of the entire nation, but because the alcohol tax funded the U.S. government, the movement stalled. It wasn't until the passage of the 16th amendment, in 1913, establishing a federal income tax, that these "dry" forces saw an opening and were able to coerce Congress into passing the 18th amendment to the constitution, which made it a crime to manufacture or sell alcoholic beverages.

The prohibition amendment went into effect in January of 1920 and kicked off a thirteen-year-long national bacchanal of epic proportions. With the stroke of a pen, prohibition made criminals of a good two-thirds of the U.S. population.

Those willfully flouting the new law included presidents, politicians, judges, policemen, and millions of American citizens from every social stratum. Nightclubs went underground as exclusive speakeasies and flourished as never before; many brazenly featured five-star dining, big bands, and floor shows.

The illegality attached to the use of so common and deep-rooted a commodity gave it an extra special allure unknown prior to the ban. The illegal manufacture and distribution of alcohol made legions of millionaires and helped turn various fraternities of big city, street thugs into highly efficient, well-financed, and utterly ruthless organized crime syndicates.

Among independently-minded Southern Californians, rum-running became a major industry—mercifully without the violence and bloodshed associated with those working in the big eastern cities.

The state government left enforcement up to the feds, who were spread way too thin to cover the 300 miles of Southern California coastline where, under the cover of the night, Canadian and Mexican merchantmen landed their illicit cargos in secluded coves from San Luis Obispo to San Diego.

Further inland, there lived so many ex-southerners that the region could boast nearly as many stills per square mile as eastern Kentucky. Every day, in broad daylight, bootleggers made regular deliveries to hotels, tourist establishments, city halls, courthouses, speakeasies, gentlemen's clubs, businesses, and private homes. Perhaps no other edict in US history failed so spectacularly.

The Bauhausers

Answering to an advertisement in a local Viennese architectural journal, Austrian Rudolph Schindler, a protégé of Adolph Loos, was hired as a draftsman in the Chicago office of Ottenheimer, Stern, and Reichert. He reported for work in the spring of 1914 and immediately began pestering Frank Lloyd Wright for a job, which had been his objective all along.

But it wasn't until 1920, when the free-spending and perpetually cash-strapped Wright was hired to design a hotel in Tokyo, that he would hire Schindler, and then only to supervise the completion of one of his unfinished projects in Los Angeles. Getting dumped in what was then considered to be architectural Siberia was not what he had in mind when he signed on with Wright, but at least he was finally working with the great master, if only indirectly. Besides, he had become disillusioned with Chicago's commitment to modernism, which he interpreted to be no more than economic.

But Schindler's completion of Wright's work led to disagreements over authorship, which resulted in a dismissal and a falling out between the two that lasted thirty years. So, with no job to return to in Chicago, Schindler decided to strike out on his own. And with the arrival of Rudolph Schindler in L.A, European modernism had spread from Austria to Southern California.

Schindler, like so many of his peers back home, was a disciple of the Bauhaus, a German art school dedicated to the creation of art and architecture shaped by the aesthetics of the industrial age. To the Bauhaus, machine-style was the new fashion statement of the working class, and as such, a deliberate affront to those believed to be their ancient nemesis—the bourgeoisie!

Machine-made was Bauhaus; handmade was bourgeois. Industrial was Bauhaus; Victorian was bourgeois. The militant Bauhausers, who operated under a strict policy of "pay up and shut up," tolerated no input from their soulless, ignorant, and more than likely, bourgeois patrons; therefore, they were forced to rely on their leftist governments for the majority of their commissions.

With no job, no prospects, limited funds, and in need of both living and working space, Shindler and a contractor friend pooled their talents and resources to build a communal dwelling to serve as both living quarters and design studio.

Even as early as 1922, the sprawling, flat-roofed, single-story Schindler House exhibited many of the design elements that would grace both the tract homes and the high-end custom designs of the 1950s and 60s. Just as Gill adapted Wright's prairie style to the culture and climate of the Southland, Schindler compromised the un-compromisable European style with California rancho and beach house bungalow.

His lightly constructed, wood-framed house had thin concrete wall sections and large, wood-framed, sliding glass panels, which opened to the gardens. On warm, summer nights, occupants could take their repose on the roof in "sleeping baskets" suspended from a grouping of decorative, spider leg supports. Yet, despite all the west-coast concessions he incorporated into his design, it was still so far ahead of its time he could only get a revocable, temporary permit to begin construction.

When his contractor friend moved out, Schindler convinced an old college acquaintance to move in. Fellow Austrian, and hard-line European modernist, Richard Neutra, came to Chicago to work with Frank Lloyd Wright in 1923, but before the year had passed, Neutra, who also took exception to Wright's organic, prairie style, had moved in with Schindler.

> **Euro-Cal**
> What distinguished this hardline, European style of modern architecture from the more malleable and whimsical strain developing in Southern California was the "shove it down their throats" overemphasis on its industrial lineage. Yet, in spite of the variance in their guiding principles, these two divergent styles would come to form the ying and yang of mid-century modern architecture in Southern California.

Neutra's first two L.A. commissions were right out of the Bauhaus playbook, but by the time these two projects were completed, the influence of the Southland's climate, culture, and clients compelled him, like his friend Schindler, to deviate from the rigid, Bauhaus formula. For even in the flush times of the roaring twenties, in the nearly anything-goes atmosphere of Southern California, modern architecture's appeal was so limited that commercial banks and home loan agencies generally refused to carry mortgages on modern-styled homes.

Star Cars

As the 1920s progressed, European aristocrats were being supplanted, in the minds of most Americans, as the arbiters of all things fashionable; the yanks now had their own royal court living in the fairy-tale kingdom of Hollywood, California.

The glamorous stars of the silent screen packed movie houses and sold a vast array of commercial products, while tales of their after-hours exploits bolstered the circulation of newspapers and magazines throughout the country. They were the nation's trendsetters and some of the highest-paid individuals on earth; and if their extravagant lifestyles were any indication, few planned to die rich.

As a symbol of their exalted social stature, they built huge estates in the hills surrounding Hollywood and toured about town in magnificently appointed, custom-built, motor coaches. These stunning vehicles were meant to be admired; they were never meant to encourage imitation, and certainly not among the hoi polloi.

But mechanically inclined commoners, dissatisfied with the appearance of their own heaps, began trying to alter them to emulate the movie star dream machines they were seeing on the streets of L.A.

Infinite varieties of hybrid vehicles were created from whatever interesting pieces turned up in the local salvage yards or were available from other second-hand outlets. One might encounter a Chevrolet with Cadillac wheels, or find the stately radiator of a Packard grafted onto the humble snout of a Dodge, or a see Studebaker coupe flaunting the elegant trimmings of a Hispano-Suiza.

And so began the early, developmental stages of a California custom car culture that would emerge full-blown on the other side of an impending depression and another world war.

Dressed to Chill
Since the coming of the conquistadors, the Southland's unique environment forced new residents to adapt nearly all their traditional modes and practices to the demands of this rarefied setting. But one of the very last customs to begin the climatization transformation was the dress code.

Buttoned up one way and down the other, Southern Californians, in open defiance of the prevailing conditions, stubbornly sported the very same heavy, woolen outer, and over-starched inner garments worn in New York, Boston, and even London. It wasn't until the 20s that the mores regarding appropriate apparel began to soften under the warm, California sun.

In America, as in Europe, upper and middle-class tradition demanded one dress up and not down. Even during the leisure hours, formal appearances were steadfastly maintained. But tradition was getting tested as sporting facilities, like golf and tennis, were becoming more common features at resorts, hotels, and spas.

While participating in these activities, men, and sometimes even women, often felt compelled to risk censure and strip down to their shirtsleeves to better facilitate the backswing. It was an act of impropriety that could likely get you written off the social registry back home. Even more shocking were the daring women swimmers who openly rejected the traditional, full-cut bathing gowns in favor of the same abbreviated, woolen "tank suits" the men were wearing.

As all this impropriety was transpiring, a handful of local milliners picked up on the spontaneous trend toward the informal and began producing lighter-weight, loose-fitting, cotton and linen shirts and trousers designed to allow for greater comfort and freedom of movement. These new, casually styled "sports togs" were intended only to be worn within the confines of the tourist enclaves, but they were so better suited to the warm, balmy, California climate that tourists, as well as locals, began wearing them as everyday street clothes.

One of the first to recognize the commercial potential of this little neighborhood, niche industry was Fred Cole, of Manchester Knitting Mills, a maker of men's knit underwear. In 1923, he changed the name of the company to Cole of California and hired Hollywood costumers to design a line of swimsuits made from a new, form-fitting, elastic material cut in the, now traditional, one-piece suit for women, and men's brief-style, bathing trunks.

Pacific Knitting Mills, another manufacturer of sweaters and knit undergarments changed its name to Catalina and began producing a line of casual sportswear featuring bright colors and bold prints that, along with Cole's swimsuits, were instantly woven into the cultural fabric of the Southern California scene.

What Catalina, Cole, and a host of other west coast outfitters did was create, not just a new brand, but an entirely new category of men's and women's apparel so unique to, and closely identified with, the Southland that the words "sportswear" and "California," would be forever entwined. In the years to follow, it would be these local labels that would completely re-dress the entire west coast, add one more crucial ingredient to the Southern Califormula, and set fashion trends worldwide.

What'll She Do?

Not only did tinsel town's trendsetters set the spark on the custom car craze, but they were also some of the first to take part in a very unique style of motorsport.

Just north of Los Angeles is the San Gabriel Mountain range, which separates Southern California proper from the Mojave Desert, where average summer temperatures hover around 120 but can reach up into the mid-130s. It was a harsh, desolate region settled only by a handful of ornery loners, aged frontier folk, and the occasional Hollywood film crew.

The area, which includes several dry lakebeds, had become a popular shooting location for desert sagas and westerns. It was while killing time between takes, that some actors discovered that the lakebeds, which were composed of a hard-packed, alkaline clay that laid flat as a tabletop and stretched out for miles, made an excellent driving surface.

For bored movie stars in three-digit temperatures with lots of downtime, powerful automobiles close at hand, and miles of lakebed before them, the stage was set for some real action. The drama might begin with a simple boast, "I bet mine's faster than yours!" Wagers were made and the cars were lined up, waved off, and hurtled straight down the lakebed, driver's feet to the floor, all the way, all she's got, he who takes and holds the lead wins.

It was an amusing diversion soon forgotten once the shoot wrapped and the players returned home. But a film crew is not made up entirely of overpaid, overbearing artist types. There's a lot of heavy lifting that goes into the making of a movie, and those underpaid grunts hired to do it were also witness to the spectacle of flat-out, wheel-to-wheel, dry lakes racing.

Soon word spread to every garage and gas station in L.A., that anyone seeking the answer to the burning question, "what'll she do," will find it just 90 miles north on the dry lakes of the Mojave desert.

The Wanderin' Waterman

After having lost his mother to disease and his father to disinterest, Tom Blake left his hometown of Milwaukee to drift wherever fate, and a passing freight might take him. He had only journeyed as far as Detroit when a chance encounter completely re-directed the course of his life. While passing through the lobby of a downtown movie house, he bumped into Duke Kahanamoku who had come to watch newsreel footage of his gold-medal victory at the 1920 Olympic Games.

Nobody knows exactly what the Olympian had to say to the young, mid-western wanderer, but whatever it was, it made an impact. A few months later, Blake turned up in Los Angeles where he planned to become a waterman like Duke. With the blessing of a sympathetic night watchman, Blake secretly trained in the pool of the very prestigious and private Los Angeles Athletic Club.

When he felt he was ready, he cornered the coach of the club's swim team and talked him into allowing a non-member to try out. Blake made the team, and right away began winning nearly all the events he entered.

There wasn't much prize money in swimming contests, but his swimming exploits led to years of occasional work when Hollywood producers, who had discovered him in the sports pages, began hiring him for stunt work, often involving underwater tussles with various rubberized sea creatures.

He also found work as a lifeguard for the Swim Club at Santa Monica Beach, where he discovered a beat-up, old surfboard in an equipment room and decided to give stand-up surfing a try. But the board refused to be ridden, and after several spectacular wipeouts, he vowed never to try again.

Then, in 1924, the Santa Monica Beach Club, adjacent to Blake's Santa Monica Club, hired a new lifeguard—Duke Kahanamoku. The two acquaintances soon became fast friends. It was Duke who goaded Blake back out into the surf, and insisted he stay out there until he could ride back in; and for the next 30 years, surfing would remain a part of his life.

After the day's guard duty was done, the two would ride the waves till the light gave out. Evenings were often spent around the fire pit where Duke beguiled listeners with tales of his halcyon days at Waikiki. For Blake, these sweet soliloquies confirmed a fear that he would never be a true waterman until he had learned the ways of the islanders; and so he stowed away on the next steamer bound for Oahu.

In Honolulu, Blake lived as a Hawaiian, surfing and spearfishing with Duke's brothers. He was made an honorary member of the "natives only" Hui Nalu Surf Club and was so well regarded by the locals that he was given permission to restore several ancient, Hawaiian surfboards belonging to a local Museum. It was while he was grappling with these mammoth beach barges that it occurred to him that there just might be a better way to build a surfboard.

When Blake returned to Southern California, in 1925, he got right to work on some innovative ideas. He rough-cut a slim-waisted board out of redwood, and carefully shaped it with a block plane and draw knife. Then, with an auger drill, he began boring holes in it. He continued drilling until he had taken out as much mass as possible, and then covered the top and bottom with a thin, wood veneer.

As expected, at 100 pounds, weight was reduced. What came as a surprise was how well it handled in the water. Because it was lighter, the hollow board could be paddled faster, which made waves easier to catch, and it also rode faster than the plank boards. It wasn't a perfect solution to the weight problem, but it was a clear indication that he was moving in the right direction.

The Lone Eagle

As a way of creating a symbolic link between the U.S. and France, and advancing aviation technology, Frenchman, and New York hotelier, Raymond Orteig put up a $25,000 cash prize for the first man to fly non-stop from New York to Paris or vice versa. The purse attracted some of Europe's most illustrious aviators as well as a 25-year-old wing-walker and air-mail pilot from Little Falls, Minnesota.

Though Charles Lindbergh was an unknown in a field that included many of the country's reigning aero-heros, a group of St. Louis businessmen were willing to put up $15,000 in hopes the notoriety associated with a successful crossing would establish St. Louis as the air capital of the nation rather than those west coast backwaters, Los Angeles and San Diego, that seemed to be drawing all the attention.

So, with cash in hand, Lindbergh went shopping for an airplane theoretically capable of making the 3600-mile trans-Atlantic flight and was turned down by every manufacturer he approached. They would sell the plane, but only if they chose the pilot; none would entrust their reputation to a boyish-looking bush pilot with a history of hard landings. He had almost given up when he came across an ad for a small company that was building some very sturdy little monoplanes way out in San Diego, California.

Ex-army pilot T. Claude Ryan and his partner, Ben Mahoney, established Ryan Airlines, in 1925. It was the first commercial airline in the U.S., running regular flights from San Diego to Los Angeles. A year later they began building their own monoplane, and a year after that, they were facing bankruptcy when Mahoney received a wire from a Mr. Lindbergh asking if he could build a plane that could fly 40 hours nonstop in just 60 days? Mahoney's answer was an emphatic yes!

In the can-do, anything-goes atmosphere of California, a deal was made with no strings attached—he who buys it flies it. Based on Ryan's own monoplane, altered to Lindbergh's specifications, the Ryan team designed and built what amounted to a flying fuel tank—a stripped-down, mail plane with just enough room for a motor, a pilot, and over 2700 pounds of petrol.

By the time Lindbergh taxied the perilously overweight *Spirit of St. Louis* onto the rain-soaked runway at New York's Roosevelt Field, on the morning of May 20, 1927, six aviators had already been killed attempting to make the same journey. Nevertheless, he pushed the throttle forward struggling to get the heavy ship airborne before running out of running room and was just barely able to clear trees and power lines by less than 20 feet.

Thirty-three and a half hours later, 150,000 Parisians greeted "Lucky Lindy," as he touched down at Le Bourget field. The next morning, Charles Lindbergh had become the most famous man in the world. The future of aviation was assured. But it was San Diego, where the Spirit was built, and not St. Louis, that reaped the glory and solidified its place as home to the nation's aviation industry.

Dark Days A' Comin'

Certainly, there could be no more appropriate symbol of America's growing omnipotence than Lindbergh's silver Spirit soaring over the Atlantic. On paper, the United States had become the richest nation on earth, and the creditor to the world. President Coolidge boasted that "the business of America is business," and by all accounts, business was very, very good. Never had the nation enjoyed so strong and prolonged a period of prosperity as it did during the decade of the 1920s.

Every segment of society seemed to be living a little better than before, but it was the women who were the real big winners of the era. After winning the right to vote, they went on a cultural tear overturning centuries-old societal norms. They bobbed their hair and took to wearing makeup; they raised their hemlines and lowered their necklines; they smoked, drank, drove cars, listened to jazz music, got college degrees, and jobs, and moved from the country to the cities where they really let loose.

Amid this mad rush to modernity, it seemed the party would last forever, but it didn't; it surprised nearly everybody and ended in late October of 1929. For too many years, too many Americans had been betting too heavily in the stock market, driving up stock prices many times higher than their actual worth.

Astute speculators, acting on a hunch that the market needed to cool down a little, cashed out, causing a dip in investor confidence. At the opening bell on October 24, 1929, known as Black Thursday, the stock market dropped 11%. Investors were astonished. Few had ever heard of a stock losing value.

The following Monday, Black Monday, another sell-off dropped market value by 13%. The next day, Black Tuesday, the market fell another 12% initiating the huge selloffs, which brought about the stock market crash of 1929. The party was over, and the hangover, that would last even longer, was just beginning.

Chapter 16
All Ahead Slow

By 1930, America had settled into the worst economic depression in its history. So pervasive and devastating were its effects that it came to be known as "the great depression." But, as always, in California, things were different. Where the rest of the nation was flattened, California was merely staggered. It's not that there weren't problems; some banks and businesses were closed, jobs were lost, and one in five Southlanders were on relief.

But the state's semi-isolated economy didn't rely on the same heavy industries and economic infrastructure as the harder-hit parts of the country. Southland business consisted of local banking, a myriad of small service industries, and a few larger ones, like oil and movies, which actually expanded their operations during the lean years of the 1930s.

Curb Service
Other depression-proof, Southern California industries were those associated with the care, maintenance, and facilitation of the automobile. On various occasions, Southlanders were conceived in automobiles, born in automobiles, and even buried in them. So compelling was the allure of automotion that main street had to restructure itself to meet the needs of the motorist on the move, and some of the earliest, and most emblematic establishments to make that transition were the roadside eateries.

The Boulevard Bistros
It had not been a year since Wayne McAllister dropped out of school to take a job designing bungalows for a San Diego building company, when, out of the blue, his boss offered him a full partnership in the business. The very next morning, the elated new partner arrived for work early only to learn that his boss had run off to Mexico with a stripper and wouldn't be arriving at all.

Stunned by the sudden turn of events, McAllister hardly had a moment to consider his options when the hotelier, restaurateur, and Hollywood bon vivant, Barron Long, popped in and asked him to design the ten-million-dollar hotel, casino, country club, sporting facility, golf course, and racetrack complex he planned to build across the border in Tijuana.

Having just made the leap from junior-grade draftsman to sole proprietor less than twelve hours earlier, McAllister could hardly comprehend the enormity of the proposition. But in the terror of the moment, he remembered his ex-boss once advising him to say yes to anything and ponder the particulars at a later date, which is exactly what he did. And so, Mr. Long left the offices of The San Diego Architectural Service Bureau unaware that he had just entrusted the most important project of his career to an unlicensed, 19-year-old, high school dropout.

In a stunning contradiction to the obvious signs that disaster was inevitable, Agua Caliente was an absolute triumph and the making of Wayne McAllister. With the successful completion of the most spectacular entertainment complex of its day, McAllister was hot, and that notoriety brought him a string of top-drawer commissions along with another of those intriguing requests from out of left field.

Bill Simon owned a couple of lunch counters, and his friend, Harry Carpenter, owned a few roadside diners. Both liked to play poker and would get together with friends for games that lasted well into the wee hours. On one such occasion, Harry offhandedly remarked that his diners were costing him too much to operate. Bill blurted out that it was his awkward layouts that were cutting into his profits and bet Harry a very large sum that he could build a much more efficient establishment.

Had Bill not been just a little bit greased, he probably would never have made such a reckless wager; and had Henry not been equally well lubricated, he probably would have kindly let the provocation pass—but he didn't. So, the next day, a bleary-eyed Mr. Simon presented the unlicensed boy wonder with his dilemma; not to worry assured McAllister, certain he could work out the thorny details at a later date.

A drive-in phenomenon was developing in response to changes in technology, regional population shifts, and basic economic necessity. In the early 1930s, more and more of the Southland's city dwellers were re-locating to the suburbs in a gradual out-migration made possible by an abundance of cheap flatland, aggressive state and local road building campaigns, and the public's relentless love affair with the automobile. As the population began to drift away from the downtown hub, business followed. The first enterprises to spring up along the outlying roadways were modest, mom & pop markets, produce stands, service stations, and roadside diners.

The early drive-in restaurants were usually just make-shift kitchens in garage-like buildings set up in the middle of a dirt lot. Although car-hop service might be available, the parking areas could be chaotic. Mr.

Carpenter's early drive-ins were examples of this slapdash, "diner in the dirt" style.

In his re-working of the drive-in formula, McAllister focused on two essential requirements: visibility and accessibility. To better facilitate a constant turnover of customers, he built his drive-ins on extra-large, corner lots that could be entered from two roadways and seen from four directions. And to make the most of the enhanced perspective and attract the attention of motorists from the furthest possible distance in any direction, he made his modest drive-ins into huge billboards.

In the center of the paved lot, he placed a half-enclosed kitchen surrounded by a circular counter; atop that he placed a huge circular, wedding cake roof mounted on lightweight steel poles; and atop the roof, the crowning glory—an enormous, vertical pylon sign as much as 50 feet high. Everything from the roof up was laced with miles of neon tubing, with the most elaborate flourishes decorating the totems on top. After dark, these comforting little bastions of light could be seen for miles. Parking spaces were laid out around the entire circumference of the building where cars nosed straight in, and cheerful carhops were waiting to greet the hungry travelers.

McAllister's first Simon's drive-in became the model for nearly all such roadside establishments of the pre-war era and represented a new wave of art-deco architecture designed specifically for the automobile. Incidentally, Mr. Simon won his bet with Mr. Carpenter, who unabashedly copied McAllister's design when he remodeled his own chain of Carpenter's drive-ins.

Blake's Water Sled

Since his return from Hawaii, Tom Blake continued in his quest to build a better surfboard. Drawing on an idea he got from a half-completed airplane wing, he began making hollow, rib-braced surfboards covered with a thin skin of plywood under multiple coats of marine varnish. Hollow from stem to stern, save for the ribs, Blake's new hollow board weighed approximately 45 pounds and was more buoyant and more manageable than anything that had come before. He patented his design, in 1931, as the "Blake Water Sled" and made licensing agreements with four small companies to manufacture them.

Lifeguards were so impressed with the hollow board that it became a standard piece of rescue equipment at

> **The Kooks**
> Though not popular with seasoned riders, Blake's light-weight hollow board was a very popular choice among novice surfers, and thus, experienced surfers began referring to these beginners as "kooks," and still do today.

beaches all over the country. As a paddleboard, the hollow was matchless; but for surfing, they were considered too skittish, too "kooky riding" to be taken seriously; and for that reason, surfers began referring to them as "kook boxes." For stand-up surfing, most seasoned wave riders still preferred the heavy, smooth-riding plank boards, especially the beautiful examples built by Blake's only real competitor—Swastika Surfboards.

Swastika Surfboards
Economic hardship, following the stock market crash of 1929, forced young Meyers Butte to leave Stanford University and work for his father's building company, Pacific System Homes, which made a line of prefab bungalows sold through Montgomery-Wards.

With the housing market gone stagnant, Meyers, who had surfed in Hawaii and was familiar with the plank board, suggested that his father manufacture surfboards as a sideline. The market was wide open, and the risk was minimal, so dad agreed to give Meyers his own corner of the shop to produce copies of the square-tailed, redwood planks he rode in Hawaii.

He called his little subsidiary Swastika Surfboards, and proudly stamped the ancient symbol of good fortune into every board that left the factory completely unaware that an obscure, political activist in Germany had already glommed onto that very same insignia. The Swastika boards were incredibly well made and quite popular among veteran surfers, but they were still quite a handful for a novice, and consequently did little to advance the sport's popularity.

Hollywood Goes Hawaiian
Even though the equipment was still way too primitive to take the sport mainstream, surfing got a major promo boost as a result of the inland activities of its two most notable devotees. By 1932, both Tom Blake and Duke Kahanamoku were veteran stunt doubles and bit players and would occasionally bring the stars out to Santa Monica for a Hawaiian-style beach bash. Of course, surfing instruction was always available.

Child star Jackie Coogan, western stars Gary Cooper and Joel McCrea, and even suave leading man Ronald Colman all took a few impromptu lessons and became near-passable, part-time surfers. Through the exploits of these and other movie stars, the studios discovered surfing, not as a subject for big-screen drama, but as an exotic backdrop for their publicity machines.

If you were under contract to one of the major studios and looked good in a bathing suit, then you were photographed holding a surfboard. These routine "sun & sand" photos, so familiar in the pages of the Hollywood fan magazines, were seen by millions of movie fans throughout the world and helped to re-enforce the Southland's image as a star-studded, tropical paradise.

The Five Dollar Ford

Not one to want to mess around with a really good thing, Henry Ford was slow to realize that, by the mid-twenties, his baby, the revered Model T, was way past its prime. In the eighteen years since the T's introduction, Ford had put 15,000,000 of them on the street, but he was losing market share to other manufacturers offering up-to-date designs and stylish features.

So, in May of 1927, he shut down production of the Model T, restructured his factory, and introduced the Model A the following December. Like the T, Ford's Model A was an overwhelming success, selling over two million units in just over a year. In fact, despite the depression, it sold so well that a whole generation of younger folks (mostly men) were finally able to afford to buy their first automobile when a glut of second-hand cars (mostly Ts) were dumped on the used car market ushering in the era of the five-dollar Ford.

For young auto enthusiasts who agonized over having to borrow the family sedan on Saturday nights, it was a dream come true. In the early 1930s, you could buy an old T for five dollars, strip it down, build it up, cruise the strip, and maybe even run it at the lake.

International Stylin' in the USA

New York's Museum of Modern Art produced the first exhibition of modern architecture in 1932, featuring models of the works of several of Europe's leading architects. The curators, in need of an elegantly descriptive title for the exhibition, highlighted the global character of the event by calling it "The International Exhibition of Modern Architecture." And from this one exhibition, the term "International Style" became synonymous with all modern architectural design.

Initially, for the Europeans, the show was something of a disappointment, for their work had lost most of its socialist significance in the crossing. In America, as in Europe, the people's architecture continued to be rejected by the working classes it

Hawaii Calls

In 1935, Webley Edwards began broadcasting a weekly radio program to the states from Waikiki Beach. His *Hawaii Calls*, stirred listener's imaginations with musical performances by the Royal Hawaiian Hotel Orchestra celebrating the beauty, adventure, and romance of the islands. In the 50s, Edward's expanded his playlist to include Hawaiian pop artists like Don Ho, and popular exotica artists like Martin Denny, broadcasting live performances to over 750 stations worldwide before the final sign-off in 1975.

was designed to liberate. However, the show was by no means a failure. Ironically, the International Style became a real big hit with the well to do, the Bourgeois—the very demographic it was designed to alienate. It seems the avant-garde imagery and leftist pedigree appealed to successful capitalists seeking to associate themselves with European, socialist chic.

And what a lucky thing it was for Europe's modernists. The following year, after several shakedowns by Hitler's SS, the Bauhaus was forced to close. The Fuhrer, having proclaimed their politics communist and their art degenerate, sent them scrambling to the U.S. where they found sanctuary in the architecture departments of America's top universities.

From there, they succeeded in spreading their brand of modernism across all 50 states; and this sterile and austere international style might have overrun Southern California as it had other parts of the nation were it not for the region's radiant atmosphere, the people's jubilant character, and the handful of independent and highly imaginative architects who made the most of it.

California Crazy

Since the days of Katherine Tingley and her Theosophical Society, no one locality had played host to as many kooks and crazy, quasi-religious sects as Southern California.

"Tip the world over on its side and everything loose will land in Los Angeles." Frank Lloyd Wright

At the time, theories as to why Southern California provided such fertile ground for these groups could, like the teachings of the cults themselves, escape the gravitational pull of rational thought:

"Cults thrived on the Pacific coast because of the wonderful transparency of the atmosphere, the heavy charges of mineral magnetism from the gold mines, which set up favorable vibrations, and the notably strong passions of the forty-niners, which had created unusual magnetic emanations." Emma Harding

With all due respect to Ms. Harding, I believe a more plausible explanation would be that the general disposition and circumstances of a growing number of recent arrivals made them particularly susceptible to the sort of spiritual and emotional salve the cultists provided.

When the early waves of migration were bringing mostly the rich and refined, there were few opportunities for quacks and spiritualists. But since the mid-1880s, many of those immigrating to Southern

California were working folk from the south and Midwest who were unaccustomed to the Southland's shallow-rooted society. It was a major culture shock for bible-toting migrants from mature districts where family and community relationships could be traced back generations.

Adding to this growing pool of potential cultists were the invalids in so desperate a fix they were willing to try anything in the hope of improving their prospects. The presence of so many alienated immigrants and incurable invalids made Southern California a haven for all manner of frauds and fakers. During the trying times of the depression, the teachings of these cultists would breach the bounds of eccentricity and soar off into the absolute outer limits of absurdity.

The sacred texts of founder Arthur Bell's "Mankind United" cult claimed that a race of metal-headed midgets from the earth's core would rise up against the corrupt "hidden rulers" of the world and establish a utopian society with a shorter workweek, higher pay scale, and larger homes with all the modern conveniences. But until that day of salvation, the cult's followers were directed to give unto Mr. Bell just about everything they had.

Then there was Guy Ballard, the Illinois check forger who claimed to have met up with a mythical deity on a hiking trip. After joining this phantom in a couple of straight shots of "pure electronic essence," the two set out on a round-the-world trip through the stratosphere. Upon his return to earth, Ballard rechristened himself as Godfrey Ray King and created the "I Am" cult, in which supernatural beings communicated their commands through select intermediaries such as Guy Ballard.

You can just imagine what the Gods had to say regarding income redistribution. Yet, in spite of the lunatic premise, Ballard made a mint preaching his gospel on a radio show, publishing spiritual books, and selling souvenir photos of himself as "the beloved messenger."

Also experiencing a depression-era renaissance were

> **The New Dealer**
>
> Acting without the aid of an extraterrestrial being, a new president, Franklin Delano Roosevelt, enacted two bundles of bills he called, "New Deals," that were designed to reverse the economy's downward drift. In New Deal One, he created the Federal Deposit Insurance Corporation (FDIC), which saved the banks by guaranteeing the safety of depositor's accounts; then he saved the bars by repealing prohibition. For New Deal Two, he established an entire alphabet's soup worth of work and relief programs, which, among many other things, gave us a Hoover Dam that pumped more, much needed, water into Southern California, and a Social Security System, which created an economic safety-net for the aged. But none of his efforts could revive the nation's collapsed economy.

a host of utopian political evangelists who promised the desperate and dispossessed a life of ease through various welfare schemes that managed to garner a surprising amount of public support. Socialist, Upton Sinclair, even came close to getting elected governor of California, in 1934, on the strength of his own "End Poverty in California" program, which called for the establishment of a communal society based on a communist command and control system.

The main attraction of these cults was the promise of freedom from want, which inevitably turned out to be a situation enjoyed only by the program's founders.

Runin' on Eight

Henry Ford once swore he would never build an engine that had, "more cylinders than a cow had teats." But since 1929, Chevrolet had been eating into Ford's market share with an excellent six-cylinder engine and an even better advertising slogan, "six cylinders for the price of four."

Taking the "more is better" approach, Ford raised the ante by two when he introduced a flathead V8 engine as an option on the 1932 Model A. Among serious gearheads, few motors have ever been so highly regarded as the legendary Ford Flathead V8; yet, at the time of its introduction, its build potential was largely overlooked by performance enthusiasts.

> *A gearhead was one of the earliest slang terms for an automobile enthusiast.*

Though it initially produced a very respectable 65hp in stock trim, it was still no match for a well-built T series four-banger, and as a recent offering, it was too expensive and had too little performance support to be of much interest.

Of course, that is not to say that Ford's new V8 did not have its early admirers—it did. Among its most notable fans was a Texas stickup artist who once took pen in hand to express his appreciation of the V8's ability to outrun the four and six-cylinder models most police departments were still using:

Dear Sir: —

While I still have got breath in my lungs I will tell you what a dandy car you make. I have drove Fords exclusively when I could get away with one. For sustained speed and freedom from trouble the Ford has got ever other car skinned and even if my business hasn't been strictly legal it don't hurt anything to tell you what a fine car you got in the V8 —

Yours truly
Clyde Champion Barrow

Nevertheless, even with that glowing recommendation, it would be a few years before a clear majority of Southern California hot rodders would come to share Mr. Barrow's opinion.

Lautnerland

As one of Frank Lloyd Wright's most promising students, John Lautner was given the responsibility of supervising the design and construction of several of Wright's own pet projects. But unlike many of Wright's other pupils who would go on to make durable careers reproducing variations on the master's own works, Lautner had visions of his own.

> **The Late V8**
> True to his word, when the law finally caught up to Mr. Barrow, and his equally lethal female accomplice, on a lonely stretch of Louisiana highway, he was indeed driving a brand new, stolen, Ford V8.

Heeding the workshop rumors he had heard of a town out west where a new idea was not always regarded as a threat, he moved to Los Angeles in 1938, opened an office, and began advancing his own distinctive approach to modern design, which one might describe as one part international, two parts prairie school, and three parts his own brand of futuristic, space-aged structuralizing.

Beholding to neither political doctrines, regional traditions, nor architectural dictums, Lautner reveled in the flagrant use of every conceivable material, texture, shape, and free-form design scheme— nothing was off-limits.

His first solo project was his own, modest, multi-level, cliff hugger, which featured a flat roof, built-in furniture, and recessed mood lighting. This house, as well as his redesigns of several at-risk Wright projects, received enough favorable media attention to attract a few more innovatively realized commissions before nearly all residential construction was shut down for the duration of the war.

But with these few projects, which featured design concepts that, to many observers, seemed to have originated in another galaxy, Lautner provided a glimpse of the jaw-dropping marvels that were yet to come once peace was restored.

The Beachcomber's Ball

After touring the world as a deckhand, Ernie Gantt settled in Los Angeles, in 1931, where he took a job running a speakeasy and bootlegging operation. When his livelihood was scuttled by the repeal of prohibition, he opened a small bar in Hollywood and dressed it up with the Polynesian artifacts and souvenirs he had picked up during his days in the South Pacific.

A little oasis in the heart of the urban jungle, Don's Beachcomber Café was a charming little dive that served up a very respectable repast.

But the house specialty wasn't the food, it was the grog. An ex-sailor, Gantt knew his rum, and he knew where stockpiles of rot-gut rum, left over from prohibition, could be had really cheap. So, he cornered the market on the cast-off contraband, and with it, created several of the world's most revered cocktails.

Using an assortment of fruit juices and syrups to soften the sting of his spirits, Gantt is said to have created the Mai Tai, the Zombie, the Vicious Virgin, the Sumatra Kula, the Missionary's Downfall, and about 80 other luscious libations. All were basically straight-up, high-proof rum, Bacardi, or tequila laced with flavorful sweeteners and topped off with a paper umbrella.

The look was festive, and the taste was saccharine, but the recoil was robustious. Men often mocked his sugar-coated cocktails as girly drinks, but only once. Like a box of Cracker Jacks, there was a surprise at the bottom of every glass.

On the strength of his cocktails, Gantt's little neighborhood bar became a favorite hangout of hard-drinking newspaper reporters and actors whose patronage and praise drew so many more customers that Gantt finally had to move across the street to a larger facility.

The name of the new establishment was changed to Don the Beachcomber, and Gantt, having assumed the colorful persona of the club's namesake, changed his name to Donn Beach.

The first Don the Beachcomber opened in 1937 as a full restaurant and bar serving a complete menu of Cantonese dishes spiced up to resemble what was thought to be island fare and Gantt's renowned rum toddies. The décor was an all-out escapist fantasy with artificial palm trees, bamboo trimmings, rattan furniture, flowered leis, jungle artifacts, nautical paraphernalia, and a simulated tropical storm that beat down on the roof at regular intervals.

Guests walked in off the street and into an island retreat an ocean away from the hectic world they left outside, or so it certainly seemed. An instant favorite among locals and tourists alike, Don the Beachcomber wasn't the first Polynesian-themed restaurant on the

---

Christian's Hut

To get mega-star Clark Gable to appear in MGM's 1935 production of *Mutiny on the Bounty*, the studio had to agree to two provisos. First, the actor would not be required to affect a British accent, and second, a tavern would be provided for the use of cast and crew while on location on Catalina Island. The crew named the Polynesian styled tavern Christian's Hut, for Gable's character in the movie, and when the shoot wrapped, the bar remained in operation. With the success of Don the Beachcomber, a group of investors bought the enterprise and opened locations in Newport Beach and San Diego. The San Diego location is still in operation and known as the Bali Hai.

west coast, but it was the first to gain widespread notoriety and the very first to franchise the "tiki bar" model and export it throughout Southern California, inspiring countless imitators.

The Lakesters

Since the early 20s, traffic out on Muroc dry lake had been steadily building. Where once a couple of swells in their Doozies might have a go every now and then, by the early 30s, a dozen or so "racing camps" would spring up every weekend.

Hot rodders would caravan out to Muroc on a Friday night and sleep in their cars. Saturday morning, they would map out a vague course, designate a viewing area, and schedule a series of heats where any and all comers could, "run what ya brung."

What they brung was their everyday rides, which were usually some pretty ragged-looking rigs. These dual-purpose lakes racers were built for speed, not comfort or appearance. They came stripped down to minimum street-legal trim and, upon arrival, were often further disassembled down to the frame rails— anything to maximize the weight to horsepower ratio.

> **None for the Road**
> According to legend, the Zombie was so debilitating that patrons were limited to just one refill.
>
> **Trader Vic's**
> In 1934, Victor Jules Bergeron, Jr. (aka Trader Vic) opened a small bar and restaurant in Oakland he called Hinky Dinks but later changed to Trader Vic's. Like his competitor, Donn Beach, he would assume the fictional identity of his club's namesake, successfully franchise his brand, and claim to have invented every exotic potable attributed to Mr. Gantt. But to this day, no one knows who really did what.

In between runs, drivers would fix what broke and make adjustments for the next heat. In the evenings, groups would gather around campfires to fraternize, discuss racing and performance theory, and swap modification and tune-up tips. Come Sunday afternoon, the cars would be reassembled and driven back to L.A. for daily driver duty.

This Southern California style of dry lakes racing, the forerunner of drag racing, wasn't anything like the contests staged in other parts of the country. It was not about handling or even explosive, off-the-line acceleration; lakes racing was all about straight line, top-speed performance.

The course was laid out in three parts. The first part (about a mile) was used to get up speed. The second part (about a third of a mile) was the "time trap" where top speed and elapsed times were measured. The third part (usually a little over a mile) was used for stopping. Contest rules were minimal and safety rules were nonexistent. They raced across the desert at speeds approaching 100mph in cars that, most likely, couldn't pass a soapbox derby safety check. A driver might hold the wheel in one hand and an "accelerator wire" in the other, while seated on an orange crate.

Racing in groups, they would take off in a cloud of dust so large that those who fell behind could lose their bearings and collide with each other. Individual groups of racers, often unbeknownst to each other, would gather miles apart for speed runs on courses that could overlap.

So, to minimize the mayhem, several L.A. area car clubs got together in November of 1937 and chartered the Southern California Timing Association (SCTA) to lay down some guidelines. And in May of 1938, the SCTA held its first race at Muroc, which attracted nearly 200 competitors and over 10,000 spectators. It was the biggest event of its kind ever held in Southern California and the last to be held at Muroc. That year, the Army Air Corps commandeered Muroc forcing the lakes racers to move their operations to other, more distant, lakebeds until those too were requisitioned by the military.

Shiner's Run
In the early days, one of Vic Edelbrock's best mail-order customers was a kid from North Carolina named Junior Johnson who used his "dual-purpose" hot rod to run moonshine on Saturday nights and race Sunday afternoons on the southern stock car circuit that would later become NASCAR.

Finned
Tom Blake made his final contribution to the design of the surfboard in 1935 when he mounted a speed boat keel on the tail of his hollow board. It was a great improvement in control and stability, but it would take years for the fin to become a standard feature. Surfers were an extremely hard-headed lot with established traditions they were reluctant to change. Therefore, most of the innovations that developed over the years were first adopted, not by the old pros, but by the newcomers.

Hot Rods West
Throughout the teens and twenties, nearly all of the specialty high-performance parts manufacturers were based where the cars were made, in the mid-west. But by the mid-thirties, a handful of small, Southland companies were emerging that would eclipse them all and solidify Southern California's ascension as the new capital of American hot rodding.

The shift coincided with the spectacular growth in the popularity of dry lakes racing. In the mid-thirties, there developed an inter-connected alliance of racers, mechanics, car clubs, garages, and auto parts suppliers. Out of this localized, hothouse environment, a handful of wiz-kids gained recognition for their exceptional talent in designing their own, very effective high-performance parts.

Word spread, and they began taking orders from friends and acquaintances. As demand continued to grow, they opened small shops, and finally, large manufacturing facilities whose names Weiand, Winfield, Moon, Cragar, Edelbrock, and Iskenderian would become household names among hot rodders throughout the country.

The Palos Verdes Surf Club

The number of regular surfers in Southern California had risen to approximately eighty by the mid-30s. Still too few to fill half the seats in an average-sized movie house, yet from that tiny, loose-knit assemblage, there emerged a select fraternity of highly enthusiastic devotees who would organize themselves around their passion for surfing and, through their union, begin to cultivate the distinctive lifestyle that would become indelibly associated with it.

The Palos Verdes Surf Club, named after a popular surf spot, was founded in 1935 by John "Doc" Ball, a dentist from Gardena. The club's meetings were held in the Doc's dentist office, and like most social circles of the period, there were strict rules. Members were expected to dress in slacks and club blazers, refrain from smoking, and behave like gentlemen.

But the rules of parliamentary procedure didn't apply when the club assembled on the beach for a weekend's surf outing. There, they composed a new code of conduct.

San O'

Along with their "home break" at the Palos Verdes Cove, the club's favorite surf spot was San Onofre, an isolated stretch of beach just south of San Clemente. With a waveform similar to Waikiki's billowing, slow rollers, San Onofre waves were ideally suited to the heavy, wooden planks of the 1930s, which made the site a major focal point for surfers from San Diego to Santa Barbara.

Club members, along with their family and friends would caravan down the old coast highway to meet up with other clubs for a few days of surfing and socializing. Nearly sixty miles from the urban centers of San Diego to the south, and Los Angeles to the north, remote San Onofre proved an ideal incubator for a west coast beach culture shaped by the islands and temporarily sustained by national insolvency.

Many who took up surfing during the 30s did so, not in spite of the depression, but because of it. Once relieved of the responsibility of having to earn a living, there was plenty of time to indulge in various idle pursuits. So, as the depression wore on, the Southland's surfing population rose, tripling by the time the war shut down the beaches in 1941.

It was during those formative years from 1935 to 1941, that most of the standards and practices that would come to be recognized as unique to the Southern California surfer were first distilled. Fashion was becoming a big part of the mystique. Women began wearing the daring new form-fitting lastex swimsuits in both one and two-piece configurations in a transitional step between the heavy, woolen bathing gowns of the past, and the string bikinis of the future. The men were taking the opposite tack, forsaking the popular, bun-hugging skivvy suits in favor of the cutoff, and fashionably frayed, white sailor pants, which inspired the creation of the baggies and jams of the late 1950s.

The suntan, once looked upon as the tell-tale sign of a common laborer, had become the hallmark of an emerging Southern California leisure class and a mandatory attribute for the surfer and his girl. Always in pursuit of a good wave and an all-around good time, the serious surfer accepted employment as a temporary condition tolerated only as long as needs dictated. The bohemian lifestyle coming together in the 1930s at San Onofre, which had crystallized into a hard-packed cliché by 1960, would have been most familiar to the Sandwich Islanders Richard Henry Dana encountered at Dana Point 100 years past and just 16 miles up the beach.

At San Onofre, the depression seemed a million miles away. In true island style, days were spent surfing, fishing, diving for lobster and abalone, sunning on the beach, drinking beer, and consorting, mainly with members of the opposite sex. Evenings were spent around the campfires dining on the catch of the day, strumming guitars and ukuleles, drinking beer, and consorting, mainly with members of the opposite sex. Whether they realized it or not, the regulars at San O' were the founding members of an entirely new and very exclusive Southern California coalition.

Hello—Goodbye

When the San Diego city council prepared to tear down the remaining Balboa Park buildings from the 1915 World's Fair, now 20 years past their expiration date, angry citizen groups descended upon the council demanding they be restored instead. So, to justify the restoration expense and hopefully add a little something to the city coffers, it was decided to host another west coast extravaganza.

Some might think it foolhardy to throw another costly intercontinental jamboree during a depression, but it was actually the inopportune timing that made it the success it turned out to be. The California Pacific International Exhibition of 1935, with its arts and science exhibits, museums, arcades, huge gardens, a mining town, international villages, a car show, and even a nudist colony, provided a most welcome diversion from the hard times for over seven million people—twice the number who visited the original Panama Exhibition. But, at the very same time this last of the great, 20th century, Southern California booster bashes was in full flower, the Los Angeles and San Diego chambers of commerce were eliminating the relocation enticement themes from their promotional programs.

> *"There is no merit to any more people coming out here."*
> Harold Wright, Los Angeles Chamber of Commerce

The chambers warned potential visitors not to come to Southern California seeking employment. Self-sustaining tourists were still welcome, but the promotional mantra had shifted from come, spend, and live, to come, spend, and then go back home where you belong. Even the ultra-boosterish All-Weather Club conceded that it might be time to slow the flow of new residents into the Southland. And a brand-new organization, the California Depopulation Commission, took the "no vacancy" theme even further, not only encouraging non-natives to leave, but distributing press releases to newspapers nationwide highlighting the region's many botherations including the most sacred of off-limits, taboo subjects—earthquakes!

For years California's boosters lied about the state's propensity for the shakes until San Francisco was rattled in 1906. Following that cataclysm, Southlanders tried to redefine the problem as limited to the northern regions:

> *"Geologists say the rock formation underlying the city of Los Angeles is of such a nature that it is as safe from any danger of earthquake as any locality in United States."*
> Los Angeles Chamber of Commerce

But the Long Beach quake of 1933 exposed that new lie and the California Depopulation Commission made sure the truth was publicized to good effect.

In the years to follow, several industries would continue to independently recruit talent from out-of-state, but by the mid-1930s, there were a great many Southlanders who felt that Southern California had already filled out nicely, and so, after 65 years of comprehensive civic boosterizin', the practice was largely abolished.

Paradise Postponed

By the early 40s, some of those Ford V8s were beginning to show up on the used market and had attracted a great deal of attention from hot rod builders, and Swastika Surfboards (now renamed Waikiki) came out with a new board made of an ultra-lightweight wood from South America called balsa. But before too much consideration could be given to the performance potential of either, the wars in Europe and Asia suddenly expanded to include the United States and all such undertakings were put on hold.

By Christmas, most of the Southland's hot rodders and surfers were either in uniform or working double shifts in defense plants. Cars were parked, and boards were stowed, and would remain so for the next 48 months.

Chapter 17
War All Over Again

Ten years before the attack on Pearl Harbor, there were warning signs that the United States was heading for a conflict with Japan. In 1931, Japan invaded Manchuria as the first step of a nation-building campaign to conquer South-East Asia, which included territory under US control.

The scheme was well executed and perfectly timed for no one was willing to get in their way, least of all the Americans whom they considered too soft and self-interested to present any serious challenge. Twelve years hence, few Japanese would characterize the Americans as soft or self-interested, but in the early 30s, they were correct in assuming the United States would do just about anything to avoid a fight.

Been There, Done That
Reluctantly drawn into the First World War twenty years earlier, Americans were determined not to let history repeat itself. And so, they declared the US to be neutral and watched history play out at the local cinema. Between screenings of *The Wizard of Oz* and *Gone with the Wind*, movie theaters ran newsreels showing the fall of Belgium followed by the fall of Holland, and then France.

Radio listeners tuned in to Edward R. Murrow reporting live from the London Blitz as Germany pummeled the city for 57 days, killing over 40,000 civilians. And though the Americans still refused to engage, they were more than willing to support the combatants they favored (China, England, and France), by selling them desperately needed supplies and raw materials.

Phoenix Rising
Getting those supplies across 3000 miles of ocean teeming with German submarines had nearly decimated Britain's merchant fleet. And so they turned to the Yanks, and American industry, idled by twelve years of depression, slowly began to sputter back to life.

Orders for big ships were received at California shipyards that hadn't turned out a vessel in over twenty years. Armies of workers were quickly hired and trained to crank out the huge, British-designed, Liberty Ships using prefabricated sections in an assembly-line process reducing production time to just over three days per ship. Speed was essential for they had to produce and deploy the ships faster than the Germans could sink them. It was a costly strategy for the British, but a win-win for the Yanks who could confront the forces of evil by proxy, and possibly put an end to the hard times in the bargain.

But the Japanese were not willing to let the United States sell goods from the sidelines while building up its industrial capacity; so, they attacked America's pacific stronghold at Pearl Harbor, Hawaii. The assault was meant to be a knockout punch, but instead, it served as a wake-up call to arms. The following day, the United States declared war on Japan; three days later, Germany, Italy, and the United States all declared war on each other, and World War II was full on.

The 97 Pound Palooka

Comparing the two nations on a map one would think the Japanese had to be crazy to attack a country so much larger than their own. But militarily, it was Japan that was the big dog. At the onset of World War II, the United States had one of the smallest, most inconsequential armed forces on the planet.

By contrast, both Japan and Germany had huge, professional armies and navies equipped with the most modern, mechanized, killing machines ever created by man. America's armory consisted of obsolete weapons dating back to World War I and before. Yet, despite this ominous mismatch, 15 million men and boys registered for the draft within hours of the Pearl Harbor attack.

Field Duty

Once accepted into the armed forces, it might be only a matter of eight to twelve weeks that separated the grocer, the salesman, the lawyer, or the high school graduate from the front-line combat assignments where they really learned their new trade.

Through a series of early, humiliating defeats in Europe and the Pacific, America's citizen-soldiers learned how to fight a modern war and came together as a battle-hardened fighting force as capable as any they would ever encounter. But the American military would not have been able to play the leading role it did in the defeat of the enemy were it not for the folks back home who, practically overnight, turned a scrappy, down-on-its-heels nation into an industrial colossus in support of their boys.

Democracy's Arsenal

The speed with which the United States shifted its slack domestic output to full-steam military production stunned both the enemy and the allies. Nearly every American industry, both large and small, modified its product line to conform to the needs of the military. The big three automakers began mass-producing bombers, tanks, trucks, guns, and ammunition in astonishing quantities. One shiny new B24 bomber came off the Ford assembly line every hour on the hour. Bantam and Willys-Overland produced the venerable Jeep. The Victor Adding Machine Company produced the famous Norden Bombsite, while the Corona Typewriter Company made Springfield rifles.

Although every region, community, city, town, and village, in one way or another, became involved in the war effort, Southern California, as "the gateway to the Pacific," was transformed into a major hub for every conceivable enterprise related to the war effort.

Billions of dollars in federal funds finally brought heavy industry to Southern California. West Coast shipyards from San Diego to San Francisco ran non-stop; dozens of small-scale aircraft manufacturers grew to become industrial giants. A growing number of military bases trained the hundreds of thousands of new recruits. Pilots and bombardiers trained in the skies above, while Marines practiced island hopping on the California beaches below.

Even local mom & pop manufacturers were called upon to produce specialized products for the war effort. Artist and designer Charles Eames, a pioneer in the use of molded plywood, who would later create some of the most iconic furniture designs of the 1950s, produced medical supplies and airplane parts. Southern California's colleges and universities trained officers and provided the talent and facilities needed to improve existing weapons systems and develop new military technology.

> **The G.I. Junket**
>
> As guests of the United States government, thousands of servicemen from all over the country, most of which had never been away from home, got an all-expenses paid trip to Southern California, where a great many fell under the spell of the soothing sunshine and the languid lifestyle. After the war, these soldiers from somewhere else would make up a significant portion of the massive, post-war migration to the west coast. 17-1
>
> **The War Store**
>
> It was during the execution of this war that a long-standing relationship first developed between the federal government (funding), the California defense industries (production), and the state's university system (research & development) that formed what a future U.S. president would identify as the Military Industrial Complex.

171

Help Wanted

World War II ended the depression. Millions of men not fit for military service were recruited for defense industry jobs. Employers with huge defense contracts, and demanding production quotas, competed for every worker. Southern California's workforce ballooned by 92%, and when the number of available jobs became greater than the number of available men to fill them, industry turned to the women.

During the war, six million women made up a third of the US workforce and were employed in factories building ships, planes, tanks, trucks, artillery pieces, light weapons, bombs, and ammunition.

In support positions, they ferried ships and planes, drove trains, felled trees, fought fires, ran farms, and successfully executed a thousand other tasks long thought to be beyond their mental and physical capability.

For many of these women, World War II was an awakening, and there would be no going back to the traditional roles when the fighting was over. The war experience opened the door to new possibilities that would be further explored in the years ahead.

West Coast Warriors

Everybody had a job to do. Kids collected scrap metal, tin cans, rubber, paper, and even cooking fat, which was used to make explosives. Celebrities not in uniform sold war bonds. The middle-aged, and even the elderly, grew victory gardens and joined the Civilian Defense Corps serving as block wardens, plane spotters, and coast watchers always on the lookout for the Japanese assault that many nervy Californians believed was inevitable.

And sure enough, on the night of February 23rd, 1942, it happened. About 100 yards off the coast of Santa Barbara, a lone Japanese submarine surfaced, took a few pot shots at some oil storage tanks, then scurried on out to sea. The owner of a local diner witnessed the shelling and called the police.

No significant property damage was done, but psychologically, the 20-minute barrage was a great victory for Japan. For the next day, all along the coast, the public was near hysterical in anticipation of a full-scale invasion. And then that night, in Los Angeles, someone thinking they had heard or seen something, hit the air-raid sirens, which set the shore batteries ablaze collectively throwing about ten tons of anti-aircraft shells into an empty night sky only to rain down upon the terrified Angelinos who mistook the

> **Faux pas on Film**
> This incident, mockingly known as "the Battle of Los Angeles," was the inspiration behind Stephen Spielberg's 1979 film, *1941*.

friendly fallout for a Japanese naval bombardment. The mayhem ran on for thirty minutes before anyone realized it was a false alarm.

The Feast of the Famished

During the 45-month-long conflict, 35 billion government dollars fueled the California war machine. In stark contrast to the many hardships faced by those men and women stationed overseas, life for those on the home front had improved dramatically. Good paying jobs were plentiful and, for the first time in years, people finally had a little money in their pockets; and that is where most of it remained, for there was little to spend it on.

With nearly every American manufacturer fully committed to war production, domestic production ground to a halt. Detroit would not produce a new car for five years. Production of consumer appliances was discontinued. Even the head of Sears Roebuck, America's department store, was reassigned to the War Production Board. Those consumer commodities still in production were strictly rationed.

The Office of Price Administration controlled the price and availability of over 8 million items from automobile tires and gasoline, to sugar, cigarettes, coffee, meat, eggs, processed foods, and textiles. Restrictions were so tight that a thriving domestic black market emerged to provide a wide variety of illicit consumer goods.

Nearly one-quarter of all transactions during the war were unlawful. Housewives determined to keep the war out of their kitchens were enthusiastically trading in back-alley butter sticks, prohibited poultry, and contraband cornbread.

The Bebop Flop

Big band music provided the soundtrack of the war years and served as one of the great moral boosters of the era. But it was during these pinnacle years of the big bands that a new style of jazz music was emerging. From L.A. to Beantown, a new generation of jazzers introduced a new style of playing built upon the art of improvisation; a spontaneous transformation was taking place away from the smooth, structured, and accessible, toward the bombastic, discordant, and experimental. The new style was called Bebop. It featured fast tempos, dissonant intervals, atonal harmonies, and was best played with fiery virtuosity. It was a mainstay in the big city nightspots of the east, but out on the west coast, the bebop flame would only flicker. There was just something about the irrepressibly buoyant nature of the sunny, Southern California scene that would not permit a comfortable fusion with the harsh, cacophonous sound of hard-driving bop. Musically, California was drifting towards a sound all its own— something cool and breezy that would lay well with the sea, and the sun, and the palm-lined suburbs.

If Tomorrow Comes

But most people were too busy working and reveling in the novelty of a steady paycheck to be too put out by the shortages and rationing. Besides, there were still some diversions available. Hollywood was still selling roughly 60 million tickets a week at theaters running 24 hours a day. People kept filling the baseball parks seemingly unaware that the draft had robbed the big-league rosters of their most capable players. People were so desperate to have a good time that nightclubs saw a near scandalous rise in patronage.

> *"It was almost as if people who weren't actually fighting the war were in some way enjoying it."* Shelley Winters

Soldiers, home on leave were often shocked to see how pleasant life was for the folks back home. Yet, in spite of the heady atmosphere whipped up by this new prosperity, the war was having a destabilizing effect on the home front.

The uncertainty encouraged a pervasive, live-for-today, attitude and a relaxation of social and moral standards. With the future in doubt, everything was done as if there would be no tomorrow. Courtships ending in marriage, and possibly a child on the way, were often carried out in the span of a two-week furlough. All this anxiety and misgiving about the future led to a dramatic rise in unwanted pregnancies and illegitimate births. Those already with children were often forced to leave them with friends, neighbors, teenage siblings, and sometimes even strangers while they worked at jobs that could be gone tomorrow.

The sadness and heartache brought on by the long separations, the sudden disintegration of underdeveloped relationships, and the steady strains on the familial bonds had a cooling effect on the general spirit of optimism that might have flourished unchecked in the face of such flush times. But what really kept the euphoric mood from boiling over was the knowledge that, at any moment, the war could hit home—hard.

> **The Wild Ones**
> In the early 50s, the wartime weakening of the family unit would be linked to an upsurge of juvenile delinquency, which would spawn a revolutionary new genre of teen-oriented films that would make true, cultural icons of Marlon Brando and James Dean.

Everyone with friends and/or loved ones stationed overseas lived in constant fear of the arrival of a telegram or the sight of a military staff car stopping in front of the house. A blue star was hung in the front window of a home to acknowledge a soldier's service; a gold star acknowledged their sacrifice. And hanging in the windows of too many of the homes along "every street USA" were the unsettling reminders that, somewhere very far away, loved ones were fighting and dying. Places with strange-sounding names like El Alamein, Corregidor, and Guadalcanal, virtually unknown before the war, had become familiar to most Americans by the time the allies had landed on Normandy Beach, which marked the beginning of the end for Germany.

In less than three months, the allies had liberated Paris. By February of 1945, they had advanced into Germany; three months later, they met up with the Russians in Berlin and the Germans called it quits on May 7, 1945. The deal on the table, for both Germany and Japan, was unconditional surrender.

The Germans did not quibble. But the Japanese refused to yield, even though the emperor and his military leaders knew the war was lost three years earlier. Adhering to the ancient warrior code of the Samurai, the Japanese fought to the death, and in the dozens of island-hopping campaigns conducted in the push towards Tokyo, that resolve had cost thousands of American lives.

Say Uncle!

The Americans took Okinawa Island in late June of 1945, in the bloodiest battle of the Pacific campaign. From there, they would launch their final assault on the home island and hope they could bring the war to an end by the spring of 1946.

The invasion (code named Operation Downfall) was to begin on November 1, 1945, and would require the participation of one and a half million American, British, and Australian combat soldiers. The planners of the invasion conservatively estimated that over two-thirds of those soldiers would be lost before Japan capitulated.

So grim were the expectations that the US government ordered up 500,000 Purple Heart medals in anticipation of the huge number of candidates eligible for the mostly posthumous honor. But their predictions were wrong; casualties were likely to be much worse. In their planning, the allies expected to face the remnants of a battered and bloodied imperial army. But the Japanese held a little something in reserve and had a much bigger surprise awaiting the invaders.

The Bonsai Bear Trap

In preparation for the inevitable invasion, the Japanese had recalled 14 divisions and numerous tank brigades. Twenty-five kamikaze destroyers along with bomb-laden, submarines, motorboats, and nearly 13,000 kamikaze planes were ready to engage American warships.

In addition to that surprisingly large assemblage of regular soldiers, the military mustered 28 million civilians armed with old rifles, longbows, swords, hatchets, clubs, spears, knives, garden tools, and cooking utensils, all ready to die for the emperor. What was in the making was a bloodbath far beyond the size and scope of even the direst predictions. But it was a battle not to be. The final curtain, in the last act of the war, would be lowered by the scientist, not the soldier.

Battle for The Bomb

Nothing motivates the development of new technology like total war. During the conflict, the jet engine was invented along with the ballistic missile, the computer, radar, sonar, synthetic rubber, plastic, and oil. But the most groundbreaking technological development, of not just the war years, but of the 20th century, was nuclear power.

In 1939, just days before the outbreak of the war in Europe, President Roosevelt received a letter from the famous mathman, Albert Einstein, warning him that the Nazis were making alarming progress in their efforts to create an atomic weapon. To FDR, the prospect of an atomic "super bomb" sounded more like science fiction than fact; but, considering the source, he couldn't dismiss the possibility.

So, he appointed a committee to study the feasibility of Einstein's claim. And while the Yanks pondered the problem of nuclear fission, a team of British scientists concluded that it was not only possible but quite probable that by firing neutrons into the densely packed atomic structure of uranium isotope 235, a chain reaction could be set off among the neighboring atoms that would gain power and momentum exponentially as it progressed and release a burst of energy several thousand times more powerful than TNT.

By the time news of their findings reached the White House, the Germans had already succeeded in proving the theory. Finding themselves years behind Nazi Germany in a race to produce a nuclear weapon, the United States, Britain, and Canada joined forces to create the Manhattan Project. The project's facilities, located in over 30 sites throughout the US, were so secret that few of the people involved had any idea what they were creating. Yet, within 28 months, they had pulled ahead of the Germans to create the first atomic bomb.

The New Chief

On April 12, 1945, President Roosevelt died. Three terms in office during the nation's most trying period in history had taken their toll. The next day, Vice President Harry Truman was sworn into office and briefed, for the very first time, on the top-secret Manhattan Project. It was decided that if the Japanese continued to stall, the bomb would be used prior to the invasion.

By July, three atomic bombs were ready. On the 16th, they tested one in the desert of New Mexico—it worked. On July 26, the United Nations demanded that Japan surrender, and warned that a refusal would result in total destruction. The Japanese refused. On the sixth of

August, the first atomic bomb was dropped on the city of Hiroshima. Beneath the mushroom cloud, 90% of the city was leveled and 66,000 of its residents were killed. Still, the Japanese refused to surrender. Three days later, a second bomb was dropped on the city of Nagasaki, killing about 80,000.

Amazingly, in the face of these two horrific demonstrations of nuclear force, some members of the emperor's council still advised him to stay the course, justifying their reckless conclusion on a hunch that the Americans had run out of A-bombs. Had the emperor followed their advice, he would have found they were right. It would take months to build another, which meant that the invasion would be launched according to schedule.

Fortunately, the emperor was not willing to risk more carnage and devastation by calling the American's bluff and cast the deciding vote to accept the allies' surrender terms. On August 14, 1945, the war finally ended.

No Place Like Home

Sixteen million Americans donned a uniform during World War II. Of that number, 2,240,000 were involved in frontline combat. Of that number, over 400,000 were killed in action. All had helped to save the world for democracy, and in the following months, there would be much fanfare celebrating that fact. There would be ceremonies, and medals, and ribbons, and parades; but for most of America's citizen-soldiers, there could be no greater reward than a salute, a handshake, a discharge, and a ride home.

Chapter 18
A World Away from Yesterday

For several days after the war's end, the country went on a wild bender that shut down nearly all enterprise and commerce; even the New York Stock Exchange closed. Servicemen were being mustered out and returning home in a steady parade that would continue for over a year. The world they were returning to would be nothing like the one they left behind.

The United States entered the war as an upstart country struggling with money problems and emerged from it the most powerful nation on earth. In the fall of 1945, America had an Omnipotent military with atomic capabilities and a gargantuan industrial infrastructure unmolested by the ravages of war, while Europe and Asia were in ruin. California alone had tripled its manufacturing capacity.

Through a series of divergent events that spawned a succession of unforeseen consequences, the Second World War set the stage for America to enter the most prosperous, productive, and influential period in its history.

Glory Days
Since the moment that golden age had passed into history, it seems that not a year goes by without some naive politician claiming their policies will return to the city, county, or state all the optimism, prosperity, and universal sense of well-being that distinguished this venerated period in American history; but they never do—they can't! For reasons so numerous and varied they're almost impossible to compile in a concise and orderly manner, this brief era of wide-ranging cheerfulness and affluence could never be even vaguely re-enacted; here's why.

The Domino Theory
The term "domino theory" is associated with a geopolitical concept that will be cited later in this chapter, but it simply implies a common chain reaction. The tipping of a single domino, within a row of dominos, sets the chain reaction in motion. It's not a perfect metaphor to describe the progression of Southern California's phenomenal post-war economic development (the process was much more chaotic than the toppling of

a neat row of dominoes would suggest) but events line up near enough to that pattern to make the term useful for our purposes. So, here is how the dominos fell—more or less.

Domino #1, Deprivation
During the great depression, industrial production dropped 50%, foreign trade fell 70%, and unemployment rose to almost 25%, which stifled consumer spending and added even more negative spin to a well-established downward spiral. During those years, much of the population was either making do, or doing without.

Domino #2, Prosperity
World War II turned the country's economy completely around. Runaway war production put the nation at full employment. People had money in their pockets and were looking to spend it on all those wonderful products they had been doing without for so many years.

Domino #3, Rationing
But nearly all consumer production was converted to war production. Maytag was making airplane parts, and Frigidaire's product line was limited to machine guns. Beyond the essentials, which were rationed, there was very little for home folks to buy.

Domino #4, Savings
So, with practically no consumer goods available, Americans bought war bonds and opened savings accounts in record numbers, collectively socking away about 150 billion dollars by the war's end. Returning soldiers also saved a substantial portion of their duty pay. Now, with the war over, and the restrictions lifted, everybody seemed to be flush with cash and desperate to begin spending.

Domino #5, Government Largesse
The Servicemen's Readjustment Act of 1944, or G.I. Bill, eased the soldier's re-acclimation to civilian life by providing ex-servicemen with low-interest home loans, business loans, college tuition loans, and even a years' worth of unemployment insurance.

Domino #6, Population Reallocation
The G.I. Bill made the vets financially independent, and that made them mobile. Many left their small towns, country farms, and big cities and headed west, to Southern California. The population surge sparked even greater demand for goods and services, which in turn, expanded employment opportunities.

Domino #7, Market Superiority
With the rest of the world shattered, the United States was left with a near-monopoly in the global marketplace. Throughout the post-war period, those in the market to buy, would buy American, and continue to do so for many years to come.

Domino #8, Industrial Superiority
Four years of all-out war had built up America's manufacturing capacity to astonishing levels of productivity. And after a brief delay in the reassignment of raw materials, industry did another quick 180° conversion from military back to domestic production, employing all the mass-production techniques they had perfected during the war.

Domino #9, Commercial Appeal
The rise in the state's population and the insatiable demand for consumer goods and services finally convinced many out-of-state enterprises (mostly retail and light manufacturing) that the time was right to establish a presence in the rapidly expanding California market. The enormous growth in new business expanded the job market beyond the limits of the labor pool.

Domino #10, Full Employment, Disposable Income, and the 8-hour Day
The ravenous consumer demand pressed industry to run at full capacity, which created a vast market for labor. The high demand, the accumulation of excess capital, and soaring population growth combined to drive wages upward to a point where even those in working-class jobs were drawing solid, middle-class incomes. With household incomes generally rising faster than expenses, many people had something left over at the end of the month, which was often spent on a host of new luxury items appearing on the consumer market.

Another new commodity now available to the post-war generation was leisure time. Workers had been pressing for an eight-hour workday since the 1860s, but it wasn't until 1938 that it became law. However, the war delayed its implementation, so it wasn't until the late 1940s that the eight-hour day finally became the norm, along with the five-day workweek and paid vacations.

Domino #11, Revolving Credit
The one-two combination of time and money touched off an explosion in the sales of luxury goods and services. Suddenly products were turning up on department store shelves that few could have imagined just ten years earlier. One such marvel was the television set, which not only brought entertainment but telemarketers right into the living room

where they preached the gospel of conspicuous consumption. And when shoppers discovered their incomes were no longer keeping pace with their buying habits, banks initiated the credit card.

For those with a hankering to keep up with the Joneses, and who had yet to learn the meaning of the words, "compound interest," it seemed as if the charge card was a magic source of free money. For many, debt would become a way of life and the credit card a ticket into the middle class.

Domino #12, Attitude!

In addition to these extraordinary circumstances, there was one other very special ingredient in Southern California's stewpot—a very strong and stirring psychological component. What really elevated this era beyond the level of a routine period of growth and prosperity and into the realm of pop-cultural legend were the veterans of World War II. The post-war era was their party; so, to understand the times, you must understand the vets.

The Soldier's Psyche

No matter where or how a soldier might have served, there was no escaping the fact that war was very dangerous business. There were no safe places; no rear areas where the war could not suddenly and violently intrude. In this environment, even those not directly engaged in combat operations restrained their expectations for the future. And then suddenly, it was over. There would be no more landings on hostile shores. Instead, they would be sent home to participate in a full-on pursuit of America's dream of life, liberty, and happiness.

Those who returned home were painfully aware of their incredibly good fortune and therefore doubly determined to leave the horrors of war behind them and reclaim the future that had been put on hold and in jeopardy.

Though they would try their best to ease back into the civilian population as if nothing had happened, there was no escaping the fact that they had become a part of an exclusive and paradoxical fraternity. Driven to succeed and do it fast, they often went back to school, married, and started families all at once. Using the G.I. Bill, they entered college in record numbers, worked harder, graduated sooner, and earned more degrees in science, mathematics, and engineering than any previous generation.

In the classroom and on the job, they were driven. Yet, at home, they longed for the tranquility and simplicity of an earlier era. To forget the turmoil and isolation of war, they aggressively sought the stability and intimacy of the family unit and embraced the domestic realm with a near-religious fervor.

In the public arena, the vets tended to be somewhat less engaged. Having done their part, they entrusted the future to those they elected to manage it, while they pursued the American Dream, which to most, amounted to no more than a job, a home, a family, and enough leisure time to enjoy the rewards of the peace and rising prosperity they had risked all to secure.

Anger and bitterness over their ordeal were rarely apparent in their demeanor; on the contrary, most returned home with an oversized sense of optimism, fun, and frivolity that would soon spread to the civilian population. This fierce determination on the part of the returning vets to seize life with both hands would energize the Southern California scene for the next two decades.

Ba, Ba, Ba Boooomm
From here, the clinking of tumbling dominos swelled up into a cacophony of booms. Southern California was booming again. The population boom led to a marriage boom, which led to a baby boom, which led to a housing boom, and boom, ba-da-boom, boom, boom...

The Wedding Bells Boom
During the late 40s, the post-war divorce rate soared. Once the fog of war had lifted, it was obvious to many young war brides and grooms that their hastily arraigned parings were terribly impetuous mistakes. Fortunately, with so little invested, either financially or emotionally, most were dissolved just as quickly as they had been established. And once the past was put right, they immediately started the whole thing all over again marrying and re-marrying in astonishing numbers. Yet, despite the "half-rushed" nature of these post-war pairings, most of the newly betrothed would keep their wedding vows for life.

The Boom in the Bassinet
There was such a rush to get back to normal that not all couples waited till after the wedding day to begin building their broods; but for those that did, the phrase "I do," was the official signal that the race towards parenthood had begun. Playing catch-up, this generation turned baby making into a national obsession. With birth rates falling since the depression, an uptick was expected, but the numbers for 1946 were remarkable.

It wasn't just a bump up in birthrates; it was a boom—a baby boom. During this period of exceptional pediatric productivity, which lasted from 1946 to 1964, over 77 million new Americans were brought into the world, with California accounting for 20% of the total. Procreation and child rearing became such a popular pastime that those without children often felt they were looked upon as low-level, cultural deviants.

So many babies, produced in so short a time, created another megaboom in the industries that served the needs of these "boomer" babies. And what a celebrated bunch they were; born into an era of extraordinary prosperity, they were the most pampered and affluent generation in history.

The boomer's influence on their parent's spending habits was so strong that the manufacturers began to cater directly to them, creating an entirely new "youth market" that would pick up many of its production cues from a new youth culture that was flourishing out on the west coast.

Boom in a Box

During the war, the housing shortage was so acute that many defense workers had to be put up in warehouses, schoolrooms, and even empty jail cells. Now, with new residents arriving daily, the demand for housing was limitless. But the old mom & pop construction outfits that once monopolized the business were not prepared to meet the need. Instead, a brand-new species of Southern Californian would arise to address the challenge— the real-estate developer.

Just as it was with the gold rush and forever thereafter, California did not evolve—it exploded! The sudden population boom set off a housing boom that would not subside for decades. Residential development companies formed by the hundreds, bought land, divided it into lots and grids, and, using mass production techniques and new materials developed during the war, erected new subdivisions faster than weeds would grow.

Suburbanation

The three most important words in the real-estate have always been, "location, location, location," and during expansive post-war years, the location that nearly 80% of Southern California's new residents considered most desirable was suburbia.

As seen in the glossy pages of popular publications like *Sunset* and *Better Homes and Gardens*, suburbia promised a family-oriented refuge away from the crime and congestion of the city and the isolation of the backcountry farm. And with the low interest, government-backed G. I. and FHA loans, returning vets fled the apartments and row houses of the pre-war period in favor of single-family homes with built-in appliances, picture windows, and yards with outdoor patios.

Will the Bough Break?

The overheated economy was spreading prosperity to every corner of the Southland, but it was a false economy based on a series of unusual and unrepeatable circumstances and certain to cool down once consumer demand was stabilized, and our foreign competitors re-grouped and re-entered the world marketplace.

When that time arrived, many worried that the US economy might, once again, sink into a depression. To support the vibrant and expansive, Arcadian-like empire that was evolving, the Southland would have to develop a solid industrial base that would take in billions and insulate the region from all the ups and downs of the real-world marketplace—an industry so wide-ranging and so scandalously lucrative that no one would even dream of such a possibility out loud.

Set em' Up Joe!

When the wheels of economic progress need a good greasing, merchants and manufacturers usually look to their elected officials to create the conditions in which business and industry can prosper. And, in a roundabout way, that's exactly what happened in the Southland; a bureaucrat did indeed facilitate unbelievable growth in the business sector. Others would do their part in the years ahead, but none would ever do more to enhance the fortunes of the Southern California region than Premier Joseph Stalin of the Union of Soviet Socialist Republics.

At war's end, the two most powerful nations on earth could not have been more diametrically opposed, with America, the capitalist, democratic republic, and Russia the totalitarian, communist regime.

The Russians took possession of Eastern Europe and the eastern half of Germany, while the allies took control of Western Europe, the western half of Germany, and the western half of the city of Berlin, which was right in the middle of Russia's half.

Seeing a democracy flourish within their own borders was not a situation that Stalin could warm up to, and so he closed all access roads through East Germany to force the westerners out. But the United States simply jumped the blockade with an around-the-clock airlift program to re-supply the western sectors and Stalin eventually backed down.

The Russians re-opened the roads and the Americans shut down their flying circus, but all had not returned to normal. Both sides had shown their hands, and the incident kicked off a Cold War between the United States and Russia, which would last for 43 years.

The War Horn of Plenty

The Berlin Airlift was considered a great victory for the west, but it was very short-lived. With both sides presenting a very clear and present danger to the other, there seemed to be only one logical course of action—arm up!

The incident in Berlin signaled the start of an arms race between the United States and the Soviet Union that would launch a second California gold rush, this time in the southern part of the state, which would bring billions of dollars in government contracts and legions of the most highly educated, highly skilled personnel to the west coast, completely restructuring the business culture from one led by the retirement and tourist industries, to one dominated by defense, aviation, and aerospace.

The Korean War

At the end of World War II, the tiny peninsula of Korea was also jointly occupied by the two great post-war superpowers. Divided at the 38th parallel, the United States held sway in the south, while the Soviets dominated the north.

One did not have to be an expert in foreign affairs to see that, here again, the possibility of another crisis erupting was very real. And on June 25, 1950, the cold war suddenly flared up red-hot in the first attempt by a communist regime to gain territory by conquest. America's answer to the problem was to implement a policy of containment—keep the communist regimes within their post-war boarders. So, to discourage any expansionist exercises, the North Koreans (who were backed by the Chinese and the Soviets) would have to be forcibly put back in their place.

> **The Domino Theory**
> This assumption that, as one country falls to communism, others will follow is the principal behind the domino theory.

Not yet five years after the end of the second war to end all wars, it was war all over again—again! As in the last one, the Southland's proximity to the battlefield, its numerous military bases, and its fully operational defense industries and infrastructure made it the focal point of another surge of military activity.

After three years of fighting, the two sides advanced and retreated themselves right back to the 38th parallel when a new warrior president, Dwight D. Eisenhower, compelled the North Koreans to agree to an armistice by implying the possibility of a nuclear response. It was a very high-stakes bluff that, for a brief few years, proved to be an effective peace-keeping strategy.

With the combatants back behind their original pre-war borders, it would appear that the fighting had accomplished nothing; but the world had tilted considerably during the three-year conflict. The communist Chinese made their presence felt in their first solo outing on the world stage. The Soviets measured the resolve of their cold war adversaries and initiated a massive arms buildup in anticipation of the perceived threat. The United States had shown they would use force to challenge communist aggression and initiated a massive arms buildup in anticipation of the perceived threat.

The Fireworks Factory

By the end of the Korean War, orders were coming in from every branch of the service for jet fighters, bombers, and support aircraft of every description; for smaller, lighter, and more powerful nuclear warheads; for ballistic missiles, and every other imaginable military contrivance known to exist or yet to be conceived.

During the next ten years, the United States would increase its defense spending by nearly 250% and award over 25% of all its manufacturing contracts and over 40% of its research contracts to California, with about 90% of those California contracts going to Los Angeles and San Diego.

All this cold war creation and construction required a huge quantity of human capital, and so the state put out the "help wanted" sign.

The Brain Pirates

Despite a dramatic rise in college enrollments, it was not nearly enough to satisfy the defense industry's insatiable need for highly trained personnel. To fill the void, defense contractors and research institutions hired recruiters, or "brain pirates," to canvas the nation in search of the most suitable prospects.

At job fairs, in newspaper ads, and on television commercials from coast to coast, those with the proper credentials were wooed out west with the promise of good jobs, affordable housing in the sun-soaked suburbs, and a chance to become a part of the new and unique civilization developing along the shores of the Pacific.

These nationwide campaigns attracted applicants from not just the nation but from all over the world. Bucolic San Diego, the sleepy little "Lisbon of the Pacific," had more PhDs than any other city in the nation. Twenty-six Nobel Prize winners in science called Southern California home. Over twenty percent of the Southland's workforce held doctorate degrees. And as the region absorbed more and more of the nation's more sophisticated, well-traveled, and well-educated citizens, the frontier gave way to the future.

"To the genre of archetypal Californians -- the 49er, the rancher, the Hollywood producer, the real estate developer -- was now added, the defense research scientist and/or engineer." Kevin Starr

And by the late-50s, this space-age, technological juggernaut was being hailed as a shining beacon of America's preeminence in the field, when, in fact, it was only one earth orbit away from a monumental public relations debacle and widespread condemnation as an association of slipshod arms merchants and second-rate scientific slackers—or words to that effect.

Sputniked!

On the evening of October 4th, 1957, US military monitoring facilities began receiving a strange signal from above. Was it a radio transmission of an approaching enemy plane, or a greeting from another galaxy? No, it was just a steady beep, beep, beep that signaled to the world that the Russians had beaten the Americans into outer space.

The following morning the headlines revealed that, for the next three months, a Russian satellite called Sputnik would circle the earth every ninety minutes. And with this puny orb no bigger than a beach ball, the Russians shook the United States to its core. On that cold day of awakening, panicked Americans had only four questions for their leaders: What is it? How did they do it? What are they doing up there? And how come we didn't do it first?

Knowing a successful launch would serve as a powerful symbol of the triumph of Soviet command and control ideology over America's free enterprise system, the Russians played it for maximum PR punch, polishing the much larger booster rocket, which trailed in orbit just behind Sputnik, to a mirror-like luster that reflected so much light it could easily be observed from any patio lounge chair as it passed overhead. 18-1

Upon realizing the implications of the Soviet's shocking accomplishment, a sudden outbreak of mild hysteria gripped the nation. If the Russians had rockets that could launch satellites into orbit, couldn't they launch warheads, or drop bombs, or shoot death rays from space! Imaginations ran wild, but the fear soon gave way to outrage over the perception that the people had been hoodwinked by their government's frequent claims that America was technologically way out ahead of those backward Bolsheviks.

> *"The beep of Sputnik is an intercontinental outer-space raspberry to a decade of American pretensions that the American way of life was a gilt-edged guarantee of our material superiority."* Clare Booth Luce

Newspapers from coast to coast mercilessly ridiculed the Eisenhower administration, the military, and the nation's defense contractors for their arrogance in dismissing the Russians as a serious threat to, what was thought to be, America's technological supremacy.

Michigan's clever governor Williams cloaked his contempt in poetic wordplay:

"Oh little Sputnik, flying high
With made-in-Moscow beep
You tell the world it's a Commie sky
And Uncle Sam's asleep
You say on fairway and on rough
The Kremlin knows it all
We hope our golfer knows enough
To get us on the ball"

And there was still a world of hurt yet to come. On November 3, 1957, not one month after the Sputnik launch, they launched a Sputnik 2 that shuttled the first astronaut (a dog) into outer space. So, while all of America looked to the heavens in shock and awe, the Russians had house pets flying rings around us.

America appeared to be totally outclassed. Public pressure to prove that the United States could challenge the Russians forced Eisenhower to push forward a launch that was not scheduled to take place for another year.

On December 6, 1957, with the entire world watching on TV, the Vanguard rocket, along with its Explorer 1 satellite, blew up on the launchpad. The media described the event as a "kaputnik," and a "flopnik," and suggested that maybe America's rocketeers should just "stayputnik." But they did not stayputnik; instead, they enlisted the aid of Nazi rocketmeister, Wernher von Braun, and with his assistance, Explorer 1 finally made it into orbit atop the more reliable Juno booster rocket on January 31st, 1958.

Had the Russians not already been there and done that, the launch of an American satellite into space might have been cause for a national day of celebration; but as it was, the launch was viewed as a "me too" stunt produced by a nation that had fallen far behind the competition.

The crisis of confidence created by the Sputnik incident prompted the federal government to inject even more government treasure into the Southland's aerospace industry. To try and catch up with the Soviets, Congress created The National Aeronautics and Space Administration (NASA) in July of 1958, and much of their work would be conducted in Southern California. Two months later, Congress passed The National Defense Education Act providing extra funding to schools and universities that placed heavy emphasis on science, mathematics, and engineering, which included nearly all Southern California learning institutions.

The United States and the Soviet Union were now fully committed to both an arms and a space race. For the next ten years, each side burned through trillions trying to top each other's manned missions into space with the ultimate goal of being the first nation on earth to place a man on the moon.

High Tide

In the Southern California of the 1950s and 60s, the defense and aerospace industries generated the high tide that lifted all other boats. So much money flowing into the Southland attracted a whole new generation of young seekers from every other state in the nation. If you had the high-tech skills necessary to work in "the industries" then you had a job—a very good job.

And even if you weren't a rocket scientist, you still had a job, for there were hundreds of acres of new businesses spreading out over the old farmlands every day. Between the war's end and the moon landing, personal average incomes would increase three-fold, making Southern California's wage scale nearly 30% higher than the rest of the nation. And upon this rock-solid economic foundation, Southern Californians would build themselves a paradise.

Chapter 19
Futurama

When the United States entered the war, in 1942, its frontline fighter plane was an underpowered, outclassed prop and piston job with a top speed of 360 mph. Just five years later, Captain Chuck Yeager flew his Bell Labs X-1 rocket plane over 800mph, breaking the sound barrier and ushering the nation into the jet age, the age of the future.

From 43,000 feet above the Mojave Desert, the supersonic boom of the X-1 signaled the start of a new, and much improved, future. After nearly two decades of depression and war, Americans were eager to forget the past and move on to what was expected to be a brighter tomorrow, and here was a sign from above that we were already well on our way.

No other single event could better illustrate the speed at which the old world transitioned into the new. Having squeezed decades of scientific and technological progress into four short years, the sheer number, significance, and speed with which these developments were now being thrust upon the public consciousness made them almost impossible to comprehend.

Overhead, vapor trails crisscrossed the sky as the Southland's leading aeronautics firms tested the latest versions of high-altitude jet planes. Two months after Yeager's historic flight, Bell Labs demonstrated the transistor— a much smaller, lighter, and cooler running device than the 40-year-old vacuum tube it would replace as the primary component in electronic circuitry, making possible a whole new array of products unimaginable just a few years earlier. And not thirty days after that, Bob Hope signed on the air for the first television broadcast of Los Angeles's new station, KTLA.

Suddenly, it seemed that the future of twenty years hence had erupted in the here and now. An outbreak of optimism swept through the population, the symptoms of which included a passionate belief in a future that promised continued improvement in the quality of life on earth through modern technology.

After all, having tapped into the power of atomic energy, how long would it be before that mysterious force would be powering every conceivable device both real and yet to be imagined. One look at Yeager's, Flash Gordon style, rocket plane begged the question, how far off can a trip to the moon really be? The moon! Why not Mars, or maybe even Jupiter?

This mass euphoria, motivated by growing prosperity, jet-age technology, and an expectation of lasting world peace, was swiftly picked up on by advertisers, marketers, and manufacturers who, along with their legions of admen and designers, would visually interpret the hopeful mood of the times through a kaleidoscope of jet-age, modernist imagery.

For the look of tomorrow, commercial artists and product designers took the sleek, aerodynamical features of jets and rockets and grafted them onto an entire galaxy of new consumer products. The future had become the fashion statement of the post-war era, and it would find representation in nearly every nuance of our existence.

Raise the Roof

The war was over, and a flood of new residents were moving into the state in search of the California Dream, which usually began with the acquisition of a home in the suburbs. Unfortunately, there weren't near enough to go around. Southern California was short about 650,000 single-family homes and the demand was only expected to increase.

Ten years earlier, the situation would have easily overwhelmed the hand-made housing industry, but the post-war developers determined that by utilizing the same standardization and mass-production techniques they had developed during the war, the Southern California housing industry would be able to catch up to the demand for new homes—in about 20 years.

> **The Cpop Era**
> The next 20 years or so are often referred to as the golden age or the glory days of Southern California. But I would like to use my own term; I'd like to call it the California Pop, or "Cpop" era, which spanned the mid to late 1940s to the mid to late 1960s, when Southern California was considered one of the nation's most attractive and desirable locations.

New Yorker, William Levitt, is often given credit for constructing the first low-cost, mass-produced, residential community in the United States; but similar developments could be found in Southern California several years before he broke ground for his legendary Levittown in 1947.

One of the first of these low-cost, worker housing projects to get underway was in Linda Vista just a few miles northeast of San Diego. On thin, concrete foundations, 40 houses a day were built in assembly-line fashion using prefabricated wall and roof sections. The development included 3000 identical, single-family homes and an adjacent 13-acre shopping center.

This arrangement of prefab, mass-produced, residential housing with neighboring shopping mall was copied several times during the war, and it became the standard layout for many of the post-war developments of the 1950s and 60s.

Mass Moderne

Out in the suburbs, countless developers bought land, subdivided it, and built endless rows of painfully plain, modest, and nearly identical, two and three-bedroom tract homes with equally modest and identical front and back yards.

Humble as they were, for many, these tract houses represented a valid entree into the middle-class and were so popular that eager homebuyers often had to wait in line to be herded through the model homes, which were already featuring many of the new marvels of the modern age like Formica countertops, vinyl flooring, built-in electric ranges, self-cleaning ovens, and frost-free refrigerators.

Of course, these were not the homes that graced the covers of *Sunset* or *Better Homes and Gardens* magazines. In the Southland's overheated real-estate market, this was the bargain basement. There were no glass walls or spacious open floor plans, but this was where most of us lived the California Dream, and did so with a surprising degree of panache thanks to a fast-growing, new industry in aftermarket home accessories that made it possible for any home, no matter how humble, to be transformed into a modernist showplace with adjoining outdoor tropical oasis—Adventureland on the quarter acre.
19-1

As for those homebuyers solidly positioned within the upper tiers of the middle class, they often opted for those iconic new California Ranch homes.

Rancho Internationale

Among the short list of celebrated Southland architects of the mid-20th century, Cliff May was an anomaly. He was not a European immigrant, but a local boy who could trace his maternal roots back to the days of the great ranchos. He was not a university-trained architect, but a college dropout with absolutely no interest in the field of architecture.

"I never ever thought of building houses—never." Cliff May

A talented saxophonist, he led a jazz band and planned on pursuing a career in music. But when it became clear that talent and hard work were no guarantee of success, he enrolled at San Diego State College, in 1932, to pursue a business degree. To support himself, the entrepreneurially inclined May designed and built reproductions of the

Monterey-style furniture he remembered from his childhood. When his future father-in-law, a real-estate agent, expressed frustration over a stubborn listing, May suggested that one of his custom-made living room sets might enhance its appeal; it did, and the house sold. The scheme was repeated on another home, and it sold as well.

Realizing he had stumbled upon a potentially lucrative enterprise, May dropped out of college to devote full-time to his fledgling furniture business, when it occurred to him that he might do even better with his furniture if he designed a house to go with it.

Having gained some local press notoriety for his entrepreneurship in the midst of a depression, he was able to find a contractor just desperate enough to back a series of spec homes designed by a twenty-three-year-old college dropout with no experience in architecture. For the design of these landmark dwellings, May would again draw upon his memories of the adobe homes of his childhood.

The result was a handful of charming, rancho-styled homes made to look even more charmingly rustic by mimicking the haphazard construction techniques and decorative flourishes of the original, Native American builders. It was this attention to authentic detail that made May's houses stand out from the numerous, faint imitations builders had been cranking out for years.

> **Son of the Sons of the Southland**
> May's mother's ancestral home was the Casa de Estudillo, aka Ramona's Marriage Place, in Old Town, San Diego.

Favorable media coverage helped to sell his little "Haciendas" before the loans came due, but their $9,500 price tag greatly limited the potential buyer pool. So, to lower costs and broaden his product's appeal, May began making design changes. He replaced the clay tile roofs and plaster walls with the shake shingles and board & batten siding of a bungalow, added the oversized windows of the International Style, and called the new model, the "Rancheria."

May's traditional-looking Rancheria homes were even more popular than his Hacienda design, which brought him to the attention of a Los Angeles developer for whom he designed real ranch homes for several upscale subdivisions. He might have continued in this exclusive vein were it not for the intrusion of the war and his experience designing mass-produced, prefabricated housing for defense workers.

Like Lautner, May was open to the use of any new process or material that would enhance the appeal and/or lower the cost of his premier creation. After the war, he had combined what he had learned building high-end estates and low-cost defense digs and turned the humble little Rancheria into the quintessential California Ranch House.

Distinguishing characteristics included ground-level foundations and Low-pitched, rough-hewn, shake shingle roofs. Wrapped in rusticated, board and batten siding, they often used non-functional farmhouse-style flourishes to round out the frontier motif. Inside, the pastoral effect was maintained with knotty-pine paneling and vaulted ceilings with exposed beams and rafters.

Incorporating the open floorplan of the International Style created an illusion of expansive square footage. From the street, the California Ranch presented a traditional appearance, but from the backside, it was all mid-century modern. Like Wright's Prairie School homes, May's ranchers focused attention on the rear of the house where the walls facing out to the patio and fenced yard were almost entirely of glass.

Driven by his own personal preferences and not design school dogma, he heedlessly mixed frontier primitive with ultra-modern, and was able to exaggerate the latter and still maintain a sense of the former by adding countrified embellishments. The public's response to May's new California Ranch House was immediate and overwhelmingly favorable. His clever blending of the familiar with the futuristic, and the cozy connection he created with the out-of-doors blended so well with the relaxed and casual California lifestyle that May's ranchers came to represent the trademark, Southern California, residential experience.

Throughout the Southland, May's own company would build about 1000 of his dream homes; and when he couldn't keep up with the demand himself, he began selling his ranch house plans, and even entire homes, in kit-form, to other builders who would best his output many times over. Gradually, as the 1940s passed into the 1950s, and the ranch house style spread throughout the region, it shed its frontier facade in favor of the new modern look; and it was through this evolution of the California Ranch house that Southlanders learned to accept, to appreciate, and even to rejoice in the mid-century, modernist milieu.

Retaking the Road

During the last quarter of 1945, and continuing into the following year, a similar scene played out over and over again. After all the welcome home hoopla had subsided, war-weary gearheads would quietly slip out the back door, jump-start the old jalopy, and take that first solemn, solo spin around town. It was a milestone event in the lives of many a returning soldier, and possibly the setting for a last few moments of quiet introspection before it was back to business as usual in a field that had broadened considerably in the years since they shipped out.

Numbering in the hundreds before the war, the number of post-war auto enthusiasts, in just the L.A. area alone, shot up into the thousands and was escalating daily. Local boys returning home were joined by an army of new hot rodders from all over the country. A lot of these guys came back with new skill sets developed in the military's motor pools, aviation facilities, and engineering units, which raised the overall level of post-war car craft immeasurably.

In addition to the returning vets, there were thousands of new, "teenaged" drivers—the first to own their own cars in any significant numbers. Established car clubs quickly regrouped and expanded, while new ones formed to absorb the younger converts to the craft.

Kustom Kalifornia

Among the most talented and imaginative of the new, post-war league of Southern California, automotive alterationists were the Brothers Barris of Sacramento.

Inauspiciously starting out with a well battered Buick, 14-year-old Sam, and his 10-year-old brother George beat the body back to near original form with bricks and stones and then laid on a fresh coat of house paint. Custom hubcaps were fashioned from dinner plates, and the grillwork was accented with drawer knobs.

Though the execution of this early Barris custom was a bit inelegant, it sold straight away and launched the careers of the most celebrated custom car builders in hot rod history.

Their first fully customized car was completed while George was still in high school; but just as momentum was beginning to build, the war broke out. Sam joined the Navy, and underage George signed on with the Merchant Marines who sent him down to L.A. for assignment aboard a ship that never came in.

When the war ended, Sam joined his brother in LA where the two opened their first body shop, "Barris Brother's Custom Shop." For the Barris boys, and the dozens of others like them, auto-art was more about style than substance. It was a

---

A Strange New Breed

Teenagers did not walk the earth until the mid-twentieth century. Prior to that time, there existed young people, youngsters, and adolescents, but there were no teenagers. It wasn't until 1941, when *Popular Science Magazine* put the word in print, that the teenager came into being. And, though the distinction might seem to be no more than a matter of simple semantics, the circumstances of the pre-war youngster, as compared to the post-war teenager, were very far removed. Prior to World War II, there was no transitional period between childhood and adulthood. Adult responsibility often intruded at a very early age. But post-war prosperity made it possible for a single wage-earner to support an entire family in reasonable comfort. Mothers stayed home, and teenagers stayed in school and enjoyed a degree of freedom and financial independence unknown to any previous generation.

"looks matter" approach to automotive styling they called "Kustom Kulture." Where the hot rodders focused on the development of the power train, the customizers lavished their attention on interior and exterior appearance.

With the emphasis on aesthetics, any car could be considered a candidate for a custom makeover. And though there were no hard, fast rules, the Barris brothers laid down some fairly rigid guidelines with their first major post-war creation, a 1941 Buick convertible.

Like the new residential housing models, the emphasis was on the horizontal. The top was chopped, and the roofline lowered. The body was lowered on the frame—nose raked upwards and the tail practically dragging on the ground.

In the smorgasbord style of those pre-war auto re-fabricators, the grillwork was Cadillac and the bumpers Oldsmobile. Taillights were mounted in the bumpers and headlights were "Frenched" or molded into the fenders, which were molded into the body. And just as if they were working from the Bauhaus book of style, all exterior ornamentation was removed.

Sculpted to perfection, and coated in several layers of deep maroon lacquer, the car was a sensation and established this mid-century California chopped, dropped, and stripped-clean style of custom makeover as a hallmark of its time that is still popular with many hot rodders today.

Strange Music

Although missionaries and traders had been facilitating some cross-pollination of musical styles between east and west since the days of the Roman Empire, the origins of the exotica music craze that swept the United States in the 1950s and 60s didn't really begin to develop until the advent of the great European expositions of the late 19th century.

In 1889, the grandest of them all, the Exposition Universelle brought much of the world to downtown Paris. Folk musicians from nearly every continent performed to the delight and amazement of the public and many of Europe's most adventurous, impressionist composers. It wasn't long after these foreign players returned home that their influence began to be heard in the works of those composers who had gone to the fair.

Strange sounding scales, modes, and intervals were integrated into the concert works of European impressionists in their own aural interpretations of far-off fantasylands. For the most part, these exotic interludes were not true interpretations of native music, but western-styled simulations of foreign folk idioms. Yet, over the next 40 years, these otherworldly musical modes became familiar elements of western music and would become even more familiar to audiences around the world when American composers used them to provide accompaniment to countless Hollywood films.

Woven into the soundtrack of any biblical epic, Arabian Nights fantasy, or Oriental dream you will hear passages influenced by the European impressionists of the late 19th century who themselves were influenced by those folk artists they encountered at the Exposition Universelle. But by the mid-1940s, these once-revolutionary musical idioms had become standard, Hollywood clichés ripe for re-interpretation. And none of Hollywood's great sound stylists ever got more re-interpretive mileage out of an old musical cliché than Les Baxter.

Smells like Moon Pop

Like most musical prodigies, Les Baxter followed the traditional trajectory of the concert artist, with years of piano lessons and recitals culminating in a serious musical education at a prestigious conservatory. And that's where this story abruptly ends—at least the traditional part. Midway through his conservatory training, Baxter went over the wall. He packed his bags and headed out west, to Los Angeles. There he dove headfirst into the multifaceted, musical jungle that was Hollywood.

He started out playing tenor sax and writing arraignments for a swing band. He sang bass in a vocal group, backing up many of the current vocal luminaries. His growing reputation as a gifted musician and arranger got him work at NBC Radio singing live commercial jingles and conducting and arraigning for the Bob Hope and Abbott and Costello Shows. From there, he began to get work conducting and arraigning recording sessions for the top artists of the day. And then, right out of the blue, Capitol Records asked him to make a record of his own. They had no particular plan in mind—just any old thing Baxter thought might catch the public's fancy.

The recording budget was modest, but as a consolation, Baxter was given a free hand in the studio, and he made the most of it. He hired a Broadway tunesmith and assembled an eclectic ensemble made up of piano, harp, flute, cello, French horn, a few odd drums, a mixed choir that sang only oohs and aahs, and a Theremin (a bizarre electronic instrument that produced eerie sounds by waving hands over its two antennae) played by a local podiatrist.

The record was called *Music Out of the Moon*, and why not. It certainly wasn't like anything anyone had heard on this planet. It was part classical concerto, part Broadway musical, part science fiction soundtrack, and all Baxter. It was light and ethereal and bold and bombastic; it was familiar as a Sunday afternoon radio show and as otherworldly as a trip through the cosmos. And the most amazing thing of all was that it was a hit.

Eager to repeat the success of *Music Out of the Moon*, RCA Records commissioned Baxter to arrange, conduct, and produce another off-the-wall project sponsored by a French perfume manufacturer. The idea was to convey a variety of scents as three-minute pop tunes. This time, along with the crew from *Music Out of the Moon*, Baxter was given a symphony orchestra to play with.

In *Perfume Set to Music*, he deftly blended light jazz styles with elements of classical, pop, and swing. It's doubtful this album had any effect on the olfactory glands, but it defiantly had an uplifting effect on RCA's bottom line. Again, in the most unlikely of circumstances, Baxter scored another hit with a new, mesmerizingly eccentric style of music not fully defined, yet clearly exposing a willingness among Southlanders of the post-war period to gamely embrace the whimsically exotic, which would encourage further experimentation in the very near future.

Surfing's Mad Scientist

It's a familiar irony that life seems to bear down harder upon those it grants the greater gifts, and Bob Simmons was no exception. In 1935, when he was 16, he developed a cancerous growth on his left ankle. When a doctor recommended amputation, his mother panicked and took him to a holistic healer who prescribed a strict diet of fruits and grains.

A dubious remedy that produced astonishing results, for, within a matter of months, the tumor was gone. But then tragedy struck again when he took up bicycling to strengthen his weakened limb and was hit by a car. Now, in addition to his withered leg, he was laid up with a broken arm, a cracked skull, and a fractured elbow. When his surgeon recommended he get back on the bike and resume his exercise program, a well-meaning fellow patient suggested he take up surfing instead. Once again, therapy would lead to tragedy; but not before he had designed nearly every feature of the modern surfboard.

When his long recovery period forced him out of high school, Simmons took the entrance exam for the California Institute of Technology, passed the test, got admitted, and maintained straight A's in engineering without ever having cracked a textbook. Finally, in 1939, after several years on the mend, he borrowed a Blake hollow board and learned to surf with the help of a surly San Onofre regular named Gard Chapin.

With his handicaps, success did not come easy; but he stuck with it and became a competent, if somewhat awkward, surfer. When the war broke out, Simmons took a job as a machinist and worked with Chapin building cabinets and a few plank surfboards.

By the time the war had ended, Simmons was working as a mathematician, cranking out aerodynamic formulas for Douglas Aircraft, when he got to wondering whether similar scientific principles might be applied to the lowly surfboard. After all, it was 1946, and he was making and riding the same plank-style boards that George Freeth rode 40 years before. So, he purchased a naval engineering manual and set out to re-invent the surfboard based on the solid, scientific principles of fluid dynamics.

He began by modifying old plank boards. Grafting an extra piece of wood onto the nose, he shaped it into something like the upturned prow of a boat. This helped to prevent its digging into the wave or pearling. He added a fin and gave the sides, or rails, a rounded, more streamlined treatment, reducing drag and increasing speed.

At about eight feet long, his boards were on the short side, and with the up-turned nose, they vaguely resembled a giant spoon, which earned them the nickname, "Simmons' Spoons." He planned to test his new designs at San Onofre, but the clannish "San O" crowd was openly hostile to the asocial Simmons and his strange-looking boards, so he followed a path of less resistance and moved his testing operation way up north to a lonely little spot called Malibu.

Simmons was not the first to surf at Malibu; Tom Blake and a friend had assayed the waves at Malibu back in 1927. However, for most surfers of the pre-war period, Malibu was a bit out of the way, and its faster, steeper waves, which tracked hard right, were not as well-suited to their old plank and hollow boards as the slow-rolling swells at Palos Verdes or San Onofre. But Simmons, in altering the specs of the surfboard, was inadvertently altering where and how it could and would be ridden.

Gettin' Glassed

As Simmons delved deeper into the pages of his engineering manual, he came across references to a process the Germans had developed during the war, in which a strong, lightweight, protective surface could be made by coating a course fabric of glass fibers with a polyester resin. He began experimenting with the fiberglass process, but only to patch damaged areas and add extra protection around the nose of his boards. It was one of his young helpers who, when confronted with the exacting requirements of a very unusual custom order, would take it to the next logical step, by using fiberglass as a protective coating for an entire surfboard.

Board Basics

Maneuverability-wise, pre-war planks and hollows would fall into the ponderous category. Their length (usually 12 to 15 feet) made them prone to pearling. They also couldn't turn very well without a fin, so it was harder to stay on a steady course. For a lot of the older surfers, Malibu wasn't worth the hassle.

Pre-war surfing style was built around the limitations of the plank board. Surfers stood upright, faced forward with feet planted shoulder-width apart, and rode straight into shore. The majestic style of the Hawaiian kings had been the Southland surfer's modus operandi for years and few of the old guard welcomed any changes to that ancient formula, but Simmons was doing just that. All the whittling down and hydro-shaping of his spoons made them a bit lighter and faster, and with the stabilizing fins, able to follow the trajectory of a wave in any direction at nearly any angle.

His presence at Malibu attracted the attention of other, younger surfers, turning his test sessions into impromptu marketing demonstrations. And as those who watched him surf, and bought his odd-looking spoons, discovered how well they performed in Malibu's more complex and challenging waveforms, San Onofre's "most favored surf spot" status began to fade. By the decade's end, Simmons' boards were the most sought after on the beach, and Malibu, the most popular break on the west coast.

Case Studies

Though the California ranch house was by far, the most popular housing model available to middle-class homebuyers, it was not the only option. Anticipating Southern California's post-war housing boom, John Entenza, the editor of *Arts and Architecture* magazine, and a committed champion of the modernist movement sponsored an experimental house-building project, which broke ground just before the war ended.

His objective was to sell the public on the merits of the International Style by demonstrating how new, modern-style homes, could be made faster and cheaper than common tract homes yet still project an image of unadorned elegance.

Knowing unrestrained modernism would face stiff resistance, Entenza hand-picked a group of architects based on their reputation for "reasonableness." These were artisans he felt he could rely on to suppress years of radical design theory for the good of his cause. Clients who took part in the program provided the financing and interested building manufacturers made donations in exchange for advertising rights. The finished homes were put on public display for a predetermined period and then turned over to their new owners.

The first few projects, more or less, held to Entenza's keep it cheap and reasonable credo, but it wasn't long before the program went off-script.

With the Case Study program, Entenza re-proved what Irving Gill had pre-proved 30 years before—the hoi polloi don't do modern! Among the usual artists and professionals willing to buy modern, reasonable wasn't a selling point, so most of the Case Study homes turned out to be larger, more expensive, and much more exotic than originally intended.

> **Little Glass Houses**
> Pierre Koenig's Case Study house #22, built in 1960, emerged as the standout of the program. Built on a cliffside overlooking the city, the L-shaped structure was walled entirely in glass. Even Julius Shulman's through-the-glass-wall photograph of two women chatting in the living room with the lights of Los Angeles twinkling in the background has itself become a familiar icon of the times.

The program lasted from 1945 to 1966, and in that time, 28 homes were built; each one an affirmation of the optimism of the moment set in stone, glass, steel, and concrete. But most of these masterworks were located in private enclaves, behind security gates, or up on hillsides high above, and far removed from the well-traveled, public thoroughfares.

Very few of us actually saw a case study house, much less lived in one. In order for the rest of us to get behind the modernist movement, a new, post-war generation of Southern California architects would have to drag it down to street level.

Heaps of Heaps

With many years' worth of savings stockpiled and new consumer products trickling back into the marketplace, Americans were buying again, and a new car was at the top of nearly everyone's shopping list. Yet, in the midst of this sizzling hot seller's market, Detroit had nothing new to offer. In the conversion back to peacetime production, it would take at least three years to turn out a new model; all they had in the pipeline was old, pre-war stock. But they were not about to miss this once-in-a-lifetime consumer rampage, so they repackaged the old 1941 models and sold them as 1946 models, and 1947 models, and 1948 models. It wasn't until the 1949 model year that Detroit began to show signs of stylistic and technological progress, but the public didn't seem to care at all; they were determined to buy a new car no matter how old it was.

As Detroit was racking up record sales numbers throughout the late forties and on into the early fifties, the used car market was flooded with the pre-war models nobody wanted. Used cars could be had cheap, and the off brands (anything that wasn't a Ford) could be had even cheaper. Any kid with a semi-liberal allowance, a part-time job, or even a paper route could buy a used car. Here, in great abundance, was the raw material for a movement that would become a centerpiece of the Southern California experience at mid-century.

Nearly half the cars sold in the 30s were Fords, and most came V8 equipped, making the once out-of-reach power plant readily available at fire-sale prices. And as more and more gearheads acquired these cars and discovered how well the flathead, or "flatty," responded to performance tweaking, it rapidly replaced the old "T mill" as the cornerstone of American hot rodding.

From 1945 to around 1958, most hot rods, no matter their original marque, were powered by the venerated Ford flathead V8.

The Girly's Man

After the war, Joe Quigg and his friend Matt Kivlin began hanging around Bob Simmon's workshop helping him build his unique creations and learning the art of surfboard design and construction as taught by the prickly, mad scientist of surf.

Like most savants, Simmons had little patience for those of lesser abilities, and perhaps it was due to his reputation for incivility that when surfer Tommy Zahn wanted to place an order for a custom surfboard, he came to the sorcerer's apprentice rather than the sorcerer.

> **Deuces Wild**
>
> With the practice of engine swapping becoming so commonplace, any model car could be transformed into a bonafide hot rod, and nearly all of them were, but the Fords were favored over all others, and among the Fords, two models stood out as the most desirable of the lot—the 1932 roadsters and coupes. Referred to as "deuces" for the number two in their model year, they were especially prized for their light weight, short wheelbase, and brawny V8 engines. Re-modeled on the stripped down, minimalist style favored by the dry lakes racers they came to symbolize the traditional California hot rod of the mid-century era.
>
> **Deuces Forever**
>
> Thirty years after these cars started showing up on the street, the Beach Boys released their 1963 hit single, "*Little Deuce Coupe*," which serves as a testament to the iconic status and enduring popularity of the 1932 Fords.

Though he had no theatrical experience, Tommy Zahn had the kind of star-quality good looks Hollywood careers could be made of, and for that reason alone, 20th Century Fox signed him to a short-term, player's contract. It was while he was at the studio being groomed for a run at stardom that he met Darrilyn, the seventeen-year-old daughter of Fox's main mogul, Darryl Zanuck. The two began dating, and when Darrilyn expressed an interest in Tommy's favorite pastime, he went to Joe Quigg with a special request—build a board light enough for a girl to carry, short enough to fit in her sporty convertible, and very easy to ride.

To meet the weight requirements, Quigg used balsa wood. He carefully selected the lightest plank he could find and shaped it to spoon specs. To protect the absorbent balsa, he decided to skip the labor-intensive fifteen coats of varnish and just seal the whole thing in a single coat of fiberglass. The result was a 10-foot squaretail that weighed only 40 pounds.

When Zahn took it out for a test run, he was amazed at how nimble it was. On a beach date, he presented his gift and then borrowed it. His friends borrowed it; even strangers borrowed it. Darrilyn did get to use it some, but as soon as she came in from the surf, the board went back out on loan. It became such a popular attraction it was christened the "Darrilyn Board," although Quigg preferred to call it his "easy rider" model.

Those seasoned surfers who took it out for a spin would never admit they enjoyed riding a "girly board," so a great show was always made to impress upon all observers that they were only out for a lark; but there was obviously something special about that board. Yet, at the time, no one, not even its creator, suspected that this beginner's toy would turn out to be the forerunner of the modern longboard, even as it was casting a spell on all who rode it.

Zahn was so beguiled by the sprightly girls' board that he purposefully "borrowed it" back just before he dumped Darrilyn for fellow Fox contract player, Norma Jean Baker. Evidently, neither he nor his new paramour had ever heard the old saying "hell hath no fury like a woman scorned," for not surprisingly, retribution was swift. Darrilyn clandestinely re-appropriated her surfboard and then arraigned to have both their studio contracts terminated. However, in the case of Miss Baker, the setback was only temporary; a few years later, she would re-up with 20th Century Fox, this time as Marilyn Monroe. But Tommy would never work in movies, and he would never get that surfboard back.

Burnin' Up the Boulevards

In April of 1946, the SCTA held its first dry lakes meet in nearly five years. Of course, the organization was eager to get its members back out on the track, but now they were getting pressure from both police and community groups desperate for them to provide an alternative to what was developing into an epidemic of impromptu street racing.

Though the pre-war gearheads often engaged in reckless behavior on the public thoroughfares, they were much fewer in number, a bit more mature and discrete, and were generally able to avoid attracting too much of the wrong kind of attention. But the post-war crew had nowhere to hide. At ten times their pre-war numbers and growing daily, it was impossible to run beneath the radar; and with the ranks filling with younger, daredevil vets who had faced down stormtroopers and kamikazes, as well as teens swept up in the spirit of youthful defiance, many were not even willing to try. And those were the good kids!

And most hot rodders really were good kids and sensible young adults who were reasonably responsible most of the time. But the cars they built were built for speed and meant to be raced—legally, when possible, but only when possible. Few were going to wait patiently for the next dry lakes meet with a hot little roadster running alongside revving up a challenge. 19-2

Hardly any evening out would be concluded without at least one good run on "the green light Grand Prix." Hot rodders would gather in burger joint parking lots, pair up, and go square off on some un-patrolled stretch of boulevard. Some guys, usually those without dates, would spend their entire evenings prowling up and down the boulevards in search of worthy opponents.

> *"All it took to arrange a racing heat was a chance encounter of two hot cars at a traffic signal. Both drivers eyeballed each other's cars, and a deadpan nod signaled the race was on."* Wetzel & Bash

Angels though they might be at home, the fact that many hot rodders habitually violated traffic laws earned them a reputation as the hooligans of the highways. An unflattering assessment, but at least one that ranks a few notches above hoodlum; but it didn't really matter, for, within the hot-rodding community, that contingent was also represented.

Driving While Delinquent

Among those sacrificed on the altar of freedom was a multitude of youngsters who grew up without adequate care and supervision, while their parents went off to war, either serving overseas or in the defense plants. They were the original latch-key kids, and they were running loose on the streets of America. The country had never witnessed such a dramatic increase in juvenile delinquency; from 1947 to 1957 the teen arrest rate increased seven-fold before finally beginning to recede.

Alienated kids from mostly broken homes and hardscrabble, working-class backgrounds, they adopted the leather and Levi fashions favored by motorcyclists and openly cultivated an outlaw image backed up by an active policy of petty criminality.

Though the truly reprobate represented only a small percentage of the whole, their activities drew most of the media attention, which turned public opinion against them all. The fact that this outlaw style and pose had also become fashionable among many of the more benign groups of gearheads only blurred distinctions and added to the tensions between the hot rod community and the community at large. It would take years of public relations work on the part of the more civic-minded members of the clan to repair the damage done, and even then, with only limited success.

The Armory Show
Officials at the SCTA were terrified that if something wasn't done to smooth over their riff with the public, the whole hot rod hobby might be legislated right off the road; so, they got together with local L.A. area car clubs, speed shops, and performance parts manufacturers and organized a little community meet and greet.

For three days in January of 1948, the SCTA held the first of its kind, big hot rod show at the National Guard Armory in LA's Exposition Park. The public was invited to get to know the hot rodders, and examine, up close, their amazing machines; and to the surprise of nearly all the event's sponsors, over 10,000 did. About 50 roadsters were on display, including one built by the young custom car legend, George Barris.

As a door prize, a 32-roadster was built from scratch in full view of the spectators. Whether the show had any real effect on the public's perception is uncertain; what is certain is that it served as the catalyst for the creation of an institution that would carry the torch for the hot rodder from that day onward—*Hot Rod* magazine.

The "Zine"
In their effort to make the most of the armory show, the SCTA hired a press agent to spread the word. After being laid-off from the MGM publicity department, Robert E. Petersen and a couple of his buddies had just set up their own PR firm when they got the armory gig. Petersen dutifully contracted for radio spots, placed ads in all the area newspapers, and attempted to do likewise with the leading hot rod magazines when he ran into a snag—there were no leading hot rod magazines; there were no hot rod magazines at all.

Petersen couldn't believe it. The hot rod craze was glowing red hot in Southern California and heating up all over the country and there wasn't one publication catering to the trend. Immediately recognizing the exceptional opportunity that lay before him, Petersen quit his PR job and hastily published hot rodding's first monthly periodical, *Hot Rod* magazine.

The initial run of 5000 copies featuring how-to articles, hot rod exposés, commentary, and mechanical tips sold out on the front steps of the armory during the show's three-day run. The next month's issue sold out as well, and the one after that, and within a year, *Hot Rod* was selling 50,000 copies a month.

From the magazine's inception, Petersen championed not only good car craft but responsible hot rodding. Always fearful the hobby was just one nasty incident away from a legislative crackdown, *Hot Rod* regularly cautioned its younger readers against taking part in high-risk horseplay on the highways. Alternatives to street racing were presented which could have been lifted straight out of the Boy Scout Handbook. Car clubs were encouraged to organize picnics, scenic tours, and fundraising events for needy charities.

Within the magazine's pages, the hot rodder was presented as a rugged, All-American individualist who, through hard work and ingenuity, could take various pieces of castoff junk and assemble them into a one-of-a-kind, mechanical marvel. The philosophy was Horatio Alger style self-determination, and the image was pure Norman Rockwell Americana.

It was an excellent example of some very crafty PR work that did manage to cast a faint aura of legitimacy and respectability over the hot-rodding scene. All great for public consumption, but to make inroads with the hot rodders themselves, Peterson had to push more than picnics, bake sales, and Sunday socials, and to that end, he would push drag racing!

Coffee Shop Crazy

According to a local legend, when John Lautner presented actor/comedian Bob Hope, and his wife with his plan for their new, Palm Springs home, Mr. Hope jibed, "well, at least when they come down from Mars, they'll know where to go." It wasn't the first time Lautner's work elicited such an incredulous reaction. For unlike most of his contemporaries who remained grounded in the familiar forms, Lautner wasn't grounded at all.

When confronted with a lot too steep to build on, he mounted a four-bedroom flying saucer-shaped house on a thirty-foot pylon, which predated the Jetson's own space-age rotunda by two years. He extended swimming pools into living rooms; he made interior walls swing out onto outdoor patios; he wrapped houses around trees, and designed structures so sinuous and serpentine that he had to hire a shipbuilder to assemble them.

His designs were always wildly imaginative, charmingly whimsical, and just plain fun! In the 1950s and 60s, nobody would design buildings that expressed the sense of pleasure and the freedom of spirit that characterized the Southern California experience better than John Lautner.

But in 1946, he just needed a job, and found one with L.A. architect Douglas Honnold, a one-time Warner Bros. set designer who made a specialty of swanky nightclubs and elaborate, movie colony mansions.

Honnold put Lautner right to work, not on one of his prestigious "film folk" palaces, but on a downtown coffee shop. Lautner's façade of horizontally stacked flagstone, oversized plate glass, copper plate siding, and upswept, cursive script for Coffee Dan's was totally out-of-sync with the 40-year-old deco edifices that surrounded it, but it was on the leading edge of a movement that was soon to sweep the Southland.

The following year, Lautner did a major facelift on one of Mr. Carpenter's old, thirties-era, circular drive-ins, and in one single stroke, ushered out the Moderne style of two decades past, and ushered in the jet-age aesthetics of ten years hence. With his first Henry's, in the unassuming little suburban outpost of Glendale, California, Lautner established the principal style elements of what would make up a new "coffee shop modern" style, for want of a better term, which he would also provide.

To fix the attention of passing motorists, Lautner used an oversized, canted roof with an integrated sign. Inside, the gleaming, ultra-modern, stainless-steel kitchen was left fully exposed. Ceiling to table-high glass walls were met by stone planters filled with luxuriant tropicals, which encircled the interior dining area and stretched out to enclose the outdoor patio. Abstract copper latticework was hung from above to add visual interest overhead and cast fanciful shadows on the scene below. Accessible to all, Henry's was an unrestrained expression of a growing belief in the power of the future—a future the common folk were becoming more comfortable with every day.

The First Foamie

From 1946 to 1949, Bob Simmons made nearly 200 experimental surfboards in which he incorporated all the features that would go into the creation of the modern longboard. All the elements were there in 1949, but it would be left to others to settle on just the right combinations. It was the same way with the foamie; Simmons would point the way for others to follow.

He became familiar with Styrofoam (used as aircraft insulation) back in 1947, but he didn't start to experiment with it until 1949. Simmons felt a surfboard performed better when it had some heft to it, and so he resisted the move towards lighter boards. But his preferences reflected those of an earlier generation of wave riders; a new generation was pulling in a different direction.

Like it or not, it was clear that weight reduction had become a major factor in surfboard design, and the nearly weightless and extremely buoyant Styrofoam looked as if it might offer some interesting possibilities. So, he got hold of the formula and began making his own foam blanks from scratch.

On the plus side, Styrofoam was indeed, light and buoyant; on the minus side, it was very fragile and dissolved on contact with resin; therefore, it could only be used as a core material. So, he sandwiched his foam blanks between sheets of mahogany veneer and then sealed them with fiberglass.

Before the end of the summer, he had sold over 100 of these "sandwich boards" and still had a backlog of orders he couldn't fill; so, he moved his backyard operation to a storefront in Santa Monica. But the routine of an obliging merchant clashed with his naturally churlish disposition and habit of disappearing whenever the surf looked promising; and in 1949, he closed the shop and moved to San Diego where he was killed in a surfing accident in 1954.

Dawn of the Drags

Just up the coast, in Ventura, the Motor Monarchs car club had been running their cars out on the old service roads around the Goleta Airport. During the war, the small Goleta field was used to train carrier pilots, but air traffic had dropped off considerably since the war's end, and so a few of the club's members dropped by the tower to beg for, and receive, permission to stage weekend drag races on the unused runways.

In April of 1948, the Monarchs, who had assumed the much more officious title of the Santa Barbara Acceleration Association (SBAA), held the first "legal" drag races in Southern California.

But the term legal applied only to use permission. Unlike the lakes meets, there was no governing body dictating proper procedure. There were no safety measures in place for either the drivers or spectators; the race format was undefined—anything on four wheels was considered race-ready.

"All that was needed was for the car to start and with luck stop afterwards, but that wasn't mandatory, and many didn't." Don Jensen

Most of the early events were pretty primitive. Using the lakes-style running start, they ran as many abreast as track-width would accommodate. Flagmen determined start and finish, and timing was done with stopwatches. Race results were generally considered to be a firm indication of what might have happened.

Using the Goleta model, C.J. Hart, convinced Santa Ana city officials to let him hold drag races at the Orange County Airport. Here, drag racing became not only a sport but a commercial enterprise. At the first running of the Santa Ana drags, on June 19, 1950, both drivers and spectators were charged fifty cents admission. There were grandstands, concession stands, restrooms, driver trophies, and real timing clocks.

> **The Dilapidated Desert**
>
> Since the first lakes meet back in 31, the crowds kept getting bigger, the cars kept getting faster, and the lakebed kept getting more and more ragged. A groundswell of new contestants entered the lists, and as they did, the scene began to transition away from the pre-war amateurism of the everyman running his regular ride, to semi-pros who trailered in their highly specialized "lakesters" racers that ran on various blends of nitro-based rocket fuels. The combination of heavy traffic and high speed scarred the lakebeds so badly they could no longer be safely used. By 1949, most of the serious speed freaks had moved on to the Bonneville Salt Flats in Utah, while the backyard builders started showing up at their local dragstrips.

Following Hart's lead, dragstrips began sprouting up all over the Southland usually sponsored by a car club, and often with the full support of police departments, city officials, and civic groups desperately hoping to cut down on street racing by providing places where kids could "get it out of their system." But the truth was that, for the most part, these sanctioned events were seen only as embellishments to the street racer's regular dance card.

Califormulatin'

At the dawn of the 1950s, dramatic cultural changes were taking place. In housing, the agrarian orchards of the past were being plowed under to make way for the suburban fields of the future, where row upon row of modernish, California Ranch houses were sweeping out over hill and dale supplanting the once traditional bungalows and Spanish colonials of an earlier vision.

On the beaches, the most imaginative watermen of the pre-war era had roughed out all the features of the modern surfboard to be perfected by a new generation of detail-oriented wave riders, bringing the old, unwieldy plank into the modern age as a tool for the masses.

Out on the outskirts of towns all over the Southland, a new style of straight-line road racing was developing into a regional obsession among young adults and teens who had turned the automobile into a modern, mid-century object d'art, while on the radio, once popular dance bands and crooners were being nudged out of the pop charts by an ultra-whimsical, symphonic breeze that came blowing over the airwaves in perfect harmony with the general giddiness of the times as memories of the depression, and even the war, faded with the growing expectations of a brighter tomorrow.

Chapter 20
Mid-Century Makeover

Not even three years of fighting in Korea, or an open-ended cold war could cool the Southland's bubbling economy, or dampen the increasingly complaisant regimen, or deter any of those who wanted to become a part of it. At the mid-century mark, the promise of palm trees and a steady paycheck continued to draw settlers from all points east like never before.

But unlike earlier generations of Westin-ers, they were not coming just to find work. Nor were they coming to escape a brutal winter, or a filthy, crowded city, or a life-threatening ailment. No, now they were coming to live the good life! In the hundred years since significant numbers of Americans first arrived in California, the environment had been steadily wearing away at the Yankee's natural aversion to idleness, a condition brought on partly by religious doctrine but mostly by economic necessity.

But now, with a robust jobs market and generous compensation packages, the economic necessity had been mitigated, fully democratizing the state of leisure in Southern California, where practically any wage earner could afford to take part in a plethora of year-round diversions. As for the spiritual considerations, they could be reconciled on Sundays.

The Detroit Dream Machine

Moving into the 1950s, Detroit automakers, for the first time since the coming of the Model T, were struggling with sagging sales brought on by post-war complacency and foreign competition. The voracious demand for new cars had been largely satisfied by the early 50s, and Detroit had not kept pace with the changing taste of the new, mid-century, American consumer.

After twenty years of doing without, the public was eager to buy Detroit's stodgy, bulbous barges. But in a new age of steadily escalating affluence and optimism, they wanted more than basic transportation; they wanted something a little stylish and maybe even a little bit fun, and Detroit was still offering stodgy, bulbous barges. To complicate matters further, American automakers, for the first time ever, were facing some real competition from European manufacturers who excelled at both style and fun.

Many of the American GIs stationed in England during the war had fallen in love with a sprightly little two-seater called the MG-T Midget. At war's end, some of them shipped their MGs back to the states where they were met with great enthusiasm. Suddenly, the American market was thrown wide open to the Brits sending the Morris Garage (MG) into a panic trying to fill orders from a new network of US dealerships.

A few years later, MG was joined in the states by a host of other sporty British marques. Detroit was besieged; even the enemy we had flattened just a few years earlier had come back at us, not with buzz bombs, but with Beetles. 20-1 As simple and austere as the Model T, Germany's peculiar-looking Volkswagen Beetle hit big in the United States where it became a counterculture icon of the 1960s.

These sporty imports could be considered the first factory performance cars, providing a spirited driving experience in a turnkey package straight from the dealer—no assembly required. They were sleek, elegant, nimble, fast, fun to drive, and, it was often imagined, conferred upon their owners an air of Euro-style panache and sophistication. By comparison, most 1948-1954 American cars were puffed-up, underpowered, ponderous handling, boulevard barges.

But the motor city's kingpins were not just sitting on their hands. Oldsmobile and Cadillac took a giant leap forward in 1949 when they introduced their modern, over-head valve, 160hp V8 engines that would immediately begin to supersede the aging Ford flathead as favorites among hot rodders.

Then in 1951, Chrysler introduced its 180hp Hemi engine that not only turned out to be another legendary performer but also started a horsepower war between all the US makers that would continue into the muscle car era. However, in stock trim, the improved performance was usually just enough to keep pace with the ever-increasing girth of the cars they powered.

> **Goin' Topless**
>
> Most European sports cars shipped to the states wound up in Southern California where their one shortcoming (limited protection from the elements) was considered a virtue in a balmy climate that invited top-down motoring nearly all year round.
>
> The term "Hemi" refers to the hemispherical shape of the combustion chamber.

Detroit's automakers hadn't gone stagnant in the style department either. Each had acquired its own cadre of flamboyant designers. General Motors' styling division was headed up by Harley Earl, a Southlander who started his design career building custom coachwork for Hollywood movie stars. But even for a true innovator like Mr. Earl, getting concepts from prototype to production was a very difficult process.

As in all top-heavy corporations, Detroit's design decisions were filtered through a committee of high-level bottom-liners beholden to the shareholders. After running the gauntlet of senior executives, even the grandest of styling gestures usually emerged upon showroom floors in basic bland.

However, occasionally a vision would slip past the style committee unmolested, like the fins Harley Earl put on the 1948 Cadillac. Like many other artists and designers of the time, Earl was beginning to feel the cultural tide turning toward the stars, and his futuristic Caddy fins were just a small sample of what would develop into "the" major automotive styling theme of the 1950s.

But a single flourish on one luxury model wasn't going to boost sales overall. Realizing they had lost touch with the tenor of the times, Detroit's decision-makers relaxed their grip on their style departments and even sent factory reps on regular pilgrimages to Southern California with clipboards in hand to attend car shows and confer with aftermarket performance specialists and well-known rod and custom builders.

By 1950, General Motors, Ford, and Chrysler each had a team of California custom consultants on the payroll. However, due to the usual lag time of two to three years between drawing board and production run, evidence of the American auto industry's efforts to re-establish themselves as trendsetters rather than followers did not begin to appear in dealer showrooms until late 1953.

The Blue Flameout

One of the most striking creations to emerge from this period of transition was the result of a little side project Harley Earl put in the works back in 1951. Annoyed by the fact that an entire segment of the American automobile market had been surrendered to the Brits, Earl assembled a small crew to put together a little something for the 1953 General Motors Motorama show in New York.

The idea was simply to gauge the public's interest in an American alternative to the British sports car. And so, what was destined to become Southern California's flagship

> **Hot Rods Under Glass**
> Earl got the idea to use a Fiberglass body on a visit to Southern California's Glasspar Company, a maker of fiberglass boat hulls, as well as the bodies for Disneyland's first fleet of Autopia cars.

sports car was originally conceived as just another long-shot concept car for this annual factory extravaganza—a one-off example of a two-seater sports car designed on the quick and assembled from standard, off-the-shelf parts and, as a cost-cutting measure, enclosed under a fiberglass body. Christened the "Corvette," it surprised everyone at GM when it turned out to be the runaway hit of the Motorama show. The public's reaction was so overwhelmingly positive that Earl's half-baked concept car was rushed into production just as it stood.

One of the show-goers smitten by the exotic-looking Corvette roadster was Zora Arkus-Duntov, a Belgian-born, Russian mechanical engineer who had twice driven the 24 hours of LeMans. Zora thought the Corvette was extraordinary—until he got a look under the bonnet. The beautiful body contours were truly beguiling, but under the hood, it was all milk truck. To his absolute astonishment, Zora found that the Corvette used the same "Blue Flame," inline six-cylinder engine, two-speed automatic transmission, and outdated suspension components found in the Chevrolet sedan, station wagon, pickup, delivery wagon, and yes, milk truck!

Soon after the Motorama show, he fired off a "what were you people thinking" letter to GM, which found its way into the hands of Harley Earl who, rather than dismiss it as the work of a crank, hired the insightful author as an assistant engineer. But that did not quell Zora's fervor.

> ### He'll Always Have Paris
> The account of Zora's early years reads like a Hollywood thriller. He fled from Berlin to Paris just before the war broke out. There, he married a dancer from the Follies Bergère and joined the French Air Force. When the French surrendered, and the Germans took Paris, he gathered his family, and in a scene right out of *Casablanca*, made a mad dash for the southern border. For five days they hid out in a Marseille whorehouse while Zora obtained the forged paperwork for the flight to Portugal where they caught a freighter bound for America sailing across a sea swarming with Nazi U-boats.

Once inside the organization, he shook up the head office again with another solemn communiqué entitled, *"Thoughts Pertaining to Youth, Hot Rodders, and Chevrolet"* in which he warned that Chevrolet was losing market share to Ford and would continue to do so unless they did something to liven up their model line and aggressively pursue the new and rapidly expanding youth market.

He pointed out that Ford had dominated hot rodding for over 40 years, and therefore, young people interested in cars were naturally drawn to Fords. He lamented that hot rod publications were full of Fords, and insightfully pointed out that, once made, the bond between man and machine can last a lifetime.

"As they progress in age and income, they graduate from jalopies to second-hand Fords, then to new Fords."

He stressed that the only way to overcome Ford's lead, which was based on decades of costly, backyard research and development, was to expedite the hot rodder's transition to Chevy by doing all that grunt work in-house, producing their own line of "ready-engineered parts for higher output."

In effect, what he was suggesting was that the Chevrolet division, backbone of the largest and most prestigious corporation in the world, begin building hot rods, an undertaking long considered to be within the exclusive purview of pump jockeys and juvenile delinquents.

Management, in a move totally at odds with their characteristic conservatism, opted to heed the advice of their wild Russian, and in 1955, Chevrolet very quietly integrated high performance into its product line. The strategy was brilliant, but not revolutionary; Ford and Chrysler, seeing sales figures rise in response to racing results coming out of the southeast, were already taking steps in that direction.

Gone Googie

Considering how significant Lautner's contributions were to the emergence of post-war, coffee-shop-modern architecture, it is surprising to note how brief his involvement with that particular sub-genre actually was.

Save for a couple of additions for the Henry's chain, Lautner's 1949 commission to design the tiny little coffee shop next to Schwab's famous drug store would be his last assignment in roadside architecture. For the remainder of his long and distinguished career, Lautner's talents would be monopolized almost exclusively in the design of spectacularly extravagant showplaces for discriminating clients.

But before he lit out for greener pastures, he left behind a masterpiece—Googies. The long, slender, single-story restaurant ran along the west wall of its much larger neighbor, yet it was Googies that commanded all the attention. Lautner had upstaged every other building on the block using hollow, non-structural, steel beams, painting them red, and laying them out, widthwise, across the low-angled roof that sharply angled up at a steep 70 degrees at street-side. Parallel, off-kilter glass and masonry sections made the entire building appear to bend upwards. Atop the raised roof, the establishment's name, "googies" was emblazoned in bold, cartoonish lettering. The utter simplicity of the device belied its mesmerizing effect on passersby.

One such mesmerized passerby was Douglas Haskell, the editor of *House and Home* magazine. When Haskell first saw the jagged, red roofline he was awestruck by the sheer audacity of the free-form, abstract composition, which he declared to be, "googie architecture." His article for the February 1952 issue of *House and Home*, presented three homes by Lautner as well as Googies restaurant. And from that single publication, the name Googie (the client's nickname for his bubbly, bespectacled wife) became the universally recognized term used to describe the flamboyant, commercial modernism of the mid-20th century.

In the Garden of Googie

By the time Mr. Haskell discovered the Sunset Strip cafe, which lent its name to the coffee shop modern movement, the movement was spreading rapidly. Driven by the demands of an increasingly crowded and competitive roadside bazaar and granted free reign by the public's growing reverence for all things futuristic, commercial architects let their imaginations run wild. Design schemes considered too extreme for residential use were freely incorporated into the layout of the Southern California commercial strip.

In sharp contrast to the strictly regulated International Style, Googie architecture existed outside the boundaries of academic convention and universally recognized standards of good taste. Forget New York and its Museum of Modern Art, or Harvard and its Ivy League school of architecture; real, spontaneous, unrestrained ultra-modernism was thriving on the commercial thoroughfares of Southern California.

As with the pre-war drive-ins, Googie designers integrated advertising elements directly into the building's structure, but the old pylon on a platter, eye-catching enough amid the orange groves, would be lost among the row upon row of competing establishments vying for the recognition of the motorist passing by at 40 miles an hour.

Instead, googie stylists relied upon huge, fanciful signs and boldly styled roofs as their primary attention getters. A Googie roof might swoop up, or droop down; it might be convex or concave; some were butterfly style, or cantilevered, or zigzagged, or scalloped, or rippled. The always generous expanse of glass curtain wall space obscured the boundary between inside and outside and made these undulating roofs appear to float in mid-air—a most desirable visual effect in this space-age milieu. When gravity demanded some load-bearing wall space, it would be covered in fanciful flagstone or lava-stone, exotic woods, ceramic tiles, or maybe even a quirky, modern art mural.

Tropical landscaping and other assorted natural wood and stone accents were mixed heedlessly with the new, man-made materials—Formica counter and tabletops, vinyl stools and chairs, and plastic lamps, screens, and fixtures—all products of the recent scientific advances, as were the new synthetic dyes, polymers, and pigments that made possible the bright, bold, primary colors that reflected off every surface. Behind the counter, a spotless, glistening stainless steel, "exhibition kitchen" conveyed to all who came within, that this was not your grandfather's greasy spoon; this was the tearoom of tomorrow.

Outside, the icing on the cake was the wonderful space-age iconography that was part and parcel of the spectacle that was Googie. Each competing establishment fielded the biggest, most elaborate banner that finances and physics would allow and emblazoned it with the quirkiest of scripting. Never did the loopy, multi-colored, off-kilter, swooping, arching, and lilting typefaces suggest anything other than pure jubilation. Re-enforcing the sensation of giddiness, the banner might feature a whimsical illustration, or caricature, or maybe one of a dozen variations on the atom, the starburst, the comet, or the sparkleburst that were used to crown rooftops and street signs, or hung from ceilings, mounted on walls or fashioned into light fixtures.

Patrons seated beneath those light fixtures were treated to an eclectic display of futuristic illustrations. Along with the jet and rocket-themed squiggles and doodles, there was a whole collection of biomorphic figures emblematic, not only of Googie style, but of the entire canon of mid-century modern design: boomerangs, amoebaes, hyperbolic paraboloids, obloids, and dozens of other highly abstract, yet equally familiar renderings too intangible to be branded with a name. These whimsical, futuristic forms and figures, which turned up on nearly everything, virtually inundated the post-war commercial environment. Primitive, yet retaining an air of cool sophistication, these childlike abstractions, presented in brash, crayon colors, were the cultural hieroglyphics that distinguished the new world of tomorrow.
20-2

Out on the Southland's commercial strips and suburban boulevards, Southern Californians (the masses of us) discovered, and fell in love with, modern design. There was just something so irrepressibly uplifting about the overt whimsicality and irreverence of the Southland's flippant strain of modernism that synced up so perfectly with the sanguine spirit of the times that it was inevitable we would want to take it home with us.

Adventures in the Interior

After receiving a fellowship in architecture at the Cranbrook Academy of Art, Charles Eame's career trajectory suddenly veered off course, in 1940, when he entered a competition in "Organic Design in Home Furnishings," sponsored by the New York Museum of Modern Art.

Charles planned to enter a chair made of cheap, construction-grade plywood. But when he tried to mold the plywood to the contours of the human body, it frayed and splintered, and he was forced to hide the imperfections under a layer of upholstery. Though technically a failure, this early prototype was still innovative and attractive enough to win the competition, and that was all the encouragement Charles needed to neglect his studies and obsess over the problem of how to bend plywood like a pretzel—and then he met her!

Co-ed Bernice Alexandra Kaiser, whom everybody called Ray, was an art student when she met Charles. The bond between the two kindred spirits eventually grew so strong that Charles left a wife and child to marry Ray and move to L.A., where, he worked in the MGM art department, and she designed covers for *Arts & Architecture* magazine; but in the evenings, in the living room of their apartment, they continued to experiment with that *@%$#&* plywood chair.

They were just beginning to make some progress when they were sidelined by a wartime, government contract to make plywood limb splints for the Navy. It was in the design of these simple splints that he discovered that slits in the right places relieved tension and allowed for much greater flexibility; and with access to new, military-grade, industrial technology and materials, he was finally able to perfect the production process. By the time the war was over, he had redesigned his signature seat into what *Time* magazine would later describe as "the greatest design of the 20th century."

As Charles had always intended, the Eames chair (now in a two-piece back and seat configuration) was elegant in its simplicity, stunningly modern, reasonably inexpensive, and easy to mass-produce; it was a perfect expression of its time. The Hermann Miller Furniture Company, a Midwestern firm that specialized in quality reproductions that perfectly expressed a time long past, sensed that the public was ready for something new and struck a deal with Eames for production and nationwide distribution of a complete line of Eames furniture that would completely transform the look of the American home.

Along with the numerous variations on the plywood chair, there were Eames tables, modular combo desks, storage cabinets, folding sofas, and sculpted wire-mesh chairs. Using the infinitely malleable new fiberglass material, he introduced a new line of one-piece, plastic shell-chairs.

A few years later he introduced the iconic Eames 670 lounge chair & ottoman, and the aluminum and leather tandem sling-seating units that can still be found in airports around the world. By the time the decade of the 50s had ended, the mid-western, middlebrow, Hermann Miller Company had become a leader in chic, ultra-modern furniture design, but they were certainly not the only players in the park. Other, once traditional, manufacturers turned out one iconic design after another.

Like the new modernist architecture sweeping the Southland, these contemporary furnishings merged the organic with the industrial, and their space-age styling, sensual textures, radiant colors, and overt whimsicality reflected the collective optimism of the time. As Southlanders relocated to the new, modern, suburban housing tracts, they often discarded their old overstuffed, claw-footed, pre-war pieces in favor of these popular new offerings. It was a transformation made all the easier by the huge number of budget manufacturers flooding the market with very credible knockoffs as well as imaginative variations on a thousand unconventional themes that were available at department stores and discount outlets. 20-3

The new wave of modernistic furnishings was an essential element in the design of the new, post-war America, and were so widely popular that they appeared nearly everywhere. If you didn't own an original piece, the chances were that you owned one of the many knock-offs available. And sprinkled throughout these modernist homes with the modernist furniture was an entire galaxy of modernist bric-a-brac. Lamps, clocks, wall hangings, sculptures, figurines, and ashtrays worthy of art gallery exhibition graced the well-appointed, mid-century domicile. Gone was the drab, cluttered aura of the Victorian age, and in its place stood the cool, clean, colorful look of the future.

Exotica

Having firmly established a reputation as a master of the eccentric, Capitol Records hired Les Baxter, in 1950, to arrange, produce, and compose a few tunes for an album featuring Yma Sumac, an exotic-looking Inca Princess with a four-octave vocal range. The *Voice of the Xtabay* was another Baxter brew in which Sumac's Peruvian folk songs were seamlessly merged with Latin-flavored jazz and swing mixed in with Baxter's own interpretations of oriental fantasy. She sang the folk songs and jammed on the pop songs.

Using her voice as a wind instrument she moaned, growled, howled, quivered, trilled, soared, screeched, and wailed. In both her musical style and appearance, Sumac really was from another world, but Baxter's pop arrangements kept the project within the bounds of popular tastes and made this most unlikely of offerings one of the top-selling records of the early 50s.

In 1951, Baxter produced a string of very successful pop singles for Capitol, and seemed to be falling into a comfortable groove, when he did something extraordinary—he created a masterpiece, and a brand-new musical genre to go with it.

Even among Baxter's previous works, *Ritual of the Savage* was a revolutionary recording on many levels. All of his prior albums were recorded on ten-inch 78-rpm discs that could hold only three to four minutes of music per side. But for *Ritual of the Savage*, Baxter used the new, "long-playing" or LP format developed by CBS Laboratories in 1948, and recorded with Bell Labs' hi-fidelity recording process, which expanded the record's frequency range to nearly the full spectrum of human hearing.

The new discs were twelve inches in diameter, were played at 33.3-rpm, and could hold up to twenty-four minutes of music per side. For the first time, Baxter wrote all twelve pieces for the album, which featured a conventional string and woodwind section, the ooh & aah mixed chorus, a vibraphone, marimbas, bongo and conga drums, timbales, and chanting natives of indeterminate anthropological origins. He took full advantage of the LP's extended format and composed, not the usual random selection of songs, but a work with a continuous theme. Today, we would call it a concept album; Baxter called it a "tone poem."

The songs, which relied heavily on Latin dance rhythms, were designed to take the listener on a musical adventure deep into the heart of a remote "jungle of the mind" without ever having to leave the safety and comfort of the living room sofa. It was clear just by looking at the album's cover that this record was going places few listeners had ever been before. In bold primary colors, four stone-faced tiki statues stand guard, while an elegant couple in formal attire wrestles with the force of their own savage passions let loose by the sound of native drums. Oh yeah! This was some sizzlingly sensual salve for suburban trailblazers.

The album was very popular with Polynesian restaurants, tiki bars, and savvy Southland suburbanites, but in 1951, Baxter was practically the lone torchbearer for this unique musical idiom. It wasn't until 1957, when an obscure, Las Vegas lounge performer covered his material, and the recording industry re-tooled for stereo, that his exotica music would truly go mainstream.

Brubeck and the West Coast Sound

By the mid-40s, the jazz world had its firmly established folklore and traditions, all of which were being trampled upon by a new breed of California musicians feeling their way towards a sound that would harmonize perfectly with the west coast experience. And although many talented players would become involved in laying the foundation of this new art form, David Warren Brubeck would be recognized above all the others as the leading figure of the new west coast jazz scene of the 1950s and 60s.

In the emergent world of 1950s jazz, Brubeck was an anomaly. He did not spend his formative years on the mean streets of an east coast metropolis; he grew up on a cattle ranch in northern California. He was not tutored by a grizzled old veteran in the backroom of a downtown gin mill; his mother taught him piano. He did not earn his stripes in smoke-filled, urban jazz joints; he studied music at the College of the Pacific.

After graduation, he joined the army and trained as an infantryman, but served as a bandleader. Discharged in 1946, he entered the graduate program at Mills College to study orchestration with Darius Milhaud, a classically trained European composer with a soft spot for American jazz. After grad school, Brubeck went on to become one of the most celebrated purveyors of what would come to be known as west coast jazz, a new style that contrasted with bebop in just about every imaginable way.

It was a hybrid style that blended swing's respect for melody with bop's improvisational zeal. It was a "cool jazz," featuring written arraignments of complex compositional structures that made liberal use of counterpoint and sophisticated harmonic shadings and was generally approached in a relaxed, upbeat manner. Emphasis was placed on a smooth, polished delivery that relied on the power of restraint and "low impact dynamics." By contrast, east coast style bebop was loud, brash, loosely arraigned, and relied heavily on improvisational virtuosity, which often strayed beyond the boundaries of conventional tonality.

The Master of None
The faculty soon discovered that Brubeck couldn't read music. Poor eyesight was the cause of the deficiency, which he concealed with an extraordinary talent for improvisation. By virtue of this exceptional ability, he was allowed to complete his studies under the condition that he promise never to teach music. It was a pledge he would honor throughout his remarkable career.

Brubeck formed his own quartet, in 1951, with Paul Desmond, a sax player he met in the army. The San Francisco based, Dave Brubeck Quartet, started out playing the usual big city clubs and then shattered convention again by taking the act out on the road to play college campuses and concert halls up and down the coast. In taking jazz out of the city and into the suburbs, Brubeck exposed west coast jazz to a more affluent, sophisticated, and very appreciative new audience. Consequently, the bookings increased, and record sales rose steadily.

The group's 1959 recording of *Take Five*, reached #25 on billboard's Hot 100; an achievement unheard of for a jazz-oriented group. And in spite of his frequent use of odd time signatures, strange polyrhythms, and numerous other ultra-modernistic underpinnings, his music achieved a gratifying measure of popularity and became a very familiar element in the musical landscape of mid-20th century Southern California.

Surf Society

At the mid-century mark, it was clear that the Southern California surfing world was undergoing a transformation. Once dominated by dedicated watermen and fun-loving, middle-class weekenders, surfing, and the beach culture developing around it, was being infiltrated by a younger crowd seeking an alternative to the regular school, job, and family merry-go-round.

Not all vets were eager to take up where they left off. Some just wanted to sit out the rat race for a while. Troubled teens from troubled families also sought sanctuary on the Southland's beaches. For many of these new converts, surfing wasn't just a part-time recreational activity, it was a full-time way of life—and why not; post-war conditions on the west coast made the "live-to-surf" lifestyle a not altogether unattractive option. The low cost of living and the booming economy, which produced an abundance of job opportunities at all levels of skill and commitment, made it possible to keep head above water and still maintain an inordinate amount of leisure time.

> *"With 18-cent cheeseburgers, cheap gasoline, and $3-an-hour jobs at Safeway loading fruit from four to seven a.m., you could be a surf bum."* Bill Jensen

Of course, the low level of workforce participation provided for only a modest living standard, but one without the hardships found in less satisfying surroundings. There were no shadowy, grey, concrete forests, no crowded ninth-floor tenements, no dark, filthy streets, and foreboding back alleys; there was only warm sunshine, blue skies, beautiful beaches, and well-mannered waves.

The Malibu Chip

As big a splash as the Darrilyn board had made three years earlier, most of the guys still stuck with their big boards and Quigg didn't get a request for another until 1950, when a group of high school girls placed orders for several of his, "starter boards." This time, what they got was a thinner, nine-foot, fiberglassed, balsa board that weighed just 25 pounds. Again, the guys would commandeer their girlfriend's "trainer boards" and completely tear up the waves at Malibu.

Nobody really likes change, but this time, Quigg's Easy Riders had evolved beyond the range of credible denial. It was no longer possible to ignore the fact that his lightweight balsa boards were the best on the beach. Yes, of course, it would mean living with the stigma of riding a girl's board, but for many of the younger guys not grounded in pre-war traditions, the benefits far outweighed any possible harm done to the machismo. But as it turned out, a random act of rebranding neatly lifted that threat of shame.

Sun exposure caused the fiberglass to turn a dirty yellow. And as some strolling beachgoer gazed down upon a cluster of boards lying in the sand, he remarked that they looked like a bunch of greasy potato chips. And that was it. The name was eagerly adopted. Now, they weren't girlie boards, they were chips, and not just chips, but Malibu Chips, taking the name of the point break they seemed to be specifically designed for.

"After we pulled in the tails, got the weight down, and the fins right, no one ever built monolithic planks again." Joe Quigg

By the following summer, everybody was riding the new Malibu Chip. 20-4

Surf Stylin'

The new boards prompted a new riding style, and the originator of the coolest style of all was Matt Kivlin, who was considered the master of what was called "performance cruising." With feet spread along the board's centerline, knees slightly bent, and arms half-extended, he would glide elegantly along Malibu's arching walls of water.

And if Kivlin was the coolest surfer at Malibu, Dewey Weber had to be the hottest. Weber, the star of national ad campaigns for Buster Brown Shoes at age seven, and a national yo-yo champion at 14, started surfing when he was four. At 15, he was one of surfing's first "hot doggers."

Beach Boutiques

Though still part of a fringe society, the number of surfers had grown to where they now made up a genuinely perceptible "niche" ripe for exploitation by anyone with a head for business. And in 1950, there were three such entrepreneurs: Dana Point high school student Hobart "Hobie" Alter started making custom surfboards in his dad's garage. That same year, Dale Velzy opened a shop in Manhattan Beach, and Joe Quigg opened one in Santa Monica.

In his bright red trunks, Weber would run up and down the length of his board while forcefully cutting left, then right, then swooping up to the crest of the wave only to hurtle back down to the bottom and start the whole sequence all over again, not necessarily in that order. Weber's kinetic style introduced performance surfing or hot dogging. He also pioneered the use of boldly colored beach apparel and was the first surfer to use peroxide bleach to accelerate the sun's natural lightening effect on the hair.

Street Scene

The NHRA and *Hot Rod* magazine preserved a competitive niche for the weekend warriors by creating several "street car" classes, but they were now relegated to what amounted to "opening act" status for the highly specialized and very expensive ultra-modifieds, so it was inevitable that many of them would begin to explore other avenues of automotive self-expression. Inspired by the customizers, whose works were regularly featured in *Hot Rod* and the dozens of other car-culture magazines, hot rodders began to lavish more attention on the appearance of their cars.

The two most potent elements used to turn automobiles into art objects were acrylic enamel paint and Hexavalent chromium, or chrome. In many instances, traffic-stopping customs were conceived using only these basic building blocks. The new acrylic enamel and lacquer paints provided customizers with an unlimited array of bold colors, and that was only the jumping-off point.

Like medieval alchemists, every customizer had his own secret formulas, blends, and ingredients. For a metallic finish, powdered metal was added to the color base. Larger flakes of metal produced the popular metal-flake finish. For an iridescent effect, ground-up fish scales were thrown into the mix. A translucent color coat sandwiched between a silver basecoat and a clear topcoat produced the legendary candy apple finish.

If one of these, or all of these finishes were not enough, one could accentuate design features with pinstripes or completely overwhelm them with scallops and flames.

And there was no need to stop with the stripes; what wasn't painted or upholstered could be chromed. Chrome on cars was common, but not in such huge quantities. On many high-concept street rods, chrome-covered more surface area than paint. Complete engines, radiators, frames, wheels, rear ends, and suspension parts were routinely bathed in mirror finish chrome. The results, when done with a reasonable measure of good taste, could be

---

The NHRA

In 1951, *Hot Rod* magazine's editor, Wally Parks, founded the National Hot Rod Association (NRHA), which would establish safety and procedural standards, and try to reserve a place for the hobbyist in a motor sport that was rapidly turning into a highly specialized, heavily sponsored, professional, multi-million-dollar entertainment enterprise.

The Pinstripe Master

Among the very best practitioners of this sinewy art was an itinerant, freelance sword-brush master called Von Dutch. Living in a converted school bus, Von Dutch roamed throughout the Southland where he painted pinstripes and flames on so many cars that the process was referred to as "Dutched."

breathtaking. Nothing else really objectified the wild optimism of the times like a fully dressed-out California roadster.

Naturally, not every effort was worthy of a magazine cover; variations ran from the completely re-imagined to practically dead stock, but no matter the car's state, a teenager had to have one. The automobile was at the center of the teen universe, and practically no social function could be properly conducted without one. However, as humble as it might be, youth had its pride, and protocol dictated that a teen's car must not resemble the parent's hack. And so nearly every teener in the Southland subjected his ride to some measure of modification.

Going on the cheap, front and rear ends could be raised and lowered; white-walled tires made a bold statement, as did a flashy set of hubcaps. Audible presence could be enhanced by drilling holes in the muffler, and mail-order parts supplier J.C. Whitney offered an inexhaustible variety of cheap, gaudy do-dads.

Whether presented in show quality or no quality, the innumerable incidents of vehicular self-expression turned common roadways into free-form art galleries where every work featured was a unique symbol of adolescent individualism meant to be exhibited, not in the pages of a magazine, or at a drag strip, but out on the streets, on those glorious cruising strips boiling over with drama, action, and romance.

Cruisin' California

The California cruising custom harkened back to the days of the Spanish ranchos when a young man would walk his lady around the town square on a Saturday night with her duenna (chaperone), following a few paces behind. Refined over a century of technological advancement and continuously evolving standards of morality, by the 1950s, the ancient, pedestrian promenade had morphed into a sparkling, slow-rolling car show and street social, while retaining the ritualistic mating motive, albeit, without the duenna. But rather than circle a square, this parade route stretched out for several city blocks along a well-traveled

---

Mercurys Rising

The pre-war coupes and roadsters would remain popular with hot rodders and customizers alike, but the preferences of the latter group leaned a little more towards the late-model, full-bodied cars, especially the 1949-51 "bathtub" Mercurys. Chopped down and dressed up with parts lifted from other cars, the 49-51 Mercs were the pinnacle of California cool in the early 1950s. Hot rodders derisively dubbed these customs "lead sleds" for their bulky appearance and ponderous performance, but they were missing the point. The custom car crowd didn't give points for performance, only style, and the style was low and slow—cruisin style.

course purposely laid out to encompass the area's most popular drive-in eateries.

On Friday and Saturday nights, blasting car radios underscored a slow and purposeful boulevard ballet staged along a measured strip of asphalt calculated to exhibit vehicles and their occupants to best advantage. Arrivals and departures were often announced through short bursts of tire-burning acceleration, and/or a throaty rumble punctuated by a deafening roar. It was customary, upon entering the strip, to take a few laps around the course before lining up in one of the select, burger stand parking lots where the real street carnivals took place. From sundown till the curfew hour, these lots were filled with a continuously revolving retinue of hot rods, customs, and carousing teenagers out for a good time.

Later in the evening, when the crowd began to thin out, the hot rodders would adjourn to a quiet stretch of road for some clandestine competition, while steady couples, and those newly made, would drift off to other, more intimate parking areas. A combination car show and teenage singles club, the cruisin' strip was a cherished, adolescent rite of passage, a world one could enter upon acquisition of a driver's license and would usually exit after the summer following the senior year.

Californulatin'

Though custom cars and motorsport would become one of the great, iconic fixtures of the region, it was only a second-tier attraction in the grand, Southlandian scheme of leisure and recreational enterprise. Ever since John Fremont disseminated his Mediterranean comparisons, Southern California has served as a rec-center for the rich, but with the hyper-expansion of the middle class, a multitude of new players entered the field, and the leisure industry, once a small segment of a minuscule economy, grew to become a leading economic force in a huge market.

Before the decade had run its course, Southern California would be awash in new entertainment venues, tourist attractions and accommodations, recreational facilities, and legendary amusement parks, all erected in a massive vacational buildup designed to appeal to the most sacred institution of the Cpop era, the American family—the average Mr. and Mrs. with their 3.7 children.

Midway through the post-war baby boom, the nation fixated on the suburban, middle-class family—the family that earned more than ever, spent more than ever, and lived better than ever; the family that was celebrated in print media and presented as the central character in numerous radio programs and television shows. But like the hit TV show that spins off an even more popular series, the family unit would be eased out of the national spotlight once those 3.7 children reached their teen years.

Chapter 21
Dreamland USA

*"Now we're ridin' a rainbow to Cloudsville, and we're makin' it —
like young." Veronica Langdon*

Midway through the 1950s, California was growing faster than any other state in the union, and as it grew, it got younger. Fifty years earlier, the population was skewed toward middle age and up; but now, nearly half the population was under 20. Amongst the young people, the dominant lifestyle trend was still to get a job, marry, and start a family right out of high school.

Though born during the depression, they were too young to be too affected by the tough times and exhibited little of the caution and frugality so common among their parent's generation. Instead, like their veteran siblings, they became rabid consumers of homes, cars, furnishings, appliances, and a multitude of luxury items—the perks of the good life.

Tops among the durable non-essentials was the television set, through which corporate sponsors presented a continuous procession of conventional dramas, comedies, and variety shows interrupted repeatedly by product advertisements peddling more wants than needs and sending many young families deep into debt trying to maintain parity with their new neighbors and their own desire to live it up and have it all.

Within the family unit, the division of labor was nearly absolute; the women stayed home with the kids and the men went off to work in a labor market rapidly expanding into the white-collar trades. Though certainly not a generation of slackers, these new hires were not the fireballs the vets turned out to be. Work was often seen as a means to an end—the weekend. There was not the drive to climb too far up the ladder of success if it meant time away from home, family, and fun.

So much emphasis was placed on leisure and entertainment that people began to identify themselves, not with their work, but with their favorite weekend activities. Largely disengaged from the traditional social and civic affairs, Southern California's young adults were turning inward in pursuit of a more congenial life starting in the home.

Tiki Time

Complimentary to, influenced by, and running in tandem with the exotica music fad was a Polynesian Pop craze that began sweeping the Southland in the early 1950s. There were no more overtly whimsical expressions of post-war euphoria than the symbiotic combination of exotica music and tiki pop décor. Southern Californians went absolutely gaga over this highly improvised design style based on, what were perceived to be, the common artistic expressions of the South Seas islanders.

Within a few short years, the playful Polynesian aesthetic had completely permeated the fabric of the Southern California experience. Yet, this tiki style was not new to the Southland. For nearly half a century, tourists, surfers, and sailors returned from their island adventures with all manner of artifacts and souvenirs, haphazardly sprinkling tropical coloration throughout the region to the extent that practically no second-hand store was ever without at least one hula-girl table lamp in its inventory.

The Pacific islands motif had been the favorite façade of the west coast tourist industry since the 1920s; however, its application had been confined primarily to restaurants, bars, and hotels; and then, in the 1950s, it seemed as if the entire populace had gone native. From bustling boulevards to suburban backyards, the image of the islands spread across the Southland like wildfire.

What could have possibly brought about this impulsive Polynesian passion en masse? Possibly it was the peace and prosperity Americans were enjoying after having emerged from one of the darkest periods in history that put them in an extraordinarily celebratory mood. Life was good, and most believed it was only going to get better. Post-war euphoria was clearly in evidence throughout the country, but in Southern California, the party assumed a distinctly tropical tone.

Those on the home front often got their first intriguing glimpse of exotic islands (and islanders) in the newsreels shown at the neighborhood cinema. Many of the vets who settled in the Southland had served in the south pacific, and, improbable as it may seem, their enthusiastic participation helped to propel the Polynesian party atmosphere to unimaginable heights of popularity.

You might assume they would want to leave the war behind them; but time often alters perspective, and within a few short years, the perspective had shifted. Wartime experiences were providing the subject matter for a host of nostalgic reminiscences, with James A. Michener's 1947-bestselling, Pulitzer Prize winner, *Tales of the South Pacific*, being the most celebrated of that new entertainment genre.

In the years ahead, many ex-servicemen would reflect on the war years as the best they would ever experience. Despite the hardships and dangers, the world seemed to be a much simpler place. The contrast between good and evil was clearly defined, and everything one did seemed to carry great consequence. All were united in a common cause, and that realization created a sense of solidarity and belonging that few would ever experience again.

Yet, inescapably mixed with the rosy, wartime recollections was the wistful sense of what had been lost. The World War II generation spent their childhood in a drab depression and their youth in a world war; and having emerged from those two calamities, they went straight into the workforce, married, bought homes, began raising children, and settle into a secure and comfortable domestic life.

By the time the dust had settled, they were nearing 30 years of age. They were adults and it seemed they always had been. Perhaps it was just a yearning to escape the daily grind and interject some fun into the lives of mid-century moms & pops, who, after having saved the world for democracy, found domestic duties, and the selling of insurance policies, stock options, and shiny new DeSotos to be a bit tedious.

Under these unique set of circumstances, an improbable fad gained widespread acceptance. All types of commercial enterprises, from banks to barber shops, with special emphasis on car washes, bowling alleys, and apartment buildings, joined the restaurants, bars, hotels, and motels in a purely frivolous tropical fantasy. Under A-frame roofs, they surrounded themselves with dense, jungle foliage, lava rock masonry, tiki totems, and flaming bamboo torches.

Amazingly, the primitive Polynesian pop styling blended so well with ultra-modern, mid-century furnishings and architecture that it was often incorporated into modern commercial and residential designs. The application of these tiki trappings could add a resort atmosphere to any structure no matter how humble. Landlords really dove headfirst into tiki-mania creating fanciful jungle outposts that catered specifically to a new and fast-growing subset of Southern Californians–singles.

Before the war, people often married early out of economic necessity, but post-war prosperity made it possible for some young adults to postpone marriage and savor the pleasures of the good life. These were just the sort of swinging bachelors and bachelorettes that inhabited the elaborately decorated Polynesian-styled apartment complexes that flourished throughout Southern California in the 1950s and 60s.

Some of these garden compounds were huge, sprawling affairs smothered in tropical vegetation that rivaled the very best resort hotels with their full complement of recreational amenities set amid cascading waterfalls, jungle pavilions, towering tiki totems, streams, lagoons, and the steaming volcanoes of a South Seas paradise. 21-1

Here, bathed in the glow of a flickering tiki torch, with the smooth sounds of an exotica record wafting on the breeze, and a multi-layered Mai-Tai in hand, it was easy to forget the problems of the day and submerge oneself in an atmosphere of artificial pagan pleasures designed to awaken the more primitive urges. Who's to say the sexual revolution of the 1960s wasn't touched off by a tiki torch?

But you didn't have to take a year's lease on a bachelor pad at the Mono-Lei, or the Kona-Kai, or any one of the many multi-unit, Polynesian pleasure palaces to join in on the fun; for the tiki tide flowed right through the suburbs as well.

A rattan furniture set with floral-print cushions and a bamboo bar often served as centerpieces of a suburban jungle, which might include a gaggle of tiki statues, some jungle masks, spears and shields, a few wild animal prints, natural tropical plantings and/or plastic replicas, reed and grass mat floor and wall coverings, nautical paraphernalia, and a jumble of assorted reproductions of primitive artifacts and curiosities representing, not only the south pacific, but the Philippines, China, India, Japan, South America, and Africa. In this jungle, diversion and amusement took precedence over authenticity. 21-2

By the mid-fifties, the tiki thing had become so pervasive that several importers started manufacturing their own tropical accents and bric-a-brac. Department stores, furniture outlets, and garden centers also began trading in tropical-themed merchandise. Do-it-yourselfers could find design tips (rumpus room jungle makeovers) and detailed construction plans (build your own tiki bar) every month in any of the California lifestyle magazines. Even hobby shops did good business with "paint-by-numbers" tiki wall art kits.

Whatever religious and cultural significance the tiki figure represented on the islands, to all of us on the mainland, it had become a symbol of leisure and recreation—the God of good times.

> **Patio Ponds**
> By the mid-fifties, there were only about 4500 swimming pools in Southern California; but improved production techniques brought the price down to just under $2000.00, and with no-down and 60 months to pay, that number grew to about 130,000 in just a few years. By 1962, one third of the nation's swimming pools were located in the Southland.

Except for the most far-gone of suburban adventurers, the tiki experience was generally relegated to the backrooms and backyards, where similarities in climate could be exploited to fortify the tropical illusion. The serious tiki worshiper could further enhance the outdoor setting by adding a backyard swimming pool with the tropical lagoon option, including natural stone trim and a functioning waterfall feature.

Of course, no backyard entertainment center would be complete without the barbecue. Out of the many regional obsessions that bloomed in middle-fifties Southern California, the tradition of cooking outdoors on a roaring fire was the most pervasive. Not every suburban home was equipped with a tiki room or a swimming pool, but very few were without a barbecue grill.

Usually, it was the man of the house that donned the traditional cook's apron and cap. Lording over the coals like a five-star Chef de Cuisine, he upheld the honor of the household with his prowess at the rotisserie. These backyard banquets were the premier, suburban social events of the summer, bringing families together with friends and neighbors to revel in the glory of the great out-of-doors.

For mid-century suburbanites, the well-appointed backyard served as a personal theme park, where the tired, work-a-day warrior could stroll out to the patio for an evening's vacation. Out there, amidst all the primordial atmospherics, it was easy to imagine that the rules of modern society had given way to the law of the jungle. In the dim glow of a near-spent tiki torch, every working stiff was Tarzan, and every harried housewife, Jane. Oh yeah—recess for adults.

The Cream Puff Cavalcade

The model year 1955 marked the point at which Detroit's design concepts finally began to reflect the lighter-than-air mood of the times. For the next decade, ultra-high style would take precedence over technology, for this was the era in which the phrase, "you are what you drive" carried the most weight.

As more and more Americans moved up into the middle class, they expected their second most costly possession to serve as a symbol of that accomplishment as well as the new era of general well-being in which they lived; and in response to their expectations, Detroit transformed their upright, boxy grocery hacks into sleek, ground-hugging, dream machines. Automakers would introduce over 100 completely new and newly restyled models in a transformation that would borrow liberally from California's custom car culture and its booming aerospace industry.

Beginning in 1955, Detroit's cars progressively adopted the longer, lower, wider look of California's street rods. In fact, so many styling cues were gleaned from visits to the Southland that Motor City design teams began to refer to LA as "Little Detroit." Many of the iconic features of the Cpop era, the lowered roof and beltlines, the integrated front facias, the hooded quad headlights, the side scoops, and the bumper port exhausts were all originally common features of California customs.

"California-inspired design has put excitement back into the automobile – moods start in California then sweep across the country."

A Detroit auto exec

California's custom color pallet also played a prominent role in this mid-century makeover. The traditional car colors of the past, the coal blacks, rust reds, and bland beiges, were banished in favor of new, west coast hues like Sea-Sprite Green, Wisteria Blue, Fantasy Yellow, aqua, coral, turquoise, and chartreuse in addition to wildly bold primaries like Bolero Red, Nautilus Blue, Regency Purple, Goldenrod, and Fireglow. A monotone finish could be ordered but, by far, the prevailing trends favored the two and even three-tone paint schemes.

Every year, the big engines got bigger and more powerful to keep pace with the inevitable increase in curb weight and the number of power-hungry convenience options added to the well-equipped dream car such as power steering, brakes, seats, door locks, windows, and air conditioning.

In fact, horsepower itself had become a luxury option aggressively advertised with flamboyant engine names (Strato-Streak, Turbo-Thrust) that suggested the convenience of limitless power. Coupled to all that power was a new breed of fully automatic transmissions whose evocative names (Gyro-Matic, Dyna-Flow, and Turbo-Glide) were meant to imply ease of operation and unrestricted forward motion.

The contours of these new dream cars were also re-designed to suggest a state of forward motion even at a standstill. The widespread incorporation of aerospace iconography into the ornamentation schemes helped to sustain this illusion, as did the obligatory, rear-mounted tailfins. There were fins on everything. There were horizontal fins, vertical fins, dual fins, and even fins on top of fins. Other re-occurring aero-themes included gun sight fender crests

---

The Mighty Mouse

Having fallen behind in technology, the Chevrolet brass allowed their engineers an unusual degree of autonomy in the design of their first overhead-valve V8 engine. The result of this "hands off" policy was the creation of the most revered power plant ever built. Chevrolet's legendary Turbo-Fire V8, was a compact, lightweight, high-revving, short-stroke motor that responded well to high-performance modifications and possessed a near infinite capacity for over-boring. Stock car drivers dubbed it the "Mighty Mouse" motor, and builders everywhere immediately adopted it as the new default swap mill, abruptly ending Ford's dominance in the field. It served as Chevrolet's primary power plant for 48 years expanding in displacement from 265 to 267, 283, 302, 305, 307, 327, 350, and 400 cubic inch variations, and it remains in production as the favorite aftermarket replacement motor of today's hot rodders.

and taillights as well as similarly styled front fender spears; side panels were decorated with imitation air scoops, Astro-badging, and sweeping comet-like side-spears in contrasting colors. And perched atop the hoods were impressionistic representations of various aerocraft.

On the inside, they offered a living room on wheels, with sofa-plush, Dial-O-Matic self-adjusting power seats, deep-pile carpeting, and a padded dash all "color-tuned" in a perfect harmony of hues. Dashboards maintained the aerospace aesthetic with Flash Gordon inspired button clusters, dials, switches, and levers. Visual contact with the outside world was maintained through Sweep-Sight, Scena-Ramic, Sea-Tinted, wraparound windshields.

To sell these over-styled dreamboats, automakers inundated the public with a torrent of incomprehensible hyperbole as absurd as the cars themselves. Chrysler opened the sloganeering sweepstakes by naming their futuristic styling "The Forward Thrusting Look." Plymouth went futuristic exclaiming, "Suddenly its 1960," three years ahead of schedule. Chevrolet countered with "Motoramic Styling," Pontiac offered a "New Direction Look," and Buick Boasted "Delta Wing Styling." The words were meaningless, but the imagery was mesmerizing.

Completely over-the-top in every way possible, these cars were the chrome-laden, multi-colored, two-ton party favors of the post-war era, the unabashed symbols of an American Dream running in high gear, each and every model a marvel of modern, mid-century, industrial design.

The NASCAR Nudge

In the early days of the automobile, most racing cars ran in stock trim, so racing played a role in a manufacturer's marketing strategy. The winning of a race, especially one of long distance or duration, was heralded as a show of superior craftsmanship and reliability, even though dumb luck usually played a more prominent role.

But as motor racing became more sophisticated, and the cars more specialized, advertising value diminished, and automakers withdrew from the sport. It would be several decades before a new organization, with an appreciation for those old conventions, would nudge them back out onto the track.

Stock car racing developed in the backwoods of the south, in the 1930s, when southern moonshine runners got together on Sunday afternoons in barren fields and cow pastures to determine who was the best driver in the county. From there, informal, dirt-track contests spread throughout the south from farmer's fields to county and state fairgrounds. And in 1948, the National Association for Stock Car Auto

Racing (NASCAR) was organized to establish some ground rules and make a legitimate business out of a moonshiner's diversion.

Unique to this new NASCAR circuit was the "showroom stock" rule which declared that only cars in stock condition were eligible. Folks really enjoyed races featuring cars like the ones they drove, and the NASCAR circuit became the most popular of them all.

Car dealers noted a bump in sales of a particular make and model after a big win and the word got back to Detroit, "when they win on Sunday, we sell on Monday." Once again, winning races helped sell cars, and so, for a very short time, automakers began openly sponsoring factory racing teams. Then, in 1957, negative publicity brought on by a few spectacular accidents forced the big three to shut down their racing programs, or so it was to appear.

None could ignore the positive impact racing success had on sales figures, and so automakers continued to clandestinely sponsor stock car racing through dealer intermediaries, quietly building high-performance into their product lines while steadfastly maintaining an illusion of respectable non-participation by producing only enough high-performance parts to meet NASCAR's stock quota (usually about 500 to 1000 units), supply their covert racing teams, and then ship the overstock to certain, "performance-oriented" dealers, many of which were located in Southern California.

These racing parts were not listed in the regular parts catalogs, but in special supplementary directories where they were deliberately miss-categorized as special purpose, heavy-duty, or police issue parts. Dealerships handled the merchandise as if it were a black-market trade, but all it took was a wink, a nod, and maybe a Boy Scout handshake, to open the gates of hot rod heaven. Now, behind the dealer's parts

> **The T-Vette**
> American manufacturers did offer a few alternatives to these dreamy "land yachts," but only one really set car-buyer's hearts aflutter—the Ford Thunderbird. An elegant two-seater similar to Chevy's Corvette but with a powerful V8 and a lower price tag. In its first year of production (1955), Ford sold three times the number of Corvettes sold since 53. GM execs were so humiliated they discontinued the hapless vette. But Zora Arkus-Duntov convinced them to replace its six-cylinder motor with their new V8 and add a three-speed manual transmission to the options list, which finally put the Corvette on course to becoming the legendary sports car it was always meant to be. 21-3 As for the Thunderbird, it evolved into another very successful full-size, luxury cruiser.

> **How to Build a Racer**
> For interested dealers, Chevrolet even distributed a detailed instruction manual on how to build a NASCAR racer to their own factory specs.

counter was everything a Southland gearhead might need to build a real hot rod.

Tubesteak and the Malibu Pit Crew

After two years as a button-down file clerk for a downtown savings and loan, Terry Tracy experienced a sudden and severe epiphany. Amid the din of ringing phones, whirring fans, veiled voices, and a dozen or so typewriters clattering away at full tilt, he heard a little voice inside his head gently whisper, THIS AIN'T YOUR LIFE! And so, he made his way to the personnel office, handed in his resignation, and hitched a ride out to Malibu, where he spent the night on the beach.

The next morning, he rose early to collect driftwood. Later that day, he paddled his surfboard up the Malibu lagoon, loaded it down with palm fronds, and ferried them back down to the beach. In the evening, with the help of some friends who scrounged up a few odd pieces of lumber, he built a good and proper beach shack. It would be his home for this, the summer of 1956, and the one after.

Tracy, who was known on the beach as Tubesteak (a nickname he picked up waiting tables at Tube's Steak and Lobster House) was a founding member, and unofficial ringleader, of a loosely structured, yet extremely influential band of Malibu regulars known as the "pit crew." Though his chunky physique did not beg comparison with any particular example of Greek statuary, in his wayfarer sunglasses and baggy shorts, he was the very essence of Southern California surfer cool. His laid-back, non-conformist approach to life made him a hero to his peers and to future generations of surfers. Like most of his cohorts, his only real ambition was to hang out on the beach and enjoy the good life.

He maintained this gloriously hedonistic lifestyle by scavenging, renting his surfboard to passing day-trippers, and graciously accepting the offerings of food and drink from well-wishers who admired his chutzpah and applauded his anti-establishment stance. His ready wit and winning personality naturally drew people to him. Wherever he would park himself, a small crowd would soon gather to hang out, to be acknowledged, and to bask in the glow of his local celebrity. Through his example, the beach bum would become a familiar, and nearly respectable, west coast cultural icon.

If Tubesteak was the embodiment of the gregarious, easy-going California surf bum, his friend, Mickey Dora, characterized the darker side of the same coin. Taught to surf by his abusive stepfather, Gard Chapin (who also tutored Bob Simmons), he met Tubesteak at San Onofre when they were teenagers. Handsome, charming, and charismatic, Dora's raffish, self-indulgent, and larcenist lifestyle characterized the iniquitous surfer. His feline grace on a surfboard earned him the nickname "da-cat," and he was indeed considered one of the best surfers of the late fifties; but he was also a shameless sociopath—surfing's first outlaw.

The rest of the crew (Mike Doyle, Mickey Munoz, Dewey Weber, Johnny Fain, Kemp Aaberg, et al), generally lacking in both Tubesteak's sociability and Dora's charisma, were recognized primarily for their surfing prowess. To them, and those deemed socially acceptable enough to be allowed to co-exist on the fringes of their exclusive society, Malibu was their turf, and woe unto thee who failed to display due deference.

When not out chasing waves themselves, recognized members would often adjourn to "the pit," an exclusive gathering place near the main entrance to the beach. From that vantage point, they could observe, and if so moved, comment on all the comings and goings as well as the various spectacles taking place in the surf. Those who demonstrated superior surfing skills might elicit a polite round of applause, whereas those who floundered could be subjected to a barrage of withering verbal critiques.

Newbies faced a tough crowd, but some were willing to risk the threat of public humiliation for the chance to become even a peripheral part of the scene. For in that summer of 1956, Malibu had become the place to be, ground zero for the development of a new social order where young surfer wannabes self-consciously assumed the cool, beach-boho demeanor of Tubesteak, Dora, and the pit crew, mimicking every discernible nuance and gesticulation and spreading that aura to the dozens of other popular breaks along the coast.

As flattering as all this imitation might have been to those who inspired it, no amount of flummery could get a suck-up an invitation into the sanctuary of the pit. Such recognition had to be earned in the wet. Many an interloper would try to bluff their way into the inner sanctum only to be rudely rebuked. The crew members knew well how to handle such blusterous incursions, but not a single one of them were equipped to deal with the cunning advances of a diminutive, determined, fifteen-year-old girl.

The Pied Piper of Malibu

Only a few days had passed since Kathy Kohner finished her freshman year of high school; the summer had just started, and already she was driving her mother crazy moping around the house all day claiming she had nothing to do; so, mom delivered a familiar ultimatum — "find something to do, or I'll find something for you!" When it became clear that Kathy had not found a fix for her funk, mom made good on her threat. She knew that several of the neighborhood boys had been going out to Malibu, and so she offered to make a daily shuttle run there and back if Kathy would agree to tag along.

Though her heart really wasn't in it, Kathy gave her consent, and the next day, Mrs. Kohner ferried a carload of teenagers out to Malibu. Once on the beach, the boys drifted away, and Kathy was left to meander up and down the beach collecting seashells.

She had waded out knee-deep in hopes of finding some more promising specimens when a bunch of guys ran past her with surfboards under their arms. Boards and bodies were launched in a single forward thrust. Landing in the prone position, they paddled out to sea and disappeared beyond the breakers. Then, one after another, they reappeared slicing across the face of the incoming waves. They would rise up to the wave's crest and then dive back down into the trough. Shuffling up and down the board's length, they would ride until the wave's energy was spent and then swivel sharply around, drop to their knees, and paddle back out again.

To Kathy, the performance was mesmerizing, and she remained transfixed until the last one returned to dry land. Right then and there, she decided how she was going to spend her summer vacation.

All the surfers had convened at the pit, so she naively sauntered on over to introduce herself. A great debate was raging over some topic of little consequence when Kathy marched into the midst of the group and announced, to no one in particular, that she would like to learn to surf. Suddenly, it seemed the whole beach went dead silent.

Kathy's glance skipped from face to face hoping to find at least one expression of encouragement, but there was none. Then a voice from the back of the pack bellowed, "beat it kid!" Several others joined in, and Kathy made a hasty exit under a hail of catcalls that continued until she was out of sight.

But the very next day she stunned everyone when she appeared in front of Tubesteak's shack and again declared that she wanted to learn to surf. This time, before the hazing could get too rough, Tubesteak stepped in and asked, "What's in the bag," referring to the brown paper bag she was carrying. "My lunch," she replied. So Tubesteak proposed a trade—her lunch for a ride on his board. Both parties agreed, and as Kathy dragged the board towards the brine, Tubesteak enjoyed a delicious repast of peanut-butter-and-radish sandwiches.

About a half-hour later, she reappeared; she had taken a few good dunkings, but the board was none the worse for the adventure. She thanked him for the ride, and he, scrutinizing her diminutive stature, replied, "Thanks Gidget" (using a conjunction of the words girl and midget he had once heard a friend use on his pint-sized girlfriend). Kathy was utterly enraptured; never mind what a Gidget was, there was something in the warmth and familiarity of his tone that suggested neither she nor her sandwiches would be unwelcome in the future.

The next day she showed up with sandwiches for all, and the day after that, and the next day, and on and on throughout the summer. Aside from having been recognized by Tubesteak and knighted with her own nickname, and the endless supply of peanut-butter sandwiches, what really won the crew over was her toughness and tenacity—she just would not give up. Neither the hazings she received on the beach, nor the beatings she took out in the surf could discourage her.

"I learned how to surf. I got my legs dinged, my knees dinged, my board dinged, but I learned." Kathy Kohner

She became a fixture at Malibu and was welcomed into the fold as the crew's un-official mascot. Now known to all as Gidget, she could take her pick of any of the surfboards strewn around Tubesteak's shack.

"On Don Pepe's board I learned how to keep in the center and paddle evenly—on Hot Shot Harrison's how to control the direction you're taking with your feet—on Malibu Mac's how to get out of a "boneyard" when you're caught in the middle of a set of breakers—and on Scooterboy Miller's hot rod I learned how to avoid a pearl dive. The great Kahoona showed me how to push the shoulders up and slide the body back—to spring to your feet quickly, putting them under you in one motion." Kathy Kohner

The summer of 1956 had been the most exciting time of her life, and so she kept detailed records of all her experiences in a diary she would refer to in the off-season, reliving the events of the summer past while she waited patiently for the summer next.

That summer of 1957, Kathy turned sweet 16, got her driver's license, a Buick convertible, a surfboard, and spent even more time hanging out at Malibu. She became a much better surfer, was finally allowed to attend some of the crew's pagan beach luaus, and even dated one of the Malibu regulars; but most of them still regarded her as everybody's kid sister.

At home, around the dinner table, she would often entertain her parents with her surf stories. Then one day, while jotting down some new entries into her log, she wistfully turned to her father and told him that, someday, she would like to write a book about her summers at Malibu. Her father, a writer himself, suggested she not wait for someday, but begin immediately and even offered to translate her oral narratives into print form.

And so, for the next few weeks, Kathy would come home from school and recite her beach tales as her father furiously scribbled. For authenticity's sake, he would often eves-drop on her conversations with friends in order to absorb all the terms, phrases, and patterns of speech characteristic of the modern, mid-century, Southern California teenager.

Mr. Kohner was a quick study, and within six weeks he had finished the final draft of the fictional teenage romance he called, *Gidget: The Little Girl with Big Ideas*. New York City publisher G.P. Putnam's & Sons purchased the publishing rights and released the book in the fall of 1957.

The coming-of-age story of a young girl traversing the male-dominated world of a Malibu surf colony became a minor hit. The romanticized portrait of Southern California living, with its sand, sun, surf, and beautiful young people, charmed readers in much the same way Helen Hunt Jackson's *Ramona* did seventy-five years earlier.

The book got reasonably good reviews and even became a best-seller on the west coast. The studio brass at Columbia Pictures were so impressed with the book's sales figures and cinematic possibilities, that they ponied up a hefty $50,000 for the film rights.

For nearly ten years, the studio had been distributing a steady stream of maudlin dramas and ticket sales were indicating the formula was going stale. *Gidget* offered a fresh, new look at American youth, not wallowing in angst, but frolicking in a beautiful,

> **Running from the Reich**
>
> Kathy's parents were German Jews who immigrated to the United States in the mid-thirties. Her father was a screenwriter in Berlin, but when Nazi propaganda minister, Joseph Goebbels, ordered his name struck from the credits of a film he had written, he wisely concluded that it was time to get out of Dodge. He arrived in Hollywood in 1933 and began writing for all the major studios and even earned an Academy Award nomination for his 1938 screenplay, *Mad About Music*.

sun-drenched, coastal paradise, and Columbia wasted no time in throwing the production wheels into motion.

To maximize commercial appeal, all the salty language from the book was excised from the screenplay, and its tough, dark-haired, Jewish protagonist was re-imagined as a naive, comely blonde. La Jolla native and veteran actor Cliff Robertson, who was bankrolling a project to make a polyurethane foam core surfboard, was cast as the Kahuna, a character based on Tubesteak. James Darren, a 22-year-old teen idol from Philadelphia, was cast as the love interest, Moondoggie, and Sandra Dee, an underage ingénue from New Jersey played Gidget.

The release of the book and the media exposure that followed in its wake had drawn so much attention to the Malibu area that, by the time cast and crew were ready to begin shooting, the actual locations had become too crowded. So, the company reconvened 20 miles further up the coast to film the exterior beach scenes. Several members of the pit crew were hired on as background and stunt doubles. Tubesteak served as a technical adviser, Mickey Dora surf doubled for James Darren, and little Mickey Munoz, donned a woman's one-piece suit and wig to stand in for Sandra Dee.

"Watch out Brigitte...Here Comes Gidget!"

Gidget opened on April 10, 1959, and in less than a fortnight, America discovered surfing. The alluring peoples, places, and premises of the book proved to be especially compelling in Cinema Scope and Technicolor. The modest summer confection was a runaway hit that swept the country and launched the image of the California surfer into the pantheon of pop-cultural icons.

Gidget was a bellwether event that marked the coming of the consumer age of the first wave of teenaged baby boomers. It signaled a passing of the torch from the WWII generation to their offspring. The first generation raised on rock 'n' roll knew nothing but peace and prosperity, enjoyed an unprecedented degree of personal freedom, and wielded enormous buying power. They were accustomed to getting what they wanted, and in the summer of 1959, a significant number of them wanted to go surfing.

The film touched off a surf-mania among teens and young adults from coast to coast that would persist for the next ten years. Before it was released, California surfers made up an obscure little micro-community of about 2000, but by the time *Gidget* had completed its initial run in theaters, that figure had exploded into the hundreds of thousands. Overnight, a mass market was created for surfboards that could never have been filled by the handful of small surf shops had it not been for Hobie Alter's determined efforts to conquer the capricious properties of polyurethane foam.

Foam Futures

Hobie Alter built nearly 100 handmade, balsa wood surfboards in the three years since he set up shop in his father's garage, and all indicators pointed to even greater growth opportunities in the future. So, in 1953, he moved his operation to a small shop at Dana Point, and it wasn't until the following year that a salesman from the Reichhold Chemical Company stopped by to show off a sample of a new product—polyurethane foam. He pulled a soap-bar-sized block of the stuff out of his pocket and handed it to Hobie.

According to the Reichhold rep, the substance was strong, light, water-resistant, and would not dissolve on contact with resin the way polystyrene did. Hobie was skeptical and demanded to see some proof; so, the man left him with the sample and a challenge to "do your worst." Hobie bathed the little block in acetone, then coated it with resin and glassed it over. It bonded tightly with the resin just like the man said. That night, at a party, he produced the hunk of fiberglassed foam and boldly announced to the rapt assemblage:

> *"This is it boys, the future of surfboards right here."*

He was right, of course, but another two years would pass before events would compel him to begin perusing that future. In 1954, the surfboard business was good, but the raw materials were getting harder and harder to find. Every builder on the west coast was competing for a consistently diminishing supply of lesser quality, higher-priced, balsa wood. To Hobie, the message was clear—find a substitute or find a new business. Builder, Dave Sweet, had already introduced a foam core surfboard that year, but the market just wasn't ready for it. As was their habit, most of the serious wave-wranglers rejected any variations from the established traditions.

> *"We had a saying, good on wood, spastic on plastic."* Phil Edwards

Nevertheless, something had to be done to keep product in the pipeline, so Hobie valiantly advanced when others were retreating, and it didn't take him long to find out why. Having built a surfboard mold, he whipped up a batch of the liquid polyurethane, poured it into his mold, and waited for it to cure; but rather than cure, it exploded and took out the whole side of his garage.

As it turned out, this polyurethane stuff had very powerful expansion properties. He made several more attempts, each time re-enforcing the strength of his mold, but he could not find a way to contain the volatile foam. Having reached a dead end on his own, he hired a friend, who had a background in chemistry and engineering, to help with the formula.

Through endless trial and error experiments, they were able to decrease the volatility of the mixture, and by reducing the size of the molds to lengthwise half blanks, they were finally able to put an end to the fireworks. The two half-blanks were then glued together and set outside for further curing.

The end results looked very much like real surfboards, but within a few days, they were looking more like giant dinner rolls. Sun exposure magnified the material's still not quite restrained expansion properties. So, they continued modifying the mixtures and found that, by filling the molds under pressure, they were finally able to produce stable foam blanks, but not without an additional quality control problem.

Air in the pressurized molds created bubbles in the foam blanks, which had to be filled with putty. To cover the putty patches, the boards had to be painted; but the only colors that would hide the patchwork were the lighter pastels.

A few years later, these aquas, corals, sky blues and such would be recognized as conventional "beach colors," but at the time, Hobie and company were horrified with the results knowing that the success of the entire enterprise rested upon their ability to sell a new and innovative product to an unyielding, male-dominated market that didn't much go for Easter bunny colors. But Hobie, having sunk every dime he had into the project, had already passed the point of no return.

Improvements continued to be made in the foam mixtures and molding process, and in the summer of 1958, Hobie introduced the polyurethane foam core surfboard to the public. Hobie's foamies generated a lot of buzz on the beach but the sales figures were not what they had hoped for. They sold best among the growing number of newbies; for them, the big selling point was the foamie's forgiving nature—they were much easier to learn on than the heavier balsa boards.

Then came that movie. The moment *Gidget* opened in theaters, in the spring of 1959, Hobie's sales figures began to arc upward and would continue on that trajectory for the next ten years. The Southern California surfing phenomenon of the 60s was the result of the dead-on perfect timing of the introduction of the foam-core surfboard occurring just in time to capitalize on the explosion of interest created by the release of *Gidget*.

Throngs of teenagers stormed the beaches, cash in hand, looking to buy their first surfboard, which, only one year before, was an obscure item laboriously hand-made by just a few very small shops.

"If that movie had come out in the balsa era, no one could have supplied them." Hobie Alter

Balsa boards required dozens of hours of gluing, clamping, sawing, and shaping, where foam blanks could be mixed, molded, cured, and ready for final shaping in 45 minutes. To keep up with the demand, Hobie hired his surfer buddies, moved his blank-making operation to a larger facility, and ran it round-the-clock, cranking out foam blanks for Hobie Surfboards and every other builder on the west coast.

With the air bubble problems solved, the 1959 models could be had in a vast array of bold primary colors as well as an unexpectedly popular assortment of delicate pastels. By mid-summer, balsa boards had gone the way of the dodo bird—everybody was riding a foamie.

The Frog Prince

In 1954, California cocktail pianist, Martin Denny, landed a choice assignment at the Dagger Bar at Don the Beachcomber's in Honolulu. By the time he had reached the end of a successful run, Denny had formed his own combo and landed another gig playing his exotically tinged cocktail jazz for the tourists at the Shell Bar, the renowned, outdoor watering hole at the Hawaiian Village Hotel, which featured a palm-lined lily pond behind the bandstand that would play a defining role in the continuing development of the exotica music fad.

One night, during a performance of Les Baxter's *Quiet Village*, the group became aware of some curious accompaniment. As the band played, the frogs in the lily pond began croaking. When the music stopped, so did the amphibious backup singers.

By evening's end, Denny had completely forgotten the peculiar incident when a patron, thinking it was the band that threw in the nature calls, complimented him on his imaginative arraignments; and to his astonishment, the next night's set began with several requests for "the song with the frogs." Not sure what to expect, they hesitantly launched into *Quiet Village*, and when the frog choir failed to come in on time, the band members began ad-libbing the wildlife effects to the delight of all in attendance.

From that night on, the jungle chorus was a part of the act with Denny taking the frog part and the rest of the group assaying a wide variety of birdcalls and wild shrieks approximating those of the lower order primates. With their jungle jazz act, the Martin Denny Group became one of Honolulu's "must-see" tourist attractions, and Liberty Records' most unlikely hit makers.

Denny's *Exotica* album was released in 1957. Five of the album's twelve songs were covers taken from Les Baxter's *Ritual of the Savage*. Denny confessed he was not the musical

> **King Crowned**
>
> On the night of June 5, 1956, Milton Berle hosted Les Baxter on his popular TV variety show, where he performed his current hit, a bright and bouncy little pop confection called, *The Poor People of Paris*. For the show's opening act, Mr. Berle booked a young truck driver from Tupelo Mississippi who belted out a brash and bluesy hit of his own called, *Hound Dog*. Among those who witnessed the spectacle, few could recall the evening's headliner, but they all remembered the television debut of Elvis Presley.

innovator Baxter was, but simply a lounge performer repackaging popular songs with exotic embellishments. Yet, it was Denny who took Baxter's music to the top of the charts, not once, but twice.

The group's spirited Exotica album was an unexpected hit for struggling Liberty Records, and a major boost for a quirky, niche musical genre that was beginning to face chart competition from a new and much more raucous style of popular music—rock 'n' roll. Yet, even as rock 'n' roll and its future king began to overshadow all other musical art forms in record sales and on radio playlists, exotica music would see a sudden rise in popularity as it was swept up on a new wave of technological innovation that would carry the craze into the next decade—the advent of stereophonic recording.

Audiomania!

Stereo technology, the recording and playback technique where multiple, independent sound sources are recorded on separate left/right channels and played back on separate left/right loudspeakers, was developed in the early thirties, but it wasn't until the mid-fifties that the technology reached the level of refinement necessary for the commercially viable consumer product that first appeared in stores in 1958.

> **Stereography**
> Several stereo systems were available in 1958. At the low end, was the portable record player with detachable speakers, but the most popular units were the higher-end consoles housed in beautifully finished wood cabinetry. These units produced exceptional sound quality, but for the true stereo enthusiast, or "audiophile," a top-quality stereo system had to be assembled with individual components (amplifier, tuner, turntable, and speakers) from the manufacturers who built, what were considered, the best examples on the market. 21-4 Magazines catering to the would-be audiophile quickly emerged to guide the novice on the path towards audio Nirvana with tips on the hottest high-performance components, the top ranked tweeters, the wildest sounding woofers, how to limit wowing and fluttering, how to maximize frequency response, the proper placement of speakers, and even the proper placement of listeners.

To herald the arrival of these marvelous machines, record companies produced and distributed a vast array of "demonstration records" with sound effects on one side and musical selections on the other.

Recorded on two independent channels and using a mix-down technique known as "pan-pot stereo," the different sounds would pass back and forth between the right and left stereo speakers like ping pong balls.

Gimmicky as it was, the buying public was absolutely entranced by the stereo experience; and soon, all the major labels were producing their own hyper-stereophonic records and establishing their own "stereo divisions" to turn out more commercially oriented product specially tailored to maximize the sonic potential of the new format, which required the purchase of an expensive new playback system.

Yet, within a very short time, the home stereo was practically commonplace. Its rapid ascension as an essential household appliance, aside from the obvious improvement in audio quality, had much to do with how well these sparkling stereo recordings fit into the Southern Californian's understanding of what the good life was all about, and how it ought to sound.

Liberty Records was so sure it sounded like Martin Denny that they re-called the group back into the studio to re-record their recently released *Exotica* album in the company's new Spectra Sonic Stereo process. Re-released in 1958, *Exotica*, in full-range stereo, became a favorite demo record in appliance and department stores and one of the biggest sellers in the record bin. Amazingly, the single, *Quiet Village*, reached number 2 on the Billboard top 40 charts, and the *Exotica* album went all the way to the number 1 spot. Before the year was out, Denny and his cocktail combo had become the world's first "stereo stars."

Striving for ever-greater stereophonic pyrotechnics with each new release, west coast record labels produced scores of whimsically effervescent, breezily upbeat albums that sonically solidified the sound of the Southland in the middle of the 20th century.

Relying solely on virtuoso musicianship and technological wizardry, rather than star power, these records rarely received radio play, yet they racked up huge sales through suburban outlets like Unimart, Fedco, and White Front, where the evocative imagery of their jacket covers presented shoppers with a promise of sensual, sonic worlds yet to be discovered.

At the dawn of the 60s, this enigmatic exotica music and unabashedly upbeat jazz, served up through brawny, hi-fidelity, stereophonic sound systems provided the soundtrack for the good life in Southern California with still one more voice yet to be added to the mix—the electrified sound of surf.

The Do-It-Yourself DeMille

Having just graduated high school, and fearful that military conscription was imminent, surfer Bruce Brown took a bold step to countermand the situation—he enlisted.

Trusting fully in a tip he had gleaned from an article in *Reader's Digest* magazine claiming that those who did well in submarine school could choose their assignment location, Brown enlisted in the Navy, went to sub school, kept his grades up, and selected Pearl Harbor as his home base.

It was while serving and surfing on the islands that he became interested in filmmaking, bought an 8mm movie camera, and began recording the surfing action on Oahu.

Mustered out, and back on the mainland, the amateur auteur was approached by board maker Dale Velzy to shoot a promo film for his surf team. Velzy put up $5000.00 for the project, which was enough to cover camera and equipment, round-trip tickets to Hawaii, room and board, production costs, and still have enough left over to finance Brown's first surf film, *Slippery When Wet*.

Bruce got the idea to make a surf movie from another surfer, Bud Brown (no relation), who made the rounds of the California beach towns screening his own 16mm home movies of Hawaiian surfing a few years earlier. Bud established the one-man-movie-mogul system adhered to by all surf filmmakers who would shoot, edit, promote, rent halls, sell tickets, run the projector, and sweep up afterward.

Like Bud, Bruce would shoot his films in the winter, edit in spring, and then barnstorm up and down the coast all summer long packing high school auditoriums and American Legion halls with audiences made up almost entirely of local surfers.

But unlike Bud, Bruce's cinematic sixth sense told him he needed to do more than just spool out a continuous parade of celluloid surfers. So, to add a little variety to his productions, he would break up the surf scenes with mini travelogues, slice of "life on the road" vignettes, and hammy, comic skits. Along with the usual stack of silent, 16mm reels, he would run a jazzy taped soundtrack while he improvised a quirky narration.

The plots never varied: a few guys embark on a journey to an exotic location in search of the fabled perfect wave. And though the productions were just as unsophisticated as his competitors, they benefited greatly from Brown's fondness for corny theatrics, dry sense of humor, and droll, laid-back narration. *Slippery When Wet* was the first of six films Brown would make in the low-key, made for surfers by surfers style that would be imitated by the half-dozen or so other surfer/filmmakers that would follow.

Surf Crazy

Gidget started the surf craze that made hallowed ground of the Southern California beaches and launched dozens of multi-million-dollar spin-off industries, the most prominent being the beach fashion industry.

After all, not everyone could be a surfer, but they certainly could look like one. In 1960, Hang Ten Sportswear emerged out of San Diego with a complete line of ultra-casual surfer trunks, shirts, and jackets. And long-established sportswear companies like Jantzen, Catalina,

Cole, and McGregor all came out with their own lightweight, loose-fitting, surfer-inspired fashions available in department stores nationwide. From there, surfer style and culture spilled over into the marketing schemes of thousands of unrelated products from automobiles to after-shave lotion.

The print media, which had always found Southern California to be good copy, ratcheted up their coverage ten-fold in the wake of the *Gidget* phenomenon. For nearly a decade, all the national news magazines (*Life, Look, The Saturday Evening Post, Newsweek* et al.), climbed onto the Southland bandwagon with the usual lifestyle and fashion mags to lay down a steady print barrage highlighting the cultural carnival that was Southern California.

The growing cult of beautiful bronze surfer boys and girls with their "bushy, bushy blonde hair do's," and the good lives they lived were the subject of countless photo-journalistic exposés. Through these, and many other media outlets, the way they looked, dressed, and talked would influence others all over the country.

Ironically, the two most celebrated players in this grand Southern California surf spectacle had already left the beach. As *Gidget* was breaking box-office records in the summer of 1959, Kathy Kohner put down her board, picked up a stack of books, and headed off to class at the University of Oregon. And in an extraordinary example of life imitating art, Terry "Tubesteak" Tracy abandoned his beach shack for a steady job, just as Kahuna, the character he inspired in *Gidget*, had done in the final reel. That same year he married his wife of 54 years and, by all accounts, lived out the rest of his days as a loving husband and devoted father to his seven children. And there would be other defections as well.

Not everybody looked with favor upon the *Gidget* movie and surf boom it ignited. Veteran surfers of the 1950s were dismayed by the huge crowds that swarmed over beaches they use to think of as their own private reserve. The lineups were log-jammed with gremmies (surf-speak for dangerously unskilled novices) and the beaches were blanketed with hodads (more surf-speak for boorish hangers-on posing as surfers). As the easy-going 50s gave way to the manic 60s, many of the original Malibu-era trendsetters drifted off in search of greener pastures. But for every old vet that opted for early retirement, a hundred new gremmies would take their place.

Califormulatin'

Of course, nobody could have this much fun and not experience a backlash. By the late 50s, bookshelves were overrun with pseudo-intellectual treatises claiming we weren't anywhere near as happy-go-lucky as we thought we were. The psychoanalyzing of the suburbs, and those who dwelled within, became the subject of a whole new sub-genre of paperback literature. Books like Sloan Wilson's *Man in the Gray Flannel Suit* and John Keats' *Crack in the Picture Window* presented the corporate workplace and the suburban housing tract as bastions of mindless, soulless conformity. And while the academics pontificated, the beatniks rebelled. In coffee houses and cellar bars, young, black-clad hipsters recited poetic works denouncing mainstream values and what they saw as the commercialism, conformity, and repression of the middle-class.

But their own self-oriented position turned out to be so untenable, and even worse, lampoonable, that the movement barely survived the 50s. Not that it really mattered; most of us living and working within the confines of the disputed territory were enjoying ourselves way too much to notice the books and the beats anyway. This was especially true of the youth contingent.

By 1959, the first wave of baby boomers entered their mid-teens as the most affluent and influential adolescents in history. With nearly every segment of the commercial marketplace catering to their every whim, no longer would kids dress like their parents, or watch the same movies, or listen to the same music. Never again would they be forced to accept the hand-me-down culture of the previous generation; from this point on, they would create their own.

Chapter 22
The New Frontier

In November of 1960, the youth movement reached the White House. On the eighth day of that month, the people elected 43-year-old John Fitzgerald Kennedy President of the United States, the youngest man ever to hold that office.

With movie star-good looks, a beautiful young wife, and four perfect children, Mr. Kennedy and clan charmed the entire nation and helped maintain the optimism of the 50s through some of the darkest days of the cold war; a cold war that would, on occasion, take us right to the brink of nuclear annihilation, but it would primarily be fought, not on earth, but in space.

Five years after the Sputnik debacle we were still struggling to catch up with the Russians when, out of the blue, the new president put the United States at the forefront of the race into space by committing the nation to land a man on the moon before the end of the decade.

"We stand today on the edge of a new frontier -- the frontier of the 1960s -- a frontier of unknown opportunities and perils -- a frontier of unfulfilled hopes and threats." John F. Kennedy

Americans were certainly all-in when it came to opportunity and high hopes, but not nearly as keen to acknowledge the many perils and threats the nation faced as Kennedy took office. In fact, some might have considered it heresy to even admit to any crises. But Kennedy was right—there were crises aplenty. Flashpoints of communist aggression were erupting all over the globe.

Politicians even feared that communists had infiltrated Washington in the east and Hollywood in the west. Racial strife and civil unrest were bubbling over in the south. Most new housing developments were equipped with air raid sirens, and the backyard bomb shelter had become one of the most popular room additions in Southern California, yet not even these vexing problems could dampen the spirits of most Southlanders. 22-1

The lyrics of a popular, war-era, tune urged Americans to "accentuate the positive and eliminate the negative," and they had been living by that credo ever since. By 1960, the United States had the highest standard of living in the world, and most people just wanted to be left alone to enjoy it. Southern Californians were entering the last phase of an Elysian transformation under construction for centuries; having finally disavowed their puritan ancestors (even those that didn't have any) they conquered their fear of fun and were pursuing the good life with unmitigated glee. Not only was it perfectly acceptable to have fun right out in the open, it was considered bad form not to. In what had become a 12,000-square mile, free-form, tropical theme park, the pursuit of happiness was practically compulsory.

This is not meant to suggest there wasn't a great deal of work going on. Southern California was one of the most innovative and industrious regions in the country and it was running at near full employment. Southlanders simply played as hard as they worked, mainly because there was just so much for them to play at.

In that glorious empire of the outdoors, every imaginable recreational outlet was available with extra emphasis placed on the aquatic diversions. The beaches, the region's main tourist attraction, were fully utilized where possible, and every suitable cove and inlet, not claimed by the Navy, was recreationalized. Where nature fell short, man intervened turning swamps into spectacular water parks and sandbars into exotic isles and peninsulas complete with all the usual amenities. 22-2

Sprinkled along the coast were the big carnivals, Belmont Park, Marineland, and Pacific Ocean Park. A few miles inland were the state's most renowned amusement centers: Disneyland and Knott's Berry Farm. Golf and tennis courses were scattered liberally throughout the landscape, but even more popular were the numerous miniature golf courses with their riotously whimsical infrastructures and associated statuary; the whole region radiated optimism. For those living along the coast of the sundown sea, it was just too easy to ignore the sound of distant thunder and lose oneself in the quest to live life to the very fullest possible measure. Kennedy dreamed big; his new frontier encompassed the world and beyond; ours was more of a local thing.

Hot Rods Ala-Cart

Even the vehicles that traversed our roadways were themselves the very image of unbounded exuberance. In the early 60s, Detroit entered the hot rod market, and it was now possible to custom order a car loaded down with every imaginable high-performance option direct from the factory — hot rods ala-cart.

Some of the customer build-sheets they were receiving were so formidable that, in order to preserve the perception of plausible deniability, manufacturers would occasionally ship the car to the dealership with the go-fast parts in the trunk and let the dealer do the final assembly work. In other instances, auto dealers would either assemble their own "dealer configured hot rods," or put in special orders that returned fully assembled, factory-built, race cars for direct sale to the public.

Since these early 60s screamers were the result of special packaged options and not actual manufacturer's models, they are not considered true muscle cars, but in effect, that's exactly what they were. Assembled ala-cart, these supercars were making serious inroads with a new, young, performance-oriented car buyer not interested in getting his hands dirty; hot rodding was going corporate. 22-3

> **Giddy-up 409**
>
> The four-speed, dual-quad, positraction 409 (a very popular special-order package) was elevated to true cultural icon status when the Beach Boys released their 1962 hit song, *409*.

The House of Roth

Like a character from a comic book, ex-high school hot rodder Ed Roth lived a double life. By day, he was a mild-mannered window dresser for Sears Roebuck & Company, but by night, he was a pinstriper for hire, who applied wildly colorful and intricate patchworks of fine-lined filigree on anything with wheels.

It was the pinstripe master himself, Von Dutch, who recognized Roth's talent and encouraged him to push it further; and when he found there weren't enough hours in the night for him to fulfill all his commitments, he quit his day job and opened The Crazy Painters custom paint shop. But the very moment he hung up his shingle, he inadvertently spun off his operation into the previously non-existent field of hot rod haute couture.

While fooling' around the shop after hours, he airbrushed a highly stylized rendering of a hot rod on one of the paint-splattered t-shirts he wore to work. The next day, he had to paint shirts for all his helpers and anyone else who came into the shop. Thinking' there might be an extra buck in it, he started bringing his easel, airbrush, and boxes of t-shirts to the Southland car shows, which had evolved since the late 40s, from informal, club-sponsored gatherings in gas station parking lots, to huge, commercially sponsored auto-extravaganzas. Here, alongside whatever car he had put up on display, Roth would paint custom t-shirts.

It was during a lull at a Disneyland show, that Roth impetuously turned his attention toward the park's main mouse and created his masterwork, re-Imagineering the Mick, as a sweaty, toothy, pot-bellied green rat with bulging, bloodshot eyes dressed in sloppy overalls.

Roth's Rat Fink was the anti-Mickey with a "screw everything" attitude, and right away people began lining up to have his subversive countenance emblazoned upon their own custom t-shirt.

Depicted solo or behind the wheel of a variety of undersized, overblown hot rods, Rat Fink was hugely popular with hot rodders and young boys still years away from driving age. Added to his stable of hot-rodding t-shirt stars were a handful of ghastly ghouls he called "the Weirdos," that kids went crazy for; and suddenly Rat Fink & Company had become a national, teen phenomenon. With this t-shirt thing developing into a major concern, he might have given up the auto-art altogether had he not discovered the unlimited creative potential of fiberglass.

Roth had always wanted to build cars like the wild ones he dreamed up in his head, but he couldn't manage the metalwork. It wasn't until he saw surfers patching their boards with the same, rock-hard, plastic plating used to make Corvettes that he realized how pliant fiberglass could be in the hands of a talented do-it-yourselfer and decided to give it a try.

> **Monster Mad**
>
> Roth's ghoulish creatures might seem odd subjects for his hot rod iconography, but they were right in line with the current trends. Hollywood movie studios had recently released their libraries of old horror films to television, which ignited a monster mania among young viewers who were seeing them for the first time. The obsession lasted several years and launched the careers of countless TV horror show hosts, a complete series of Universal Pictures monster models from Aurora, two television series (*The Munsters* and *The Adams Family*), and a hit song (Bobby "Boris" Pickett's *The Monster Mash*).

On huge molds sculpted from Paper Mache and casting plaster, he shaped a roadster-like fiberglass body shell, painted it pearl-white with candy-apple green inserts, and then mounted it on a solid chrome chassis and drive train assembled from a diverse collection of parts representing nearly every automobile manufacturer in the United States.

Christened "The Outlaw," Roth's wundercar took top honors for several years running at nearly every show it appeared in and was featured on the cover of *Car Craft* magazine in 1960. But Roth lost interest in the car and was about to sell it when the Revell Toy Company contacted him with a proposal to immortalize it in precision molded plastic. This represented a major shift in Revell's, and every other model maker's, product line away from the conservative (ships, planes, trains, and store-bought cars) towards the outrageous (hot rods, monsters, customs, and ghoulish, cartoon characters) that young boomers were so taken with.

Revell's rival, AMT, had just made a deal with George Barris to produce scale models of his celebrated custom cars, and if Revell wanted in on what turned out to be a very hot market, they had to get their own California customizer, and so a deal was struck with Roth, and the Outlaw became the first of five 1/25th scale models of Ed "Big Daddy" Roth's original custom cars. The "big daddy" moniker was tacked on at the request of the Revell people who felt Roth needed to project an image as hip as his cars, to which he gleefully added the thrift shop top hat and tails that became his trademark.

For the 1961 show season, Big Daddy Roth presented his latest and craziest creation, The Beatnik Bandit. It was a bubble-top two-seater with a tiller for steering, acceleration, and gear shifting that looked like a cross between an elegant European sports car and a space-age lunar rover. The bubble top was heated in a pizza oven and then blown up to size like a balloon. The handmade fiberglass body was layered in 20 coats of candy-appled metal flake, and most everything else was dipped in chrome.

The Bandit was a milestone for Roth and for custom culture that would stand alongside Barris' magnificent Ala Kart as two of the most iconic customs of the Cpop era, but it also marked the point at which Roth's engineering skills could no longer keep pace with his lively imagination. Having built a reputation for outlandish, freeform designs, the public, and now Revell Inc., expected each new Roth creation to be more fantastic than the last. But the demands of his burgeoning t-shirt empire left him barely enough time to sort out the cosmetics before the start of the next show season, and so the increasingly complicated operational logistics were left unresolved. Though the Bandit was technically "drivable," the partially realized tiller assembly made handling erratic and so it was trailered to events. Roth's future creations would be designed only to show, to draw crowds to the t-shirt booth, and to serve as big models for toy models—the tribal tokens of California's custom culture that were flying off store shelves all across the country.

King of the Surf Guitar

Born in Boston, in 1937, to a Lebanese father and a Polish mother, Richard Monsour showed such promise on the piano and ukulele that his uncle, a Lebanese folk musician, taught him the tarabaki (a small lap-drum), and the oud (an Arabic stringed instrument) so he could play in his band.

He accompanied his uncle at various Lebanese restaurant and heritage festival gigs until he was 17 when his father took a machinist's job in the Southern California aerospace industry and moved the family to the beach community of El Segundo, in 1954. In California, Richard took up surfing and guitar, and within a year had become a decent surfer and an exceptional country guitar picker, performing regularly on *Town Hall Party*, a local country and western variety show broadcast on KTLA TV.

Television exposure brought him to the attention of local record mogul, Bob Keane, who signed the budding country star to a recording contract with his own Del-Fi records, only to drop him after cutting just two songs when Richard's father, who had assumed the role of artist's manager, tried to manage his son's recording sessions. Undeterred, Richard and his dad formed their own record label they called Deltone and opened a record store in Newport Beach, also called Deltone. Then, acting on the advice of a local radio DJ, Richard Monsour changed his name to Dick Dale, and put together his own band called, what else, "The Del-tones."

Dick Dale and the Del-tones got their first gig as the house band at the Rinky Dink Ice-Cream Parlor on the Balboa Peninsula in Newport Beach. News traveled fast throughout the beach areas and Dale and company were soon attracting overflow crowds to the pint-sized ice-cream emporium. Right away, he found himself in the enviable position of having to find a larger venue to accommodate his rapidly expanding fan base, and there just happened to be a defunct old dance hall right across the street.

Built in 1928, the Rendezvous Ballroom was one of the premier showplaces for the big-name swing bands of the 1930s and 40s. In its heyday, as many as 3000 dancers would pack the floor to do the Lindy Hop and the Jitterbug to the big band strains of Tommy Dorsey, Woody Herman, and Stan Kenton. But the Rendezvous had been shut down for years when Dale approached the city fathers with his request to stage what he called, a "musical revue," in the cavernous, old dancehall. The city cautiously granted his request under the condition that no liquor would be sold and that a strict dress code would be enforced. Dale agreed to the terms, and thus added concert promoter to his growing list of entrepreneurial endeavors.

He then took the Del-tones around to the local high schools with a brief presentation he called "The Sands of Time," in which they played a selection of popular tunes the kid's parents had danced to twenty years earlier and closed with an invite to the Rendezvous the following Saturday night. Only the faculty were fooled.

Dick Dale and the Del-tones opened their first show at the Rendezvous Ballroom on the first of July 1961. As in their promo shows, they started off slow with a few ancient pop tunes, then eased into some mid-tempo country numbers followed by a handful of harmless R&B hits; and before any of the civic sentinels stationed throughout the hall had wised up, the band launched into an evening of full bore, loud and raucous rock 'n' roll.

Dale's bluesy vocal renditions of R&B-tinged rock songs were reminiscent of the popular performers of the day; it was only on his instrumental tunes that he broke away from the pack, laying the groundwork for an entirely new musical sub-genre. With his Fender Stratocaster cranked up full, he used a percussive, rapid-fire, staccato picking technique he gleaned from his uncle's oud playing, with generous amounts of tremolo effect laid on to emulate the sensation he claimed he got from surfing.

> *"There was a tremendous amount of power I felt while surfing, and that feeling of power was simply transferred from myself into my guitar when I was playing surf music." Dick Dale*

The roar brought the crowd to their feet. Over the band's solid beat, Dale would wail away in hyper-drive and dancers would respond by pounding out a two-step "surfer's stomp" that shook the hall. Among the beach crowd up and down the coast, Dale's surfer stomps became 'the' social event of the week, drawing over 4000 revelers to the Rendezvous every Saturday night. Yet, as his popularity grew, so did his problems.

Though his shows brought revenue into the Newport area, they were also responsible for traffic congestion and a rise in petty crime, curfew violations, assaults, and public drunkenness, which got Dale in trouble with a city hall that regularly threatened to shut him down. And the overcapacity crowds he packed into the Rendezvous kept him off the fire marshal's list of leading citizens as well.

> **The Surfer Stomp**
> This spontaneous reaction to Dale's surf inspired instrumentals resulted in the creation of the world's simplest modern dance. Put your right foot back, then foreword, and then stomp twice. Repeat the same sequence with the left foot and you're doing the surfer stomp.

Then there were the technological problems that consistently plagued his performances. Like all trailblazers, with his Rendezvous shows, Dale had gone where no rocker had gone before. In this huge venue, in order to maintain the sense of power and authority his playing was known for, he pushed his guitar amplifier well beyond the limits of its endurance.

The primitive, low-watt amps of the day were just not able to deliver the hours of maximum volume and power output rock artists were demanding of them. Therefore, Dale's performances were often punctuated by spectacular equipment failures, which elicited cheers from the audience who interpreted his fiery malfunctions as sacrifices on the altar of rock 'n' roll. But for a balding, middle-aged radio repairman observing the scene from the back of the house, these equipment breakdowns were of very grave concern, for it was he who built them.

Let's Get Fenderized!
In 1938, Clarence Leonidas Fender, a self-taught electronics tinker, borrowed $600.00 and opened a small radio repair shop in Fullerton California. Fender Radio Service repaired and sold appliances, phonograph records, sheet music, and carried a small assortment of musical instruments.

One afternoon, the leader of a dance band came in and asked him to build a public-address system. Less than a week after the bandman took delivery of his special order, six more orders had come in, and Leo Fender, an unassuming electro-geek who would never pluck a note himself, had begun his journey toward rock 'n' roll immortality.

Having heard of his expertise in amplification, guitarists began bringing in their underpowered and overworked amplifiers for repair, and in many cases, complete resurrection. From this experience, Leo began making minor design improvements to enhance roadworthiness and even built a few of his own custom guitar amplifiers.

Then, in 1945, he teamed up with another radio repairman, Doc Kauffman, to form K & F Manufacturing Company to produce a simple, "frying pan" style, lap-steel guitar, and a small amplifier to go with it. Right away, they got a distributor for their products and were doing much better than either had expected; but the demands of their success were more than Kauffman bargained for and he bowed out before a year had passed.

Renaming the company, The Fender Electric Instrument Company, Leo continued producing his line of steel guitars and amplifiers, which had become very popular with the western swing bands that passed through town. If fact, Leo's instruments were moving so well that his distributor began pressing him for more product and suggested that he consider producing a standard electric guitar.

The Gibson Company, of Kalamazoo Michigan, produced the first electric guitar in 1936, which they sold through the Montgomery Ward's mail-order catalog. The Gibson ES-150 was an arch-top guitar with a single pickup mounted on top. For years, this was the only type of electric guitar available, but it had a significant limitation. At high volumes, hollow body electrics "feedback" causing the amplifier to wail like a banshee. Thirty years on, this effect would become eminently fashionable, but in those early days, guitar feedback was a disruption most players sought to avoid.

Since the acoustic properties of the hollow-body guitar were greatly de-emphasized through an amplifier, the fix for the problem seemed obvious—make the guitar's body from a solid piece of wood that didn't resonate. But in the 1930s and 40s, the notion of a solid-body guitar was too radical a departure from the original concept of the instrument to be given any serious consideration.

Guitar makers felt they had a tradition to uphold; however, there were a growing number of guitar players that felt it was high time for a new tradition. One of those early malcontents was Lester Polsfuss, better known to radio audiences in the Chicago area as Les Paul, who was not only a gifted artist but also a very accomplished tinker and musical innovator.

To address the feedback problem, Paul built a guitar using a solid, 4x4 piece of pinewood for a body. He called his creation "the log." A description so painfully appropriate that he felt compelled to attach the upper and lower body bouts of a guitar just to make it halfway presentable. Even with the cosmetic appliqués, it still wasn't much to look at, but it did solve the feedback problem, and as an added bonus, the solid mass under the pickups increased the instrument's sustaining properties.

> *A guitar pickup is a magnet(s) wrapped in a coil of copper wire mounted under the strings. When an electric current is passed through the coil, it picks up the string vibrations and transforms them into an electronic signal. That signal is passed along the guitar cable and through the amplifier to the speaker, which reproduces the string vibrations.*
>
> *Guitar feedback is caused by sound waves from the amplifier passing back through the guitar's sound holes and re-vibrating its top, which transfers the sound back to the guitar's pickup and then back to the amplifier creating a cacophonous sound loop.*

It was a major breakthrough, and Paul was so thrilled with the results that he took it straight to the Gibson Company, whose shortsighted representatives dismissed it as "a broomstick with pickups." The Gibson people were not about to sully their reputation for distinctive, finely crafted instruments, with such a monstrosity.

But back in Fullerton California, Leo Fender, who had no traditions to protect, nor the resources necessary to produce the kind of labor-intensive, handcrafted instruments the competition was turning out, was more than willing to consider the unconventional approach. In fact, he had inadvertently taken the first step in that direction when he built himself a very simple, one-off, solid-body guitar as a test platform for the new pickup designs he was tinkering with.

It was a primitive-looking instrument made of a solid, two-inch-thick slab of ash wood with a one-piece maple neck joined to the body with four large screws. But even with the unrefined look of a high-school woodshop project, visitors to his radio shop just couldn't leave it alone. The guitar was constantly out on loan to players who raved about its high-volume capabilities, its slippery maple neck, and its brilliant, biting tone.

The guitar was not a stunner and was never intended for the marketplace, but players seemed to like it, and the simple design meant it could be mass-produced cheaply. So, with practically no start-up capital, and guided only by his own inclinations and his customer's feedback, Leo decided to build a line of electric guitars. He made an initial run of about 50 solid-body, single pickup guitars, patterned after his homely little test guitar, which he called the Fender Esquire.

He sold some and loaned others out to local players in exchange for their input, which, save for a recurring suggestion to add a second pickup to expand the instrument's tonal range, was overwhelmingly favorable. The recommended upgrade was duly incorporated into the second version of the guitar, which he renamed the Telecaster. And in the fall of 1950, it became the world's first commercially available solid-body electric guitar.

At first, music stores refused to sell it, complaining of its strange design and plain appearance.

> "...It was called everything from a canoe paddle to a snow shovel."
> Don Randall, Fender sales rep

But when the Telecaster started showing up in the hands of Leo's beta testers on the bandstand, on television shows, and in the local recording studios, demand picked up considerably.

The small, upstart company was becoming a huge success, especially among the country & western artists who would gradually work the Telecaster's piercing, trebly tone into the DNA of the modern country music sound. The Telecaster marked a quantum leap in electric guitar design and there was still more to come. The next year he came out with the revolutionary Fender Precision bass guitar. It was another, simple, solid-body design that was such a godsend to bass players that it practically eradicated the cumbersome double bass from the pop music scene overnight.

The Fender Sound

Leo designed his guitars and amplifiers to favor the treble frequencies, voicing them in a manner he thought best suited the country & western sound. He had no idea at the time that his distinctive, "Fender sound," would also make an indelible imprint on the sound of rock 'n' roll as well.

The sudden emergence of Fender guitars and amplifiers caught the major manufacturers completely off guard. Within two years, some anonymous appliance repairman from some Southern California hamlet no one had ever heard of had soundly trumped the biggest names in the business.

Gibson responded by summoning Les Paul back to the plant to help design their first solid-body guitar. Bearing the name of the man who inspired its creation, the Gibson Les Paul hit the market in 1952. It was a fine instrument, but it cost more than a Telecaster and therefore sold in fewer numbers.

By 1953, Leo Fender's guitars and amplifiers were considered among the very best available. Had he sold the farm right then and there and retired to Florida he would still be a legend today. But he didn't retire; he went back to his drawing board to remake the electric guitar all over again—this time, with a vibrato.

Paul Bigsby developed a very popular vibrato unit that all the big guitar makers were using. But Leo, an engineer at heart, was not content to simply license Bigsby's design; instead, he designed a unit of his own and a new guitar to go with it. The curvaceous Fender Stratocaster, introduced as an alternative to the homely Telecaster, was Leo's masterpiece. Making its market debut in 1954, it was a marvel of engineering, functionality, and mid-century, modernist style.

The Stratocaster sported three, hi-output pickups, and of course, Leo's new vibrato unit, which not only lowered pitch but raised it when the player yanked up on the handle.

The body was contoured and sculpted to where it practically wrapped around the player's waist, and its futuristic form was a triumph of space-age, modern design worthy of the very best interpreters of the art.

Though it would prove versatile enough for any musical setting, simply coupling it up

> **Disassociation**
>
> Though it would become the world's quintessential rock guitar, the Stratocaster's first celebrity devotees were Buddy Merrill of television's *Lawrence Welk Show*, and Mary Kay, a guitar wielding chanteuse popular on the Las Vegas lounge circuit.
>
> *A vibrato is a spring-loaded guitar bridge with a handle attached. When the player pushes down on the handle, the string tension is relaxed, which lowers the guitar's pitch to simulate the sound of a steel guitar.*

with one of Leo's tweed-covered amplifiers was all one need do to evoke the familiar, crystalline sound that would become the hallmark of the Southern California surf-rock scene.

But good sound alone was no longer good enough. By 1960, loud had become an essential element of the rock 'n' roll experience, and none of the amps available at the time were able to deliver the copious quantities of volume required, Leo's included. Rock 'n' Roll was evolving from an adolescent fad into a multi-million-dollar industry; and as Dick Dale was making agonizingly clear with every Rendezvous performance, the gear was going to have to evolve along with it.

Using Dale as his beta-tester, Leo set to work on an all-new 30-watt amp, which Dale promptly deconstructed. Every week Leo would build a new, more powerful amp, and every Saturday night, Dale would blow it up. And so, the cycle continued with Leo adding more and more power until he built the 85-watt amp that was able to pass the torturous Dick Dale stress test. He called it the Fender Showman, and in the cavernous Rendezvous Ballroom, it was practically a force of nature. Not only could you hear Dale's Stratocaster from the back of the house, you could feel it—all night long.

While he was struggling with the development of the Showman amp, Leo was also tinkering with another interesting contraption called a reverb unit, which produced an echo effect adjustable from subtle wavering to full-on surfverb. He intended it to be used with his vocal PA systems, but when Dale got hold of a demo unit, he plugged it into his guitar and thus nailed down the final ingredient of the classic Southern California surf sound.

But the 24-year-old veteran performer, the man dubbed the "King of the Surf Guitar" by his legion of fans, would not be the first to get the surf sound down on record. That distinction would go to a bunch of high school kids up the coast at Redondo Beach.

Surf Bands a Go-Go

Also included among Leo's legion of honky-tonk field testers were the Bel Airs from the South Bay area. Their gigs at the Club Bel Air were frequented by surfers who had declared the band's R&B-flavored repertoire to be surf rock. Musically, there wasn't a great deal of distance between the Bel Airs or Dick Dale and the other popular rock instrumentalists of the day.

What really distinguished the Southern California beach bands was the unique sound of their trebly, twangy Fender guitars and amplifiers. Add to that formula a liberal use of reverberation and delay effects, and the coastal scene from which the sound emerged, and you have surf rock.

In the summer of 1961, the Bel Airs cemented that classification when they recorded their first single called *Mr. Moto*, released on the small Arvee label. Many aficionados consider it to be the world's first surf song, beating Dick Dale to the radio waves by two months. With their Fender guitars out front swimming in tremolo and reverb, and punctuated with a bit of wavy vibrato work, the song set the surf sound in stone (or vinyl, which is practically the same thing).

Dale's first single, *Let's Go Trippin*, released on his own Deltone label, hit the airwaves in September of 1961. Though it too was a milestone in the annals of the surf-rock sub-genre and climbed all the way to number 4 on the regional charts, it only reached number 60 on the national charts, clearly emphasizing the fact that surf music was primarily a local phenomenon.

The surf sound may not have had much of an impact east of Riverside County, but within the confines of the Southland, it was all-pervasive. In 1962, if you were under 18 years of age, and you weren't in a surf band, then you knew someone who was.

It Came from the Garage

With their records climbing the local charts, the Bel Airs and Dick Dale set a spark that spontaneously ignited in 1001 suburban garages all over the Southland. The music was loud, flashy, fairly simple to play, and didn't involve any sissified singing, which made it enormously popular with suburban teenage boys who developed it into a genuine Southern California folk idiom. 22-4

Nearly the entire canon of surf rock hits was composed by pimply-faced high-school kids who had yet to pass their driver's tests. The Chantays, from Santa Ana High School, recorded a single called *Move It* that never moved onto radio playlists. It wasn't until a bored DJ flipped the disc to the B-side and played *Pipeline*, that the Chantays had their one-and-only top-40 hit.

The Surfaris were a group of Glendale High School kids who had scraped together $12.50 for one hour of studio time to record their one original song, *Surfer Joe*. The band was so inexperienced they had forgotten to prepare a second song for the B-side; a fine point brought to their attention by the recording engineer. The thirty minutes left on the clock was just enough time to run through two quick takes of an instrumental tune improvised on-the-spot featuring classic drum fills lifted from the repertoire of their high school marching band.

Unable to decide on a title, one of the dads in attendance suggested Wipeout and helped record a lead-in by breaking a piece of plywood into the microphone to suggest a splintering surfboard, while the engineer manically cackled the song's title. Again, it was the record's B-side, *Wipeout*, which became, not only the Surfaris biggest career hit but the highest-charting instrumental surf song ever, reaching number two on the Billboard Hot 100.

Fairfax High Schoolers, The Marketts, scored a hit with *Surfer's Stomp*. The Lively Ones from Orange County had great chart success with *Surf Rider*. And then there was that bunch from Hawthorne High, The Pendletones, who, with their first single, *Surfin*, would turn the whole surf rock thing completely on its ear.

A Surfin Safari

"We're loadin' up our woody with our boards inside, and headin' out singin' our song." Mike Love

It's very unusual for a true musical prodigy to go undetected for nearly twenty years, but Brian Douglas Wilson wasn't like your average run-of-the-mill wunderkind. Where others were discovered early through spontaneous displays of instrumental virtuosity, Brian, for the most part, kept his talent hidden between his ears, where he often heard strange voices harmonizing in six parts.

Oh, he had his outward moments of musical exceptionalism singing in the church choir, in holiday sing-a-longs, family get-togethers, and performing in school assemblies and pep rallies; but the real flashes of brilliance came behind closed doors.

Alone in his room, he spent hours at the record player singing along with Gershwin's sophisticated arraignments in a soaring falsetto that elicited so much teasing from his pals at school that, for years, he refused to exercise it anywhere else.

Gershwin was fun, but his favorite artists were the Four Freshmen—one of several popular vocal quartets of the late 50s. He bought all their records, learned every part of every song, and then taught them to his family for their occasional living room jam sessions. In these settings, Brian clearly showed himself to have an exceptionally keen ear for music; but neither he, nor his parents, really considered his musicality to be much more than a preoccupation of youth.

Perhaps it was their comfortable, suburban upbringing that tempered any grandiose dreams of stardom. The Wilson family was living the middle-class, post-war, California dream. Brian's father, Murry, married his high school sweetheart, Audree, and built up a small business renting machine lathes to the aerospace industry. They bought a typical tract home in Hawthorne, California, and raised three boys: Brian, and his two younger brothers, Dennis and Carl.

It wasn't the kind of unsettled existence that stimulates the sort of steely determination that sometimes results in spectacular achievements. Besides, real pop stars came from big towns in the east, or small towns in the south, not the salubrious suburbs of Southern California.

Indeed, most of his classmates at Hawthorne High School knew Brian only as a good guy with an easy-going, fun-loving personality who could carry a tune when the situation warranted. And by the time he had entered the final stretch of his senior year, his interest in both school and music was already fading. For his musical comp class final, he turned in a partially realized pop tune in place of the assigned sonata and received a C minus for what should have been a very easy A. In the brief summer of transition between high school kid and college man, he drifted, spending most of his free time hanging out with his buddies at the Foster's Freeze drive-in.

Ballad of the Pendletones

With September 1960 looming on the horizon, and no specific plans for the future, Brian enrolled at El Camino Community College declaring a psychology major—a popular choice for those still weighing their options. Then one day, while crossing campus on his way to class, he bumped into Al Jardine, an old classmate from Hawthorne High.

Al, who was into folk music and played in a band, and still remembered Brian's impressive performances at school functions, coaxed him into a practice room at the music department where they spent the afternoon going over some of Al's favorite folk tunes.

By the time the session had ended, Al had wheedled a commitment from Brian to put a group together with the proviso that Brian's brother Carl, who had a nice voice and could play a few Chuck Berry guitar riffs, and his cousin Mike Love, who liked to sing doo-wop, could also be in the band. Dennis, who wasn't much of a singer and had no real interest in folk music, was initially left out of the lineup.

Practices were held in the Wilson's living room where, on several occasions, Dennis urged the guys to write a song about his newest favorite pastime—surfing.

> **Singin' for Suppers**
>
> Brian had another, more altruistic reason for wanting to include his cousin Mike. Married at 19 with a child on the way and working two low-wage, part-time jobs with no plans to further his education, Brian thought he could use the extra money they might earn.

When the Southern California surf craze exploded, Dennis bought a surfboard and joined the revolution, becoming a familiar face among the south bay regulars. However, his passion for the surf scene was not shared by either his brothers or Al, and therefore his suggestions went unheeded.

What they were interested in doing was making a record, and when Brian's father, Murry, overheard them discussing strategy during a break between songs, he stepped in and offered to help.

Odd though it was, Murry Wilson, the portly, bespectacled, suit and tie businessman was not a stranger to the music business. Back in his salad days, Murry tried his hand at pop songwriting, and not without some modest success, for he had written a few songs and even found a publishing house willing to promote them.

Hite and Dorinda Morgan ran Guild Music, a modest, storefront publishing and recording service on Hollywood's Melrose Ave. In

1951, they managed to get a couple of Murry's songs recorded by a local country singer, and even get Lawrence Welk to play his *One Step, Two Step Polka* tune on the radio; but the momentum soon fizzled, and Murry went back at his day job. Now ten years down the road, the Morgan's were still in the business, and as a favor to Murry, willing to spend a few hours on a Saturday afternoon listening to his son's band, "the Pendletones," which now included Dennis at his mother's insistence.

The group assembled in Guild's tiny front lobby and ran through a handful of well-worn folk songs. When it was all over, the Morgans complimented the boys on their polished presentation but turned them down for their lack of originality—the country was already crawling with Kingston Trio clones.

Murry and the boys thanked the Morgans for their time and were making their way to the exit when, out of the blue, Dennis wheeled back around and asked the Morgans if they had heard of the new surfing craze that was sweeping over the Southland, because he and Brian were working on a new song about it called *Surfin*.

Hearing this, the rest of the boys froze dead in their tracks; Brian was so stunned he couldn't speak. Murry, who was not privy to the group's day-to-day activities, didn't know what to think. The Morgans, on the other hand, seemed to be genuinely interested, which emboldened Dennis to continue on and explain that surfers had their own culture with their own lingo, their own music, and their own surfer stomp dance, which he eagerly demonstrated.

> **Out of the Fire**
> After getting expelled from school for fighting and getting involved in a few other dustups with the law, Audree thought that Dennis' involvement with the group might keep him out of trouble.
>
> **Branded**
> The group's name was taken from the brand name of a woolen shirt that was popular with the teenagers.

The Morgans were so intrigued with the novelty of this surfing thing that they made the boys promise to come right back to perform their new song as soon as it was completed. They sheepishly nodded in agreement and hurriedly exited the premises before Dennis could dig them in any deeper.

By the time they arrived home, Brian's inclination to want to strangle his little brother had passed, and he began to warm up to the idea of writing a song. Of course, the way Dennis put it, it couldn't be just any song; he had specifically promised a surf song. Brian didn't know anything about surfing, but he still had that C minus pop tune he wrote the year before in high school, so he began working with that, throwing in some vocal harmonizations, and a doo-wop chorus for Mike to sing. For lyrics, he and Mike put together a simple "let's go surfin" narrative built upon Dennis's knowledge of common surfer terms and practices.

It was while they were working through the final few drafts of the song that Murry and Audree departed on an extended, Labor Day weekend trip to Mexico City, leaving the boys with $100.00 to cover living expenses and strict instructions not to get into any trouble.

Though all three brothers readily agreed to the terms, alternate plans had already been made well in advance of the parent's departure, and the moment their cab disappeared around the corner, the whole group loaded into the Wilson family car and headed for Hollywood.

Wallich's Music City, on the corner of Sunset and Vine, was one of the Southland's first entertainment superstores offering a full line of televisions, stereos, sheet music, records, and musical instruments, which they also rented. With the Wilson boys $100.00, the Pendletones rented a whole carload of guitars, amps, drums, and microphones, and set them up in the Wilson's living room.

For three days straight, they hammered their one song into a presentable state and were congratulating themselves for a job well done when Murry and Audree returned home a little ahead of schedule. When he learned how they acquired the equipment, Murry flew into a rage throwing Brian against the wall and choking him blue-faced. Al and Mike, having never seen the dark side of Murry, were terrified, but for the Wilson boys, these scenes were just an unfortunate part of their upbringing.

Like his roughneck father before him, Murry had a fierce, uncontrollable temper. Years later, Brian would claim, that as a child, he lost most of the hearing in his right ear due to a backhand from Murry. But this time, Audree was able to calm the situation before any real damage was done by suggesting he let the guys play their new song for him. And in the span of a two-and-a-half-minute pop song, Murry had forgiven all and appointed himself the band's manager.

Within a few weeks of their first visit, the Pendletones were back at Guild Music to play *Surfin* for the Morgans. In truth, it was not a great piece of work. The music was not original, and the lyrics were a little clumsy, but the theme was indeed unique. There had never been a song about Southern California's beach phenomenon, and just the novelty might be enough to get it on the pop charts. And so, the Morgans agreed to sign the band to a standard, minor league publishing contract.

Two weeks later, (10/3/61) the Pendletones were booked into World Pacific Studios to record *Surfin* and one of Hite's songs, *Luau*, for the B-side of their first record, which Hite arraigned to be released on the small Candix Records label. And about five weeks later, the Wilsons received a package from Candix containing copies of their newly released single. Bubbling over with excitement, the whole family gathered at the kitchen table for the unboxing of the 45s; but with the records spread out on the table, the jubilant mood evaporated. None could believe their eyes.

The record labels read, "*Surfin*, by The Beach Boys." Who the #@$% were the Beach Boys? With his face turning a bright beet red, Murry got on the phone to Hite Morgan, who pled ignorance and referred him to the label's A&R man, who referred him to the record distributor, who referred him to the distributor's agent, who brazenly admitted that it was he who changed the group's name to something, he thought, was more suggestive of their music. Murry's pitch rose an octave as he countered with the obligatory threat to sue everyone involved and then slammed down the receiver.

That evening, Brain took his brothers to Foster's Freeze where, over burgers, fries, and shakes, they commiserated with each other over the capriciousness of the music business and the indignity of being so callously disregarded. With the radio volume set to an uncharacteristically low level, the ride home was somber and nearly silent until the word "surfin'" seemed to suddenly pop right out of thin air. Brian immediately lunged for the radio's volume knob giving it a hard twist in time to catch the DJ announce that the evening's debut single with the most listener requests was *Surfin*, by the Southland's own Beach Boys.

Having been so preoccupied with the unsolicited name change, they forgot that the local radio stations also received promo copies of *Surfin*, and one of the biggest, radio KFWB, had been playing it all day long.

Brian was so startled he nearly sideswiped a parked car; Carl upchucked in the back seat, and Dennis jumped out and ran the rest of the way home screaming, "We're on the radio!"

It's one thing to hear your song on the record player at home, and quite another to hear it on the radio and know that half of L.A. County is listening along with you. By the following day, *Surfin* was in regular rotation on the two biggest stations in L.A., the Pendletones were history, and the Beach Boys were on their way to becoming the Southland's foremost pop-cultural icons.

"Surfin" ... launched, however tentatively, was one of the most important mythic brandings of Southern California since the creation of the orange crate label." Kevin Starr

To get them out into the public eye while they had a song on the radio, the Morgans got them booked into the Rendezvous Ballroom to play their two songs during the intermission in Dick Dale's show. But the inexperienced, and visibly nervous, Beach Boys were not well received by Dale's rabidly partisan fans who were already wise to the fact that their surfer image was just a façade.

> *"They dressed in silly matching outfits, sang like girls, and didn't even surf."* Pat Ganahl

The band was humiliated, but fortunately, there was little time to dwell on the rough spots. Eight days later, they opened for Ike and Tina Turner at the Long Beach Municipal Auditorium, and despite the cultural incongruity of five lily-white suburbanites playing to a predominantly minority audience, the band played well, and the crowd genuinely seemed to enjoy their set.

Everything seemed to be coming together for them until they received their first royalty check. After selling over 40,000 singles in just a few weeks, and reaching number three on the local charts, and seventy-five on the nationals, the band's cut of the take was a measly $200.00.

They were not yet in the music business six months and already they were being robbed blind. Murry again promised to sue all responsible parties, but before any action could be taken, Candix Records, overwhelmed by the demand for Beach Boys records, went bankrupt.

> **Too much Monkey Business**
>
> How does too much business drive a business out of business? Retailers are notoriously slow to pay their wholesalers. Because Candix couldn't produce more records until they were paid for those they had already delivered, they couldn't meet the demand for new product and were forced out of business.

Al was so disgusted he quit the group to go back to college and was replaced by David Marks—the 13-year-old neighbor kid from across the street who took guitar lessons from Carl's instructor. 22-5

As the group's self-appointed manager, Murry assumed the responsibility of finding the boys another record label and booked a studio to record new demos of Brian's latest batch of original songs.

Though his musical aspirations and abilities lay well beyond the simple, surf rock formula, *Surfin* had done well enough to justify further variations on that same theme. And so, taking his cues from personal experience and the passing parade, he continued writing

> **Sound Check**
>
> In one of the great ironies of pop cultural history, Brian Wilson, whose music immortalized the Southern Californian's preoccupation with surfing, cars, and girls, was terrified of the ocean, timid behind the wheel, and somewhat awkward in dealings with the opposite sex.

songs that celebrated the Southern California experience as seen through the eyes of the typical teenager.

Along the melody lines of his simple, three-minute pop sagas, he revealed the life at home, at school, on the boulevard, and on the beach. Like thousands before him, he would explore the universal themes of love won and lost, and the everyday trials and triumphs of youth, but always with a very keen sense of place.

Among his new songs was a beautiful ballad called *Surfer Girl*, another "Surfin'esque" California anthem called *Surfin Safari*, and a song about a souped-up Chevy called *409*, which he wrote with Gary Usher, a bank teller and hot rod buff who had wandered into one of their living room rehearsals.

With these songs, the group returned to the recording studio, for only the second time, and it was during this "spec session" that Brian really began to refine the sound that would set them apart from all others, blending the smooth, intricate harmonies of a sophisticated vocal group with rock 'n' roll instrumentation.

With the band's new tapes in hand, Murry went knocking on doors, pitching the band to every label in L.A., and got rejected by all until he met with Nick Venet at Capitol Records. At twenty-three, Venet was the youngest A&R rep at Capitol, which put him in a much better position to appreciate the group's potential than his middle-aged counterparts. After hearing just eight bars of *Surfin Safari*, he knew it would be a hit and signed the group to a recording contract making them Capitol's very first rock 'n' roll act.

But it was an acquisition the upper management was not entirely comfortable with. Capitol made its mark with a roster full of solid, seasoned performers like Frank Sinatra, Nat King Cole, and Peggy Lee. With the success of these, and many other entertainment veterans, the company could afford to take a few chances; but rock 'n' roll, a musical genre entirely dependent upon the whims of teenagers, was considered almost too big a risk.

And so, for the entirety of their tenure with Capitol Records, the company relentlessly pushed them to produce their records as fast as possible before the bottom fell out of the teen music market.

As the first of many cost-saving measures, Capitol issued the *Surfin Safari/409* demo recordings as their first single.

The Sound of Sunshine

Like the west coast jazz and exotica practitioners, the Beach Boys distinctive, California sound was spirited and upbeat. Later described as a herald of, "the Sunshine Sound," liberal measures of Wilson's pop-rock recipe would add sweet flavoring to the repertoire of several other Southern California acts like the Mommas and Poppas, the 5th Dimension, the Association, and Harper's Bizarre, as well as countless, 60s era, movie and television themes.

The company's pick for the record's A-side, *409*, stalled at number 76, but the B-side, *Surfin Safari*, reached number 14 on Billboard's Hot 100. With the release of this, their first single with Capitol, the Beach Boys not only had a hit, but they also launched two distinct and regionally specific sub-genres of rock 'n' roll: vocal surf and hot rod rock. For the next half-dozen years, each category would inspire numerous imitators and account for millions in record sales for the L.A.-based labels.

"At Capital, liberty, Decca, Columbia, Tower, RCA, Warner Bros., Mercury, and dozens of smaller labels there was a feeding frenzy afoot for anything that smelled of sea air, surf wax, and West coast fuel exhaust, all hands riding the emblematic shirttails of a certain Hawthorn group." Timothy White

Now that Capitol had a major chart success on their hands, they rushed the band out on a bare-bones, 40-date tour of the mid-west chaperoned by a libertine tour manager only a few years Brian's senior. They left L.A. as boys but returned as seasoned road warriors having sampled all the forbidden fruits that their newly established rock star status availed them. But once back home, Capitol had them go right back into the studio to record their first album featuring the hits *Surfin, Surfin Safari*, and *409*.

For the album's no-budget cover, Nick Venet took the boys down to Paradise Cove, near Malibu, in their matching Pendleton shirts and Chino pants to pose for a few pictures with Dennis's surfboard. But while the photographer was clicking away, Venet noticed an old Model A pickup in the parking lot he thought might add some gravitas to the surfer image he was crafting, so he paid the owner a few bucks rent and adorned the old beater with palm fronds, the surfboard, and the five Beach Boys.

On the command "smile," the shutter was snapped on the iconic photo that would grace their first album cover, introduce their likeness to the world, and advance their rising status as the Southland's foremost representatives of the new Southern California youth scene.

Califormulatin'

In addition to the regionally specific music pouring out of the Southland, television shows began to reflect a very pronounced west coast aura when the three major networks moved the bulk of their operations from New York to Hollywood. In the early 1960s, gritty, urban cop shows like *Naked City* and *The Detectives* gave way to sun-drenched, suburbanized, California-centric cop shows like *77 Sunset Strip, Hawaiian Eye*, and *Surfside 6*. Also, airing nightly, amongst a whole slew of primetime cowboy shows, were the "tropical escape fantasies." *Adventures in Paradise, Follow the Sun*, and *The Beachcomber* featured dropout protagonists livin' the good life as it was meant to be lived—on that mythical island paradise far from the demands and pressures of civilized society.

Though the fictional settings would vary, they were all made in Hollywood, and it showed to very good advantage. Like the old Keystone Cops serials that brought Southern California into the local movie houses back in the 20s, these swingingly stylized TV shows brought it right into America's living rooms often rousing wistful notions of how one might spend a summer's vacation.

If by chance, that notion blossomed into a definite travel plan, the excursionist would find that there had never been a better time for a trip out west. Six years into a ten-year federal program to build 40,000 miles of interstate super-highways and freeways, it seemed that all roads led west.

A century before, one risked all to make the trip; now, anyone with a reasonably sound automobile could set out on a whim, pull onto the interstate, let loose the horses, and glide across deserts and over mountains at speeds twice that possible just a few years earlier. And as fast as they could, they came, and came, and came.

In 1962, 114 years after gold was discovered, and 90 years after the railroads began their monumental efforts to stimulate westward migration, California had overtaken New York as the most populous state in the nation. The milestone was received with great fanfare, which gradually ebbed away as it became apparent the achievement did not come without a price—yet still the crowds kept coming.

Chapter 23
The American Riviera

In the lustrous splendor of early 1960s Southern California, the land of sunny blue skies, sea-scented breezes, and sandy-white beaches, it would have been very difficult to convince either the native, the outlander, or the tourist of the unimaginable efforts undertaken over many decades to persuade people to come and live along the southwestern coast of the United States.

Amidst the pageantry of the palms, few had any idea they were living in a desert, or that the whole shebang was precariously dependent on water pumped and piped from better-balanced ecosystems hundreds of miles away.

Everything they saw and experienced ran counter to the truth. By 1963, the multi-generational, regional art project begun back in the 1870s had finally reached its zenith; Southern California had crystallized into a fully developed, coastal civilization as distinct and recognizable as any of the great hamlets of yore. Along the highways, byways, and boulevards of the big burgs and small towns lay an architectural patchwork of fancifully ornamented edifices interweaving pre-war charm with post-war chic.

And though not every structure was completely adorned in the whimsical Googie-mod/Poly-pop mode, the trend was so pervasive that enough of it bled over from one property to another that it appeared to be absolute, which bestowed upon the entire region a perennial sense of levity.

This trend toward idiosyncrasy and frivolity gained even more momentum within the confines of the average, suburban tract development, where form also followed fun rather than function. For those of us truly in tune with the times, no opportunity to commemorate the exuberance of the moment would be squandered.

We commemorated at home, we commemorated on the road, and we most certainly commemorated along the Southern California shoreline where there emerged one of the most illustrious coastal cultures on earth. Names like Silver Strand, La Jolla, Laguna, Newport, Santa Monica, and Malibu were known throughout the world, and scattered in-between those renowned points of interest were over 100 others, including at least two dozen storied surf sites. Along these shores, the bronzed and beautiful Southern Californians of legend cavorted amongst the legions of the not so "tall, tan, young, and lovely." The stunners were outnumbered, of course, but there were more than enough to give credence to the myth.

As for those 200 miles of coastline, there was nothing at all mythical about that; it was a magnificent spectacle from one end to the other. Visitors came to Southern California for many reasons, but few returned home without putting in at least one appearance at one of the many oceanfront playgrounds along the coast if only to gaze out upon the Pacific, stroll barefoot in the sand, or stretch out on a towel with a good magazine.

Pulp Depiction

Of all the good reading rags available to Southern California beachgoers in that summer of 63, one of the most relevant to the coastal scene was a slick new monthly called *Surfer*, which fortuitously came into being through one surfer's errant efforts to promote a flagging film career.

Surfer and amateur filmmaker John Severson had a master's degree in art and a steady job as a teacher when the army came calling. Though certainly not thrilled to be pressed into service, his outlook improved when he found he was to be shipped out to Schofield Barracks, on Oahu, where he would be placed on the army surf team and be paid to surf for the U.S. government. For the next few years, he surfed, soldiered, and sold his paintings in grand boho style on the boardwalk behind the Royal Hawaiian Hotel.

Like Bruce Brown, Severson returned home with several reels of 16mm surfing footage, which he forgot about until he attended a screening of Brown's *Slippery When Wet*. By the time the house lights came back up, Severson had convinced himself that he could make a film every bit as engaging as the opus he had just witnessed. So, he put together his own rudimentary film called *Surf*, and hit the road. The film did just well enough to encourage a second attempt, entitled *Surf Fever*, which Severson heavily promoted with handbills featuring several of his impressionistic renderings.

Beachgoers admired his artwork so much, that they stole the flyers almost as fast as they could be posted. So, to ensure that he got some advertising value for the money and effort spent, he improvised a 36-page program to be sold at screenings featuring photos, cartoons, a little surf talk, and even a few ads. In the spring of 1960, Severson printed 5000 copies of the promo publication he called, *The Surfer*. Surprisingly, even at the steep price of two dollars per issue, booklet sales surpassed ticket sales. Severson began selling *The Surfer* at surf shops and beach area bookstores, which marked the sideways launch of what would become *Surfer* magazine.

His original idea, to publish an annual photo journal, was soon scrapped in favor of a quarterly magazine, but it didn't take long to figure out that, in the aftermath of *Gidget*, a solid market existed for a much more comprehensive publication and, by 1963, *Surfer* magazine had evolved into a super-slick monthly, becoming the first of a handful of glossy, Southern California based publications dedicated solely to surfing and the surf culture it spawned.

Tri-Fives and Wooden Sides

Out on the streets, the heavily modified, 30s era roadsters, bucket T's, and coupes the Beach Boys immortalized in song were losing ground, among a new generation of boomer drivers, to the more contemporary-looking and technologically advanced coupes and two-door sedans of the mid-50s, especially Chevy's Tri-Five models — the 1955, 56, and 57 Bel Airs, 210s, and hardtops.

Huge sellers when they were first introduced, they were now six to eight years old, relatively cheap on the used car market, and due to the vast array of interchangeable performance parts Chevy produced for its, "we're not racing, racing program," infinitely buildable.

The classic look included a custom paint job, a tail-end jacked up high above the extra-wide rear tires, a full set of chrome, Cragar SS mag wheels, and black leatherette upholstery either in the straight back or Tijuana tuck & roll style. Of course, the drive trains were always developed as far as ability and bank account would allow.

For the surfers, the Tri-Five models also included some very desirable wagons. Though most truly dedicated surfers were generally low on funds, and therefore any vehicle at the right price would have to do, station wagons, with their added carrying capacity were favored, and the Tri-Five wagons were favored above all others, save for the iconic woodies.

An integral part of the surfer mystique, the woodies, (or wood-paneled station wagons), were built during the 30s and 40s and used primarily as "station hacks" ferrying tourists and their luggage between train depots and hotels. The expensive wood siding was an attractive feature but did not hold up as well as sheet steel, and in the early 50s, automakers dropped them from their lineups.

Those still on the road in the 60s were pretty well worn and weathered and could usually be had cheap, which made them ideal conveyances for surfers, and some of the old woodies did see service as beach buggies, though they were never quite as common as the old songs and sagas suggest. 23-1

Revell-ing

In the spring of 1963, Big Daddy Roth hit the road again with his latest creation, the Mysterion, which ratcheted up the fantastical factor by two—two engines and two transmissions. The fiberglass body was coated in a highly reflective yellowish-green lacquer and crowned with another bubble top, retaining the futuristic, space-age aura he created with the Beatnik Bandit.

A cosmic roadster under glass, the Mysterion wowed audiences wherever it appeared, even though, like the Bandit, it was too fantastic to function. But rumors of its infirmity did nothing to diminish its appeal. Show goers didn't come to see ordinary, they came to see over-the-top, and on that count, Roth led the pack.

The King Midas of the custom car craze, Roth was winning accolades on the concourse and magazine covers, while at the same time, turning plastic into gold for Revell Inc. Both the Outlaw kit,

> **Custom Crutches**
> The Mysterion's frame couldn't support the weight of its twin engines, so they were gutted of their internal workings and the frame was re-enforced with wooden 2x4s.

released in 1962, and the Beatnik Bandit, released in early 63, were selling so well that Revell had the Mysterion kit on store shelves while the original was still making its first appearance on the summer show circuit. Revell even issued scale models of Rat Fink and the rest of Roth's cartoonish creatures.

Hugely popular with males under the age of sixteen, Roth's outlandish t-shirts and do-it-yourself, plastic miniatures became the wardrobe essentials and fashionable bedroom accents of kids from every corner of the country who wished to share in a bit of the mad magic of Southern California and its crazy custom car culture.

California Carnival

Of the many events Roth participated in during the 1963 spring and summer season, the biggest and the best of them all was the annual California Teen-Age Fair, a ten-day extravaganza staged during the spring break, celebrating the Southland's youth culture.

Sponsored by L.A.'s radio stations, the Teen Fair was part carnival and part teen trade show featuring the usual rides and attractions alongside scores of commercial booths and pavilions exhibiting an endless array of products designed specifically to appeal to the American teenager.

Any company seeking entry into the teen market, from small startups to long-established corporations, set up an exhibit at the fair. Coke and Pepsi, Chevrolet and Ford, Honda and Yamaha, Clairol and Yardley, and local legends Catalina and Hang-Ten sportswear, Hobie and Hansen surfboards, and Fender and Rickenbacker guitars all hawked their wares at the fair. Sideshow attractions included battles of the bands, dance contests, teen fashion shows, surf films, hot rod films, a Miss Teen USA beauty pageant, and a custom car show.

Performing on the main stage were the Beach Boys, Dick Dale and the Deltones, and Frankie Avalon, a nearly forgotten pop singer who had just finished shooting some crazy movie about a beach party.

Though the isles were overflowing with unique and trendy consumer goods, what was really on display here was the rapidly rising social, cultural, and economic power of the modern-day teenager, which was already altering the lay of the land we lived in, and never more thoroughly as in the fields of fashion, film, and popular music.

California Road Rock

With the enormous success of the Beach Boys *Shut Down* album, every record company in Los Angeles rushed to capitalize on this new west coast phenomenon. But rather than beat the bushes in search of the next great hot-rodding beach band, the middle-aged label execs created their own "Hotrod Rock" sub-divisions, marshaling in-house talent to mass-produce records bursting forth with the electrified, high-energy sounds of Southern California's custom culture.

Over the next couple of years, the L.A. labels released a barrage of singles and albums by, what appeared to be, a whole slew of new, Southland rock bands that were actually made up of the same studio aces that were laying down the backing tracks for nearly every pop artist on the west coast.

The Hondells

One of the few rod-rock projects to penetrate the national pop charts was built around one of Brian Wilson's throw-away tunes called *Little Honda*, inspired by a series of Honda TV ads "You meet the nicest people on a Honda" introducing their new, lightweight "motorbikes" to the American market. Brian considered it album filler, but when Usher heard it, he heard a hit and called in the Wrecking Crew and a few singers to record the song and release it as a single by the fictional Hondells. When the song did become a hit, Usher hastily put together a touring band and sent them out on the road, while he and his studio crew recorded material for an album so rushed that the photographer hired to do the cover photo had to recruit a quartet of bank clerks on lunch break as stand ins for the band that never was.

The Band's Band

Unbeknownst to most record buyers at the time, it was the Wrecking Crew, the informal assemblage of about two-dozen of L.A.'s top session players, that provided the instrumentation on most of the pop/rock records that came out of L.A. during the 1960s and 70s.

And of all the many contract producers grinding out this assembly-line rod-rock, one of the most prolific was Brian Wilson's old songwriting partner, Gary Usher. Freelancing for several different labels, Usher produced over a dozen different "car bands," with the Wrecking Crew accompanied by a revolving roster of contract singers. With songs like *Cheater Slicks, Hot Rod High,* and *Dragin' Duce,* bands like the Superstocks, the Four-Speeds, and the Kustom Kings became the Southland's pop purveyors of California's car culture.

Usher and crew even made novelty albums for Big Daddy Ed Roth and Capitol Records under the pseudonym of Mr. Gasser and the Weirdos. Designed mainly to cash in on the nation's fascination with the Southern California scene, these recordings rarely made it to the top of the pop charts, but they became a staple in discount record bins all over the country where they sold very well and were especially popular with teen and pre-teen boys dreaming of their first car, their first kiss, and maybe even a first trip out west.

Beach Blanket Bonanza

With the emergence of television, fewer and fewer grown-ups were going out to the movies, yet the Hollywood studios continued to tailor most of their output toward that vanishing demographic. This oversight was recognized by James Nicholson, a film distributor's rep, and his associate, Samuel Arkoff, an entertainment lawyer, who together formed one of the most prolific and profitable production companies in the history of filmed entertainment, American International Pictures (AIP).

Launched in 1954, AIP specifically tailored its films to appeal to the fastest growing demographic in the United States—teenagers. Their independent productions, unapologetically low budget and sensationalist, with plenty of gratuitous action, romance, sex, violence, and gore became the mainstay of grindhouse double bills and drive-in theaters throughout the county.

By 1962, AIP had over-exploited nearly every possible film genre imaginable: westerns, *Flesh and the Spur*; delinquent dramas, *High School Hellcats*; horror, *The Screaming Skull*; sci-fi, *Earth Vs. the Spider*, and were preparing to go full circle by resurrecting the delinquent teen genre when they sent for director William Asher. 23-2

A veteran director in the fast-paced, high-pressure world of episodic television, Asher built a reputation as a man who could get things done quickly and under budget; therefore, he was an ideal choice for an AIP project. In the office of the two producers, Asher was presented with a pitch to direct, what he considered to be, another stale "switchblades and sideburns" potboiler.

So, as tactfully as he could, Asher explained to the two, now middle-aged, execs that they had lost touch with the times and then rose to his feet, expecting to be shown to the door. But instead of throwing him out, they asked him to stay and share his opinion as to what he thought might light up the box office.

Asher, a Malibu resident and part-time surfer himself, knew exactly where the action was, and argued that the American public wasn't interested in ugly urban dramas, they wanted to enjoy themselves on vicarious vacations to bright sunny climbs with beautiful girls and handsome guys living as if they hadn't a care in the world.

To back up his claim he pointed out that every major studio in Hollywood had already repackaged Gidget's surfin', singin', dancin', and romancin' formula and scored a hit every time out. MGM moved the scene to Fort Lauderdale, Florida, for *Where the Boys Are* and was rewarded handsomely; Columbia's *Gidget* sequel, *Gidget Goes Hawaiian* out grossed the original. And in Paramount's *Blue Hawaii*, Elvis broke box office records just by laying on a surfboard.

Though not completely convinced that Asher was on to the next big thing in movies, Nicholson and Arkoff agreed to gamble on one film if Asher could shoot it in two weeks and deliver the finished product on a budget of $300,000, which was less than one-quarter of the budget for a B picture at a major studio. Asher signed on, and the three principals began putting all the wrong pieces together. To fill the roles of the lead beach boy and bunny, AIP went way against type with two raven-haired Italians from the east coast.

Philadelphia born and raised; teen idol Frankie Avalon scored several top 40 hits in the late 50s. But with his teen years behind him, and his 40s-era crooner's style losing ground to pop acts like the Beach Boys, he sought to extend his career by branching out into films.

He had some early success with supporting roles in a few major productions like *The Alamo* and *Voyage to the Bottom of the Sea*; but by 1962, he was under contract to AIP appearing in, *Operation Bikini* and *Panic in Year Zero*, before being tapped to star in what would become *Beach Party*.

Annette Funicello's star had once shown far brighter thanks to her legendary stint on Walt Disney's TV variety show *The Mickey Mouse Club*. In the late 50s, Funicello, who hailed from Utica, New York, was the most popular teenager on the planet. Every girl from six to sixteen wanted to be her, and every boy in that same demographic had a major crush on her.

After the run of the Mouse Club, Disney kept her under contract recording pop songs for the house label, Buena Vista, and appearing in several Disney films and TV shows. But like Avalon, her career was losing momentum when AIP offered her the lead in *Beach Party*.

As Southern California surfers, Avalon and Funicello were hopelessly miss-cast. Neither was fond of the beach, nor at ease in the water; but they brought some name recognition to the project at an affordable price, and, as a bonus, the genuine chemistry between them easily transferred to film.

Arkoff's brother-in-law, Lou Rusoff, who had written several of AIP's "teens gone wrong" and "monsters on the loose" pictures was assigned script duties even though the balding and bearded 52-year-old writer knew absolutely nothing about surfers and surfing. To plug this gaping hole in his knowledge base, Rusoff went out to Malibu to absorb the local color.

Wandering up and down the beach, he listened for surf-specific jargon and observed teen behavioral patterns as expressed both in sand and surf. It was while he was reconnoitering that he hit upon the idea of incorporating his researching into the plot of the script. Taking Gidget's beach backdrop and mixing in the communal vacation theme from *Where the Boys Are*, Rusoff built his story around an anthropologist studying the sex life of the Southern California teenager.

The plot centered on the conflict between Dolores (Funicello), who wants to save herself for the wedding day, and her boyfriend, Frankie (Avalon), who would rather she didn't. In the remaining 90 minutes, Dolores is menaced by a slapstick motorcycle gang, rescued by the professor whom she uses to make Frankie jealous, which makes the professor's amorous assistant jealous, while Frankie uses a Hungarian barmaid to make Dolores jealous.

In-between the jealous spats there's some surfing, singing, and frug dancing before the misunderstandings are resolved and we arrive at the inevitable happy ending.

For background and surf doubles, AIP hired many of the same Malibu crewmembers that lent their skills to *Gidget*. And except for a ringer or two (a few sons and daughters of Hollywood stars made their screen debut in *Beach Party*), most of the younger players were recruited right on the beach.

To hedge their bet and add some weight to this lighter-than-air affair, the producers salted the cast with Hollywood veterans, Bob Cummings, Dorothy Malone, Morey Amsterdam, Harvey Lembeck, and in a cameo role, Vincent Price. In fact, the casting of older, established stars that still had some name recognition, yet worked for a fraction of their old studio salaries, had been AIP's casting strategy since the company's inception, and it paid substantial dividends. This

> **Navel No-No**
>
> According to legend, Disney refused to loan Annette out to AIP unless they promised she would not wear a bikini and not reveal her belly button. And although she never appeared in anything more revealing than a sensible two-piece suit, her navel is visible in *Beach Party* and several other films, suggesting the story was most likely a fiction dreamed up by the AIP publicity department.

was especially true of their immensely popular horror films, which launched new careers for Hollywood scary men Boris Karloff, Peter Lorrie, and Vincent Price, all of whom were featured in the beach party films.

Dick (King of the surf guitar) Dale and his Del-tones were hired on as the house band, playing songs written for the film by Beach Boys co-writers Gary Usher and Roger Christian, and orchestral sound cues were produced by Hollywood soundtrack specialist and exotica maestro Les Baxter.

Beach Party presented a world of sunshine, sandy beaches, and crystal-clear waters where there were no parents, no authority figures, and no problems of any kind; just good, clean-cut, attractive kids having nothing but fun, fun, fun.

"It's all good clean fun; no hearts are broken, and virginity prevails." William Asher

A gala première was held in San Diego and the film was very well received, but it was practically a home-town crowd, and that little coup could not dispel the producer's fears that the film was so California-centric it would never be anything but a regional attraction and that financing a costly nationwide release would prove disastrous.

So, in July 1963, *Beach Party* was released in just three mid-western cities. But the film broke the house records at all three theaters and word soon spread to other exhibitors around the country who began pressing the producers for prints, and by the following month, *Beach Party* was released nationwide and became AIP's highest-grossing film to date.

Beach Party was such an overwhelming success that AIP immediately rushed a sequel into production to be released in the spring of 1964. This follow-up was so rushed the producers had to re-use the same cast, the same crew, the same script, and practically the same title, "*Muscle Beach Party.*"

With its second beach party film, AIP would establish a solid formula. The casts, which remained fixed right down to the stunt doubles and background players, were rounded out with an assortment of familiar, Hollywood veterans. The basic storylines never strayed from the *Beach Party* model: An attractive transgressor comes between the two lovers, jealousy ensues, misunderstandings abound, and all is sorted out and forgiven in the end.

Variety came in the form of settings and leisure activities. In *Bikini Beach*, the gang took up drag racing; in *Beach Blanket Bingo* it was sky diving, and motorcycle racing in *How to Stuff a Wild Bikini*. In *Ski Party*, the whole beach party road show was moved to the wintery slopes of Sun Valley, Idaho. Box office receipts suggested the audience hardly noticed the deviation.

Despite the inane plots, the flawed acting, and the dated musical numbers, nothing could stop this AIP juggernaut; the beach movies were absolutely bulletproof at the box office, and every major studio and grade Z-movie hack in Hollywood began producing *Beach Party* knockoffs.

What made these awkward films so popular? The beach films evoked a sun-soaked fantasyland purged of any real-world responsibility where beautiful young people co-existed in communal harmony in a world of their own. It was high-octane escapism and American teens teetering on the brink of adulthood swallowed it whole.

The Endless Summer

In the fall of 1962, Bruce Brown began preparing to shoot his sixth surf film. Although he was entertaining some vague notion to break out of the "surf film" mode and reach out to a larger, more general audience, he had not formulated a specific game plan by the go-date, and so he patterned the project on the same familiar formula he had used five times before.

On paper, everything was business as usual except for the intended shooting location, West Africa. It wasn't until he visited the travel agency that the project developed into something out of the ordinary.

Brown intended to purchase three round-trip tickets for himself and his two protagonists, Robert August and Mike Hynson, when his travel agent pointed out that he could save $50.00 if he just continued eastward making a complete trip around the world.

Suddenly, there it was all laid out before him; the hook that would make this film stand out from all the others: not only would they search for the perfect wave, they would do it by following the summer season around the world. Brown walked out of the travel agency with a new flight plan, a new shooting plan, and an iconic new title for his next film, *The Endless Summer*.

Arriving in Senegal, West Africa, Brown and company worked their way down the coast towards Cape Town, dropping in at any beach that looked promising. At each stop, they fraternized with the locals and appreciated the natural wonders of the locality. After declaring Cape St. Francis to be the site of the perfect wave, they hopped on over to west Australia, to east Australia, to New Zealand, to Tahiti, and finally back to Hawaii, where the film began.

Though still similar in format to earlier efforts, the scope was grander, the camerawork was more imaginative and self-assured, the surf shots had greater immediacy and presence, and the extended travelogue sequences had a reverence and authority worthy of National

Geographic. Everything about *Endless Summer* showed vast improvement over his earlier films; even his trademark corny skits radiated a little Hollywood sheen. All in all, it was an amazing accomplishment for one man with a wind-up, newsreel camera.

Pulling out all the stops in hopes of attracting a national distributor, Brown pre-recorded his narration without sacrificing the folksy, Southern California charm that helped to make his films "best of breed."

After viewing a rough cut, he knew he had something special, so he shelved the traditional pre-recorded jazz track and hired an unknown surf band from San Clemente to compose and record an all-original score. Taking into account all the hazards he faced shooting the film, few could have measured up to the risk he took with this decision.

How easily things could have gone so very wrong, especially when considering the slim direction Brown gave the band, "Write me a sunset." That was it–write a sunset, and they did. The Sandal's sentimental, *Theme from the Endless Summer*, elegantly expressed all the bittersweet longing of a summer's evening as the sun sinks below the horizon and another matchless day in a life passes into memory.

Brown took no less of a risk with the artwork when he hired an untested art student to design his publicity poster. But once again, the surf gods were smiling. John Van Hamersveld's silk-screened, surfers silhouetted against a day-glow sunset, was so simple, yet so bold, and so thoroughly representative of its milieu, it was practically a Southern California cultural icon before the paint dried.

With The Endless Summer, Brown & company had created the stuff of legend—a legend that would include a three-year delay in the film's release date while Brown struggled to convince Hollywood to invest in what they considered to be a cleverly conceived and constructed home movie.

Beach Boys Metamorphosis

Always fearing the fad would fail at any moment and leave them with a warehouse full of unsold records, Capitol kept up the pressure on the Beach Boys. Sandwiched between numerous local appearances and tour engagements, the group recorded material for their next album, *Surfin USA,* released just six months (3/25/63) after *Surfin Safari*. And just twenty days after the release of their double-hit single, *Surfin' USA/Shutdown*, on March 4, 1963, Capitol released *Surfin' USA*, which became the first of many gold albums.

By the spring of 1963, after less than eight months with the label that relentlessly pushed them to produce, Brian's music had broken into Billboard's Hot 100 four times, the top 40 twice, the top ten once; his second album had gone gold, and he wrote a number one hit for Jan and Dean. Now, he figured, it was time for a little pushback.

Frustrated at having to work with producers who couldn't produce the arraignments he heard in his head, Brian demanded that the Capitol brass give him complete autonomy in the studio as both artist and producer. It was an outrageous request. No artist had ever been given that level of control, much less a 20-year-old kid who had not even been on the roster a year.

Yet, after logging in a reasonable measure of face-saving opposition, the suits folded. The easy win was probably an indication that the management was not entirely certain that the assessment of many in the business that Brian was the most gifted musician in pop music was not without merit.

So, in June of 1963, singer, songwriter, arraigner, and now producer Brian Wilson rolled tape on the first two cuts for the *Surfer Girl* album. Now he would make records sound the way he heard them in his head, with strings, and horns, and harps, and even pizzicato violins added to the usual mix of rock instrumentation. His signature vocal arraignments were never more precisely plotted and performed. Every track exhibited a level of musical sophistication unheard of in the rock 'n' roll milieu.

The single *Surfer Girl/Little Deuce Coupe* was released on August third and hit number seven and fifteen respectively. The *Surfer Girl* album also climbed to the number seven spot on the album charts confirming Brian's debut as a record producer to be an unequivocal success.

And then, as if to prove it wasn't just a freshman's fluke, three weeks later they released *Little Deuce Coupe*, an album of original hot rod songs that did even better.

> **Rise of the Surf Clones**
>
> After appearing in concert with the Beach Boys, and witnessing the screaming frenzy that accompanied their set, Jan & Dean, a 50's style doo-wop duo, decided to try to catch this wave of popularity by re-inventing themselves as Southern California surf-rockers. V-neck sweaters, penny loafers, and jelly-roll hairdos gave way to bright colored tees, huarache sandals, and bushy, bleach blond coiffures. The aural transformation from doo-wopers to hot rodding Southern California surfers was so convincing that when their new songs hit the airwaves, local radio stations began getting irate calls from Capitol Records reps who thought they were playing un-released and unauthorized Beach Boys recordings. They even beat the Beach Boys to the top of the charts with one of Brian's own songs, *Surf City*. And the hits just kept coming until the day Jan was seriously injured in a car wreck, which was ironically foreshadowed in their 1963 hit, *Dead Man's Curve*.

In just over a year, these five regular Joes from Hawthorne CA. had gone from jamming in the Wilson's living room to the top ranks of the pop music industry. Their rise to prominence was so sudden there wasn't time to smooth over youth's rough edges.

They exhibited none of the suave sophistication of a Bobby Darin, or the ultra-confident swagger of an Elvis Presley. Instead, they were very much like the majority of their teenage fans—shy and a little bit unsure of themselves, which further cemented the bond between them.

To kids in other parts of the country, they were foreign emissaries from the land of eternal summer. To Southlanders, having grown up in similar circumstances, they were as familiar as the neighbors next door. And by the summer of 1963, they were the hottest group in the nation.

Califormulated

In the years since Helen Hunt Jackson first described Southern California as "an island on land," the label had only become more relevant. Not because of the vast distances and topographical barriers that once separated it from the rest of the country, but because of the pronounced cultural differences that propagated during its development, where, in this most favorably endowed swath of Mediterraneated desert, a distinctly regional society arose forged by sun and sea. Visitors recognized the differences right away.

These Southlanders didn't live, dress, drive, work, play, or even speak the way others did. Descended from two centuries worth of pioneers and fortune hunters, they were stubbornly independent and possessed of an unyielding, "can-do" spirit.

They spent so much of their lives outdoors, that the colloquialism "outdoorsy," had no meaning. They never walked when they could ride, and they could always ride. They dressed for comfort rather than commerce and in a style all their own.

They placed an unusually high value on health, fitness, and youth, and went to great lengths to maintain them. Education was also revered as the gateway to the good life in Southern California's suburban middle-class.

Transient within the locally preferred precincts, they would move as frequently as the upward trajectory of a hot jobs market would permit, in a constant quest for self-improvement. Their demeanor was informal and generally upbeat; they were friendly but not overly so. Social circles were usually limited to immediate family and close friends.

Though known to be a tolerant society, they were not quite as tolerant as they were disinterested, preferring to confine their attention to their own interests and enterprises. As for the non-natives, the acculturation process from outlander to Southlander was so forceful that, within a matter of months, most newbies had succumbed fully to the recreational ideology so deeply rooted among the more established residents of these far western provinces.

Between the native-born and the naturalized, they built a promised land—a winsome, impetuous place where the atmosphere was charged with a sense of limitless possibilities for all. In the years to come, this time, here in this summer of 1963, would be acknowledged as the period most representative of the mid-century Southern California of popular mythology.

This was our "Kodak Moment." Having made the transition from "worthless, burnt over desert" to "world renown playground of the pacific," Southern California had truly become America's Riviera, and to its most fervently devoted residents, it seemed reasonable to assume that it always would be.

Chapter 24
California Popped!

"To everything there is a season, and a time to every purpose under heaven." Book of Ecclesiastes

A Bad Day in Dallas

We were just a few minutes into our morning recess at Rolando Elementary when all students were summoned back into their classrooms. Our Teacher, Mr. Tibbits, was standing up front, next to his desk, with a transistor radio in his shirt pocket with the earpiece cord dangling from his right ear. Once we were all settled in our seats, he told us that President Kennedy had just been shot.

Visibly shaken, he tried to engage the class in a discussion about the president as he listened to the news bulletins coming out of Dallas, Texas, where the incident occurred. With his attention divided between the radio and a room full of confused sixth graders, the open discussion stumbled along until he suddenly raised his hand for quiet; he listened intently for a moment, and then pulled the earpiece from his ear to relay the news that the president was dead.

Many historians and social scientists have claimed that on that 22nd day of November 1963, the 1950s abruptly ended—and they are right. Nothing would ever be the same again. The next day might have looked like the one before, but it wasn't, for our collective faith in humanity, not to mention our unflappable faith in the future, was shattered. The optimism that energized the nation since the war's end seemed to evaporate overnight.

Throughout the days and weeks that followed, the general mood remained somber; it wasn't until the next year was underway that people began to adjust to the idea that, even in the greatest nation on earth, the birthplace of freedom and democracy, evil could arise anywhere and claim anyone.

We Loved Them Yeah, Yeah, Yeah

It was during those dark days, in the aftermath of the Kennedy assassination, that we cherished our little diversions just a little bit more than usual, and one of our most beloved amusements was a Sunday night variety show broadcast live from New York City. From 1948 to 1971, anybody who was anybody in the world of entertainment performed on the Ed Sullivan Show. And on the evening of February 9, 1964, among the usual clowns, magicians, acrobats, and stage acts, Mr. Sullivan presented us with a real surprise: "Ladies and gentlemen, the Beatles!" And with those five words, the balance of pop-cultural power shifted to the Brits as millions of American teens were captivated by the Merseybeat sound. What the British Empire couldn't do in two wars, four blokes did in fifteen minutes of airtime.

They would play two concerts and appear an unprecedented two more consecutive Sundays on the Sullivan show before returning home, by which time they had turned the American music industry upside down. Dozens of other English bands, duos, and solo artists followed in the wake of the Beatles, and by the summer of 64, the British sound dominated America's airwaves.

Suddenly, every other pop group in the country looked like an oldies act. Many of yesterday's headliners were reduced to lounge act status, while others opted for early retirement. The Southland's exotica and jazz artists were already drifting into studio work, cutting tracks for movies and TV shows, and now America's rock groups were all doing their best to look and sound like the Englanders.

Of the Southern California based pop groups, only the Beach Boys could even halfway whether the storm. They would go on to produce some of the most memorable and best-loved songs of the 1960s, but in the wake of the British Invasion, the classic California sound they created would gradually lose its appeal with teen record buyers, radio DJs, and record companies.

But of course, this sort of adjustment was nothing new. Within the normal ebb and flow of time, things do change. The Southern California of mid-century legend was, for the most part, a construct of a World War II generation that was beginning to settle into a comfortable middle age when their cultural hegemony would naturally begin to fade; but rarely during peacetime, would life change as fast and as forcefully as it did in the early 1960s, for the era of the boomer was firmly at hand.

Twilight of the Rods

Nearly all commercial enterprises had shifted their attention toward the boomer generation with the auto industry leading the charge. But sadly, their successful introduction of an entirely new product line would result in the decline of another of our most venerated Southland traditions—homespun hot rodding.

With the first wave of boomers already out on the road, every automaker in Detroit was trying to come up with a new "youth-oriented" model and Pontiac was first to the showroom with the GTO in the fall of 1963.

Guided by the street rodder's maxim, "low weight to high horsepower," the GTO (a mid-size Pontiac Tempest with an oversized 350hp V8 engine) was every high-school boy's dream come true—all power and no finesse. Yet, in spite of the ungainly handling, Pontiac did very well with the GTO; in baseball parlance, they hit a triple—Ford hit a grand slam!

In the spring of 1964, just as those first-line baby boomers were preparing to graduate high school, Ford came out with the Mustang. It was fast, sporty, affordable, and half a million of them were sold in the first year, launching the era of the "pony/muscle car."

Straight from the factory, these new performance cars were such a hit with car buyers that, within a few years, Detroit automakers would be cranking out 36 different high-performance models, presenting Southern California teens with a dilemma: to build it, or to buy it. In droves, boomers chose buying over building, and the traditional coupes and roadsters, and a good many of the Tri-Fives, began to vanish from our roadways; and with them would eventually go a lot of the once-ubiquitous drag racing events and custom car shows.

In the summer of 64, boomers were not very interested in cars;

> **Stuck in Reverse**
>
> The bottom fell out of the custom car scene so suddenly that Ed Roth got word from Revell that his model series was being cancelled while en-route to their headquarters to have his latest creation measured for another kit. *"After the Beatles, kids stopped building models and started playing guitars."*
>
> **No Fair**
>
> After passing through a hippie phase in the late 60s, the Los Angeles Teen Fair shut down in 1972.

their thoughts were of the future; of going off to college to further their education in reading, writing, and a brand-new subject not listed in the curriculum—rebellion!

Bedlam at Berkeley

To most other Americans, Californians appeared to be too deeply immersed in their excesses to concern themselves with events occurring outside the bounds of their own dominion. That made it all the more shocking when news spread of students rioting on the campus of the University of California at Berkeley.

The trouble started when the dean shut down the campus free speech plaza after it was discovered that non-student activists were using it to promote their causes and recruit students to take part in off-campus demonstrations.

When one of these non-students refused to leave, he was arrested. A large crowd gathered around the patrol car and a spontaneous demonstration broke out on that first day of October 1964. For 32 hours, students took turns standing atop the police car and sermonizing on what they alleged to be the failings of "the system."

Over the next three months, there would be more demonstrations, and sit-ins, and hundreds of arrests, but in the end, the powers that be, the protectors of the status-quo, would bend to the will of the new, liberated armies of the young.

The Berkeley Free Speech protests marked a great awakening of America's youth to the power of their overwhelming numbers; it was a realization that unleashed an irresistible tidal wave of youthful idealism from which would emerge the two distinct, yet intertwined, movements that would define the decade of the sixties.

Counterculture Crusade

Among college students all over the country, an activist fever spread. Disenchanted with the established leadership and the boundless chicanery of nations, suburban teens took up the mantle of civil rights, environmentalism, women's liberation, and the most compelling of all 60s causes, opposition to a rapidly escalating war in Viet Nam. This altruistic compulsion to march, demonstrate, sit-in, or be-in anywhere, at any time for a good cause, was a hallmark of the children of the 60s, but even more characteristic was their capacity for self-indulgence.

> **Viet Nam**
> We entered the Viet Nam conflict as military advisors to the semi-democratic South Vietnamese in their struggle against communist North Viet Nam. When they proved unequal to the task, the United States stepped in hoping to stop the spread of communism in Southeast Asia. But efforts to bolster the South and diminish the North proved futile. After ten years of fighting, at a huge cost in blood and treasure, we left Viet Nam without a victory.

Intoxicated with the power of youth and its infinite possibilities, they abandoned the social mores of the past to freely pursue the ultimate gratification of body and soul. And though these two attributes of activism and hedonism might seem to be at odds, within this new "counterculture" of socially aware young people, they coexisted in near-perfect harmony.

At its essence, the youth movement of the 1960s was simply another attempt to create a Utopian society. The concept was not a novel one. There had been many such efforts dating back hundreds of years, but they were small, isolated efforts. This, on the other hand, was a global crusade boasting millions of young followers spread throughout the United States and Europe. The movement gained traction in 1965, built momentum throughout 1966, and exploded onto the world stage in the summer of 1967, the legendary "Summer of Love," at the momentary epicenter of the youth movement—San Francisco, CA.

"We saw it as a staging area for changing the world." Peter Berg

The philosophy of these new utopians, which the media called "hippies," advocated the complete freedom to do, and experience, just about anything in the quest for self-fulfillment.

"Life should be about ecstasy." Gabe Katz, San Francisco Oracle

In this pursuit of unlimited freedom and euphoric experience, the hippie doctrine encouraged the comprehensive use of marijuana, hashish, a select assortment of prescription pills, and the hallucinogenic compounds, mescaline and lysergic acid diethylamide (LSD) as a means of raising the consciousness, turning the hum-drum into a happening, and, it was imagined quite strenuously, ridding the world of its anti-social tendencies.

"The more people who turn on, the better the world would be." Phil Lesh, the Grateful Dead

Their politics registered hard left; they rejected most of the established customs, traditions, and institutions of modern society, and instead, imagined an alternative, communal society where everything was shared, and everyone was loved. They scorned materialism and avoided work when possible; authority was flouted, and eastern mysticism was embraced along with a fundamental, "back to nature" impulse.

To the bewildered parents of these "new Aquarians," it was a rejection of everything they stood for and held dear. Never had there been such a divide between one generation, tempered by depression and war, and the next, nurtured in peace and comfort, who were going to make the world a better place through drug use, hyper-hedonism, and very good intentions.

> **60s Astrologics**
> The "age of Aquarius," in counterculture lore, is just a fanciful term for the hippie era.

But not all 60s youth were hippies, and not all hippies were hardcore counterculturalists. Within the movement, there were varying levels of commitment. I was one among a great many of the Southland's middle-class, suburban faction. We went to school and had jobs and worked very hard at both. Most of us were against the Viet Nam War, for civil rights reform, and sympathetic to environmental concerns, yet we distanced ourselves from hippiedom's more absurd sociological and political positions. What we did not distance ourselves from were the drugs. We used drugs regularly, exhibited the same, libertine attitudes towards sex, and gorged ourselves on rock 'n' roll in all the various new flavors that were served up at the Monterey Pop Festival.

Monterey Pop

Running for three days in mid-June of 1967, the Monterey Pop Festival revealed just how much pop-rock music had changed in the three years since the Beatles first appeared in prime time.

With over 30 acts, every variety of pop music was represented, including two new California factions—the electric folk rockers from the south (Byrds & Buffalo Springfield, et al), and the psychedelic rockers from the north (Jefferson Airplane & Grateful Dead, et al), though it should be noted that these were generalized classifications. Both factions worked both genres with great success.

This folk-rock sound, which blended folk-ish songs and sensibilities with upbeat, electrified, Beatlesque instrumentation emerged from the Hollywood clubs along Sunset Boulevard and helped to re-establish an American presence on the U.S. pop charts when the Byrd's *"Turn, Turn, Turn"* reached the number one spot in April of 1965. The new folk-rock scene offered a second chance for the Southland's ex-surf rockers and coffeehouse troubadours.

> **Surfer cum Folkie**
> The Chantays and the Surfaris each released folk-rock albums in the mid-sixties. Several members of the popular west coast groups, the Buffalo Springfield, the Byrds, the Doors, the Turtles, the Strawberry Alarm Clock, Gary Lewis and the Playboys, and Harper's Bazaar started out as surf rockers. David Crosby, of the Byrds, was even a member of Les Baxter's Balladeers.
>
> **Beyond the 60s**
> In spite of their many setbacks, the Beach Boys would soldier on for decades to eventually become one of the most beloved nostalgia acts of all time, proudly playing all the hits that originally made them favorite sons of the Southland.

Even America's foremost folkie, Bob Dylan, made the switch to folk-rocker when he strapped on a Stratocaster at the 1965 Newport Folk Festival and walked out onstage to a hail of boos and jeers served up by a traditionalist audience that refused to see that "the times they are a-changing."

The Beach Boys' attempt to leave their illustrious past behind them was not nearly as successful. Their latest album, *Pet Sounds*, was a major critical success, but a commercial disappointment. In December of 1966, their single, *Good Vibrations*, hit the top of the charts but the accompanying album had to be scrapped when Brian, who had suffered a few breakdowns and had succumbed to the same drug abuse problems that were beginning to plague a great many rock artists, couldn't finish the project.

With no new material to play and fearing their old hits would not hold up well in front of a counterculture crowd, the Beach Boys dropped out of the lineup for the Monterey Pop Festival, effectively abdicating their position as the musical ambassadors of a Southern California scene that many young people felt was no longer relevant.

End of the Endless Summer

Another favorite son, Bruce Brown, was also experiencing the negative effects of this seismic cultural shift. Three years after completing *The Endless Summer,* he was still struggling to get the film picked up for distribution. When no offers came his way, he hit the beach circuit playing to packed houses at every showing, yet no studio would back the film's release claiming that without the customary pop stars, dance numbers, and wacky heavies, it would never play east of interstate 5.

To prove they were wrong, he went to the heartland of America, Wichita, Kansas, and booked a theater for a two-week run. And, in spite of a projectionist's strike, and an opening night blizzard, the house was filled to capacity for the entire run. Still Hollywood refused to budge. So, he took the film to New York and played it for the owners of the Kip's Bay theater chain, who agreed to give it a trial run.

On June 15, 1966, *The Endless Summer* opened in New York City to a sell-out crowd and continued to sell out for the remainder of its 48-week run. The New Yorkers loved it; even the tough-as-nails New York critics showered Brown with praise. The *New York Times* hailed him as "the Fellini of Foam," and *Time* magazine dubbed him "the Bergman of the boards." Finally, Cinema V Inc. bought the distribution rights and put the film into nationwide release where it continued to break box-office records for many more months.

But by the time America discovered *The Endless Summer*, the film was an anachronism, showcasing a golden era that was already passing into history.

Storm Surf

Even on the Southland's beaches, the spirit of revolution was in the air. In the mid-sixties, a handful of backyard builders began producing mini boards as much as three feet shorter than the average longboard. These "shortboards" were skittish, difficult to ride, and required more wave space than a longboard, but they provided a more manic surfing experience, which had an enormous appeal among the younger practitioners of the art. Suddenly, the old longboard wasn't cool anymore.

"The 9'6" nose rider, by the spring of 1968, had become the Edsel of surfboard manufacturing." Matt Warshaw

It had been nearly ten years since surfing emerged from near obscurity to become one of the coolest pastimes on the planet; naturally the original, "Gidget gang" would thin some as the years passed, but during those years, the number of new recruits willing to take their place was also dwindling, due, in part, to the unforgiving nature of the new platform.

What was always a difficult and demanding sport was made even more so by the shortboard. The result was a slow, weeding out of part-timers, leaving the field to those of a more singular mind, purpose, and opportunity.

The change in technology also ushered in an unfortunate change in attitude. The kinetic nature of the shortboard demanded a more aggressive style of surfing, which seemed to encourage a more aggressive style of surfer. With wave space at a premium, hard-core short boarders became less tolerant of the crowds of tourists and weekenders.

At some of the more popular surf spots, this antagonism developed into an ugly, localist posture that poisoned the atmosphere around some of the most beautiful seascapes on the coast. In addition to the behavioral problems, heavy drug use was also casting a shadow over the Southern California beach scene. By the summer of 68, it was clear that Gidget and Tubesteak were long gone.

Also, absent from the scene were Frankie and Annette, who made their final beach flick for AIP in 1965.

None could match AIP's success in the beach party genre. Even as Beatlemania was gaining momentum, both of their offerings for 1964, *Muscle Beach Party* and *Bikini Beach*, were huge hits, and they did very well in 1965 with *Beach Blanket Bingo* and *How to Stuff a Wild Bikini*. Director William Asher called the era of the beach party films, "the longest summer on record," but the summer finally reached its end in 1966.

Nothing could have been more out of sync with the changing times than those crazy, campy beach movies. After *The Ghost in the Invisible Bikini* (1966), failed at the box office, AIP abandoned the beach and moved on to another successful series of exploitation films featuring outlaw bikers and stoned hippies.

Castoff Cool

Tied for the number one spot in the category of mid-century, pop-cultural kitsch now regarded as trivial, dated, and irrelevant were the tokens of the tiki trend, the festive ornaments left over from a nearly two-decades-long World War II wrap party, along with all the great, Googie styled roadside architectonics. Even the more serene and sensible of the modernist themes were fading from the field.

Without a universal belief in a better tomorrow, all that lighthearted artifice seemed insignificant. By the early 70s, public taste in residential architecture turned sharply toward the traditional styles, and many of the mid-century modernist structures were raised to make room.

On Main Street, the look went from the overtly festive, one-off facades to corporatized chain stores housed in generic strip malls. Style, at least the extraordinarily exuberant style that defined the Southern California of the post-war years, was dead. 24-1

The Population Bomb

And it was not only in the areas of pop-cultural expression where the Southland was showing signs of wear. There were fissures running throughout the very foundation of the empire. After nearly 100 years of unrestrained boosterism, from railroad booklets and orange crate labels to top-40 pop ballads and wide-screen, technicolored beach bashes, the message that life was lived better in Southern California had thoroughly sunk into the global consciousness.

Beginning with the end of World War II, from all over the world, true believers in the life-affirming powers of the California sun began arriving at a rate of about 3000 a day, every day. By 1962, the population had passed the 20,000,000 mark, and by 1969, it had risen another 3,000,000, which was about the time that Southlanders were beginning to finally acknowledge that their growth problems had long ago shifted from too few to far too many.

Southern California was being loved to death; the huge growth in population was pushing the region further and further away from its partly mythical identity as a terrestrial paradise. Urban and suburban sprawl now dominated many of the once picturesque landscapes. Los Angeles had become a big city with all the usual big-city problems of urban blight, high crime, traffic congestion, and suffocating smog. Even in geranium-minded San Diego, more and more space was forcibly ceded to the unsightly, and not just at ground level.

The Southern Californian's long-standing obsession with the automobile had always come at a progressively escalating price, but it had finally reached the point where it could no longer be ignored. With nearly as many cars as people, all freely blowing their toxic emissions out into the atmosphere, the air was usually filled with a beige photochemical haze. On the bad days, this "smog" could get so dense the sky would turn brown. Local radio and television stations began broadcasting smog alerts warning residents of the risk levels associated with exposure to the once great out-of-doors. The situation was not only a public health hazard but a threat to the once-mighty Southern California economy.

Since the mid-50s, Congress passed many "clean air acts," but they didn't really come down hard on the main culprit, the automobile, until they passed the Clean Air Act of 1970, and established the entity charged with enforcing it, the Environmental Protection Agency (EPA). The 1970 Clean Air Act required auto manufacturers to reduce vehicle emissions 90% by 1975. To hit that mark, automakers were forced to install power-robbing smog devices, de-tune engines, and lower compression ratios, which dropped some horsepower ratings by half.

Though these measures would not eliminate the smog problem, they did improve the air quality; what they did eliminate was the muscle car. In the October issue of *Popular Hot Rodding* for 1971, the headline read, "The Detroit Supercar is Dead," and, by 1973, it was, in effect, buried alongside the American hot rod.

Downsized

Not quite dead, but on full life support, were the Southland's defense and aerospace industries. In 1968, the federal government began the first of a series of drastic cuts in defense spending, which hit California especially hard. After having put men on the moon in July of 1969, even NASA's budget began to shrink; and commercial jet sales were slipping for the first time since their introduction in the late 50s. All of these setbacks led to mergers, downsizings, bankruptcies, and of course, huge layoffs, which sent a ripple effect throughout the entire Southland economy.

At the same time, the steadily rising population pushed consumer demand for goods and services ahead of supply, which drove prices up along with the taxes required to keep pace with the constantly rising demands on the infrastructure. Known as one of the least expensive places in the country to live and do business just a dozen years back, Southern California was fast becoming one of the most expensive.

Many businesses were finding that the higher operating costs, the higher taxes, and the increasingly stringent EPA standards they had to operate under were offsetting the advantages they once enjoyed doing business in California; and one by one, they began a slow, steady exodus from the golden state to one of the more accommodating southwestern states California had usurped in the territorial process 100 years before.

Conduct Unbecoming

The Southland was also found to be awash in a sea of societal ills. Lauded as the archetype of the good life just a few years earlier, Southern California had become a media treasure trove of lurid, domestic horror stories and cautionary tales of excess, which were gleefully put forth in a torrent of sensationalist narratives.

By the late 60s, we were on top of all the wrong lists with more crime, more divorce, and more alcohol and drug addiction than anywhere else in the nation. We were only just edged out of first place in the suicide sweepstakes by Nevada.

But with sixty percent of the population uprooted from somewhere else, you must expect some measure of psychosis. We had always had our kooks, but the side effects were much more benign during the good times. Things began to change as the jobs market shrank, the cost of living soared, and the California Dream slipped further and further out of reach.

So many came expecting so much. When reality set in, some adjusted, some moved on, and some slipped deep into the darker regions of the soul.

Not six months after the close of the summer of love, the country would embark upon one of its most violent years on record—1968. It seemed that all news was bad news. The Viet Nam War, as well as the numerous race riots and student demonstrations, were featured every evening on the nightly news.

Amidst all the chaos, the hippies were desperately trying to convince themselves, and the rest of the world, that love would conquer all. But was anyone paying attention? Certainly not the assassin who killed Martin Luther King in Memphis, or the one who shot down Bobby Kennedy in Los Angeles, nor the rioters at the conventions, nor the bombers of the college campuses and government buildings. Could it be that the hippies, with their grand, utopian vision of a perfect world were not factoring into the equation the very imperfect nature of the people within it?

And then, in August of 1969, there appeared a slight ray of sunshine. The Woodstock Music and Arts Fair, an outdoor rock concert in upstate New York, which inadvertently drew over 400,000 attendees, and could have easily turned into an epic catastrophe, was instead, hailed by authorities as one of the largest gatherings of well-behaved, respectful, and law-abiding (aside from the rampant drug use) young people in recent history.

It made real big news everywhere except the west coast; there, the stories of exemplary conduct on the part of 400,000 hippies were eclipsed by the news coming out of Los Angeles of the horrifying conduct of just five.

The Garden of Evil

Shockwaves shot throughout the nation as news spread of the horribly savage murders of four prominent Angelinos in a very sadistic and apparently random bloodletting. The following night, there was another similarly grisly murder, and the Southland went into a panic that wouldn't subside until the perps were finally caught in October at a hippie commune north of Los Angeles.

The trial of Charles Mason and four of his disciples lasted eight months and exposed the American public to the absolute depths of madness and depravity lurking within the darkest precincts of the counterculture. Manson, and his equally demented and drug-addled "family," put faces to the nation's fears regarding the youth culture of the late 1960s.

> **Devil's on the door step**
> Manson came to Los Angeles dreaming of rock stardom and briefly managed to push his way into the Beach Boys inner circle, and even got them to record one of his own songs. But his creepy, threatening behavior got him exiled from their presence just months before his infamous murder spree.

But possibly, even more rattled than the parents, were the kids. How many times had even those who operated on the suburban fringes of hippie society come across "brothers" or "sisters" who were not the least little bit groovy? People who were, in fact, just the kind of lying, cheating, stealing, and yes, murdering reprobates you might find out there in the real world. Manson revealed what many of us were already beginning to suspect—that the Age of Aquarius was a sham.

The counterculture was like any other culture; it had its heroes, its villains, and all those in-between. And to drive that point home, there was Altamont—the free concert up San Francisco way in December of 1969. Billed as Woodstock West, it turned out to be an exceptionally bad trip in which four were killed.

Coming just days before the decade's end, this unfortunate event was interpreted by many as the death knell of the counterculture dream.

Hippie Hiatus

But it wasn't just the one incident that brought down the dream; it was a whole host of hang-ups that would turn many of the hip, young apostles towards the realization that a Utopia without Utopians, could not endure. Real-life caught up with the revolution, and in real life, you can't stay young, feckless, and vainglorious forever.

By 1970, the majority of that first wave of baby boomers, the contingent most committed to the cause, had completed their education and were entering the workforce, getting married, renting apartments, buying consumer goods, and preparing for a middle-class future. Many of these new wage earners, who had mercilessly ridiculed their parents for their devout materialism, would go on to best them on that very same score by a huge margin.

Others would remain true to the cause and continue to wage war on the system from within it, relentlessly pulling the nation to the left. Still, others would drop out of society completely. But most just got jobs and left the turbulent 60s, and much of what they stood for, behind them.

Almost lost amongst the pomp and pandemonium of the flower power era was the quiet passing of that other Southern California. The colorful picture-postcard Southern California had also passed into history at the close of the 1960s.

It was a slow process; there were no alarm bells to sound a warning. Distracted by the novelty of the new, one hardly noticed the slow, wearing away of the old and familiar. The macro transformation ebbed and flowed in micro increments, and by the time the senses were piqued, it was gone. 24-2

All Things Considered

And what was it really all about? I guess you could say it was simply a fluke of good fortune in a calm period between storms, where, in an exceptionally well-endowed landscape, during an extraordinary span of time, the nation's most ideally situated inhabitants were treated to a decades-long gala of good living.

But the scene was fragile and entirely dependent upon the most favorable of social and economic conditions; when those conditions began to erode, the show folded. Oh, for a while, the stalwarts would find ways to pleasantly persevere, but never again with the same, iron-clad conviction that tomorrow would always be better than today. The period of universal jubilation that shaped that particular mindset had passed.

Throughout the next couple of decades, the remarkable reputation the Southland cultivated during the golden years of its ascension would become just another chapter in

Babylon West

In spite of decreasing levels of domestic migration, the state's population has grown to nearly 40 million, largely through foreign migration.

its expansive mythology. The 1970 California census, for the first time in over 120 years, revealed a declining rate of population growth. People would still be drawn out to the west coast, but in the years ahead, though it would retain its popularity as a vacation destination, for those settlers with all their options open, there was a growing sense that there might be better places to sink roots.

Song of the Southland

For those of us steeped in the mid-century, Southern California traditions, this reversal of fortune, coupled with an equally disheartening reversal of fashion, was an affirmation that paradise was indeed lost; like Margaret Mitchell's old South, the Southland as we once knew it was "a civilization gone with the wind."

It was a calamity deeply lamented by many of the kids who grew up in the midst of the California Carnival and whose sense of symmetry was lastingly shaped by the experience. But astonishingly, no sooner had the mid-century era passed into history than it almost immediately re-emerged as nostalgia.

With so much that was going so wrong in the 70s, the Viet Nam War, the Watergate scandal, the energy crisis, and rising rates of unemployment and inflation, the country was in no mood to wait out the usual 20-year-long fallow period before rediscovering a past that seemed to glow brighter than the future that lay ahead.

In the time between the Kennedy assassination and the Watergate break-in, that brief period of post-war promise and prosperity had become America's golden age of record, and it has remained so to this day.

Beginning with Universal Pictures' 1973 release of George Locus's warm-hearted homage to mid-century youth culture, *American Graffiti*, the nation's mid-century era has been persistently memorialized in books, movies, television shows, and on classic rock radio stations.

And then, in the 1990s, almost on cue, young "generation Xers" rediscovered the modernist, mid-century chic of their parent's generation.

Tiki bars, mid-century-styled cocktail lounges, and similarly themed restaurants began to reemerge along suburban boulevards that hadn't seen their like in nearly 30 years. Even some of the era's original participants joined in the celebrations, periodically driving their rusty old chariots to pre-determined meets at burger joint parking lots and assembling with their cracked and faded longboards along some of the more forgiving stretches of coastline in rituals of reverence and remembrance.

In the years that followed, "urban archeologists" located and preserved all the old mid-century structures and artifacts they could find. Today, the whimsical old bric-a-brac that once littered thrift store shelves now turns up in antique emporiums and uptown auction houses. Longboards of any particular note are often displayed in museums, and most of the iconic, custom cars of the period have, long ago, been restored to their original splendor.

The only thing that hasn't been resurrected is the optimism that was such an essential part of the scene. That, I fear, is gone forever. In the end, all that remains are the mementos, the myths, and the memories.

California Pop Foot Notes

Chapter 3
1 The good Father Serra and I were practically neighbors. My house was within walking distance of the mission, and Rolando Elementary School made a pilgrimage to the site, as well as the presidio, for all of the six years I was in attendance.

Chapter 11
1 The first five years of my life were spent on my Grandpa Mac's lemon farm & turkey ranch located in Jamul out in the San Diego outback on one of the original Spanish land grants.

Chapter 13
1 In the mid-eighties, my wife and a friend had a trendy little clothes boutique at Nine Market Street, just off the boardwalk. By that time, nearly everything Kinney created was either gone or altered beyond recognition. Their shop was in a walled-in section of the colonnade (which has since been liberated) at the southwest corner of what was the bathhouse. But the one thing that has remained intact for all these years is the carnival atmosphere. Then as now, at Venice Beach, the circus is always in town.

2 Long before it became the poster child for ecological calamity, this "accidental ocean," was ringed by dozens of resort communities, and often referred to as the Riviera of the desert. Sinatra and the Rat Pack hung out at Salton City. Just up the road, my Grandpa Mac had a place at the Marina Mobile Estates at Desert Shores. It was there, at the Salton Sea, that I learned to ride a motorcycle, water ski, and salt-water fish. From 1964 to 70, this was our regular, every weekend or so, family getaway.

3 Even with these extra infusions, Southern California would never escape its water problems. In the mid-50s, one of my earliest childhood memories was sitting on my Grandpa Mac's lap while he drove his big, diesel-powered, Caterpillar tractor. What fun we had mowing down row after row of gnarly dead trees. It wasn't until many years later that I learned we were plowing under his lemon orchards that had died when the scarce water resources were re-directed from agricultural use to the growing suburbs.

Chapter 14
1 For Southern Californians, and especially farm families like ours, the automobile was considered such an essential contrivance that it was

often regarded as a part of the family unit. Evidently, the everyday conversations taking place in our house during my rug-rat days were so thoroughly interspersed with references to our 1939 Chevrolet Deluxe Coupe that my very first infantile utterance was not the usual da-da or ma-ma, but Chevrolet—all three syllables.

Chapter 15
1 In keeping with the emergent migration patterns, my great grandparents, on my father's side, moved from Mississippi, to Arkansas, and finally to San Diego, California, around 1900.

Chapter 17
1 My father-in-law, George Bakich, was a classic example of these "New Californians" of the mid-20th century. While training as a Navy radio operator in San Diego, he developed an appreciation for California living. After the war, in answer to an ad in the *Youngstown Vindicator* seeking trained mechanical engineers, he moved his family to Serra Mesa California, and began working for Convair Aeronautics in their new Kearney Mesa plant.

Chapter 18
1 I can still remember standing out in a field on Grandpa Mac's citrus farm in Jamul and watching what appeared to be just another star race across the Southern California sky.

Chapter 19
1 My first five years were spent on Grandpa Mac's citrus/turkey farm in Jamul. But when it came time for school, my parents bought one of these spartan domiciles in an indistinguishable development called Dennstedt Terrace in La Mesa California, just east of San Diego. Built in 1950, it was a simple, stripped-down, vaguely modernish re-interpretation of the traditional 2br/1ba layout. The only nod to mid-century modern style was the three-panel picture window in the front room.

2 The street racing habit was pervasive and persistent. Twenty years later, at the intersection of College Ave. and 54th Street, a Porsche pulled alongside my MGA and we had us a go. (Yes, my first car was an MG, so I ran in the under 100hp sports car class) The Porsche got the lead and got away; I got the ticket and had my driver's license suspended for six months, which at the time, was four months longer than I had it.

Chapter 20

1 While working for a Hollywood auto restoration firm in the early 80s, I got to spend some time behind the wheel of a 1952 Jaguar XK120 (rumored to have once belonged to actor Clark Gable); and 30 years on, it was still a very impressive machine that would have certainly run rings around the competition back in its day.

2 In the Cpop era, bowling was as popular with the parents as surfing was with the kids. Nearly every community had its own space-aged bowl-A-rama, and nearly every mom in the neighborhood, mine included, was a member of a bowling team. Games were a weekly affair and my friends and I would often tag along, not to bowl, but to be let loose amidst a surplus of opportunities for dedicated mischief-makers. Our neighborhood "fun center" was University Lanes at 60th and University Ave.—a 64-lane behemoth with a game room, pool parlor, and the adjoining Red Coat Inn restaurant and nightclub. The most alluring diversion for my gang of marauding 12-year-olds was not the game room or even the pool parlor; it was the nightclub. One could enter the Red Coat's ultra-swanky nightspot either through the elegant front entryway or through the massive, padded double doors off one of the bowling alley's side corridors, which, during the morning hours when the bar was closed, were left unlocked. Set'em up, Joey!

3 Like many Southlanders of the era, our family edged into the forefront of the modernist movement when, while browsing with my parents at a discount furniture outlet on West Morena Blvd., I managed to steer them towards a light-gauge, teakwood living room set with thin, square cushions in a bold tropical print and a space-age lounge chair in a solid olive green with matching ottoman. I thought it was so very chic and sophisticated—like something out of a James Bond movie. But I admit, with its minimalist composition, it probably lacked the comfort qualities of those old, full-size davenports. When my parents moved a few years later, the teakwood set mysteriously disappeared, and was replaced with a traditional sofa along with a couple of those lazy boys; and as I now recall, they never took decorating advice from me again.

4 My first surfboard was a well-battered, ten-dollar example of an early Malibu Chip presented in a very unfortunate shade of Kelly Green. It was heavy, riddled with dings, and got so waterlogged it took days of drying before it could be reused. Grandpa Mac would take me out to Torrey Pines, where, through much trial and error, I managed to develop a rudimentary surf style and continued to surf sporadically for

several years, but I was never the fanatic most of my friends were; I was more of what you'd call a "tag-along-surfer."

Chapter 21

1 In the early 90s, I was lucky enough to spend about six months in one of the grandest of all tiki apartment villages, The Shelter Isles Apartments, in Arcadia California. Built in 1960, by Hollywood husband and wife dancers/choreographers Madge and Gower Champion, it was truly a marvel of west coast whimsicality sporting all of the Polynesian paraphernalia one could imagine. Sadly, this mid-century shrine was replaced years later with a very unremarkable townhouse tract.

2 To dress up our own little backyard tiki hut, I painted tiki faces on the palm fronds that fell off our tree and carved Easter Island tiki heads out of Plaster-of-Paris blocks molded from half-gallon milk cartons. In fact, in nearly all my art classes, throughout all my school days, the Plaster of Paris tiki totem was my go-to class project.

3 In the late 60s, I use to hang out with one of the older boys in the neighborhood—a twenty-one-year-old Viet-Nam vet who bought and sold performance cars, which I often helped to ferry around town. Naturally, he was a very accomplished street racer, yet he rarely did the driving. Instead, he seemed to take perverse pleasure in being chauffeured around town in his own scintillatingly fast 58 Corvette by an unlicensed fifteen-year-old. I never really understood that. Maybe he was acting out a death wish—who knows. Whatever the psychosis, I sure did love driving that vette.

4 My father succumbed early, building a fairly typical modular setup, which included a Marantz amplifier, a Scott tuner, a Garrard turntable, and mammoth Bozak speakers, which he exercised frequently with near maniacal zeal.

Chapter 22

1 Our air raid siren was located at the corner of Tower Street and Terry Lane, right next to Rolando Elementary. Every Monday at noon, it would be tested and we would respond by diving under our desks under the false, government-sponsored, assumption that a nuclear attack was survivable.

2 One of my favorite beaches was not a surf-site, but a picaresque little inlet called La Jolla Cove. After dinner in the village, a romantic, moonlight stroll along the cove was a must. On my first date with my

wife of over 40 years, we visited Ye Old Bratskeller, took a turn around the cove, and shared a bottle of champagne in my favorite watering hole—the La Jolla Cove lifeguard tower.

3 My hot rod flipper friend once had one of these custom-built supercars in his stable. It was a 1962 Ford Galaxie with a 406 tri-power motor, four on the floor, and a nine-inch locking rear end. What I remember most about that car is how quickly it could get you into trouble. But then God never intended it to be driven by a fifteen-year-old. How I managed it without loss of life, limb, or property is a mystery for the ages.

4 In my neighborhood, on any given Saturday or Sunday afternoon, you could step outside and hear the strains of a local surf band, maybe even more than one, wrestling with the intricacies of the standard repertoire. The garage door would rise, the band would play, and a very appreciative audience of neighborhood kids would gather in the driveway.

5 The obligatory music lessons were a familiar part of the suburban curriculum. Nearly all the kids on my block were required to participate. I took guitar lessons at Ozzie's Music on El Cajon Blvd. with Danny Weis—a 17-year-old guitar virtuoso and founding member of the Iron Butterfly.

Chapter 23

1 Back in the day, an acquaintance once offered to sell me his 1948 Packard woody, which he had christened the "Packard Pig," and not without reason. It was a barge and handled like it, and its antiquated straight-eight sucked gas, not through a straw, but through a drainpipe. I gave it some thought but eventually opted for a much more manageable and economical VW van.

2 In the late 70s, I got to appear in several stage productions directed by Steve Terrell, star of some of the coolest camp films Hollywood ever made including *Drag Strip Girl, Runaway Daughters*, and *Invasion of the Saucer Men*.

Chapter 24

1 Of all the Southland's great Polynesian-styled commercial establishments, San Diego's Hanalei Hotel was one of the most magnificent. Built in 1954, at the dawn of the tiki craze, the Hanalei had absolutely everything in the way of whimsical, Polynesian trimmings. The structures, the grounds, and especially the Hotel's

Islands Restaurant were equal to anything one might find anywhere on the Hawaiian archipelago. On occasion, after a hard day at the beach, my friends and I would stop in at the Hanalei to enjoy the atmosphere, the amenities, and possibly the company of one of the hotel's lovely guests. During the summer months, the beautiful Hanalei was so well-patronized that no one ever noticed a few over-tanned locals among the fairer-skinned out-of-towners. Unfortunately, like nearly all of the delightfully ludicrous old leisure lodges that are still in existence, the Hanalei, renamed the Crown Plaza, has been genericized beyond recognition.

2 My own heads-up moment came in the spring of 1971, behind the wheel of a killer 55 Chevy. I had been out of high school for eight months, and after a false start in the fall, was finally resolved to make a decent showing in college. Like most freshmen, I was focused on the future; I was not aware that Irving Gill's futuristic "Dodge House" was torn down the year before, or that modernist maestro Richard Neutra had died. It didn't occur to me that I hadn't heard an exotica tune on the radio, or seen a deuce coupe on the road, or visited a backyard tiki tavern, or even sat in an Eames chair outside of an airport boarding lounge in several years. As a part-timer stubbornly clinging to his longboard, I wasn't completely aware of how far surf culture had strayed from its original construct, much less that my days as even an occasional practitioner had already ended. It wasn't until I took custody of that killer 55 that I truly began to realize that an era had passed.

Most of the guys I hung out with drove some sort of self-modified performance car. I was one of the few exceptions. Being of a somewhat dispassionate temperament, I was never able to make the commitment necessary to maintain so demanding and spirited a ride. Instead, I settled for a series of unremarkable, foreign four-bangers—basic transport. My friend Scott, on the other hand, was a genuine true believer in the doctrine of high-performance. It was through him that I acquired most of my own firsthand knowledge of, and experience with, the hot rod calling. For years, Scott drove a 1962 Chevy Nova with a mighty mouse small block built up from bolt-on parts that proved to be quite a decent little runner; and then he got that killer 55.

It was one hell of a car, but not in the looks department. In fact, it was a painfully ordinary-looking two-tone model, white over green, that had long ago faded to a flat, chalky-looking patina. The chrome was dull and pitted and the interior, though still sound, had also lost its original luster. Even up close, it appeared to be just another over-the-hill hand-me-down. The veil was lifted only when the ignition key was turned hard right. After a quick tic-off of the electric fuel pump, the engine exploded to life. The sounds of the volcanic exhaust note, the rough idle, the clatter of precision machinery, and the sucking of voluminous amounts of air was absolutely disconcerting to the senses when taken together with the car's pedestrian appearance.

It's been so long ago that I no longer recall the engine's size, but I'd like to think it was the big one, the 427. What I do remember is that, under the hood, it was tricked out to the twelve's; everything that could be done to a performance engine was done right down to the balancing and blueprinting. Gears were selected with a Hurst shifter connected to a Muncie four-speed trans. I can't recall the rear-end specs, but I do know it was capable of maintaining traction and trajectory under hard load. To sustain the very deliberate deception, the tachometer was mounted below the dash, and the twin, three-inch exhaust cannons were mounted up into the wheel wells, just out of sight. It was a real sleeper designed specifically for street racing. On paper, an insurance company saw only an old coupe. On the road, a cop saw only an old coupe. But on the green light Grand Prix, guys saw only an old coupe's taillights. But Scott's barnstorming days came to an end when he got his draft notice, and before he left for basic training, he asked me to look after his killer 55 while he was away.

On alternate days, I would drive the killer 55 the eleven miles from Rolando Blvd. to Grossmont College and back. But I only got as far as the first stoplight before I realized I had lost my bearings. Peering out at the world over that baroque dashboard, it was as if I had gone back to a time I had yet to fully acknowledge had passed. Inside that killer 55 it was still 1963, and suddenly, the contrast between what had been, and what was, came into sharp focus. I was all alone out there. Volkswagens, Datsuns, and Saabs to my right; Volvos, Peugeots, and Fiats to my left. Where was the Scalphunter, that wicked supercharged 56 Pontiac that regularly prowled this section of El Cajon Blvd? Or that flaming 406 Hi-Po Ford? Or the yellow mako-vette with the tri-power rig protruding through the hood? Or all those other go-boys we used to run with. They were nowhere to be found.

There I sat, like a rodeo rider atop a Brahma bull waiting for the chute door to open, firmly gripping the wheel with the left hand and the shifter with the right—motor vibration surging throughout the entire chassis, the windows rattling, the seat quivering. A whole hurricane's worth of horsepower lay at my feet waiting to be loosed at the sudden turn of a traffic signal, and I'm sharing the pole position with a girl in a VW microbus adorned with a colorful assortment of flowered appliqués. The light turned green, and as meekly as a matron on her way to an all-day bingo bash, I proceeded along the boulevard right in step with the regular flow of traffic.

And so it was to be for the rest of my tenure. Street dueling had gone out of fashion. I never did cross paths with the Scalphunter, or the flaming Ford, or the yellow mako-vette, or any of those old runners that use to haunt these very same highways. That was when I realized that what had gone before, had gone for good. So, with the street racing opportunities all dried up, there was time for reflection while driving around in the killer 55. And whenever I ventured out, though the destinations might vary, the route was always the same—straight down memory lane.

In the brief interim between basic training and his deployment to Viet Nam, Scott spent his time visiting with friends and cruising around in his killer 55. And I wouldn't be a bit surprised if, during those solo wanderings, he didn't take some of the same side streets that I had frequented.

Then, on the eve of his departure, he sold the killer 55. He handed over the keys and listened to it roar one last time before disappearing into a rose-colored past—token of a bygone era under the golden glow of the California sun.

California Pop Bibliography

Armstrong, Elizabeth. *Birth of the Cool: California Art, Design, and Culture at Midcentury*. Orange County Museum of Art and Prestel Publishing, 2007.

Adinolfi, Francesco. *Mondo Exotica*. Duke University Press, 2008.

Aron, Cindy S. *Working at Play: A History of Vacations in America*. Oxford University Press, 1999.

Badman, Keith. *The Beach Boys: The Definitive Diary of America's Greatest Band, on Stage and in the Studio*. Backbeat Books, 2004.

Bailey, Harry P. *Weather of Southern California*. University of California Press, 1966.

Barron, Stephanie. Burnstein, Sheri. Fort, Ilene Susan. *Made in California: Art, Image, and Identity 1900 – 2000*. University of California Press, 2000.

Bash, Kent & Witzel, Michael Karl. *Crusin': Car Culture in America*. Motorbooks International, 1997.

Bean, Walton E. *California: An Interpretive History*. McGraw-Hill Book Company, 1968.

Beck, Warren A. and Williams, David A. *California: A History of the Golden State*. Doubleday & Company Inc. 1972.

Beers, David. *Blue Sky Dream: A Memoir of America's Fall from Grace*. A Harvest Book, Harcourt Brace and Company, 1996.

Bell, Horace. *Reminiscences of a Ranger: Early Times in Southern California*. Yarnell, Caystile, & Mathes Printers,1881.

Betrock, Alan. *The I was a Teenage Juvenile Delinquent Rock 'N' Roll Horror Beach Party Movie Book*. St. Martin's Press, 1986.

Bottles, Scott L. *Los Angeles and the Automobile: The Making of a Modern City.* The University of California Press, Berkeley, 1987.

Brilliant, Ashleigh. *The Great Car Craze: How Southern California Collided with the Automobile in the 1920s.* Woodbridge Press, 1989.

Bronson, William. *How to Kill a Golden State.* Doubleday & Company Inc., 1968

Bryson, Bill. *The Life and Times of the Thunderbolt Kid: A Memoir.* Broadway Books, 2006.

Burt, Rob. *Surf City – Drag City.* Sterling Publishing Co. Inc., 1986.

Carlin, Peter Ames. *Catch a Wave: The Rise, Fall, and Redemption of the Beach Boys Brian Wilson.* Rodale, 2006.

Casdorph, Paul D. *Let the Good Times Roll: Life at Home in America During WWII.* Paragon House, 1989.

Cashill, Jack. *What's the Matter with California?* Threshold Editions, 2007.

Chidester, Brian & Priore, Domenic. *Pop Surf Culture: Music, Design, Film, and Fashion from the Bohemian Surf Boom.* Santa Monica Press LLC, 2008.

Collected Essays. *The Work of Charles and Ray Eames.* Harry N. Abrams Publishers, 1997.

Colburn, Finney, Stallings, Stecyk, Stillman, Wolfe. *Surf Culture: The Art History of Surfing.* Laguna Beach Art Museum & Ginko Press, 2002.

Cottrell, Robert C. *Sex, Drugs, and Rock 'N' Roll: The Rise of American's 1960s Counterculture.* Rowman & Littlefield, 2015.

Crowley, Kent. *Surf Beat: Rock 'N' Roll's Forgotten Revolution*. Backbeat Books, New York, 2011.

Culver, Lawrence. *The Frontier of Leisure: Southern California and the Shaping of Modern America*. Oxford University Press, 2010.

Dana, Richard Henry Jr. *Two Years Before the Mast*. Grosset & Dunlap Publishers, 1927.

Dasmann, Raymond F. *The Destruction of California*. Collier Books, 1966.

Denton, Sally. *Passion and Principle: John and Jesse Fremont, the Couple Whose Power, Politics, and Love Shaped Nineteenth Century America*. Bloomsbury Publishers, 2007.

DeWitt, John. Cool Cars, *High Art: The Rise of Kustom Kulture*. University Press of Mississippi, 2001.

Diggins, John Patrick. *The Proud Decades: America in War and Peace, 1941-1960*. W.W. Norton & Company, 1988.

Dregni, Michael (editor). *The All-American Hot Rod: The cars, The Legends, The Passion*. Voyageur Press.

Elwell, John & Schmanuss, Jane. *Surfing in San Diego*. Arcadia Publishing, 2007

Engstrand, Iris. *San Diego: California's Cornerstone*. Sunbelt Publications, 2005.

Fitoussi, Brigitte. *Eames*. Assouline Publishing, 2004.

Flammang, James M. *Cars of the Fabulous 50s*. Publications International, 2002

Flink, James J. *The Automobile Age*. The MIT Press, 1988.

Fradkin, Philip L. *The Seven States of California*. Henry Holt and Company, Inc. 1995.

Friedman, Alice T. *American Glamour and the Evolution of Modern Architecture*. Yale University Press, 2010.

Gaines, Steven. *Heroes and Villains: The True Story of the Beach Boys*. New American Library, 1986.

Galbraith, John Kenneth. *The Affluent Society*. Houghton Mifflin Company, 1958.

Gentry, Curt. *The Last Days of the Late, Great State of California*. G.P. Putnam's Sons, 1968.

Gibbs, Jocelyn and Olsberg, Nicholas. *Carefree California: Cliff May and the Romance of the Ranch House*. Rizzoli International Publications, Inc., 2012.

Gioia, Ted. *West Coast Jazz: Modern Jazz in California 1945-1960*. University of California Press, 1992.

Gordon, Richard E. & company. *The Split Level Trap*. Dell, 1959.

Goulden, Joseph C. *The Best Years 1945-1950*. Atheneum, 1976.

Greene, Bob. *Chevrolet Summers, Dairy Queen Nights*. Viking/Penguin Putnam Inc. 1997.

Greene, Bob. *When We Get to Surf City*. St. Martin's Press, 2008.

Gunnell, John A., Sieber, Mary L., editors. *The Fabulous 50s*. Krause Publications, 1992.

Hall, Marian. *California Fashion: From the Old West to New Hollywood*. Harry N. Abrams Inc., 2002

Hanson, Victor Davis. *Mexifornia: A State of Becoming*. Encounter Books, 2007.

Harris, Edward D. *John Charles Fremont and the Great Western Reconnaissance*. Chelsea House Publishers, 1990.

Hartman, Kent. *The Wrecking Crew: The Inside Story of Rock 'N' Roll's Best Kept Secret*. St. Martin's Griffin, 2013.

Hayward, Philip (editor). *Widening the Horizon: Exoticism in Post War Popular Music*. John Libbey & Company Pty Ltd., 1999.

Heimann, Jim. *Car Hops and Curb Service: A History of the American Drive-in 1920-1960*. Chronicle Books, 1996.

Heitmann, John. *The Automobile and American Life*. McFarland & Company, 2009.

Hemmings, Fred. *The Soul of Surfing*. Thunder's Mouth Press, 1997.

Hess, Alan. *Forgotten Modern: California Houses 1940-1970*. Gibbs Smith Publisher, 2007.

Hess, Alan & Weintraub, Alan. *The Architecture of John Lautner*. Rizzoli International Publications, Inc., 1999

Hess, Alan. *Googie Redux: Ultramodern Roadside Architecture*. Chronicle Books, 2004.

Hinckley, Jim & Robinson, Jon G. *The Big Book of Car Culture: The Armchair Guide to Automotive Americana*. Motorbooks, 2005.

Hine, Thomas. *Populux*. Overlook Press, 1986.

Hine, Thomas. *The Great Funk: Falling Apart and Coming Together in the Seventies*. Sarah Crichton Books, 2007.

Horn, Huston. *The Pioneers*. Time-Life Books, New York, 1974.

Hunter, Don and Pearce, Al. *The Illustrated History of Stock Car Racing*. MBI Publishing Company, 1998.

Issitt, Micah L. *Hippies: A Guide to an American Subculture.* Greenwood Press, 2009.

Johnson, William W. *The Forty Niners.* Time-Life Books, New York, 1974.

Kampion, Drew. *Stoked: A History of Surf Culture.* Salt Lake City: G. Smith, 2003.

Kampion, Drew. *The Way of the Surfer: Living it 1935 to Tomorrow.* Harry N. Abrams Inc., 2003.

Kaplan, Fred. *The Year Everything Changed: 1959.* John Willey & Sons, Inc. 2009.

Keats, John. *The Crack in the Picture Window.* Ballantine Books, New York, 1956.

Keats, John. *The Insolent Chariots.* J.B. Lippincott Company, 1958.

Keller, Michael A.; Lane, L.W. Jr.; Lane, Melvin B.; Starr, Kevin; Jaehn, Thomas. *Sunset Magazine: A Century of Western Living 1898-1998.* Stanford University Libraries, 1998.

Kieley, Genny Zak. *Green Stamps to Hot Pants: Growing Up in the 50s and 60s.* Nodin Press, 2008.

Kirsten, Sven A. *Tiki Modern.* Taschen, 2007.

Kirsten, Sven A. *Tiki Style.* Taschen, 2004.

Kirsten, Sven A. *Tiki Pop: America imagines its own Polynesian Paradise.* Taschen, 2014.

Kling, Rob & Olin, Spencer & Poster, Mark. *Postsuburban California: The Transformation of Orange County Since World War II.* University of California Press, 1991.

Koeing, Gloria. *Eames*. Taschen, 2005.

Kohner, Frederick. *Gidget*. Berkeley Publishing Group, 1957.

Lamprecht, Barbara. *Neutra*. Taschen, 2009.

Lavender, David. *De Soto, Coronado, Cabrillo*. Division of Publications, National Park Service, 1992.

LeCorbusier. *Towards a New Architecture*. Dover Publications, 1986.

Lifson, Hal. *Hal Lifson's 1966: A Personal View of the Coolest Year in Pop Culture History*. Bonus Books, Chicago, 2002.

Lisanti, Thomas. *Hollywood Surf and Beach Movies: The First Wave 1959-1969*. McFarland & Co. Inc. 2005.

Lockwood, Herbert. *Fallout from the Skeleton's Closet: a light look at San Diego History*. The San Diego Independent, 1967.

Lucsko, David N. *The Business of Speed: The Hot Rod Industry in America, 1915-1990*. John Hopkins University Press, 2008.

Lummis, Dayton. *Captain Midnight and the California Dream*. iUniverse, Inc., 2005.

Lutz, Tom. *Doing Nothing: A History of Loafers, Loungers, Slackers, and Bums in America*. Farrar, Straus, and Giroux, 2006.

Makinson, Randell L., and Heinz, Thomas A. *Greene & Greene: Creating a Style*. Gibbs Smith Publisher, 2004.

Marcus, Ben. *Surfing USA: The History of the Coolest Sport*. Voyageur Press, 2005.

Marcus, Ben. *The Surfboard: Art, Style, Stoke*. MVP Books, 2007.

Mathews, Joe & Paul, Mark. *California Crackup: How reform broke the golden state and how we can fix it*. University of California Press, 2010.

May, Kirse Granat. *Golden State, Golden Youth: The California Image in Popular Culture, 1955-1966*. The University of North Carolina Press, 2002.

Maynard, John Arthur. *Venice West: The Beat Generation in Southern California*. Rutgers University Press, 1991.

McCoy, Esther. *Five California Architects*. Reinhold Publishing Corporation, 1960.

McWilliams, Carey. *Southern California: An Island on the Land*. Gibbs Smith, Publisher, 1946.

McWilliams, Carey. *California: The Great Exception*. University of California Press, Berkeley, Los Angeles, 1949.

McWilliams, Carey (edited by). *The California Revolution*. Grossman Publishers, Inc. 1968.

Menzer, Joe. *The Wildest Ride: A History of NASCAR*. Simon & Schuster, 2001.

Michaels, Leonard (edited by). *West of the West: Imagining California*. Harper Perennial, 1991.

Michener, James A. *Tales of the South Pacific*. The MacMillan Company, 1947.

Miller, Judith. *Mid-Century Modern: Living with Mid-Century Modern Design*. Octopus Publishing Group Ltd., 2012.

Moorehouse, H.F. *Driving Ambitions: A Social Analysis of the American Hot Rod Enthusiasm*. Manchester University Press, 1991.

Morgan, Neil. *The California Syndrome*. Prentice Hall, Inc., 1969.

Morgan, Neil. *San Diego: The Unconventional City*. Morgan House, 1972.

Morgan, Neil. *Westward Tilt: The American West Today*. Random House, 1963.

Moruzzi, Peter. Palm Springs Holiday: A Vintage Tour from Palm Springs to the Salton Sea. Gibbs Smith Publishers, 2009.

Nadeau, Remi. *California: The New Society*. David McKay Company, Inc. 1963.

Nadeau, Remi. *The Water Seekers*. Crest Publishers, 1997

Nichols, Chris. *The Leisure Architecture of Wayne McAllister*. Gibbs Smith, Publisher, 2007.

Nordhoff, Charles. *California for Health, Pleasure, and Residence: A Book for Travelers and Settlers*. Harper & Brothers Publishers, New York, 1874.

Oakley, Ronald J. *God's Country: America in the 50s*. Barricade Books, 1990.

O'Neill, William L. American High: *The Years of Confidence 1945-1960*. The Free Press, New York, 1986.

Ortlieb, Patricia & Economy, Peter. *Creating an Orange Utopia: Eliza Lovell Tibbets and the Birth of California's Citrus Industry*. Swedenborg Foundation Press, 2011.

Packard, Vance. *The Status Seekers*. David McKay Company, New York, 1959.

Palm, Carl. *The Great California Story: Real-life Roots of an American Legend*. Northcross Books, 2004.

Phoenix, Charles. *Southern Californialand: Mid-Century Culture in Kodachrome*. Angel City Press, 2004.

Post, Robert C. *High Performance: The Culture and Technology of Drag Racing 1950 – 1990*. The John Hopkins University Press, 1994.

Pourade, Richard F. *The History of San Diego: The Explorers*. The Union-Tribune Publishing Company, 1960.

Pourade, Richard F. *The History of San Diego: Time of the Bells*. The Union-Tribune Publishing Company, 1961.

Pourade, Richard F. *Gold in the Sun: The History of San Diego*. Union-Tribune Publishing Company, 1965.

Pourade, Richard F. *The Glory Years, 1865-1899*. Copley Press, 1964.

Pourade, Richard F. *The Rising Tide: The History of San Diego*. Union-Tribune Publishing Company, 1967.

Pourade, Richard F. *City of the Dream: The History of San Diego*. Copley Books, 1977.

Priore, Domenic. *Riot on Sunset Strip: Rock 'N' Roll's Last Stand in Hollywood*. Outline Press Ltd. 2007

Quinn, Bradley. *Mid-Century Modern*. Conran Octopus Limited, 2004.

Rawley, Donald. *The View from Babylon: The Notes of a Hollywood Voyeur*. Warner Books, 1999.

Rayner, Richard. *The Associates: Four Capitalists who Created California*. W.W. Norton & Company, 2008.

Remington, Roger R. *American Modernism: Graphic Design 1920-1960*. Yale University Press, 2003.

Rensin, David. *All for a Few Perfect Waves*: The Audacious Life and Legend of Rebel Surfer Miki Dora. It Books, 2008.

Rice, Richard B. Bullough, William A. Orsi, Richard J. *The Elusive Eden: A New History of California*. McGraw-Hill, 1988.

Rolle, Andrew F., *California: A History*. Harlan Davidson Inc., 1978.

Roth, Ed and Thacker, Tony. *Hot Rods by Ed "Big Daddy" Roth*. MBI Publishing, 1995.

Satin, Joseph. *The 1950s: America's "Placid" Decade*. The Riverside Press, 1960.

Schrag, Peter. *California: America's High-Stakes Experiment*. The University of California Press, Berkeley, 2006.

Schrag, Peter. *Paradise Lost: California's Experience, America's Future*. University of California Press, 1998.

Smith, Elizabeth A.T. *Case Study Houses*. Taschen, 2007.

Starr, Kevin. *Inventing the Dream: California Through the Progressive Era*. Oxford University Press, 1985.

Starr, Kevin. *Americans and the California Dream 1850-1915*. Oxford University Press, 1973.

Starr, Kevin. *California: A History*. Modern Library Chronicles, 2005.

Starr, Kevin. *Golden Dreams: California in an Age of Abundance 1950 – 1963*. Oxford University Press, 2009.

Starr, Kevin & Richard Orsi (editors). *On Barbarous Soil: People, Culture, and Community in Gold Rush California*. University of California Press, 2000.

Starr, Kevin. *Embattled Dreams: California in War and Peace 1940-1950*. Oxford University Press, 2002.

Starr, Kevin. *Material Dreams: Southern California Through the 1920s*. Oxford University Press, 1990.

Stebbins, John and Marks, David. *The Lost Beach Boy*. Virgin Books Ltd., 2007.

Thompson, Mark. *American Character: The Curious Life of Charles Fletcher Lummis and the Rediscovery of the Southwest*. Arcade Publishing, 2001.

Toop, David. *Exotica: Fabricated Soundscapes in a Real World*. Serpent's Tail Publishers, 1999.

Truman, Major Ben C. *Semi-Tropical California: Its Climate, Healthfulness, Productiveness, and Scenery*. A. L. Bancroft & Company, Publishers, 1874.

Waite, Heather. *Calling California Home*. Wildcat Canyon Press, 1999.

Waldie, D. J. *Holy Land: A Suburban Memoir*. St. Martin's Griffin, New York, 1996.

Waldie, D.J. *Where We Are Now: Notes from Los Angeles*. Angel City Press, 2004

Warner, Charles Dudley. *Our Italy*. Harper & Brothers Press, 1891.

Warshaw, Matt. *The History of Surfing*. Chronicle Books, 2010.

Warshaw, Matt. *Photo/Stoner: The Rise, Fall, and Mysterious Disappearance of Surfing's Greatest Photographer*. Chronicle Books, San Francisco, 2006.

Weingarten, David; Howard, Lucia; Fletcher, Joe. *Ranch Houses: Living the California Dream*. Rizzoli International Publications, Inc., 2009.

White, Timothy. *The Nearest Faraway Place: Brian Wilson, The Beach Boys, and the Southern California Experience*. Henry Holt and Company, New York, 1994.

Wilentz, Amy. *I Feel Earthquakes More Often Than They Happen: Coming to California in the Age of Schwarzenegger*. Simon and Schuster, 2006.

Wolfe, Tom. *The Kandy-Kolored Tangerine-Flake Streamline Baby*. Farrar, Straus and Giroux, New York, 1963.

Wolfe, Tom. *From Bauhaus to Our House*. Farrar, Straus, & Giroux, 1981.

About the Author

Dorian MacDougall was born and raised in the suburbs of San Diego, California, during the heady days of the Cpop era. A true dabbler of arts, he has, at various times, worked as an actor, a musician, a documentary filmmaker, and a writer for television, technical publications, and works of non-fiction. Between writing projects, he restores and repairs old guitars.

www.ingramcontent.com/pod-product-compliance
Lightning Source LLC
Chambersburg PA
CBHW071217080526
44587CB00013BA/1410